Cognition
Theory and Applications

Second Edition

Brooks/Cole's Series in Experimental Psychology

Introduction to Measurement Theory, Allen/Yen

Psychological Theories of Motivation, *2nd ed.*, Arkes/Garske

Psychology of Language, Carroll

Introduction to Statistics for the Social and Behavioral Sciences, Christensen/Stoup

Methods of Psychological Research, *2nd ed.*, Craig/Metze

Principles of Learning and Behavior, *2nd ed.*, Domjan/Burkhard

Human Motivation, *2nd ed.*, Franken

Motivational Explanations of Behavior: Evolutionary, Physiological, and Cognitive Ideas, Hoyenga/Hoyenga

Psychobiology: The Neuron and Behavior, Hoyenga/Hoyenga

Psychological Testing: Principles, Applications, and Issues, Kaplan/Saccuzzo

Experimental Design: Procedures for the Behavioral Sciences, *2nd ed.*, Kirk

Psychological Theories and Human Learning, *2nd ed.*, Lefrancois

The Practical Statistician: A Simplified Handbook of Statistics, Linton/Gallo

Directed Readings for Principles of Learning and Behavior, Marlin

Doing Psychology Experiments, *2nd ed.*, Martin

The Game of Science, *5th ed.*, McCain/Segal

Principles of Everyday Behavior Analysis, *2nd ed.*, Miller

Experimental Psychology, *2nd ed.*, Myers

Statistics: Applications for the Behavioral Sciences, Porter/Hamm

Basic Statistics: Tales of Distribution, *3rd ed.*, Spatz/Johnston

Statistics: An Intuitive Approach, *4th ed.*, Weinberg et al.

Cognition
Theory and Applications

Second Edition

Stephen K. Reed
Florida Atlantic University

Brooks/Cole Publishing Company
Pacific Grove, California

Brooks/Cole Publishing Company
A Division of Wadsworth, Inc.

Printed in the United States of America

10 9 8 7 6 5 4 3 2

Library of Congress Cataloging-in-Publication Data

Reed, Stephen K.
    Cognition: theory and applications.

    Bibliography: p.
    Includes indexes.
    1. Cognition.   I. Title.
BF311.R357   1987   153   87-11785
ISBN 0-534-08172-X

Sponsoring Editor: *C. Deborah Laughton*
Editorial Assistants: *Monique Etienne and Amy Mayfield*
Production Editor: *Fiorella Ljunggren*
Production Assistant: *Dorothy Bell*
Manuscript Editor: *Rephah Berg*
Permissions Editor: *Carline Haga*
Interior and Cover Design: *Roy R. Neuhaus*
Cover Illustration: *Roy R. Neuhaus*
Art Coordinator: *Sue C. Howard*
Interior Illustration: *Judith L. Macdonald*
Typesetting: *Omegatype, Champaign, Illinois*
Cover Printing: *The Lehigh Press, Pennsauken, New Jersey*
Printing and Binding: *Arcata Graphics/Fairfield, Fairfield, Pennsylvania*

(Credits continue on p. 345.)

To my parents:

Anita M. Reed
Kenneth D. Reed

Preface

The most exciting development in the field of cognitive psychology is not a particular theory or experimental finding but a general trend. Cognitive psychologists have demonstrated an increasing interest in studying complex, real-world tasks and are making significant progress in understanding how people perform on these tasks. I hope that one result of this trend is that undergraduates discover the direct relevance of cognitive psychology to many of their daily activities. A course about cognition should be useful not only to psychology students but to those who have selected other fields of study.

In this book I have attempted to place a greater emphasis on the application of cognitive psychology than is typically found in an undergraduate text. The study of reading, for example, is discussed in the chapters on pattern recognition, attention, language, and text comprehension. Efficient learning strategies are major topics in the chapters on long-term memory and visual imagery. The chapter on classroom problem solving shows how the study of problem solving is currently being extended to include the kinds of problems students encounter in their courses. The chapter on language discusses how the implications of sentences influence legal testimony and advertising, and the chapter on decision making includes a section on medical decision making. In order to help students relate the study of cognition to popular articles they are likely to read, I have included many magazine and newspaper clippings on such contemporary topics as playing blindfolded chess and formulating the odds that someone would be injured by the fall of Skylab.

In presenting this material, I have attempted to avoid overwhelming students with more information than they need. The chapters are each about 25 pages long and include a summary. They cover a wide range of topics, and instructors should be able to expand on whatever topics interest them. The 14 chapters are divided into three parts: Information-Processing Stages, Representation and Organization of Knowledge, and Complex Cognitive Skills. The first part consists of an introductory chapter followed by chapters on pattern recognition, attention, short-term memory, and long-term memory. The chapters describe what occurs during the different information-processing stages and how the stages interact. The second part contains chapters on levels of processing, visual imagery, categorization, and semantic memory. The first two chapters in this part describe qualitatively different memory codes, and the next two chapters discuss the organization of knowledge in long-term memory. The final part consists of chapters on language, text comprehension, problem solving, classroom problem solving, and decision making. The discussion of these complex cognitive skills is often related to ideas presented earlier in the book.

The organization of a book on cognition should perhaps reflect what we actually know about cognition. Research suggests that a hierarchy is a particularly effective way to organize knowledge (see Chapter 9). Recall is facilitated when information is partitioned into categories, which are further partitioned into smaller categories. Hierarchical organization seems to be particularly effective when the number of partitions varies from two to five. I deliberately selected such a structure for this book in the hope that the material will thereby be more accessible to students.

I wrote the first edition of the book while spending a sabbatical year at the University of California at Berkeley. I am grateful to Case Western Reserve University and the Group in Science and Mathematics Education at Berkeley for providing financial support during this year. The Group in Science and Mathematics Education also furnished me with a stimulating environment, and the Institute of Human Learning provided an excellent library.

Shortly after arriving at Berkeley, I had the good fortune to meet C. Deborah Laughton, a psychology editor at Brooks/Cole. She expressed confidence in the book long before it was deserved and, with the assistance of an excellent staff at Brooks/Cole, helped in the development of the book. The development was also facilitated by a number of first-rate reviewers. I would like to thank Ian M. Begg of McMaster University, Bruce K. Britton of the University of Georgia, Dennis Egan of Bell Laboratories, Judith P. Goggin of the University of Texas at El Paso, Richard A. Griggs of the University of Florida, David T. Hakes of the University of Texas at Austin, Kenji Hakuta of Yale University, Robert Haygood of Arizona State University, Stephen M. Kosslyn of Harvard University, Stephen E. Palmer of the University of California, Berkeley, Stan Parkinson of Arizona State University, John W. Payne of Duke University, John Pittenger of the University of Arkansas at Little Rock, Peter Polson of the University of Colorado, James R. Pomerantz of the State University of New York at Buffalo, Eleanor Rosch of the University of California, Berkeley, and Robert E. Till of Eastern Illinois University for their insightful comments.

The second edition retains the same organization as the first edition. I had two objectives in revising the book: I wanted to make it more readable by making the figures easier to interpret, by clarifying some points that needed clarifying, and by eliminating several sections that may have been too advanced for an undergraduate course; and I wanted to include some of the new research that had occurred since the book's initial publication.

Examples of new material include an expanded discussion of structural theories of pattern recognition, emphasizing their application to three-dimensional objects. I have also included additional material on memory retrieval in Chapters 5 and 6, and I show how guided retrieval can be used in place of hypnosis to improve eyewitness recall. The chapter on visual imagery contains new material on alternative interpretations of mental scanning and on reality monitoring. Sections on goal-derived categories and person perception have been added to the chapter on categorization. New sections on goal-directed events are included in the chapter on text comprehension, and recent work on context effects is discussed in the chapter on language. I have also added sections on analogical reasoning, computer-based tutoring, and business decisions to the chapters on problem solving and decision making.

I am grateful to the following reviewers for their insightful comments on the second edition: James Chumbley of the University of Massachusetts, Richard A. Griggs of the University of Florida, Andrea R. Halpern of Bucknell University, Don MacKay of Pomona College, Lucinda McLain of Marquette University, John Mueller of the University of Missouri, Gregory Murphy of Brown University, Lloyd Peterson of Indiana University, David Riefer of California State University–San Bernardino, and Laurence D. Rust of the State University of New York at Potsdam. The comments of others are always welcome, and I would appreciate receiving suggestions from readers.

Stephen K. Reed

Contents

xii Contents

4 Short-Term Memory 55

Forgetting 56
Capacity 61
Rehearsal and Acoustic Codes 67
Recognition of Items in STM 74
Summary 78
Recommended Reading 79

5 Long-Term Memory 81

The Atkinson-Shiffrin Model 82
Automatic Encoding 89
Memory Retrieval 92
Summary 98
Recommended Reading 99

PART 2 Representation and Organization of Knowledge 101

6 Levels of Processing 103

The Levels-of-Processing Theory 104
Supporting Evidence 107
Criticisms and Modifications 110
Encoding Specificity and Retrieval 115
Summary 120
Recommended Reading 120

7 Visual Images 122

Evidence for Images 123
Visual Imagery and Learning 135
Mnemonic Strategies 141
Limitations of Images 146
Summary 150
Recommended Reading 151

8 Categorization 152

Concept Identification 153
Natural Categories 158

Cognition
Theory and
Applications

Second Edition

PART 1

Information-Processing Stages

1

Introduction

Cognitive psychology refers to all processes by which the sensory input is transformed, reduced, elaborated, stored, recovered, and used.

ULRIC NEISSER (1967)

Cognition is usually defined simply as the acquisition of knowledge. However, the acquisition and use of knowledge involve many mental skills. If you glanced at the table of contents at the beginning of this book, you saw a list of some of these skills. Psychologists who study cognition are interested in pattern recognition, attention, memory, visual imagery, language, problem solving, and decision making.

The purpose of this book is to provide an overview of the field of cognitive psychology. The book summarizes experimental research in cognitive psychology, discusses the major theories in the field, and attempts to relate the research and theories to cognitive tasks that people encounter in their daily lives—for example, reading, driving, studying, judging advertising claims, evaluating legal testimony, classroom problem solving, and medical decision making.

Neisser's definition of cognitive psychology quoted above reflects how psychologists study cognition. Let me repeat it for emphasis: "Cognitive psychology refers to all processes by which the sensory input is transformed, reduced, elaborated, stored, recovered, and used."

This definition has several important implications. The reference to a sensory input implies that cognition begins with our contact with the external world. Transformation of the sensory input means that our representation of the world is not a passive registration of our physical surroundings but an active construction that may involve both reduction and elaboration. We can attend to only a small part of the physical stimulation that surrounds us, and only a small part of what we attend to can be remembered. Reduction occurs when information is lost. Elaboration occurs when we add to the sensory input. For example, when you meet a friend, you may recall many shared experiences.

The storage and the recovery of information are, of course, concerned with memory. The distinction between storage and recovery implies that the storage of information does not guarantee recovery. A good example of this distinction is the "tip of the tongue" phenomenon. Sometimes we can almost, but not quite, retrieve a word to express a particular thought or meaning. Our later recall of the word proves that the earlier failure was one of retrieval rather than one of storage. The word was stored in memory; it was simply hard to get it back out.

The last part of Neisser's definition is perhaps the most important. After information has been perceived, stored, and recovered, it must be put to good use—for example, to make decisions or to solve problems. We will learn more about problem solving and decision making in Part 3, after we review the progress that has been made in understanding perception and memory.

The Information-Processing Approach

The fact that cognitive psychology is often called *human information processing* reflects the predominant approach to the subject used by cognitive psychologists. The acquisition, storage, retrieval, and use of information involve a number of separate stages, and the information-processing approach attempts to identify what happens during these stages (Haber, 1969).

Figure 1.1 identifies the stages that researchers most commonly include in information-processing models. They are arranged in temporal order; however, since information flows in both directions, as indicated by the two-headed arrows, an earlier stage can be influenced by information in a later stage. For example, in order to recognize a pattern in the pattern recognition stage, we need to store information about patterns in long-term memory.

A brief consideration of the model in Figure 1.1 will give you a superficial account of the stages, each of which will be elaborated in later chapters. The *sensory store* provides a brief storage for information in its original sensory form. Presumably, a sensory store exists for each of the senses, although the visual and auditory stores have been the most widely studied. The sensory store extends the amount of time that a person has to recognize a pattern. If a visual pattern is flashed on a screen for 5 msec (5 milliseconds, or 5/1000 of a second), the observer has more time than 5 msec to identify it if the visual information can be briefly maintained in a sensory store. Although the sensory store for vision lasts only about one quarter of a second (250 msec), this is much longer than the 5-msec exposure.

The information in the sensory store is lost at the end of this time unless it can be described during the *pattern recognition* stage. Most of the patterns we encounter are familiar, and recognition consists in classifying a pattern as a cat, the letter *a*, the word *ball*, and so on. When we recognize a familiar pattern, we are using information that we have previously stored in memory. If the description does not

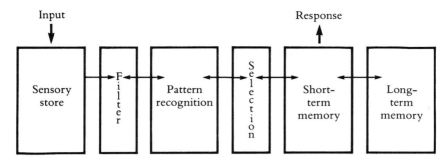

Figure 1.1 Stages of an information-processing model

match a description of a familiar pattern, the observer may want to store the new description in memory.

The relation between pattern recognition and attention has been a topic of much debate. Some theorists have claimed that we can recognize only one pattern at a time. They argue that attention acts as a filter that determines which patterns will be recognized when many patterns arrive simultaneously. Other theorists have argued that simultaneous patterns can all be recognized but that only some of the recognized patterns will be remembered whereas others are immediately forgotten. The latter view states that attention controls which patterns will be selected into memory. Since the most popular current view is that both theories are correct, depending on the circumstances, attention is represented in Figure 1.1 by both the *filter* and the *selection* stages. The filter limits the amount of information that can be recognized at one time, and the selection limits the amount of material that can be entered into memory.

Memory is represented in Figure 1.1 by *short-term* and *long-term* memory. We use short-term memory (STM), for example, to remember a telephone number as we are dialing it. STM is limited in both the amount of information it can hold (capacity) and the length of time it can hold the information (duration). Most adults can remember a seven-digit number, but they find it very difficult to remember a ten-digit number, such as an unfamiliar area code in addition to the telephone number. The limited duration of STM is illustrated by the fact that we may quickly forget the number if we don't repeat it to ourselves by using verbal rehearsal. Long-term memory (LTM) has neither of the two limitations of STM. It has no limitations on the amount of information it can hold, and forgetting occurs relatively slowly, if at all.

The "higher" cognitive skills such as decision making and problem solving do not have a stage in our information-processing model. However, they depend greatly on the other stages. For example, pattern recognition skills are important in playing chess, a very demanding intellectual task. The limited capacity of STM is a major determinant of performance on tasks that require complex decision making or problem solving. The role of problem solving in learning new information is receiving increasing emphasis as cognitive psychologists discover more about the active nature of learning. Specifying the interactions among perception, memory, and thought is one of the challenges that confront cognitive psychologists.

The Beginning of Cognitive Psychology

It is difficult to pinpoint the exact beginning of any field of study, and cognitive psychologists would likely offer a wide variety of dates if asked when cognitive psychology began. William James's *Principles of Psychology,* published in 1890, included chapters on attention, memory, imagery, and reasoning. F. C. Bartlett's book *Remembering: A Study in Experimental and Social Psychology,* published in 1932, contained a theory of memory for stories that is very consistent with current views. We could find other important articles or books that would seem modern but did not cause a major shift toward the way cognitive psychology is currently studied.

One book that did have a major impact was *Behaviorism,* published in 1924 by John B. Watson. The book's central theme was that psychologists should study only what they could directly observe in a person's behavior. Watson's argument lent support to a stimulus-response (S-R) approach, in which experimenters measure how people respond to stimuli. The stimulus-response approach is consistent with Watson's view because the stimulus and response are both observable. The problem with this approach is that it does not reveal exactly what the person does with the information presented in the stimulus. By contrast, the information-processing approach seeks to identify how a person transforms the information between the stimulus and the response. Psychologists who follow the latter approach seek to understand what occurs during each of the stages shown in Figure 1.1. Finding out what occurs during each of these stages is particularly important when a person has difficulty performing a task, for the psychologist can then try to identify which stage is the primary source of the difficulty.

Information Processing Gathers Momentum

The change from the S-R to the information-processing approach began to gather momentum in the middle to late 1950s, stimulated by the growing popularity of computers and computer programs that illustrated the different operations in the processing of information. Psychologists became interested in using the computer as an analog of how people process information and tried to identify how different stages of processing influence performance. One stage that can have a dramatic influence on how people perform mental tasks is STM. George Miller argued in a classic paper published in 1956 that STM capacity limited performance on many cognitive tasks. Miller's paper was important in demonstrating how a single stage—STM—can influence performance on a wide variety of tasks.

Two years later Donald Broadbent (1958) proposed one of the first models based on an information-processing analysis—a filter model to account for performance on selective listening tasks. When subjects were asked to listen simultaneously to different messages played in each ear, they found it difficult. Broadbent proposed that many sensory inputs can simultaneously enter the sensory store, but only a single input can enter the pattern recognition stage. The filter model proposes that the listener can attend to only one message at a time; attention is controlled by the filter. The purpose of the filter is to determine which message is heard. Two simultaneous messages can both be recognized only if the unattended message passes through the filter before it decays from the sensory store. The filter model implies that a perceptual limitation prevents people from comprehending two messages spoken at the same time.

The year after Broadbent's filter model appeared, George Sperling completed his doctoral dissertation at Harvard. In one of Sperling's (1960) tasks, observers viewed a very brief exposure of an array of letters and were required to report all the letters in one of the rows of the display. The pitch of a tone signaled which row was to be reported. Sperling designed the procedure to determine whether perception or memory limited the number of letters people could report from the brief exposure. His analysis of this task resulted in an information-processing model that proposed how the sensory store, pattern recognition, and short-term memory combined to influence performance on the task (Sperling, 1963).

Both Broadbent's and Sperling's models had an important influence on subsequent information-processing theory, the former on models of auditory attention and the latter on visual recognition.

Higher Cognitive Processes

The information-processing analysis of perceptual tasks was accompanied in the late 1950s by a new approach to more complex tasks. The excitement of this new approach is described by Newell and Simon (1972). The development of digital computers after World War II led to active work in artificial intelligence, a field that attempts to program computers to perform intelligent tasks such as playing chess and constructing derivations in logic. A seminar was held at the RAND Corporation in the summer of 1958 with the aim of showing social scientists how computer simulation techniques could be applied to create models of human behavior. The RAND seminar had a major impact on integrating the work on computer simulation with other work on human information processing.

One consequence of the RAND seminar was its influence on three psychologists who spent the 1958–1959 academic year at the Center for Advanced Study in the Behavioral Sciences at Stanford University. The three—George Miller, Eugene Galanter, and Karl Pribram—shared a common dissatisfaction with the then-predominant theoretical approach to psychology, which viewed the human being as a bundle of stimulus-response reflexes. Miller brought with him a large amount of material from the RAND seminar, and this material, along with other recent work in artificial intelligence, psychology, and linguistics, helped shape the view that is expressed in their book *Plans and the Structure of Behavior* (Miller, Galanter, & Pribram, 1960).

The authors argued that much of human behavior is planned. A plan, according to their formulation, consists of a list of instructions that can control the order in which a sequence of operations is to be performed. A plan is essentially the same as a program for a computer. Since the authors found it difficult to construct plans from stimulus-response units, they proposed a new unit called TOTE, an abbreviation for Test-Operate-Test-Exit. A plan consists of a hierarchy of TOTE units.

Consider a very simple plan for hammering a nail into a board (see Figure 1.2). The goal is to make the head of the nail flush with the board. At the top of the hierarchy is a test to determine whether the goal has been accomplished. If the nail is flush, one can exit. If the nail sticks up, it is necessary to test the position of the hammer. The position of the hammer determines which of two operations, lifting or striking, should be performed.

The ideas expressed by Miller, Galanter, and Pribram were influenced by earlier work in two areas outside psychology. The work of Newell, Shaw, and Simon (1958a) in the area of artificial intelligence identified strategies that people use to perform complex tasks such as playing chess. A second major influence came from the linguist Noam Chomsky, who argued that a stimulus-response theory of language learning could not account for how people learn to comprehend and generate sentences (Chomsky, 1957). His alternative proposal—that people learn a system of rules (a grammar)—was consistent with Miller, Galanter, and Pribram's emphasis on planning. We will return to both contributions, as well as the contributions of Miller, Broadbent, and Sperling, in the following chapters.

The ideas expressed by these theorists have continued to be developed and refined over the past 30 years. Neisser's *Cognitive Psychology* (1967) brought many of these ideas together into a single source; other books on cognition have followed.

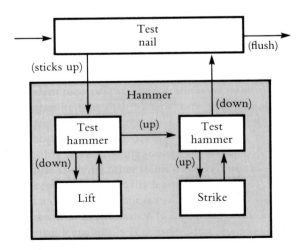

Figure 1.2   A hierarchical plan for hammering nails

Although some of the early ideas about the stages shown in Figure 1.1 have proved oversimplified, the model still provides a good explanation of how people perform on many cognitive tasks.

Our understanding of cognition has greatly increased over the past 30 years, even though cognitive psychology is still a young science. Elliot Aronson, in the introduction to his popular book *The Social Animal* (1972), explained the major reason he wrote the book: he once told one of his classes that social psychology was a young science, and it made him feel like a coward. He went on to write that labeling social psychology as a young science was a gigantic cop-out—a way of pleading with people not to expect too much, a way of avoiding the responsibility for applying findings to the problems of the world we live in. Aronson wrote his book to demonstrate that social psychology does have a lot to contribute. I hope you feel the same way about cognitive psychology after reading this book.

Organization of the Book

This book is divided into three major parts. The first part discusses information-processing stages; the second part discusses the representation and organization of knowledge; and the third part discusses complex cognitive skills.

In this chapter I have presented a brief overview of the information-processing approach to the study of cognition. One of the primary objectives of that approach, as was illustrated in Figure 1.1, is to identify the major information-processing stages. The first part of the book summarizes our knowledge of what occurs during each of these stages. Chapters 2 and 3, on pattern recognition and attention, are both concerned with perception. Theories of pattern recognition seek to specify how people recognize and store descriptions of patterns in memory. These theories also seek to determine why performance limitations occur when a person cannot report all the letters in an array of letters and why it is easier to perceive letters when they form a word. Theories of attention are needed to explain performance when too much perceptual information arrives at the same time. Usually a person can respond to only some of the information. Experiments designed to measure how much is processed have resulted in theories about whether a particular stage causes the limitation or whether the tasks simply require too much mental effort to be performed at the same time.

Chapters 4 and 5 are both concerned with memory, and they discuss STM and LTM, respectively. STM is a "working memory" that enables us to combine information that is retrieved from LTM with information that arrives from the environment. STM's limited capacity and fast decay rate make it necessary for us to enter into LTM new information we want to remember over a long period. The chapter on LTM discusses various strategies that can be used in learning and focuses on verbal rehearsal. Both chapters distinguish between recall and recognition tests and show how theories of recognition memory differ depending on whether the information is retained in STM or LTM.

The second part of the book is concerned with the representation and organization of knowledge in memory. Chapters 6 and 7 illustrate different kinds of memory codes; our ability to remember depends on the kind of memory code that is constructed. An influential theory of memory has been the levels-of-processing theory proposed by Craik and Lockhart (1972). Their theory was stimulated by research showing that a person's ability to remember a word depended on what characteristics of the word were emphasized in a judgment task. Memory codes can also be distinguished by whether they emphasize verbal information or visual information. The study of visual and verbal codes has resulted in many findings that have implications for how efficiently people can perform different tasks.

Chapters 8 and 9 emphasize the organization of LTM. Chapter 8 is primarily theoretical; it examines how knowledge is organized into categories and how categories are organized into hierarchies. The ability to categorize is a skill that is frequently used in pattern recognition. Identification usually occurs when an item is classified as a member of a particular category. The organization of knowledge in LTM can also be studied by measuring how quickly people can make classification decisions. Chapter 9 examines how psychologists have used this and other techniques to study the relations among concepts in semantic memory, the part of LTM that represents the meaning of words.

The last part of the book contains five chapters on cognitive skills. The section begins with a discussion of language in Chapter 10. Language involves not only the meaning of individual words but the combination of words to form sentences that are grammatically correct and convey the intended meaning. Chapter 11, on text comprehension, focuses on our ability to comprehend paragraphs rather than individual sentences. Over the past several years psychologists have made significant progress in identifying factors that influence the comprehension of text. They have even developed some rather detailed models of how the organization of ideas in a text interacts with STM and LTM to determine what is remembered.

Chapter 12, the first of two chapters on problem solving, shows how cognitive psychologists have studied this area. The chapter describes attempts to identify the skills needed to solve different kinds of problems, identify general strategies, and examine the role of memory in problem solving. Chapter 13, on classroom problem solving, discusses performance on material typically encountered in a classroom, such as mathematics. Topics include the initial analysis of a problem, the use of planning, and the role of instruction in teaching solution strategies and identifying mistakes.

Chapter 14 discusses decision making. The study of decision making has shown that people often find it difficult to combine information in an optimal way when evaluating alternatives. The term *risky decision making* is used to describe situations in which there is uncertainty regarding possible outcomes. People's estimates of probabilities are often biased. The study of how people make probability estimates, how they revise their estimates when they receive new information, and how they use their estimates to make decisions constitutes most of the research on risky decision making.

Recommended Reading

An early statement of the assumptions of the information-processing approach is given by Haber (1969). Estes (1978a) provides a more recent overview of this approach. Lachman, Lachman, and Butterfield's (1979) book on cognitive psychology contains an excellent discussion of how other disciplines—behaviorism, verbal learning, human engineering, information theory, and linguistics—contributed to the information-processing paradigm. An interesting paper by Roediger (1980) discusses how people have used familiar analogies to help them understand memory. Roediger begins with Aristotle's and Plato's comparison of memory to a wax tablet and ends with the computer analogy that is currently emphasized. Readers interested in how other major theoretical approaches influenced the history of psychology should read Heidbreder's *Seven Psychologies* (1961). The book contains chapters on prescientific psychology, the beginning of scientific psychology, the psychology of William James, functionalism, behaviorism, dynamic psychology, Gestalt psychology, and psychoanalysis. A recent book by Howard Gardner (1985), *The Mind's New Science: A History of the Cognitive Revolution,* provides a very readable account of the evolution of cognitive psychology.

2

Pattern Recognition

About patterns, philosophers and psychologists have been strangely silent; yet most interesting phenomena are almost certainly patterned. Of course, this silence is really not at all strange, for patterns are amazingly complicated things to come to grips with. Even a consensus of what we mean by the word "pattern" is lacking, but a growing number of people are beginning to feel that many of the central problems of behavior, intelligence, and information processing are problems that involve patterns.

LEONARD UHR (1966)

We begin our study of cognitive psychology by starting with a skill that people use very well—pattern recognition. The study of pattern recognition is primarily the study of how people identify the objects in their environment. Our ability to recognize patterns should seem impressive if we stop to consider how much variation there is in different examples of the same pattern. Each letter of the alphabet, for example, is one kind of pattern. Figure 2.1 shows various styles of handwriting. It is obvious that not all people have the same style of writing and that some handwriting is much less legible than others. However, unless it is very illegible, we usually are successful in reading it—that is, in recognizing the words.

The ease and accuracy with which we can recognize patterns make it difficult to study this ability. It is not very interesting or revealing if someone easily identifies all of a variety of patterns. In order to make the task more difficult, psychologists often resort to using a tachistoscope—a device for presenting patterns very rapidly under controlled conditions. If the patterns are presented for only a few milliseconds, people start to make mistakes, and psychologists start to take notes about the kinds of mistakes they make.

A large part of the literature on pattern recognition is concerned with alternative ways of describing patterns. The first section of this chapter discusses three

We all read different styles of handwriting so easily and so commonly that it is easy for us to overlook what an extraordinary ability this is. Note the extreme discrepancies in the way different people write certain letters of the alphabet. Now consider what kind of a machine would be necessary to "recognize" all these LETTERS. IN PART, WE ARE ABLE TO READ THESE SAMPLES OF HANDWRITING because of the context and redundancy in the passage. But to a page typer, our ability to read this passage is also due to the remarkable capacity the human organism has for "perceptual generalization".

Figure 2.1 Variations in handwriting

kinds of descriptions that represent different theories of pattern recognition. The second section is about information-processing models of visual pattern recognition. We will take a more detailed look at Sperling's research and how his results influenced later theories. The third section deals with word recognition and will give us the opportunity to consider some of the factors that influence reading.

Describing Patterns

Consider the following explanation of how we recognize patterns. Our LTM contains descriptions of many kinds of patterns. When we see or hear a pattern, we form a description of it and compare the description against the descriptions stored in our LTM. We are able to recognize the pattern if its description closely matches one of the descriptions stored in LTM. Although this is a plausible explanation, it is rather vague. For example, what form do these descriptions take? Let us consider three explanations that have been suggested: (1) templates, (2) features, and (3) structural descriptions.

Template Theories

Template theories propose that patterns are really not "described" at all. Rather, they are holistic, or unanalyzed, entities that we compare with other patterns by measuring how much two patterns overlap. Imagine that you made a set of letters out of cardboard. If you made a cutout to represent each letter of the alphabet, and I gave you a cutout of a letter that I had made, you could measure how my letter overlapped with each of your letters—the templates. The identity of my letter would be determined by which template had the greatest amount of overlap. The same principle would apply if you replaced your cardboard letters with a visual image of each letter and used the images to make mental comparisons.

There are a number of problems with using the degree of overlap as a measure of pattern recognition. First, the comparison requires that the template be in the same position and the same orientation, and be the same size, as the pattern you are trying to identify. Thus the position, orientation, and size of the templates would have to be continuously adjusted to correspond to the position, orientation, and size of each pattern you wanted to recognize. A second problem is the great variability of patterns, as was illustrated in Figure 2.1. It would be difficult to construct a template for each letter that would produce a good match with all the different varieties of that letter. Third, a template theory doesn't reveal how two patterns differ. We could know from a template theory that the capital letters P and R are similar because one overlaps substantially with the other. But in order to know how the two letters differ, we have to be able to analyze or describe the letters. By contrast, the feature theory, considered in the next section, allows us to analyze patterns into their parts. A fourth problem is that a template theory does not allow for alternative descriptions of a pattern. The pattern in Figure 2.5, for example, can be perceived as either a sting ray or a full-blown sail, depending on which lines are grouped together. The structural theory, considered later, will allow us to specify the relations of parts of the pattern.

These weaknesses of a template theory make it very unpromising as a general theory of pattern recognition, and it is usually quickly dismissed. There are, however, some situations in which a template theory might provide a useful model. Remember from Chapter 1 that the sensory store briefly preserves sensory information to give the observer more time to recognize patterns. But how are the patterns preserved in the sensory store if they are unrecognized? One possibility is that the patterns can be represented as unanalyzed templates, which are analyzed into their features during the pattern recognition stage.

This interpretation of the sensory store is most clearly presented by Phillips (1974). Subjects in Phillips's experiment viewed patterns made by randomly filled cells in a square matrix. The first pattern was presented for 1 sec and was followed after a variable interval by either an identical or a similar pattern. The subject's task was to decide, as quickly as possible, whether the two patterns were the same or different. On half of the trials, the second pattern occurred in exactly the same location as the first. Since the second pattern was exactly superimposed over the sensory image of the first pattern, it might be possible to use the sensory store to make a template match. On the other half of the trials, the second pattern was moved horizontally by the width of one cell. The slight shift in position should prohibit a template match because the two patterns are not correctly aligned.

Figure 2.2 shows the results of Phillips's experiment. The interstimulus interval—the time separating the two patterns—was 20, 60, 100, 300, or 600 msec. When the two patterns were presented in identical locations (labeled *still* in Figure 2.2), accuracy declined as the interstimulus interval lengthened. This finding suggests that the subjects were making use of a sensory store that was rapidly decaying. When the second pattern was moved, subjects could not use the sensory store to make a template match, and so accuracy was not influenced by the interval separating the patterns. It should be noted that the use of the sensory store resulted in more accurate performance when the interstimulus interval was less than 300 msec. This result suggests that the sensory store lasts only about a quarter of a second. When the separation was only 20 msec (the data points to the extreme left on the graph) and the patterns were presented in the same location, performance was almost perfect.

When the second pattern was moved, subjects had to rely on a description of the first pattern rather than a sensory image. The description might be in the form

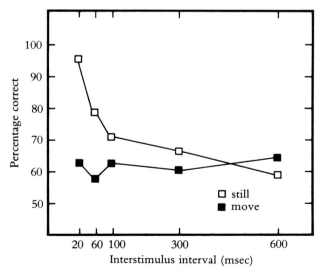

Figure 2.2   Percentage of correct responses for an 8 × 8 matrix as a function of the interstimulus interval and movement

of a visual image, but unlike a sensory image, in which the pattern still appears to be physically present, a visual image has to be retrieved from memory. Thus the description was less accurate than the sensory image. Since comparing the descriptions of two patterns takes longer than making a template match, the speed of response was highly correlated with accuracy. The reaction time results would look very much like the accuracy results in Figure 2.2 if we were to replace "Percentage correct" with "Speed of response." Reaction times were very fast for the "still" condition but became slower as the interstimulus interval increased. Reaction times were slower for the "move" condition and were uninfluenced by the interstimulus interval. Both the accuracy and reaction time results suggest that the sensory store can be used for a rapid template match if the two patterns are separated by less than 300 msec and are presented in the same location.

Feature Theories

The success of the template theory in accounting for Phillips's results depends on matching the second pattern to a sensory image of the first pattern. The sensory image can be thought of as a kind of afterimage in which the pattern still appears to be physically present until the sensory store decays away. But it is questionable whether the sensory store plays an important role outside the laboratory, and even if it did, the information would be quickly lost. Since we usually cannot rely on the sensory store to match patterns, we must compare descriptions of patterns. Feature theories allow us to describe a pattern by listing its parts. For example, we might describe a friend as having long, blond hair, a short nose, and bushy eyebrows.

Feature theories are convenient for describing perceptual learning, and one of the best discussions of feature theories is contained in Eleanor Gibson's *Principles of Perceptual Learning and Development* (1969). The theory proposed in Gibson's book is that perceptual learning occurs through the discovery of features that distinguish one pattern from another. Children learn to identify an object by being able to identify differences between it and other objects. For example, when first confronted with the letters *E* and *F,* the child might not be aware of how the two differ. Learning to make this discrimination depends on discovering that the lowest horizontal line is present in the letter *E* but not in the letter *F.* The lowest horizontal line is a *distinctive feature* for distinguishing between an *E* and an *F*; that is, it enables us to distinguish one pattern from the other.

Perceptual learning can be facilitated by a learning procedure that highlights the distinctive feature. An effective method for emphasizing a distinctive feature is initially to make it a different color from the rest of the pattern and gradually change it back to the original color. Egeland (1975) used this procedure to teach prekindergarten children how to distinguish between the confusable letter pairs *R–P, Y–V, G–C, Q–O, M–N,* and *K–X.* One letter of each pair was presented at the top of a card with six letters below it, three of which matched the sample letter and three of which were the comparison letter. The children were asked to select those letters that exactly matched the sample letter.

One group of children received a training procedure in which the distinctive feature of the letter was initially highlighted in red—for example, the stem of the *R* in the *R–P* discrimination. During the training session, the distinctive feature was gradually changed to black to match the rest of the letter. Another group of children viewed only black letters. They received feedback about which of their choices were correct, but they were not told about the distinctive features of the letters. Both groups were given two tests—an immediate test at the end of the training session and a delayed test one week later. The "distinctive features" group made significantly fewer errors on both tests, even though the features were not highlighted during the tests. They also made fewer errors during the training sessions.

Emphasizing the distinctive features produced two benefits. First, it enabled the children to learn the distinctive features so they could continue to differentiate letters after the distinctive features were no longer highlighted. Second, it enabled them to learn the features without making many errors during the training session. The failure and frustration that many children experience in the early stages of reading (letter discrimination) can impair their interest in later classroom learning.

Evaluating Feature Theories

Although most pattern recognition theorists make use of the feature concept, it is often a challenging task to find a good set of features. Gibson (1969) proposed the following criteria as a basis for selecting a set of features for upper-case letters.

1. The features should be critical ones, present in some members of the set but not in others, so as to provide a contrast.
2. The identity of the features should remain unchanged under changes in brightness, size, and perspective.
3. The features should yield a unique pattern for each letter.
4. The number of proposed features should be reasonably small.

Gibson used these criteria, empirical data, and intuition to derive the set of features for upper-case letters shown in Figure 2.3.

A set of features is usually evaluated by determining how well it can predict perceptual confusions, since confusable items should have many features in common. For example, Figure 2.3 reveals that the only difference in features for the letters *P* and *R* is the presence of a diagonal line for the letter *R*; therefore, the two should be highly confusable. The letters *R* and *O* differ in five features, and so they should seldom be confused.

There are several experimental procedures for generating perceptual confusions. The feature set shown in Figure 2.3 was initially tested by examining confusion errors made by 4-year-old children (Gibson, Osser, Schiff, & Smith, 1963). Since these children made errors on a perceptual matching task, it was possible to determine which pairs of letters were likely to be confused. One problem with this procedure was that even 4-year-old children made few errors, and many letters were never confused at all.

Features	A	E	F	H	I	L	T	K	M	N	V	W	X	Y	Z	B	C	D	G	J	O	P	R	Q	S	U
Straight																										
horizontal	●	●	●	●		●	●								●					●						
vertical		●	●	●	●	●	●	●	●	●				●		●		●	●			●	●			
diagonal /	●							●	●		●	●	●	●	●											
diagonal \	●							●	●	●	●	●	●	●												
Curve																										
closed																●		●			●	●	●	●		
open V																			●							●
open H																	●				●	●			●	
Intersection	●	●	●	●			●	●				●				●						●	●	●		
Redundancy																										
cyclic change		●					●			●						●									●	
symmetry	●	●		●	●		●	●	●		●	●	●	●	●	●	●	●			●					●
Discontinuity																										
vertical	●		●	●	●		●	●	●	●			●									●	●			
horizontal		●	●			●	●									●										

Figure 2.3   A possible set of features for capital letters

A second procedure projected a pair of letters on a small screen and required that subjects respond whether the two letters were the "same" or "different" by pushing one of two buttons as soon as they could make their decision (Gibson, Schapiro, & Yonas, 1968). The subjects were college students and 7-year-old children. Since all the possible combinations of "different" pairs and an equal number (to prevent a response bias toward saying "different") of "same" pairs required too many judgments, two sets of nine letters were used. The assumption of this procedure is that it should take longer to decide that two rather similar letters are different than to decide about two very dissimilar letters. The results supported this assumption. The average time for adults to decide that G and W are different was 458 msec, compared with 571 msec to decide that P and R are different.

The reaction times were analyzed by hierarchical cluster analysis (Johnson, 1967). The analysis partitions letters into finer and finer categories on the basis of their perceived similarity. The letters in each category are difficult to distinguish from each other, as revealed by the longer reaction times to discriminate between any pair of letters in a category. An analysis of the children's reaction times revealed that the letters C, G, P, and R belonged to one category and the·letters E, F, M, N, and W to another (see Figure 2.4). By looking at the letters in each category, we can infer the features of the letters that were important in determining perceived similarities: all the letters with curves were grouped into one category and the letters

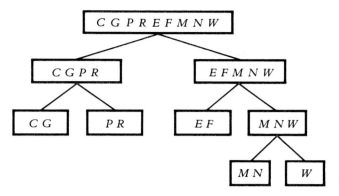

Figure 2.4   A hierarchical cluster analysis illustrating perceived similarities among letters

composed of straight lines into another. This grouping reveals that people are slower in responding that two letters are different when both letters contain curves or when both letters contain only straight lines.

The cluster analysis next partitioned the curved letters into the two confusable pairs C G and P R, distinguished by the presence of a vertical line. The other branch was then partitioned into E F and M N W, distinguished by the presence of either a horizontal line or a diagonal line. Finally, the pair M N was established as a confusable pair. The analysis of the adult reaction times yielded very similar results. The cluster analysis for both groups showed that the straight/curved contrast was the major determinant of perceived similarity. The presence of a particular line orientation (vertical, diagonal) also influenced reaction times.

A third method for measuring perceived similarity is to ask an observer to identify letters that are presented very rapidly in a tachistoscope (Townsend, 1971). It is often difficult to discriminate physically similar letters under these conditions, and the errors provide a measure of perceived similarity. Holbrook (1975) compared two feature models to determine how successfully each could predict the pattern of errors found by Townsend. One was the Gibson model shown in Figure 2.3, and the other was a modification of the Gibson model proposed by Geyer and De Wald (1973). The major change in the modification was the specification of the number of features in a letter (such as "two" vertical lines for the letter H) rather than simply a listing of whether that feature was present. A comparison of the two models revealed that the feature set proposed by Geyer and De Wald was superior in predicting the confusion errors made both by adults (Townsend, 1971) and by 4-year-olds (Gibson et al., 1963). The prediction of both models improved when the features were optimally weighted to allow for the fact that some features are more important than others in accounting for confusions. Since the straight/curved distinction is particularly important, it should be emphasized more than the others.

A potential source of embarrassment for proponents of feature models is that even the best-predicting model did not predict Townsend's data as well as a template model that measured the physical overlap of each pair of letters. The correlation between predicted errors and obtained errors was .70 for the template model and .50 for the Geyer model using optimally weighted features. The higher correlation for the template model means that it was more successful than the feature model at predicting correct responses. Why did the template model do better if it is not a very good theory of how people recognize patterns? Perhaps one reason it predicted well in these circumstances is that all the letters came from the same type font and there were no variations of each letter. A more important reason is that a template preserves the relations among the features. The letters E and F would produce considerable overlap because the vertical line and two horizontal lines in the letter F are connected in the same way as the vertical line and the upper two horizontal lines in the letter E. However, the similarity of two letters is determined not only by what features each contains but by the way the features are joined together. In order for feature theories to predict more accurately, the relations among features would have to be made more explicit. This is the main objective of structural theories.

Structural Theories

The importance of the relations among the features of a pattern was a guiding principle of Gestalt psychology. To the Gestalt psychologists a pattern was more than the sum of its parts. The relations among pattern features were later formalized by people working in the field of artificial intelligence who discovered that the interpretation of patterns usually depended on making explicit how the lines of a pattern were joined to other lines. I pointed out previously that a template theory would be unable to distinguish between the two interpretations of Figure 2.5. A feature theory would also have problems because although it could identify the four sides as features, the features are identical for the two interpretations. Structural theories, however, emphasize the relations among the features, and Clowes (1969) used Figure 2.5 as an example of why structural theories are often necessary to produce adequate descriptions of patterns. Perceiving the pattern as a sting ray requires grouping adjacent lines: line *a* with line *d* and line *b* with line *c*. Perceiving the pattern as a sail requires grouping opposite lines: line *a* with line *c* and line *b* with line *d*.

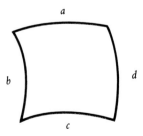

Figure 2.5   An ambiguous pattern, showing a sting ray or a sail

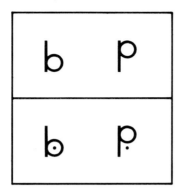

Figure 2.6   Normal (top) and dotted letters

Structural theories build upon feature theories. Before we can specify the relation among features, we have to specify the features. A structural theory allows for specification of how the features fit together. For example, the letter H consists of two vertical lines and a horizontal line—But we would make many different patterns from two vertical lines and a horizontal line. What is required is a precise specification of how the lines should be joined together: the letter H consists of two vertical lines connected at their midpoints by a horizontal line.

A simple experiment shows how creating a relation between features can facilitate rapid discrimination between two patterns. The bottom pair of letters in Figure 2.6 differs from the top pair by the addition of a dot. The dot appears in the same physical location for each letter, but it creates a different relation for each letter. It falls inside the curve for the letter b and outside the curve for the letter p. If people can use this relation, it should be easier to discriminate between the two dotted letters than between the two normal letters.

Lockhead and Crist (1980) tested this prediction by asking kindergarten children to sort a deck of cards into two bins. The deck contained either the two normal letters or the two dotted letters, arranged in a random order. The children sorted the dotted letters significantly faster than the normal letters, indicating that the addition of the dot made it easier to discriminate between the b and the p. The children also made fewer errors on the dotted letters. These results showed that adding the same feature to a pair of patterns made it easier to distinguish the two patterns because of the differing relation between features.

The features that we have considered thus far are features of two-dimensional shapes such as letters. However, it may be more convenient to describe three-dimensional objects in terms of simple volumes such as cylinders, blocks, wedges, and cones. Like the features of letters, these components can be combined in many different ways to produce a variety of objects. For example, the mug and the pail in Figure 2.7 contain the same two components in a different arrangement.

(a)   (b)   (c)   (d)

Figure 2.7   Different arrangements of the same components can produce different objects

The advantage of being able to form many different arrangements from a few components is that we may need relatively few components to describe objects. Irv Biederman (1985) has proposed that we need only about 35 simple volumes to describe the objects in the world. If so, then pattern recognition consists mainly in describing the relations among this limited set of components, rather than in discriminating among hundreds of components.

One consequence of Biederman's argument is that deleting information about the relation of features should reduce people's ability to recognize patterns. To test this hypothesis, Biederman removed 65% of the contour from drawings of objects, such as the two cups shown in Figure 2.8. In the cup on the left, the contour was removed from the middles of the segments, allowing observers to see how the segments were related. In the cup on the right, the contour was removed from the vertices so observers would have difficulty recognizing how the segments were related. When drawings of different objects were presented for 100 msec, subjects correctly named 70% of the objects if the contours were deleted at midsegments. But if the contours were deleted at the vertices, subjects correctly named fewer than 50% of the objects (Biederman, 1985). As predicted, destroying relational information was particularly detrimental for object recognition.

In conclusion, we have seen how structural theories extend feature theories by specifying how the features are related. Sutherland (1968) was one of the first to argue that if we want to account for our very impressive pattern recognition capabilities, we will need the more powerful kind of descriptive language contained in a structural theory. The experiments in this section show that Sutherland was correct. We will now look at how pattern recognition occurs over time.

Figure 2.8   Illustration of 65% contour removal centered at either
midsegments (left object) or vertices (right object)

Information-Processing Stages

The Partial-Report Technique

In order to understand how people perform on a pattern recognition task, we have to identify what occurs during each of the information-processing stages discussed in Chapter 1. Sperling (1960) is responsible for the initial construction of an information-processing model of performance on a visual recognition task. Subjects in Sperling's task saw an array of letters presented for a brief period (usually 50 msec) in a tachistoscope and were asked to report all the letters they could remember from the display. Responses were highly accurate if the display contained fewer than five letters. But when the number of letters was increased, subjects never reported more than an average of 4.5 letters correctly, regardless of how many letters were in the display.

A general problem in constructing an information-processing model is to identify the cause of a performance limitation. Sperling was interested in measuring the number of letters that could be recognized during a brief exposure, but he was aware that the upper limit of 4.5 might be caused by an inability to remember more than that. In other words, subjects might have recognized most of the letters in the display but have forgotten some before they could report what they had seen. Sperling therefore changed his procedure from a whole-report procedure (report all the letters) to a partial-report procedure (report only some of the letters).

In the most typical case, the display consisted of three rows, each containing four letters. Subjects would be unable to remember all twelve letters in a display, but they should be able to remember four letters. The partial-report procedure required that subjects report only one row. The pitch of a tone signaled which of the three rows to report: the top row for a high pitch, the middle row for a medium pitch, and the bottom row for a low pitch. The tone sounded just after the display disappeared, so that subjects would have to view the entire display and could not simply look at a single row.

Use of the partial-report technique is based on the assumption that the number of letters reported from the cued row equals the average number of letters perceived in each of the rows, since subjects did not know in advance which row to look at. This turned out to be a faulty assumption, but it seemed reasonable at the time, so let's accept it for a while for purposes of discussion. The results of the partial-report procedure indicated that subjects could correctly report three of the four letters in a row, implying that they had recognized nine letters in the entire display.

Sperling's Model

It often happens that what is best remembered about a scientist's work is not what that person originally set out to investigate. Although Sperling designed the partial-report technique to reduce the memory requirements of his task and obtain a "pure" measure of perception, his work is best remembered for discovery of the importance of a visual sensory store. How did this come about? The estimate that subjects had perceived 9 letters was obtained when the tone occurred immediately after the termination of the 50-msec exposure. In this case, subjects could correctly report about three quarters of the letters, and three quarters of 12 is 9. But when the tone was delayed until 1 second after the display, subjects' performance declined to the point that the estimated number of letters perceived was only 4.5. The estimates showed a gradual decline from 9 letters to 4.5 as the delay of the tone increased from 0 to 1 second (Figure 2.9).

The most interesting thing about the number 4.5 is that it is exactly equal to the upper limit of performance on the whole-report task, as represented by the black bar in Figure 2.9. The partial-report procedure has no advantage over the whole-report procedure if the tone is delayed by 1 second or more. To explain the gradual decline in performance illustrated in Figure 2.9, Sperling proposed that subjects were using a visual sensory store to recognize letters in the cued row. When they heard the tone, they selectively attended to the cued row in the store and tried to identify the letters in that row. Their success in making use of the tone depended on the clarity of information in the sensory store. When the tone occurred immediately after termination of the stimulus, the clarity was sufficient for recognizing additional letters in the cued row. But as the clarity of the sensory image faded, it became increasingly difficult to recognize additional letters. When the tone was delayed by 1 second, subjects could not use the sensory store at all to focus on the cued row, so their performance was determined by the number of letters they had recognized from the entire display that happened to be in that row. Their performance was therefore equivalent to the whole-report procedure, in which they attended to the entire display.

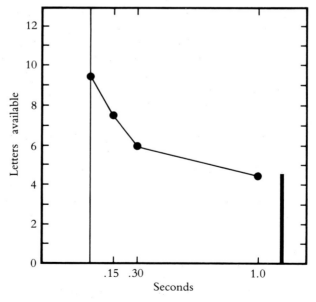

Figure 2.9   Estimated number of "letters available" as a function of delay of the tone

In 1963 Sperling proposed an information-processing model of performance on his visual report task. The model consisted of a visual information store, scanning, rehearsal, and an auditory information store.

The *visual information store,* VIS, is a sensory store that preserves information for a brief period lasting from a fraction of a second to a second. The decay rate depends on such factors as the intensity, contrast, and duration of the stimulus and also on whether exposure of the stimulus is followed by a second exposure. Visual masking occurs when a second exposure, consisting of a brightly lighted field or a different set of patterns, reduces the effectiveness of the visual information store.

In order for pattern recognition to occur, the information in the sensory store must be scanned. Sperling initially considered *scanning* to occur for one item at a time, as if one had a sheet of cardboard with a hole in it just large enough for a single letter to appear.

The next two components of the model were *rehearsal* (saying the letters to oneself) and an *auditory information store,* AIS (remembering the names of the letters). In order to remember the items until recall, subjects usually reported rehearsing the items. Additional evidence for verbal rehearsal was found when recall errors often appeared in the form of auditory confusions—in other words, producing a letter that sounded like the correct letter. The advantage of the auditory store is that items can be continuously recycled by means of rehearsal. Sperling's auditory store is part of short-term memory, a topic we will consider later in the book.

Sperling revised his initial model in 1967. By this time evidence had begun to accumulate suggesting that patterns were not scanned one at a time but were analyzed simultaneously. Sperling therefore modified his idea of the scan component to allow for pattern recognition to occur simultaneously over the entire display, although the rate of recognition in a given location depended on where the subject was focusing attention. Another change in the 1967 model was the inclusion of a *recognition (R) buffer* for converting the visual image of a letter into a program of motor instructions for pronouncing the names. Sperling added the recognition buffer to the model because a person would not have time to actually rehearse the letters during the brief exposure of the stimulus. Recognition of a letter would therefore activate the program for rehearsal, which would be carried out after the visual information store had decayed. Figure 2.10 shows a diagram of the revised model.

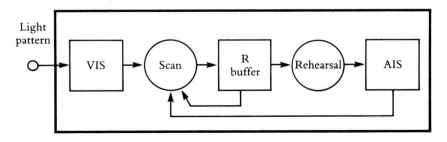

Figure 2.10   Model of processing stages in Sperling's paradigm

Rumelhart's Model

In 1970 Rumelhart proposed a detailed mathematical model of performance on a wide range of information-processing tasks, including the whole-report and partial-report procedures studied by Sperling. Rumelhart's model assumes that recognition occurs by identification of the features of a pattern. Feature recognition occurs simultaneously over the entire display, but it takes time to recognize features, and the more time the observer has, the more features can be recognized. Imagine that you are looking at the screen of a tachistoscope and the experimenter presents a brief exposure of the letters F, R, and Z. If the exposure is very short, you might see only the vertical line of the letter F, the curve of the letter R, and the diagonal line of the letter Z. If forced to guess at this point, you would most likely use this information. You might guess that the R was an R, P, or B because these letters have curved segments at the top. If the exposure is a little longer, you will be able to see more features, and it will be easier to guess or even recognize the entire letter.

Your success in identifying the letters will be determined not only by the length of the exposure but also by how quickly you can recognize the features. The rate of feature recognition in Rumelhart's model is influenced by both the clarity of the information and the number of items in the display. When the exposure terminates, the clarity declines as the visual information store decays. The number of items in the display affects the rate of feature recognition because the model assumes that people have a limited amount of attention, which is divided across all the items in the display. As the number of items increases, the amount of attention that can be focused on each item declines, and this slows down the rate of recognizing that particular item.

The assumption that the rate of feature recognition depends on both the number of items in the display and the clarity of the information is used by Rumelhart to account for performance on Sperling's task. Rumelhart's model proposed that people can report an average of only 4.5 letters in the whole-report procedure because of a perceptual limitation rather than a memory limitation. As the number of letters is increased up to 12, people continue to try to recognize all the letters simultaneously. But the rate of recognizing each letter slows down as more letters are added to the display. Although there are more letters that could be recognized, the increase is compensated for by the lower probability of recognizing each letter.

Rumelhart's model assumes that in the partial-report procedure the observer tries to recognize letters over the entire display before hearing the tone. Then, on hearing the tone, the observer attends only to the cued row in the visual information store and tries to recognize additional letters in that particular row. The rate of recognition is faster because the observer now has to attend to only 4 letters rather than 12. But as the visual information store decays, not only is there less time to use it, but it becomes harder to use because of decreasing clarity. Success in focusing on the cued row therefore depends very critically on the delay of the tone, as is illustrated in Figure 2.9. Rumelhart's assumptions were adequate for making quantitative predictions about performance not only on Sperling's tasks but on a number of other tasks as well.

One difference between Rumelhart's interpretation and that suggested by Sperling is that Sperling claimed that performance in the whole-report task was limited by memory and Rumelhart claimed that performance was limited by perception. The relative roles of perception and memory as limiting factors in this task should depend on the number of letters in the display and the exposure time. We will see in the next chapter that STM could limit performance if the number of letters in the display exceeded the limited capacity of STM. However, if people could recognize only 4.5 letters because of the very brief exposure, the limiting factor would be perception rather than memory.

Because memory is a limiting factor when people have time to recognize more letters than they can remember, the whole-report procedure is no longer used to measure perception. A better procedure, called the *detection paradigm*, was designed by Estes and Taylor (1966). This procedure requires that the observer report which one of two target letters is in a display of letters. For instance, the subject might be told that a display will contain either a *B* or an *F*, and the task is to report which letter is present. The memory requirements are minimal because the subject must report only a single letter. By using the percentage of trials on which the observer was right, and correcting for guessing, Estes and Taylor were able to calculate the average number of letters perceived on each trial. The detection procedure has also been analyzed by Rumelhart (1970) as a part of his general model—a model that provided an impressive account of performance on the visual information-processing tasks studied during the 1960s.

Word Recognition

The Word Superiority Effect

Much of the research on pattern recognition during the 1970s shifted away from how people recognize isolated letters to how people recognize letters in words. This research was stimulated by a finding that has been labeled the *word superiority effect*. Gerald Reicher (1969), in his dissertation at the University of Michigan, investigated a possible implication of the scan component in Sperling's 1967 model. If the observer tries to recognize all the letters in an array simultaneously, is it possible to recognize a four-letter unit in the same amount of time as it takes to recognize a single letter? To answer this question, Reicher designed an experiment in which observers were shown a single letter, a four-letter word, or a four-letter nonword. The task was always to identify a single letter by selecting one of two alternatives. The exposure of the stimulus was immediately followed by a visual masking field with the two response alternatives directly above or below the critical letter. For example, one set of stimuli consisted of the letter *D*, the word *WORD*, and the nonword *OWRD*. The two alternatives in this case were the letters *D* and *K*, which were displayed above the critical *D* (see Figure 2.11). Observers indicated whether they thought the letter in that position had been a *D* or a *K*.

This example illustrates several characteristics of Reicher's design. First, the four-letter word has the same letters as the four-letter nonword. Second, the position

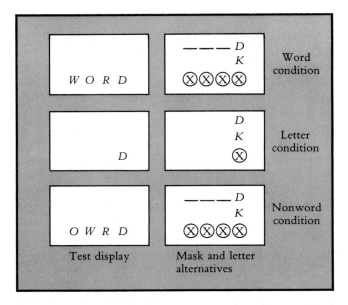

Figure 2.11 Example of the three experimental conditions in Reicher's (1969) experiment. The mask and response alternatives followed the test display. The task was to decide which of the two alternatives had appeared in the tested position.

of the critical letter is the same for the word and the nonword. Third, both of the response alternatives make a word (*WORD* or *WORK*) for the word condition and a nonword for the nonword condition. And fourth, the memory requirements are minimized by requiring that subjects identify only a single letter, even when four letters are presented.

The results showed that subjects were significantly more accurate in identifying the critical letter when it was part of a word than when it was part of a nonword or when it was presented alone. Eight of the nine subjects did better on single words than on single letters. The one subject who reversed this trend was the only subject who said that she saw the words as four separate letters, which she made into words; all other subjects said that they experienced a word as a single word, not as four letters making up a word.

This word superiority effect can possibly tell us something useful about reading. Over the nine years following Reicher's experiment, the effect was the subject of numerous investigations, which have been reviewed by Baron (1978). Baron points out that it is still unresolved which of several possible explanations of the effect is the best. The explanation that Baron seems to favor is simply that more features of letters are identified when the letters are parts of words than when they are parts of nonwords.

A detailed model of how people's knowledge of words can facilitate their perception of letters in words has been proposed by McClelland and Rumelhart (1981).

In their model; perception results from excitatory and inhibitory interactions among features, letters, and words. Presentation of a string of letters begins the process of activating detectors for letters that are consistent with the presented letters. As some letters begin to be recognized, they begin to activate detectors for words that are consistent with the recognized letters. The activated words then produce feedback, which reinforces the activations of the detectors for letters in the word. Letters in words are more perceptible because they receive more activation than single letters or letters in nonwords.

An alternative explanation—the inference view—is that the perceptual information is easier to interpret for words than for nonwords (Krueger & Shapiro, 1979; Massaro, 1979). This view implies that the same number of features is perceived for words as nonwords. Imagine that you saw a four-letter word and identified the first three letters as WOR. You didn't have time to identify the fourth letter but noticed that it contained a curved segment. The curved segment suggests that the fourth letter must be either a D, an O, or a Q. Since only the letter D completes a word, you can eliminate O and Q. If you identified ORW and a curved segment in a nonword, you wouldn't know whether the last letter was D, O, or Q. The correct inference in the first case depends on using knowledge of what letters occur in words.

Reicher's procedure attempted to limit the use of inferences by requiring that people choose between only two alternatives, such as the letters D and K in the above example. It is not obvious how well the inference view can explain his results when there are only two alternatives, both of which form a word. The detection of a curved segment, for example, should result in selecting a D rather than a K regardless of whether the letter occurred in a word or a nonword.

Some of the studies on the word superiority effect have used variations of Reicher's procedure, and the inference view may provide a better explanation of their results (see Krueger & Shapiro, 1979; Massaro, 1979). We also know that inferences are important during normal reading, since we can use both our knowledge of language and the perceptual information to identify words. Let us look at how an interactive model of reading combines these two sources of information.

An Interactive Model of Reading

Recognition of words during reading is determined by both the information in the text and the reader's knowledge of the world. A major problem is how the skilled reader puts all this information together to make reading an easy task. Although we do not yet have a detailed answer to this question, we do know the general form a model should take.

It is clear from the many studies on reading that a model of how people recognize words will have to be an interactive model in which different sources of information are combined. Figure 2.12 shows an interactive model proposed by Rumelhart (1977). As the reader scans the text, letters are registered in the visual information store (VIS), where the reader attempts to identify the features of the letters. This perceptual information is then combined with the reader's knowledge to recognize words.

Figure 2.12   An interactive model of reading

The knowledge includes information about the orthographic structure of the language, lexical items in the language, syntactic possibilities, and semantic context.

Orthographic knowledge is knowledge about the probability of various strings of letters—for example, knowing that a *u* typically follows a *q* and that a *z* is unlikely to follow the letter *t*. *Lexical* knowledge is knowledge of which letter combinations form a word in a language. The constraint that the letters must form a word places restrictions on which letters can occur.

Syntactic knowledge concerns the grammar of a language. It helps us use the previous words in a sentence to determine whether the next word is likely to be a noun, a verb, an adjective, or some other grammatical unit. Children make use of grammatical information quite early in learning to read (Weber, 1970). Observers who classified oral reading errors made during a first-grade reading class found that about 90% of the errors were grammatically acceptable within the preceding context. An error was judged grammatically acceptable if the child's response could be completed to form a grammatical sentence. If the child reads *Spot and* for the words *Spot can,* the error is grammatically acceptable because *Spot and* can be completed to form a grammatical sentence. Substitution of *she cold* for *she could* would be classified as ungrammatical.

Semantic knowledge refers to the meaning of what we are reading. Consider the experience of trying to read handwriting that is almost illegible. If we isolate single words from their context, we may not be able to recognize them at all, even if we have very good orthographic and lexical knowledge. If a word appears in a sentence, we can make use of grammatical knowledge to determine whether the word is likely to be a noun, verb, or adjective. This would provide some help, but each of these grammatical classes is very large, so we would most likely resort to semantic knowledge for further help. The meaning of the sentence and surrounding sentences should help us identify the illegible word.

An example might help to show how all this information can be combined (Rumelhart, 1977). Consider the following procedure. You view the picture shown

Figure 2.13   A scene illustrating a context

in Figure 2.13 for a few seconds and are then given a tachistoscopic presentation of a noun phrase, which you know will refer to one of the objects in the picture. The picture provides a semantic context for the noun phrase. The noun phrase is *THE CAR*, but because of the fast exposure, you identify only some of its features—shown in Figure 2.14.

Since the perceptual information is rather meager, you must use other sources of knowledge to interpret the stimulus. The syntactic knowledge that a noun phrase usually starts with a determiner (*a, an, the*) makes it relatively easy to identify the first word as *THE*. This decision is also facilitated by the orthographic knowledge that *TH* is a frequent letter pair. Orthographic knowledge is represented at the letter cluster level in Figure 2.14. The syntactic knowledge that the second word of a noun phrase is a noun or an adjective is much less restrictive, and the words *FAT, CAT,* and *CAR* are considered at the lexical level as being consistent with the perceptual information. The fact that *AT* is a frequent letter pair is counterproductive because it suggests an incorrect answer. If you gave the correct answer in this case, it would likely be because of the influence of the semantic context. Identifying the second word as *CAR* is consistent with the fact that there is a car (a Volkswagen) in the picture.

We might want to question whether this example overemphasized the importance of nonperceptual knowledge by providing so little perceptual information. Don't we usually have time to recognize all the features of a letter when we read? I have two answers to this question.

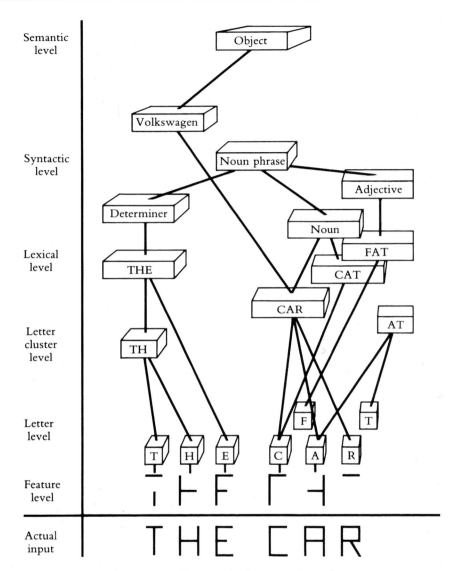

Figure 2.14   Sources of information for reading

First, the features can often be very difficult to recognize when we are reading handwriting, making it necessary to use nonperceptual information. In fact, we may not even realize that a letter or word is ambiguous, because the context makes it clear which word is intended. The two sentences in Figure 2.15 contain a physically identical word, yet we have little difficulty in identifying the word as *went* in the upper sentence and as *event* in the lower sentence.

Second, even when we read typewriting and therefore have very legible letters before us, the use of nonperceptual knowledge can reduce the amount of perceptual

Jack and Jill event up the hill.

The pole vault was the last event.

Figure 2.15 The dependence of letter perception on context

analysis we have to perform. The difficulty of doing a very careful perceptual analysis is illustrated by proofreading errors. I was surprised to find about three or four errors in each of the chapters of this book even after I had carefully read the manuscript on two previous occasions in an attempt to identify errors. And proofreading is done much more carefully and slowly than normal reading.

The purpose of normal reading, of course, is to extract meaning from text. This section illustrates that the extraction of meaning not only depends on pattern recognition but also helps to guide pattern recognition. The way people manage to comprehend text is one of the most challenging problems in cognitive psychology. We will return to this issue in a later chapter. Our immediate task is to continue examining the perceptual aspects of cognition by studying the role of attention in limiting the amount of information we perceive and enter into memory. You will notice as you read the next chapter that most of the experiments in this area use auditory messages. Our ability to process many visual patterns simultaneously and control what we are looking at by moving our eyes makes it easier to study attention by using auditory messages. The findings reported in the next chapter will generalize some of the ideas expressed in this chapter. The role of context, for example, is as important in understanding speech as it is in reading written material. As you read further, look for related ideas and concepts. I will try to make your task easier by pointing out some of the similarities between visual and auditory perception.

Summary

Pattern recognition is a skill that people perform very well. The three most popular explanations of pattern recognition are template, feature, and structural theories. A template theory proposes that people compare two patterns by measuring their degree of overlap. A template theory has difficulty accounting for many aspects of pattern recognition, but it is a useful way of representing information in the sensory store before it is analyzed during the pattern recognition stage. The most common theories of pattern recognition assume that patterns are analyzed into features. Feature theories are often tested by determining how well they can account for perceptual confusions. Structural theories state explicitly how the features of a pattern are joined together. They provide a more complete description of a pattern and are particularly useful for describing patterns consisting of intersecting lines.

Sperling's interest in the question of how many letters can be perceived during a brief tachistoscopic exposure resulted in the construction of information-processing models for visual tasks. Sperling proposed that the information is preserved very briefly in a visual information store, where all the letters can be simultaneously analyzed. When a letter is recognized, its name can be verbally rehearsed and preserved in an auditory store (short-term memory). Rumelhart's model proposed that we recognize patterns by identifying their features. The rate of feature identification depends on both the clarity of items in the visual information store and the number of letters in a display. The model accounts for performance on Sperling's partial-report task by assuming that the observer focuses attention on the cued row as soon as the tone is heard. The probability of recognizing additional letters in the row depends on the clarity of the visual information store.

Recognition of letters while reading is influenced by perceptual information and the context of the letter. The finding that a letter can be recognized more easily when it is part of a word than when it is part of a nonword or is presented by itself has been called the word superiority effect. A perceptual explanation of this finding assumes that recognition of some letters can facilitate recognition of other letters that frequently occur together or form a word. An alternative explanation assumes that it is easier for people to infer what letter occurred when the letter is part of a word. An interactive model of reading proposes that perceptual information interacts with orthographic, lexical, syntactic, and semantic knowledge to influence word recognition and thus facilitate reading.

Recommended Reading

Kolers's (1983) chapter provides a recent overview of issues related to perception and representation. Townsend and his colleagues (Townsend & Ashby, 1982; Townsend, Hu, & Evans, 1984) have evaluated formal models of pattern recognition in which feature detection has a major role. Garner's book *The Processing of Information and Structure* (1974) reviews research on the structural characteristics of patterns. The relation between his work and Eleanor Gibson's is discussed in his chapter on letter identification (Garner, 1979). Palmer (1977) shows how structural descriptions influence the analysis and synthesis of patterns, and Bower and Glass (1976) demonstrate how structural descriptions determine the effectiveness of memory cues. The characteristics of the visual information store are described by Long (1980) and Loftus, Shimamura, and Johnson (1985). Articles by Baron (1978) and Adams (1979) discuss the theoretical attempts to explain the word superiority effect. Recent models of word recognition have been proposed by McClelland and Rumelhart (1981; Rumelhart & McClelland, 1982), Paap, Newsome, McDonald, and Schvaneveldt (1982), and Grossberg and Stone (1986). Other areas of research on pattern recognition include the recognition of speech (Marslen-Wilson & Welsh, 1978), faces (Pittenger & Shaw, 1975), scenes (Biederman, 1981), and maps (Tversky, 1981).

3

Attention

Everyone knows what attention is. It is the taking possession by the mind, in clear and vivid form, of one out of what seem several simultaneously possible objects or trains of thought. Focalization, concentration, of consciousness are of its essence.

WILLIAM JAMES (1890)

The above words from William James's famous *Principles of Psychology*, published in 1890, refer to two characteristics of attention that continue to be studied today—focalization and concentration. *Focalization* implies selectivity. We are usually bombarded by all kinds of perceptual stimuli and must decide which of these are of interest to us. The selective nature of attention is illustrated by the behavior of subjects in Sperling's partial-report task: when a cue signaled which row to report, subjects were able to attend selectively to the cued row and ignore the information in the other two rows.

The selective nature of perception is necessary to keep us from becoming overloaded with information. This is particularly true in large cities. According to Stanley Milgram (1970), a well-known social psychologist, it has been calculated that in midtown Manhattan it is possible to encounter 220,000 people within a ten-minute radius of one's office. This kind of overload, Milgram argues, can affect our life on several levels, influencing role performance, the evolution of social norms, and cognitive functioning. Adaptive responses to information overload include spending less time on each input, disregarding low-priority inputs, or completely blocking off some sensory inputs. The first part of this chapter is concerned with theories that try to locate the stage at which this selection occurs. Do we block off the sensory input before it reaches the pattern recognition stage, or do we make the selection after recognition? Theories that attempt to answer this question are called *bottleneck*

35

theories because they assume that selection is necessary whenever too much information reaches a bottleneck—a stage that cannot process all of it.

The second aspect of attention is *concentration*. Imagine that you are the first to arrive at a cocktail party, and you carry on a conversation with the hostess. As long as there are no other conversations in the room, it will require little concentration or mental effort to follow what the hostess is saying. If she were not speaking in your native language, however, comprehension would be less automatic and would require more mental effort. You would also have to concentrate more to follow what she was saying if you were surrounded by many other conversations. If you wanted to eavesdrop on one of the other conversations while you were listening to the hostess, still more concentration or mental effort would be required.

The second section of this chapter discusses *capacity theories* of attention, which try to determine how capacity or mental effort is allocated to different activities. Such theories propose that attention is limited in capacity, and when we try to attend to more than one event—studying while watching television, for instance—we pay the price of doing each less efficiently. Rumelhart's model, discussed in Chapter 2, is a theory that assumes a limited capacity. According to his model, feature recognition slows down as the number of items increases because a limited amount of attention must be distributed over more patterns.

An important area of research related to capacity theories is the study of automatic processing. *Automatic processing* occurs when the capacity required for carrying out a task is minimal. If a task requires very little capacity to perform, it should not interfere with other tasks. The third section of this chapter examines the characteristics of automatic processing and illustrates how the concept can be applied to the acquisition of reading skills.

The final section presents some research on using selective listening tests to predict success in a pilot training program and the accident rate of commercial drivers. There are other potential applications of research on selective attention. One example is the diagnosis of heart murmurs. Rushmer (1970) pointed out that it is difficult for medical students to learn how to classify heart murmurs. Part of the difficulty results from the demands of selective attention—it is hard to hear the murmur embedded in the sound of a heartbeat. Perhaps we will see still more applications of selective attention research in the future.

Before I talk about attention in my own course on cognitive psychology, I have the students try to listen to two verbal messages at once. Two volunteers come to the front of the class and read different passages from one of their books. The rest of the class usually finds it very difficult to comprehend both of the messages simultaneously. It is easier to try to comprehend only one of the messages, but the difficulty of the task depends on physical characteristics such as pitch and separation. The difficulty increases as the pitch of the two speakers becomes more similar or the two speakers stand closer together. If you have the opportunity, try to participate in such a demonstration and observe some of these effects for yourself. It will give you a better understanding of the listener's task.

[handwritten annotations in top margin: "sub filter PR ST m"; "when in Sys does bottleneck occur, selectin filter PR etc."]

Bottleneck Theories

Broadbent's Filter Model

As you will recall, the discussion of information-processing models in Chapter 1 included a summary of Broadbent's (1958) filter model. The model could account for much of the data on attention that had been collected at that time. One example is an experiment in which enlisted men in England's Royal Navy listened to three pairs of digits (Broadbent, 1954). One member of each pair arrived at one ear at the same time that the other member of the pair arrived at the other ear. For example, if the sequence were 73–42–15, the subject would simultaneously hear 7 and 3, followed by 4 and 2, followed by 1 and 5.

Left ear	Right ear
7	3
4	2
1	5

The pairs were separated by a ½-second interval, and the subjects were asked to report the digits in whatever order they chose. They were able to report 65% of the lists correctly, and almost all the correct reports involved recalling all the digits presented to one ear, followed by all the digits presented to the other ear. In other words, if 741 had been presented to the left ear and 325 to the right ear, the subject would recall either in the order 741–325 or in the order 325–741.

Another group of men was instructed to recall the digits in the actual order of their arrival: the first pair of digits, followed by the second pair, followed by the third pair. The time between successive pairs of digits varied from ½ second to 2 seconds. Figure 3.1 shows the percentage of lists correctly recalled as a function of the interval between pairs. Performance was better at the longer intervals; nevertheless, it was much worse than when subjects could recall the digits heard in one ear and then the other ear.

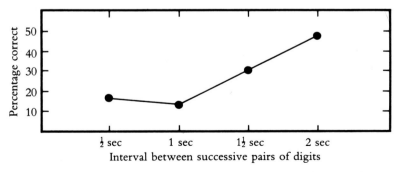

Figure 3.1 Recall of digit sequences as a function of the interval between pairs

To account for these findings, Broadbent (1957) used the filter model, which can be represented by the mechanical model shown in Figure 3.2. The mechanical model consists of a Y-shaped tube and a set of identifiable balls. The tube has a narrow stem that can accept only a single ball at a time (the limited-capacity perceptual channel) but upper branches (the sensory store) that are wider and can accept more than one ball at a time. At the junction of the stem and branches is a hinged flap (the filter), which can swing back and forth to allow balls from either branch of the Y to enter the stem.

In this case the balls represent digits, and the two branches represent the two ears. Two balls are simultaneously dropped, one into each branch. The flap door would be set to one side to allow one of the balls to enter the stem, while the other ball would be held in a sensory store. If the observer wanted to report all the digits entering one ear, the flap would stay to one side until all three balls from one branch entered the stem. The flap would then be shifted to the other side, allowing the three balls from the other branch to enter the stem. If the observer were forced to report the digits as they arrived, the flap would have to be shifted back and forth to allow balls to enter the stem in the order in which they arrived.

The model accounts for performance on Broadbent's (1954) task by assuming that it takes time to switch attention (represented by the flap, or filter) from ear to ear. If the interval separating pairs of balls is too short, the flap will not have time to switch back and forth, and performance will deteriorate as it did when the interval was 1 second or less (Figure 3.1). The easiest case should be when the listener can report all the digits entering one ear before reporting all the digits entering the other ear. In this case, the listener can recognize all the digits entering one ear before recognizing the digits entering the other ear, and only a single shift of attention is required. But the shift has to occur before the information entering the unattended

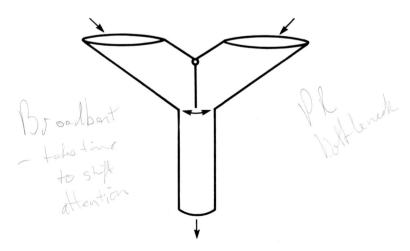

Figure 3.2   A mechanical model of attention

ear decays from the auditory sensory store. A limitation of the filter model is that the sensory store would have to last fairly long in order to operate as proposed; otherwise, the information would decay before it could be recognized.

Treisman's Attenuation Model

A common experimental paradigm for testing Broadbent's assumption that the listener can recognize information on only one channel at a time is to present a different, but continuous, message to each ear and ask the listener to "shadow," or repeat aloud, one of the messages. Shadowing a message provides proof that the listener is following instructions and attending to the correct ear. The initial findings from shadowing experiments supported the filter model. As predicted, subjects were almost completely unaware of the content of the message played to the unattended ear (Cherry, 1953).

However, later research indicated that listeners occasionally could report information on the unattended channel. Moray (1959) discovered that subjects sometimes heard their own names on this channel. Treisman (1960) found that the contextual effects of language would sometimes cause subjects to report words on the unattended channel and therefore shadow inappropriately. The following are two examples of the intrusions that occurred:

> 1. . . . I SAW THE GIRL / song was WISHING . . .
>   . . . . me that bird / JUMPING in the street . . .
> 2. . . . SITTING AT A MAHOGANY / three POSSIBILITIES . . .
>   . . . . let us look at these / TABLE with her head . . .

so much for Broadbent. — context was important

The first line in each example is the message that the listener was asked to shadow. The second line is the unattended message. The words in capital letters are the words actually spoken by the subjects. The intrusions from the unattended channel fit the semantic context better than the words on the attended channel. The contextual cues were not sufficient to cause subjects to change permanently to the unattended message in order to follow the meaning of the passage, but the results did raise some questions for the filter theory. If the filter completely blocks out the unattended message, how could subjects report hearing their names or shadow words on the unattended channel?

To answer this question, Treisman (1960) proposed a model consisting of two parts—a selective filter and a "dictionary" (Figure 3.3). The filter distinguishes between two messages on the basis of their physical characteristics, such as location, intensity, or pitch. However, the filter in Treisman's model does not completely block out the unattended message but merely attenuates it, making it less likely to be heard. The recognition of a word occurs in the dictionary if the intensity or subjective loudness of the word exceeds its threshold (the minimum intensity needed for recognition). The thresholds have two important characteristics. First, they vary across words. Some words have permanently lower thresholds than others and thus are more easily recognized—for example, important words such as a person's own name and perhaps danger signals such as *fire*. Second, the thresholds can be momentarily lowered by the listener's expectations. For instance, if the words *sitting at a mahogany* are heard, the threshold for the word *table* will be momentarily lowered, making recognition of that word more likely.

The model proposed by Treisman was able to explain why usually very little is heard on the unattended channel, but occasionally some words are recognized. The attenuation of words on the unattended channel implies that they will be subjectively less loud than words on the attended channel. They will usually not be loud enough to exceed their threshold unless they have a very low threshold or their threshold is momentarily lowered. Figure 3.3 shows a schematic representation of this effect. The height of the arrows represents the subjective loudness of the two messages, and the height of the thresholds represents the loudness that is necessary for recognition of the word. Since important words have permanently low thresholds, they can occasionally be heard on the unattended channel, as was found by Moray (1959). A word like *table* normally has a high threshold, but its threshold can be momentarily lowered by expectations. This aspect of the model could account for Treisman's (1960) finding that words on the unattended channel were sometimes incorrectly shadowed if they better fit the context of the message on the attended channel.

Figure 3.3   Treisman's attenuation model

The Deutsch-Norman Memory Selection Model

The models proposed by Broadbent and Treisman placed the bottleneck at the pattern recognition stage. Attention was represented by a selective filter that completely blocked out the unattended message in Broadbent's model and attenuated it in Treisman's model, with the implication that very few words should be recognized on the unattended channel. An unattended message could be recognized, in Broadbent's model, only if attention switched to that message before it decayed from the sensory store. In Treisman's model, words in the unattended message could be recognized only if their thresholds were low enough to be exceeded by the attenuated message.

We have previously seen that a frequent problem in constructing information-processing models is identification of the stage at which a performance limitation occurs. Constructing models of attention is no exception. According to the models proposed by Deutsch and Deutsch (1963) and Norman (1968), the bottleneck occurs after pattern recognition. The problem is not one of perception but one of selection

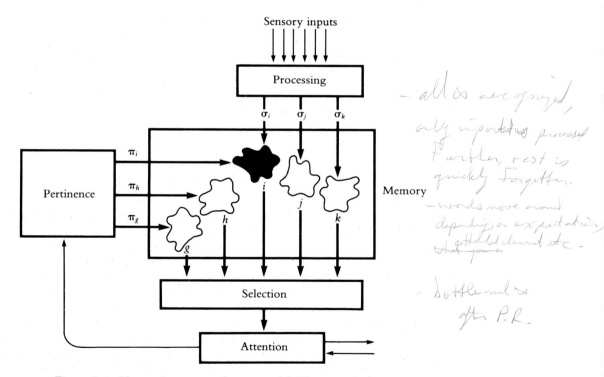

Figure 3.4 Norman's memory selection model. The example shows five words, represented by the subscripts, g, h, i, j, and k. Words g, h, and i are important, and words i, j, and k are consistent with the sensory input. The word selected for further processing is the one with the greatest combination of pertinence (importance) and sensory activation.

after perception occurs. In their models attention is equivalent to the selection stage in Figure 1.1 (Chapter 1).

The model proposed by Deutsch and Deutsch involves two different conversations (messages). The model assumes that words in both conversations are recognized but are quickly forgotten unless they are important. Words on the attended channel are important because people have to shadow them. Words on the unattended channel are usually unimportant because the listener is asked to attend to another channel. Although recognized, they are quickly forgotten unless they are important—a person's own name, for instance. The probability that information will enter memory depends on the general level of arousal in addition to the importance of the material. Much more will enter memory when a person is alert than when the person is drowsy.

Norman expanded the Deutsch and Deutsch model in a 1968 paper. Figure 3.4 is a schematic diagram of Norman's model. Three sensory inputs—i, j, and k—are recognized by being matched to their representations in memory. They will be quickly forgotten, however, unless they can be selected for more permanent storage. Selection is determined not only by the strength of the sensory input but also by the pertinence, or importance, of each input. Certain words have a permanently high level of importance, whereas others have low levels but can fluctuate as a result of expectations formed from contextual, grammatical, or semantic cues. The input that is acted on or stored more permanently in memory is determined by a combination of sensory activation and importance (labeled σ and π in Figure 3.4). Stimulus i has the highest combination in the example, so it is the one selected for further processing.

Capacity Theories

The models proposed by Broadbent, Treisman, Deutsch and Deutsch, and Norman stimulated many experiments and arguments regarding the location of the bottleneck. Some data seemed to support the assertion that the bottleneck was caused by the limitations of perception, whereas other data supported the assertion that the bottleneck occurred after perception. The failure to agree on the location of the bottleneck has had two consequences. First, psychologists have become more interested in studying the capacity demands of different tasks than in locating the bottleneck (Kahneman, 1973). Second, it now seems reasonable to assume that the observer has some control over where the bottleneck occurs depending on what is required in a particular task (Johnston & Heinz, 1978).

We will look first at a capacity model of attention proposed by Kahneman to see how a capacity model differs from a bottleneck model. Then we will review the theory proposed by Johnston and Heinz (1978), which suggests that attention is flexible and that the observer has control over where the bottleneck occurs. The Johnston and Heinz theory is particularly interesting because it shows how a bottleneck theory can be related to a capacity theory, since the location of the bottleneck determines how much capacity is required to perform a task.

Example of a Capacity Model

Capacity theories are concerned with the amount of mental effort required to perform a task. Daniel Kahneman's *Attention and Effort* (1973) helped to shift the emphasis from bottleneck theories to capacity theories. Kahneman argued that capacity theory assumes there is a general limit on a person's capacity to perform mental work. It also assumes that a person has considerable control over how this limited capacity can be allocated to different activities. For example, we can usually drive a car and carry on a conversation at the same time if both activities do not exceed our capacity for attending to two different tasks. But when heavy traffic begins to challenge our skills as a driver, it is better to concentrate only on driving and not try to divide our attention between two activities.

A model of the allocation of capacity to mental activities is shown in Figure 3.5. Any kind of activity that requires attention would be represented in the model, because all such activities compete for the limited capacity. Different mental activities require different amounts of attention; some tasks require little mental effort and others require much effort. When the supply of attention does not meet the de-

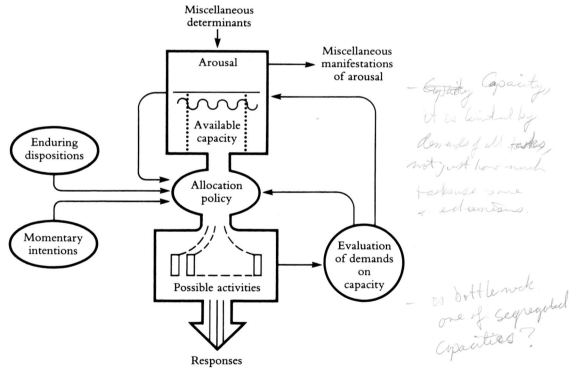

Figure 3.5 A capacity model for attention

mands, the level of performance declines. An activity can fail entirely if there is not enough capacity to meet its demands or if attention is allocated to other activities.

Kahneman's model assumes that the amount of capacity available varies with the level of arousal; more capacity is available when arousal is moderately high than when it is low. However, very high levels of arousal can interfere with performance. This assumption is consistent with the Yerkes-Dodson (1908) law that performance is best at intermediate levels of arousal.

Level of arousal can be controlled by feedback from the attempt to meet the demands of ongoing activities, provided that the total demands do not exceed the capacity limit. The choice of which activities to support is influenced by both *enduring dispositions* and *momentary intentions*. Enduring dispositions reflect the rules of involuntary attention. A novel event, an object in sudden motion, or the mention of our own name may automatically attract our attention. Momentary intentions reflect our specific goals or objectives at a particular time. We may want to listen to a lecturer or scan a crowd at an airport in order to recognize a friend.

The use of alarm systems to automatically attract attention is one way to help people cope with situations that overload their limited capacity. Recently a Boeing 707 was flying in clouds toward the World Trade Center at an altitude that was 200 feet below the top of the North Tower Mast. An alarm system buzzed in the control tower to signal that the plane was flying at a dangerously low altitude. Instantly the controller radioed the crew to turn around and climb to 3000 feet. The controller did not initially notice the low altitude because he was responsible for controlling seven other planes at the time of the near accident, a situation that overloaded his limited capacity.

The capacity model proposed by Kahneman was designed to supplement, rather than to replace, the bottleneck models. Both types of theories predict that simultaneous activities are likely to interfere with each other, but they attribute the interference to different causes. A bottleneck theory proposes that interference occurs because the same mechanism is required to carry out two incompatible operations at the same time, whereas a capacity model proposes that interference occurs when the demands of two activities exceed the available capacity. Thus a bottleneck model implies that the interference between tasks is specific and depends on the degree to which the tasks use the same mechanisms. A capacity model, in contrast, implies that the interference is nonspecific and depends on the total demands of the task. Both kinds of interference occur, and both kinds of theories are therefore necessary.

Capacity and Stage of Selection

The flexibility of attention and the interaction between a bottleneck and a capacity theory have been demonstrated by Johnston and Heinz (1978). They used selective listening tasks to develop their theory, so a bottleneck would be likely to occur. However, unlike the early bottleneck theories, their theory proposed that the listener has control over the location of the bottleneck. The location can vary along a continuum ranging from an early mode of selection—in other words, before recognition (as represented by Broadbent's theory)—to a late mode of selection—in other words, following a semantic analysis (as represented by Deutsch and Deutsch's theory). Johnston and Heinz call their theory a multimode theory because of its flexibility: the observer can adopt any mode of attention demanded by, or best suited to, a particular task.

Although a listener can attempt to understand the meaning of two simultaneous messages by adopting a late mode of selection, use of a late mode is achieved at a cost. As the perceptual processing system shifts from an early to a late mode of selection, it collects more information about the secondary message, but this reduces the capacity to comprehend the primary message. The predicted result is that comprehension of the primary message will decline as the listener tries to process a secondary message more fully.

Johnston and Heinz tested these predictions in a series of five experiments. A common procedure for measuring the amount of capacity required to perform a task is to determine how quickly a person can respond to a subsidiary task. The main task in their research was a selective listening task. A light signal occurred randomly throughout the listening task, and as the subsidiary task, subjects were instructed to respond to it as quickly as possible by pushing a button. The experimenters assumed that the greater the portion of capacity allocated to selective listening, the less should be available for monitoring the signal light, causing longer reaction times.

One of the experiments used a paradigm in which subjects heard pairs of words presented simultaneously to both ears. Undergraduates at the University of Utah were asked to shadow words defined either by the pitch of a voice or by a semantic category. One set of stimuli used a male and a female voice, and the undergraduates were asked to shadow the words spoken by either the male or the female. These subjects could use an early, sensory mode of selection because the two messages were physically different. Another group of undergraduates heard two messages spoken by the same voice. One message consisted of words from a category such as names of cities, and the other message of words from a different category, such as names of occupations. Subjects were asked to report the words from one of the categories and ignore the words from the other category. These subjects had to use a late, semantic mode of selection because it was necessary to know the meaning of the words in order to categorize them.

The multimode theory predicts that more capacity is required to perform at a late mode of selection. Use of the semantic mode should therefore cause slower reaction times to the light signal and more errors on the selective listening task. The theory also predicts that listening to two lists should require more capacity than listening to and shadowing one list, which should require more capacity than listening to no lists. Reaction times for the subsidiary task supported the predictions. The average time to respond to the light signal was 310 msec for no lists, 370 msec for one list, 433 msec for two lists that could be distinguished by using sensory cues (pitch), and 482 msec for two lists that could be distinguished by using only semantic cues (categories). These results were accompanied by different levels of performance on the shadowing task. The percentage of errors was 1.4 for a single list, 5.3 for the two lists that could be separated using sensory cues, and 20.5 for the two lists that could be separated using only semantic cues.

The authors interpreted the results as supporting their view that selective attention requires capacity and that the amount of capacity required increases from early to late modes of selection. The first assumption received support from the consistent finding across experiments that reaction times were slower when the listener had to listen to two lists rather than only one. The second assumption received support from the consistent finding that reaction times were slower when the listener had to attend on the basis of semantic cues rather than sensory cues. This latter finding, when combined with the performance results on the selective listening task, suggests that a person can increase the breadth of attention, but only at a cost in capacity expenditure and selection accuracy. But there are two silver linings to this otherwise dark cloud. First, if attention is as flexible as suggested by the multimode theory, a person at least has the choice of how best to use it. And second, psychologists have demonstrated that, with sufficient practice, some tasks can become so automatic that they do not appear to require any of the precious capacity postulated by a capacity theory.

Automatic Processing

The work of Johnston and Heinz and other cognitive psychologists has shown that tasks vary considerably in the amount of mental effort required to perform them. Some skills become so well practiced and routine that they require very minimal capacity. Psychologists have used the term *automatic processing* to refer to such skills.

Acquisition of automatic processing is often an advantage. It allows us to perform routine activities without much concentration or mental effort. However, automatic processing can be a disadvantage. We may put so little thought into what we are doing that we make a silly mistake or fail to remember what we did.

We will begin by examining criteria that people can use to determine whether they are using automatic processing. We will then see how automatic processing is useful in performing complex tasks such as reading.

When Is a Skill Automatic?

Posner and Snyder (1975) have proposed three criteria to determine whether a skill is automatic. A skill is automatic if it (1) occurs without intention, (2) does not give rise to conscious awareness, and (3) does not interfere with other mental activities.

Learning to ride a bicycle is a familiar example that we can evaluate by using these criteria. Most of us have learned how to ride a bicycle, and perhaps we can still remember the early experience of wobbling back and forth for a few feet before stopping and having to start over. Balancing the bicycle initially required intention, conscious awareness of what we were trying to do, and mental effort that could interfere with our concentration on other activities. Once we learned how to balance, it became hard to imagine why we had had so much trouble initially. We could then ride a bicycle without consciously intending to balance, we had little conscious awareness of the movements we used to achieve balance, and we became more able to attend to the scenery or our thoughts because we no longer had to concentrate on balancing.

Another task that initially requires a lot of mental effort or capacity is reading a word. But like riding a bicycle, reading a word eventually becomes a fairly automatic skill. In fact, it becomes so automatic that it is difficult to stop, even when reading would be a disadvantage. Consider a task in which you are shown words that are printed in either red, green, or blue ink and your objective is simply to name the color of the ink. If the words are names of colors that cause a competing response (such as the word *RED* printed in blue ink), it is better to avoid reading the words, because it makes the task much harder. However, people cannot completely avoid reading the words, as is revealed by the fact that they perform the task more slowly when there are competing responses. This finding is called the Stroop effect after its discoverer (Stroop, 1935).

The Stroop effect provides a partial answer to the question asked by Posner and Snyder (1975) at the beginning of their article: To what extent are our conscious intentions and strategies in control of the way information is processed in our minds? The fact that people could not avoid reading words illustrates that we cannot always adapt our thought processes to the strategies required by the task. Because automatic processes occur without intention, they may occur even when they are a nuisance. Fortunately, automatic processes usually are advantageous and allow us to perform complex skills that would otherwise overload our limited capacity. Reading a word with little effort allows us to become good readers, but achieving automatic processing requires extensive practice.

Automatic Processing and Reading

One of the most demanding cognitive skills that face the young child is learning how to read. Learning to read requires many component skills, some of which we considered in the previous chapter. The child must analyze the features of letters, combine the features to identify the letters, convert the letters into sounds for pronouncing words, understand the meanings of individual words, and combine the meaning of the words to comprehend the text. According to a theory proposed by LaBerge and Samuels (1974), the ability to acquire complex, multicomponent skills such as reading depends on the capability of automatic processing. Their criterion for deciding when a skill or subskill is automatic is that it can be completed while attention is directed elsewhere. The rationale behind this argument is that unless at least some of the component skills can be completed without requiring capacity, the total demands of all the component skills will be simply too great for the individual to perform the task.

As we saw in the previous chapter, an initial component skill for successful reading is the ability to identify the features of a letter. The features must then be organized or combined to form a letter, a process that initially requires attention, according to LaBerge and Samuels. However, after sufficient practice in recognizing letters, the features can be combined automatically to form a letter, freeing some capacity for the other necessary component skills. Learning to read depends not only on learning the component skills but on learning them so well that they make very little demand on the limited capacity of attention.

LaBerge and Samuels used a letter-matching task to illustrate the acquisition of the automatic processing of letters. They studied how quickly people could decide whether two letters were the same or different. The pairs were either familiar letters (*b d, p q*) or artificial letters (↳ ↓ ↾ ↿). When subjects were shown letters from one of these sets, they could match the artificial letters as quickly as they could match the familiar letters; familiarity didn't make any difference as long as the subjects were attending to the correct set of letters. However, when subjects matched a different set of letters (*a n u v*) and were occasionally shown one of the above pairs, they could match a familiar pair faster than an artificial pair. The time to match the artificial pairs declined with practice, however, and after five days of practice, the subjects could match artificial pairs as quickly as familiar pairs (see Figure 3.6).

LaBerge and Samuels interpreted these results as demonstrating the acquisition of automatic processing. When subjects were expecting a different group of letters,

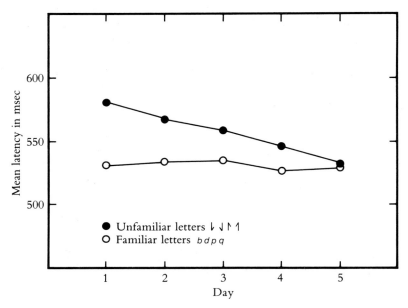

Figure 3.6   Average response times for matching familiar and unfamiliar letters when subjects were expecting a different letter set

they had to switch their attention to the appropriate set when artificial letters were presented. This would require additional time and delay their response. But a switch of attention was not required for the familiar letters, because these letters could be identified automatically, without attention. The finding that artificial letters eventually were compared as quickly as familiar letters suggested that something was being learned about the unfamiliar letters over the five days of practice. Since there was no difference in matching pairs when subjects were expecting the correct set of letters, LaBerge and Samuels proposed that subjects were learning to automatically process the artificial pairs when their attention was directed elsewhere. They suggested that acquiring the ability to carry out a component skill automatically is an important part of learning that should be tested in addition to accuracy. Accurate performance of a component skill (such as recognizing letters) could nonetheless hinder the acquisition of a new component skill (such as pronouncing words) if the performance required so much capacity that little was left for learning the new component.

LaBerge and Samuels argued that the automatic processing of letters became possible when people could recognize a letter as a unit rather than attend to its individual features. To extend their argument, words should require less capacity to recognize if we can recognize the word as a unit rather than as a string of individual letters. You may recall that almost all the people who participated in Reicher's (1969) experiment reported that they perceived a four-letter word as a unit rather than as four separate letters.

One consequence of perceiving a word as a unit is that it should cause us to attend less to the individual letters in the word. You can test your own ability to perceive individual letters in words by reading the following sentence. Read it once and then read it again, counting the f's.

> FINISHED FILES ARE THE
> RESULT OF YEARS OF SCIENTIFIC
> STUDY COMBINED WITH THE
> EXPERIENCE OF MANY YEARS.

There is a total of six f's in the sentence. If you counted fewer than six, please try again.

Most people find this a difficult task because they fail to detect the f in one of the words (of) even though it occurs three times in the sentence. One explanation of why we overlook this particular f is that it is pronounced like the letter v. Although this may be a contributing factor, results obtained by Healy (1980) indicate that we often recognize frequently occurring words as units and therefore find it difficult to focus on their individual letters. Healy asked people to read a prose passage at normal reading speed but to circle the letter t whenever it occurred in the passage. She found that people were more likely to miss the letter when it occurred in common words than when it occurred in rare words. In particular, they often missed the letter t in the word the, which is the most common word in the English language.

Healy's results are consistent with the theory advocated by LaBerge and Samuels. Since people encounter frequent words more often than rare words, they should be better able to recognize a frequent word as a unit. This explanation is analogous to the explanation that familiar letters are more likely than unfamiliar letters to be recognized as units. Less capacity should be required to recognize a frequent word because the reader does not have to pay as much attention to the individual letters. If less capacity is required to recognize a familiar word, the reader should have more capacity available for comprehending the meaning of the sentence.

Individual Differences and Applications

The preceding section showed how a capacity theory can help us understand complex skills such as reading. Research on the selective nature of attention also has potential applications. Effective design of emergency instructions, for example, depends on making certain that people attend to the instructions. When the emergency could create a panic, this requirement is not trivial (see Box 3.1). Another application is the evaluation of individual differences in order to select people who will perform well in occupations that require selective attention. We will now look at studies that have successfully applied the selective listening task to predict flight performance and road accidents.

Predicting Flight Performance

The ability to selectively attend is important in many activities outside the laboratory. For example, Gopher and Kahneman (1971) found that flight instructors frequently emphasized the importance of selective attention in learning to fly high-performance aircraft. Flight cadets often failed because they could not appropriately divide their attention among simultaneous activities or were slow to recognize crucial signals that arrived on unattended channels. Although the selective listening paradigm was a popular laboratory task, psychologists had not developed it to study individual differences or to predict performance outside the laboratory. Gopher and Kahneman tried to remedy this situation by determining whether a test of selective listening would help them predict progress in a flight training program.

The subjects were 100 cadets in the Israeli air force. The test consisted of a series of messages that simultaneously presented different information to the two ears. Each message contained two parts: an 8-second period that contained 16 pairs of words (a mixture of verbs and digits), followed by 3 pairs of digits. Each part was preceded by a tone that signaled which ear was relevant. The task was to report every digit on the relevant ear as soon as it was heard. There were either two or four relevant digits during the first part of the message and three relevant digits during the second part.

The 100 cadets were divided into three groups according to how far they had progressed during flight school: (1) 17 cadets had been rejected during initial training on light aircraft; (2) 41 cadets had been rejected early in training on jet aircraft; and

Box 3.1   Emergency instructions

Our May colloquium speaker, Dr. Elizabeth Loftus, spoke at the Document Design Center about her pioneering work on the design and testing of emergency instructions for public places. Dr. Loftus, a cognitive psychologist at the University of Washington, began working in the field of public messages in 1973, when she and a colleague, Dr. Jack Keating, were asked by the Government Services Administration to develop emergency evacuation messages for a 37-story Federal building. They extracted what they could from the published psychological literature on perception, attention, memory, and crowd behavior and began to answer questions about the design of messages: Should there be a warning tone? Should a male or a female voice speak the message? How should the message be logically constructed? What types of sentences should be used? What words should be included or avoided?

Their initial success with applying psychological principles to the design of emergency messages led the National Bureau of Standards to request Loftus to extend her findings to hospital situations, where the words of emergency messages must be carefully chosen to avoid panic among patients. Loftus found still another way to develop and apply cognitive principles when San Francisco's subway system, BART, asked her to redesign their evacuation instructions following a disastrous fire. Three recommendations that emerged from that project were: parts of the message must be repeated, since there is no assurance that people are attending to the message the first time it is uttered; the message should be pre-recorded, since a conductor's accent or emotional state can interfere with intelligibility; the structure and timing of the message need to be coordinated with the movement of people as they are obeying the instructions—too much information given too soon can prevent people from carrying out the instructions. In most of these emergency situations, designers must also carefully coordinate vocal and written instructions to make them most effective.

From the May 1980 issue of *Fine Print* (now called *Simply Stated*). Reproduced with permission from the Document Design Center, American Institutes for Research.

[handwritten margin note: Highlight]

(3) 42 cadets had reached advanced training on jet aircraft. The cadets' performance on the second part of the selective listening task was the best predictor of their progress in flight school. Cadets who made three or more errors on this part of the test included 76% of those rejected during training on light aircraft, 56% of those rejected early in jet training, and 24% of those who had progressed to advanced training. The findings indicate that selective listening tasks have promise as a test, particularly since these results were obtained from a select group of people who probably all possessed good attentive skills relative to the general population.

Predicting Road Accidents

Kahneman, Ben-Ishai, and Lotan (1973) evaluated the generality of these findings by testing the validity of the task as a predictor of the accident rate of bus drivers.

The study involved three groups of drivers. The accident-prone drivers had had at least two moderately severe accidents during a single year; the accident-free drivers had had no accidents during the same time period; and the intermediate group fell between these two extremes. The drivers from the three groups took the selective listening test, and their performance was correlated with their driving records. Performance on the second part of the test again produced the highest correlation with the accident rate. Kahneman and his coinvestigators concluded that the test should enable a company to reject from 15% to 25% of the accident-prone drivers with a relatively negligible cost in rejecting potentially safe drivers.

The potential usefulness of the test was confirmed by Mihal and Barett (1976), who included a slightly modified version in a battery of seven tests. The test that best predicted the accident involvement of 75 commercial drivers was the selective listening test. Mihal and Barett's findings are interesting because we might think that some other test, such as a visual test of selective attention, would have produced the highest correlation, as driving would seem to emphasize visual skills over auditory skills. However, an embedded figures test was not as good a predictor, nor was a simple reaction time test.

The results suggest that the selective listening test has merit as a predictor of driving records, particularly since accidents depend not only on driving skill but also on various chance factors in the environment. However, exactly what is being measured by the test is not entirely clear. Kahneman and his associates argue that the test measures how quickly a person can switch attention. They base their argument on the finding that the second part of the test—during which the subject has to decide whether to switch attention to the other ear—produced the highest correlations. But the second part of the test also differed from the first part in what stimuli occurred on the irrelevant channel. A relevant digit was never paired with another digit on the first part but was always paired with another digit during the second part. This may make a difference if some subjects use a late mode of selection, as defined by Johnston and Heinz (1978). Furthermore, Mihal and Barett's results were obtained using only the first part of the test. The attempt to discover what selective attention tests measure is a good example of the kind of interaction that should occur between theoretical and applied areas of psychology.

We are now ready to consider the two memory stages in the information-processing model. Let us assume at this point that information has been successfully identified during the perceptual analysis stages: it has been attended to, recognized, and entered into a temporary store called short-term memory (STM). What will happen next? To answer this question, let us turn to the investigation of the characteristics of STM in Chapter 4.

Summary

Two characteristics of attention are selectivity and mental effort. Selectivity is necessary to keep us from becoming overloaded with too much information. The initial theories developed within the information-processing approach proposed that selectivity occurred at a bottleneck—a stage that could process only one message at a time. Broadbent's filter theory specified that the bottleneck occurred at the perception or pattern recognition stage, and attention was represented by a filter that preceded this stage. Treisman modified the filter theory to allow for the occasional recognition of words on the unattended channel. She proposed that the filter attenuated the unattended message and did not completely block it out. Important words or expected words could be recognized on the unattended channel if their thresholds were low enough to be exceeded by the attenuated message. Unlike Broadbent and Treisman, Deutsch and Deutsch suggested that the bottleneck occurs after perception and determines what is selected into memory. Norman further developed the latter theory and argued that the quality of the sensory information is combined with importance to determine what enters memory.

The results of many experiments on selective listening failed to agree on the location of the bottleneck. The effect was to shift the emphasis to capacity theories of attention and to encourage a more flexible view of the stage at which selection occurs. Capacity theories emphasize the amount of mental effort that is required to perform tasks and are concerned with how effort is allocated to different activities. A capacity theory supplements a bottleneck theory by proposing that the ability to perform simultaneous activities is limited when the activities require more mental effort than is available. The interaction between a capacity theory and a bottleneck theory is illustrated by results obtained by Johnston and Heinz. They effectively argue that a person has control over the stage at which selection occurs, but late modes of selection (following recognition) require more capacity than early modes. The attempt to comprehend two messages therefore results in a decline in accuracy on the primary message and slower responses to a subsidiary task designed to measure capacity.

Automatic processing occurs when a task requires very little capacity to perform. Posner and Snyder proposed three criteria to determine whether a skill is automatic: (1) it occurs without intention, (2) it does not give rise to conscious awareness, and (3) it does not interfere with other mental activities.

The work on selective attention has implications for performance outside the laboratory. LaBerge and Samuels suggested that the acquisition of complex, multicomponent skills such as reading depends on the ability to carry out some of the skills automatically, without attention. Ability to perform some components correctly does not necessarily mean that a person is ready to acquire new components if all the available capacity must be used to perform the already-learned components. The performance of flight cadets and commercial drivers on selective listening tasks is one of the best predictors of success in flight school and of accident rates. It is not entirely clear, however, what the tests measure; further research linking theory and applications may prove beneficial to both areas.

Recommended Reading

Kahneman's *Attention and Effort* (1973) provides a comprehensive discussion of attention in addition to presenting a capacity theory. Chapters by Johnston and Dark (1986), Shiffrin (in press), and Wickens and Kramer (1985) also summarize much of the work on attention. Neisser and Becklen (1975) studied selective attention by using a visual task that was somewhat analogous to the selective listening tasks we have looked at. Schneider and Shiffrin (1977; Shiffrin & Schneider, 1977) describe their research on the acquisition of automatic processing through extensive practice and present a general theoretical framework for integrating a large number of experimental findings. Hirst, Spelke, Reaves, Caharack, and Neisser (1980) evaluate different theoretical explanations of how people can perform two complex tasks (dictation and reading) at the same time. Navon and Gopher (1979) propose a general theory of how people allocate their attention when the demands of a task exceed their capacity. The role of conscious awareness during perceptual processing is discussed by Marcel (1983) and Klatzky (1984). Treisman's work (Treisman & Gelade, 1980; Treisman & Schmidt, 1982) on the importance of attention for integrating the features of a pattern is related to the theory proposed by LaBerge and Samuels (1974).

4

Short-Term Memory

My problem is that I have been persecuted by an integer. For seven years this number has followed me around, has intruded in my most private data, and has assaulted me from the pages of our most public journals. This number assumes a variety of disguises, being sometimes a little larger and sometimes a little smaller than usual, but never changing so much as to be unrecognizable. The persistence with which this number plagues me is far more than a random accident. There is, to quote a famous senator, a design behind it, some pattern governing its appearances. Either there really is something unusual about the number or else I am suffering from delusions of persecution.

GEORGE A. MILLER (1956)

The quotation above is the first paragraph of George Miller's famous paper "The Magical Number Seven, plus or minus Two: Some Limits on Our Capacity for Processing Information." Miller found that people are limited in the number of items they can keep active in memory and that this limited capacity influences their performance on a variety of tasks. The previous chapter, on attention, also dealt with a capacity limitation, but our concern there was with simultaneously arriving information. The capacity model of attention proposed that our ability to carry on several activities at the same time is restricted by the total amount of mental effort that is available for distributing to these activities.

The tasks in this chapter do not require that people recognize simultaneously arriving information. There is no perceptual overload, and there is enough time to recognize each item and enter it into short-term memory (STM). The problem is that STM can hold only a limited number of items, having a profound effect on the many tasks that require use of STM. The implications of this limitation are evident throughout the book—not only in this chapter but in later chapters on text comprehension, problem solving, and decision making.

55

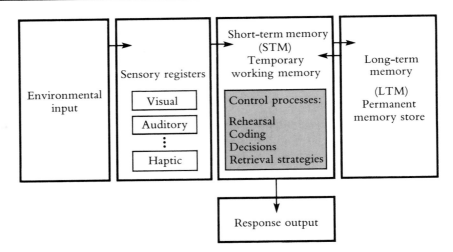

Figure 4.1 Flow of information through the memory system

The fact that STM will be referred to throughout the book reflects its important role as a working memory. Figure 4.1 shows that STM can combine information from both the environment and LTM whenever a person tries to learn new information, make decisions, or solve problems. When you add the numbers in your checking account, you are receiving some information from the environment (the numbers in your account) and other information from LTM (the rules of addition). Getting a correct answer depends on using both sources of information appropriately.

The goal of this chapter is to summarize the major characteristics of STM. We begin by examining both the rate and the cause of forgetting. The emphasis will be on interference as the primary cause. The second section discusses the capacity of STM. After looking at Miller's (1956) insights about capacity, we will learn how the formation of groups of items in LTM can partly compensate for limited capacity. The third section deals with acoustic codes and rehearsal, as acoustic codes are often used to maintain information in STM. We will examine whether they are necessary for reading. The final section presents a model of how people recognize whether an item is in STM. In particular, we will consider how quickly people can examine the contents of their STM.

Forgetting

Rate of Forgetting

The label *short-term memory* indicates that information in STM is lost rapidly unless it is preserved through rehearsal. The rapid rate of forgetting from STM was established by Peterson and Peterson (1959) at Indiana University. They tested undergraduates on the ability to remember three consonants over a short retention interval. To prevent subjects from rehearsing the letters, Peterson and Peterson required them to count backward by threes, starting with a number that occurred after the consonants. For example, a subject might hear the letters *C H J* followed by the number 506. She would then count backward until she saw a light, which was a signal for recalling the three consonants. The light went on 3, 6, 9, 12, 15, or 18 seconds after the subjects began counting.

Figure 4.2 shows the results of the experiment. The probability of a correct recall declined rapidly over the 18-second retention interval. The rapid forgetting rate implies that we must rehearse verbal information to keep it available in STM. It also shows why it is very likely that if we are momentarily distracted after looking up a telephone number, we will have to look it up again before dialing.

This rapid rate of forgetting can be very frustrating when we are trying to learn new information, but it can also be beneficial. There are many occasions when we need to remember something only briefly. Think of all the phone numbers you have dialed. Most of these you dialed only once or twice and will never need again. If all these numbers were permanently stored in LTM, it could be very difficult to retrieve the few numbers that you constantly use.

Decay versus Interference

One question raised by Peterson and Peterson's findings is whether the loss of information from STM is caused by decay or by interference. Try to remember the consonants *R Q W* over a short interval without thinking about them. Since it's difficult not to think about them if you have nothing else to do, subjects in memory

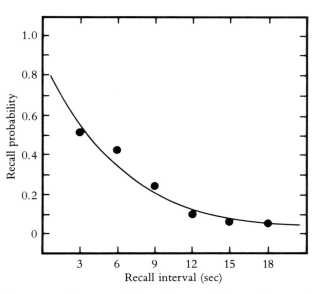

Figure 4.2   Correct recall as a function of the recall interval

experiments are asked to perform some other task. An interference theory proposes that memory for other material or the performance of another task interferes with memory and causes forgetting. A decay theory proposes that forgetting should still occur even if the subject is told not to do anything over the retention interval, as long as the subject does not rehearse the material.

A decay theory and interference theory make different predictions about whether the passage of time or the number of interfering items is the primary cause of forgetting. If memory simply decays over time, then the amount of recall should be determined by the length of the retention interval. If memory is disrupted by interference, then recall should be determined by the number of interfering items.

Waugh and Norman (1965) tested whether the loss of information from STM is caused mainly by decay or by interference. They presented lists of 16 single digits. The last digit in every list (a probe digit) occurred exactly once earlier in the list. The task was to report the digit that had followed the probe digit. For example, if the list was 5 1 9 6 3 5 1 4 2 8 6 2 7 3 9 4, the probe digit would be 4 and the correct answer (the test item) would be 2. For this particular example, there are 7 digits that occur after the test item. The number of interfering items is therefore 7. Waugh and Norman varied the number of interfering items by varying the location of the

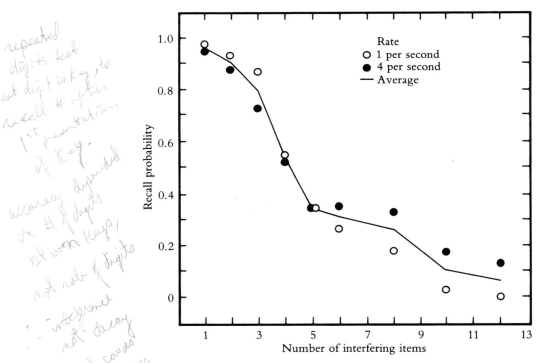

Figure 4.3 Effect of rate of presentation and number of interfering items on recall probability

test digit in the list. There were many interfering items if the test item occurred early in the list and only a few if the test item occurred late in the list.

The experimenters also varied the rate of presentation in order to determine whether the probability of recalling the test digit would be influenced by the length of the retention interval. They presented the 16 digits in a list at a rate of either 1 digit or 4 digits per second. A decay theory would predict that performance should be better for the fast rate of presentation because there would be less time for the information to decay from memory. Figure 4.3 shows the results. The rate of presentation had very little effect on the probability of recalling the test digit. Consider the case in which there are 12 interfering items. The retention interval would be 12 seconds for the 1-per-second rate and 3 seconds for the 4-per-second rate. Memory is only slightly (and insignificantly) better for the shorter retention interval. In contrast, the number of interfering items has a dramatic effect on retention. The probability of recall declines rapidly as the number of interfering items increases.

Waugh and Norman's findings support the contention that interference, rather than decay, is the primary cause of forgetting. Although some decay may occur (see Reitman, 1974), the amount of forgetting caused by decay is substantially less than the amount caused by interference. As Reitman and many others have shown, the extent of forgetting is determined not only by the number of interfering items but also by the degree of similarity between the interfering and test items. Increasing the similarity makes it harder to recall the test items.

The finding that interference is the chief cause of forgetting is good news. If information spontaneously decayed from memory, we would be unable to prevent its loss. If information is lost through interference, we can improve retention by structuring learning so as to minimize interference. A phenomenon called "release from proactive interference" illustrates how interference can be reduced by decreasing the similarity among items.

Release from Proactive Interference

Psychologists have distinguished between two kinds of interference—proactive interference and retroactive interference. *Retroactive interference* is caused by information that occurs after an event. The Waugh and Norman (1965) study demonstrated the effect of retroactive interference; the number of digits that followed the probe digit influenced how well it could be recalled. *Proactive interference,* in contrast, is caused by events that occurred before the event that someone attempts to recall.

Keppel and Underwood (1962) had previously demonstrated the effect of proactive interference in the Peterson STM task. They found that people initially performed very well in recalling three consonants after a short retention interval, but their performance deteriorated over subsequent trials. The reason is that the consonants they had tried to remember during the initial trials began to interfere with their memory for consonants during the later trials. People found it increasingly difficult to distinguish between consonants that were presented on the current trial and consonants that had been presented on earlier trials.

Reduction of this interference is called the *release from proactive interference* (Wickens, Born, & Allen, 1963). The study by Wickens and his colleagues was the first of many studies to show that the recall of later items can be improved by making them distinctive from early items. Figure 4.4 shows a clear illustration of release from proactive interference. Students in this particular experiment were required to remember either three numbers or three common words over a 20-second interval, during which time they performed another task to keep from rehearsing. The control group received items from the same class (either numbers or words) on each of four trials. The interference effect is evident from the decline in performance over trials. The experimental group received items from the same class over the first three trials but on the fourth trial received items from the other class. If they had been remembering words, they now remembered three numbers; if they had been remembering numbers, they now remembered three words. The shift in categories caused a dramatic improvement in performance, as Figure 4.4 illustrates. The interference effect was specific to the class of material being presented and was greatly reduced when three distinctive items occurred.

Release from proactive interference also occurs when people are asked to remember more complex events (Gunter, Clifford, & Berry, 1980). The events consisted of television news items that people heard while they viewed a videotape of the same events. People heard three items during each trial and attempted to recall them after a one-minute delay. The control group received items from the same class (either politics or sports) over a series of four trials. The experimental group received items from the same class over the first three trials, but on the fourth trial they received items from the other class. If they had been recalling sports events, they now recalled

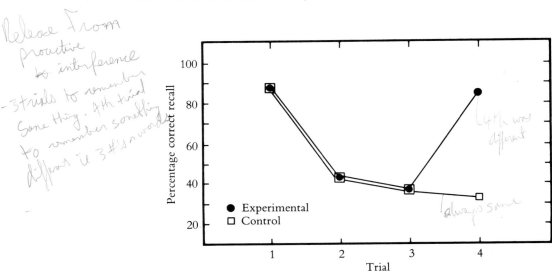

Figure 4.4   Release from proactive interference is demonstrated on Trial 4 for the experimental group

political events, and vice versa. The results were very similar to the results shown in Figure 4.4. The proportion of correct responses declined for the control group over the four trials—87% on the first trial, 67% on the second, 55% on the third, and 43% on the fourth trial. The recall of the experimental group showed a similar decline over the first three trials but improved dramatically on the fourth trial, when they heard items from a different category. The experimental group recalled 82% of the items on the first trial, 67% on the second, 55% on the third, and 74% on the fourth.

The practical implications of these results are simply that, whenever possible, we should try to reduce interference by ordering material in an appropriate sequence. Items that are likely to interfere with each other should be studied at different times rather than during a single session. Reduction of interference through appropriate sequencing can partly compensate for the rapid forgetting from STM. Let us now look at how we can partly compensate for the limited capacity of this store.

Capacity

The Magic Number Seven

A second limitation of STM is that it can hold only about seven items. The limited capacity of STM is demonstrated by a task that is often used as a measure of its capacity. It is called a *digit span* or, more generally, a *memory span* task. The task requires that a person recall a sequence of items in their correct order. Memory span is the longest sequence that a person can typically recall. An example of a memory span task is shown below. Read each row of letters once; then shut your eyes and try to recall these letters in the correct order.

T M F J R L B

H Q C N W Y P K V

S B M G X R D L T

J Z N Q K Y C

If you are like most other adults, you could probably easily recall a string of seven letters (Rows 1 and 4) but not a string of nine letters (Rows 2 and 3). It was this number seven that plagued George Miller. The "magic number seven" kept appearing in two different kinds of studies: experiments on absolute judgment and on memory span. In the absolute judgment task, an experimenter presents stimuli that vary along a sensory continuum, such as loudness. The experimenter selects different levels of loudness that are easy to discriminate and assigns each a label. The labels are usually numbers that increase as the values on the continuum increase: if there were seven stimuli, the softest stimuli would be labeled 1, the loudest 7. The subject's task is to learn to identify each stimulus by assigning the correct label. The experimenter presents the stimuli in a random order and corrects mistakes by providing the correct answer.

The experimenter is interested mainly in how many stimuli the subject can label correctly before the task becomes too difficult. The results vary depending on the sensory continuum, but Miller was impressed with the finding that the upper limit for a single dimension was usually around seven, plus or minus two. The upper limit was about five for loudness, six for pitch, five for the size of squares, and five for brightness. The average across a wide variety of sensory tasks was 6.5, and most of the upper limits were between five and nine.

It is important to point out that these results are not caused by an inability to discriminate adjacent values of the stimuli. All the stimuli would be easy to discriminate if the subject had to judge which one of two adjacent stimuli was louder, larger, brighter, or higher in pitch. The limitation was caused by the inability to keep more than about seven sensory values available in STM because of its limited capacity. The results represent performance during the early stages of learning, before the different sensory stimuli are stored in LTM. With sufficient experience, the upper limits can be increased, as is illustrated by a musically sophisticated person who can accurately identify any one of 50 or 60 pitches. However, that person is using LTM, which is not limited in capacity.

The upper limit found in the absolute judgment experiments corresponds very well with the upper limit found in memory span tasks. Miller cited the results found by Hayes (1952), which indicated that the memory span ranged from five items for English words (*lake, jump, pen, road, sing*) to nine items for binary digits (0 0 1 0 1 1 1 0 1). The memory span for numbers or letters fell in about the middle of this range.

Miller's paper was important for drawing attention to how little the upper limit varies in performance on absolute judgment and memory span tasks. His paper was also important for suggesting that recoding the information to form chunks can help one overcome the limited capacity of STM. Chunks consist of individual items that have been learned and stored as a group in LTM. You can demonstrate for yourself how chunking can increase the number of letters that can be recalled from STM. Tell someone that you will read 12 letters to him and that you would like him to repeat them back in the correct order. Then read the 12 letters grouped in the following way: *FB–ITW–AC–IAIB–M*. Next read to another person the same 12 letters grouped in a different way: *FBI–TWA–CIA–IBM*. You will likely find that the second person can recall more letters. The first person has to recall 12 separate letters, but the second person can recall four chunks, each containing three letters. Miller argued that the capacity of STM should be measured in chunks rather than in individual items. The 12 letters should be easy for the second person to recall because they take up only 4 "slots" in STM rather than 12.

Individual Differences in Chunking

There is increasing evidence that a major determinant of individual differences in memory is how effectively people can group material into familiar chunks. The initial evidence for this conclusion came from the study of how chess players reproduce the pieces on a chessboard. The classic study of this task was begun by de Groot, a Dutch psychologist, during the 1940s and was later published in his book *Thought and Choice in Chess* (1965). The main conclusion of his study was that the difference between the skills of the chess master and lesser players results more from differences in perception and memory than from differences in the quality of their operational thinking.

Empirical support for de Groot's conclusion came from a series of clever experiments that required players of different abilities to reproduce a chessboard as it might appear 20 moves into a game (de Groot, 1966). Figure 4.5 shows two of the board configurations that were used in the study. The subjects were given five seconds to view the board. The pieces were then removed, and the subjects were asked to place the pieces back on the board to reproduce what they had just seen. When the subject was finished, the experimenter removed the pieces that were incorrectly placed and asked the subject to try again. The subjects continued to try to replace the incorrect pieces until they correctly reproduced the board or until 12 trials were completed.

The average performance of five master players and five weaker players is shown in Figure 4.6. The master players correctly reproduced about 90% of the pieces on their first attempt, compared with only 40% for the weaker players. To determine whether the results were caused by the masters' ability simply to guess where the pieces should be located, de Groot chose other board configurations and asked the players to guess where the pieces were located, without ever seeing the board or receiving any clues. Figure 4.6 shows that the master players were only slightly better at guessing where the pieces were located. The weaker players, in fact, did about as well guessing as when they actually saw the board. De Groot argued that the master players depended on their ability to code the pieces into familiar groups. When the

From: Janosevic-Krisnik;
Zenica 1964

From: Bannik-Geller;
Moskou 1961

Figure 4.5   Examples of experimental positions used in the guessing and reproduction experiments

Figure 4.6   Percentage of correctly located chess pieces

players viewed pieces that were placed randomly on the board, the master players no longer had an advantage over the weaker players, and the two groups performed about the same.

Chase and Simon (1973) extended de Groot's paradigm in order to identify the groups of pieces (chunks) that presumably produced the superior coding ability of master chess players. A master chess player, a Class A player, and a beginner were tested on de Groot's reproduction task. Chase and Simon assumed that pieces belonging to the same chunk would be placed on the board as a group. They measured the time between successive pieces and classified pauses greater than two seconds as indicating chunk boundaries. The latencies suggested that, for middle-game positions, the average number of chunks per trial was 7.7 for the master player, 5.7 for the Class A player, and 5.3 for the beginner; the number of pieces per chunk averaged 2.5, 2.1, and 1.9, respectively. There was some tendency for more skilled players to use more chunks, particularly for end-game positions, in which the average number of chunks per trial was 7.6, 6.4, and 4.2, respectively.

A simulation program (Memory-Aided Pattern Perceiver, or MAPP) of the chess reproduction task was developed by Simon and Gilmartin (1973) to gain further insight into the kinds of chunks stored in LTM. The memory of the program contained 572 chunks, with two to seven chess pieces in each. The simulation program was somewhat more effective than the Class A player in coding the configurations but less effective than the master player. There was, however, a substantial correlation between the pieces that MAPP remembered and those the master player remembered, even though the patterns stored by MAPP were selected independent of a detailed knowledge of the master's performance. Extrapolating from the performance of the simulation model, Simon and Gilmartin estimated that master players have between 10,000 and 100,000 chunks stored in LTM. Their estimate implies that there is no shortcut to becoming a chess master.

Recall of Circuit Diagrams

Skill in reading nonverbal symbolic drawings is important for a wide range of occupations, including electronics, engineering, chemistry, and architecture. A skilled electronics technician, for example, must be able to understand circuit diagrams and relate the symbols to hardware in need of repair or to circuit design problems. Egan and Schwartz (1979) conducted a study to determine what differences distinguish the novice and the skilled technician in their ability to reproduce a circuit diagram. Discovering what the skilled technician actually knows should be useful for assessing skill levels, developing job aids for skilled performance, or improving training in such skills.

The earlier work of de Groot, Chase, Simon, and Gilmartin on chess influenced the design of the experiments. Chunks were determined by asking an expert (a skilled electronics technician at Bell Laboratories who had over 25 years of experience working with electronic circuits) to mark off meaningful groups of symbols in circuit drawings by circling symbols that served a common function. Figure 4.7 shows an example of a circuit drawing. The enclosed groups and verbal labels indicate how the technician organized the diagram.

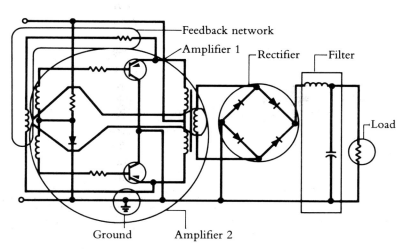

Figure 4.7   An example of a circuit drawing. Enclosed groups and verbal labels indicate the organizational description provided by a skilled technician.

The subjects in one of Egan and Schwartz's experiments were six skilled electronics technicians and six novices. The technicians had been employed at Bell Laboratories for at least six years. The novice subjects were college students who had little knowledge of electronics. Each subject participated in 12 meaningful recall tasks, 12 random recall tasks, and 12 construction tasks, all involving different circuit diagrams. The meaningful recall tasks used actual circuit diagrams copied from texts. The random recall tasks used drawings that had the same wiring pattern and circuit symbols as the meaningful diagrams but with the symbols positioned randomly in the spaces. After viewing the diagrams for either five or ten seconds, subjects tried to reconstruct the drawings from memory by placing magnetized circuit symbols on the blank spaces of the answer sheet. The construction task required that subjects guess the location of the symbols on the answer sheet without having seen the diagrams.

Figure 4.8 shows how well the two groups of subjects did on each of the three tasks. The technicians did significantly better than the novices in reproducing a meaningful configuration but did no better in reproducing a random configuration. Both these findings replicate the results obtained for chess (de Groot, 1965; Chase & Simon, 1973). Although an expert's opinion, rather than latencies, was used to determine chunk boundaries, the time between replacing successive symbols was significantly shorter for pieces belonging to the same chunk. This finding is consistent with the research on chess, as is the finding that the recall of circuit diagrams by skilled technicians (whether measured by number correct, chunk size, or number of

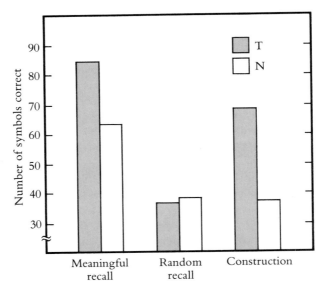

Figure 4.8   Performance by technicians (T) and novices (N) on meaningful recall, random recall, and construction tasks

chunks) was very similar to the recall of chess positions by chess players in the Class A to master range (Chase & Simon, 1973). One difference between the results obtained by de Groot (1966) and those obtained by Egan and Schwartz (1979) is that the skilled technicians, but not the master chess players, did significantly better on the construction task. This finding raises the question whether the superior performance of the skilled technicians was caused by more sophisticated guessing rather than by encoding more information into memory. Egan and Schwartz present several arguments against the guessing interpretation; more research might prove beneficial in answering this question.

Rehearsal and Acoustic Codes

Rapid forgetting rate and limited capacity are the two most important characteristics that distinguish STM from LTM. Psychologists once emphasized a third distinction based on differences in memory codes. They argued that acoustic codes are the predominant memory codes in STM, and semantic codes are the predominant codes in LTM. The emphasis on acoustic codes occurred because of the nature of the material used to study STM and because of the usefulness of verbal rehearsal for retaining information. The material usually consisted of sequences of letters, numbers, or nonsense syllables, all of which could be labeled but were not very meaningful. It is therefore not surprising that a person would use acoustic codes rather than visual or semantic codes to maintain information in STM.

The emphasis on acoustic codes declined when psychologists used material that would activate other kinds of codes. Release from proactive interference, for example, is often cited as evidence that semantic codes influence STM, as recall improves greatly when the material changes to a different semantic category. There is also evidence that people can use visual images to maintain information in STM, particularly when trying to remember the details of visual patterns. We will examine this evidence in Chapter 7.

Although the acoustic code is no longer considered the only code that influences STM, it continues to be studied extensively. The acoustic code is important because verbal rehearsal is an effective way of retaining information in STM. However, one limitation of rehearsal is that it can result in acoustic confusions. Let us now look at the evidence for acoustic confusions and then at a model that demonstrates how they can occur.

Acoustic Confusions

We saw in Chapter 2 that one of the early information-processing models provided for the translation of visual information into acoustic information (Sperling, 1963). Evidence for this translation included Sperling's finding that subjects made acoustic confusions—errors that sounded like the correct response. The subsequent work of

Conrad (1964) also established that acoustic confusions occur in STM. Conrad selected two groups of letters that had high within-group confusability but low between-group confusability: B C P T V and F M N S X. Conrad used a film projector to present visually six-letter sequences consisting of letters from both sets. After each sequence subjects had to write the six letters in their correct order.

If acoustic confusions occur, an error would be more likely to involve substitution of a letter from the same group than substitution of a letter from a different group. Conrad found that 75% of the errors involved one of the other four letters belonging to the same acoustic group, and 25% of the errors involved one of the five letters in the other acoustic group. It is particularly easy for acoustic confusions to occur when all the letters in a sequence sound alike. Try to recall the letters in each of the two following rows. You should find that the letters in the second row are easier to recall than the letters in the first row.

G Z D B P V C T

M J Y F H R K Q

The finding that acoustic confusions occur in an STM task shows that acoustic codes are important, but it does not reveal how the errors occur. One way of accounting for the errors is to use auditory components to represent the names of items. For example, the name of the letter C ("sē") has two components—namely, the s and ē sounds. The components—called *phonemes*—are the basic sounds of the English language.

Table 4.1 lists the phonemes used in English. Notice that some letters are represented by several phonemes because they can be pronounced in different ways. The letter *a* is pronounced differently in the words *father, had, call,* and *take;* each pronunciation is represented by a different phoneme. The letter *e* has two pronunciations: the long *e* sound in *heat* and the short *e* sound in *head.* It is also possible for two letters to combine to form a phoneme—for example, *ch* and *th.*

Table 4.1   Phonemes of general American English

Vowels	Consonants	
ee as in heat	t as in tee	s as in see
I as in hit	p as in pea	sh as in shell
e as in head	k as in key	h as in he
ae as in had	b as in bee	v as in view
ah as in father	d as in dawn	th as in then
aw as in call	g as in go	z as in zoo
u as in put	m as in me	zh as in garage
oo as in cool	n as in no	l as in law
ʌ as in ton	ng as in sing	r as in red
uh as in the	f as in fee	y as in you
er as in bird	ө as in thin	w as in we
oi as in toil		
au as in shout		
ei as in take		
ou as in tone		
ai as in might		

It is convenient to use phonemes to account for acoustic confusions because words that sound alike usually have some phonemes in common. Let's look again at the two sets of letters in Conrad's experiment. The names of the letters in the set F M N S X (ĕf, ĕm, ĕn, ĕs, ĕks) have the same initial phoneme—the short e (ĕ) sound—but their second phoneme differs. The letters in the set B C P T V (bē, sē, pē, tē, vē) all share a common phoneme—the long e (ē) sound—but have different first phonemes.

The major assumption of a model proposed by Kenneth Laughery (1969) is that each of the auditory components representing an item can be independently forgotten. In other words, if a name consists of two phonemes, a person might remember one phoneme but not the other. The model also assumes that the auditory components can be forgotten at different rates; the decay rates were determined from experimental results (Wickelgren, 1965). Laughery makes the reasonable assumption that a person who cannot recall all the auditory components of a letter uses whatever is recalled to limit the number of possible responses. It is therefore easy for the model to account for acoustic confusions. Whenever only the ē phoneme is recalled, the subject will guess one of the letters in the B C P T V set. If only the ĕ phoneme is recalled, the subject will guess one of the letters in the F M N S X set. An incorrect guess in either case will result in an acoustic confusion.

Although acoustic confusions occasionally occur, it is usually advantageous to use verbal rehearsal when we want to maintain information in STM. Translation of visual material into an acoustic code is not limited to remembering strings of letters or digits. The most common example of converting visual material into acoustic codes occurs when we read.

Acoustic Codes in Reading

Most of us read by subvocalizing (saying to ourselves) the words in the text. Although subvocalizing can help us remember what we read, it limits how fast we can read. Since covert speech is not much faster than overt speech, subvocalization limits reading speed to the rate of speaking; we could read faster if we didn't translate printed words into a speech-based code (see Box 4.1).

When I was a graduate student, I attempted to improve my reading rate by enrolling in a speed-reading course. A prerequisite for increasing my speed was that I learn to eliminate subvocalization. The trick is to go directly from the printed word to its meaning without covertly pronouncing the word. I was successful at increasing my reading rate while maintaining comprehension when the material was fairly simple. However, I found it quite difficult to read more complex or technical material without using subvocalization. I soon returned to my slower rate. I don't know how representative my experience was or what percentage of graduates from speed-reading courses successfully eliminate subvocalization. However, the experimental analysis of speech processing during reading has produced results that seem consistent with my own experience. The results suggest that although we can comprehend the meaning of words without subvocalization, subvocalization is useful in facilitating detailed recall of a text (Levy, 1978).

Box 4.1   Does speed reading really exist?
ALEXANDRA D. KORRY

Begin reading now.
Use your hand to guide your eyes.
Don't regress.
Stop subvocalizing.
Faster.

This is the message of Evelyn Wood Reading Dynamics, the California company that has made millions teaching Americans how to glide through that pile of bestsellers sitting on the shelf.

Evelyn Wood claims it will have you reading at up to 5,000 words a minute at the conclusion of a seven-session course. They'll triple your reading, they say, or your money back.

More than one million speed-reading aspirants, including President Carter, John F. Kennedy's military advisers, actor Charlton Heston, and a host of members of Congress have enrolled in the courses since they were first offered in 1959.

But now a growing number of reading specialists are raising serious questions about speed reading. They dispute the value of the $395 Evelyn Wood course and others like it, saying simply that no one—regardless of training—can read that fast.

"They have the illusion of improving their reading when in fact they are skimming," charged John Guthrie, director of research for the 70,000-member International Reading Association. To Evelyn Wood officials, those are fighting words.

"Skimming is a nasty word in our business," said M. Donald Wood, husband of the woman who founded the system and helped organize a national franchise system that teaches speed reading in 26 cities around the country. "It works. We know that."

"I think it's the greatest invention since the printing press," said Evelyn Wood, now 72, and recovering from a stroke in her native Salt Lake City. She was a graduate student at the University of Utah when she discovered the technique after years of observing naturally fast readers.

Many reading experts challenge the system. Although they differ as to what is the proper upper limit for reading speed, most agree that anyone who claims to be reading more than 900 words a minute is, in fact, skimming.

"I can't imagine that someone reading 4,000 words a minute is reading," said Keith Rayner, a professor of psychology at the University of Massachusetts in Amherst. "Given the anatomy of the eye . . . I have a hard time believing that people can read beyond 900 words per minute."

Ronald Carver, an education professor at the University of Missouri, says tests he gave students there tend to support that notion. When the students were tested at 600 words a minute, they were "simply getting an idea of what they were reading," in effect, skimming.

Box 4.1   *(continued)*

Evelyn Wood officials, who regularly claim to have students reading at 2,000 words a minute, said such studies ignore a basic premise of their approach. At Evelyn Wood, people learn a new way to read—one that teaches readers to take in whole ideas rather than single words, they said.

"It's a visual form of reading," said Verla Nielson, director of the program's Salt Lake City operations. "It's seeing words in chunks—reading as the author thought it. It's like learning to read music—you can see many notes at the same time."

To prove that the method works, the company cites the results of comprehension tests given to their students at the beginning and end of the course. Some reading specialists take issue with those multiple-choice quizzes.

Carver, a reading specialist for 13 years, told a group of college students to imagine they were reading material from the Wood course and then gave them the Wood tests. The students averaged a 60% comprehension level without ever reading the material, a reflection of what Carver says is the tests' shortcomings.

"They claim you can increase your perception of the number of words taken at once. That's absurd," said the Reading Association's Guthrie. "There's a lot of scientific evidence that shows you can only take in 20 characters at a time."

Carlos Garcia Tunon, a Washington marketing consultant and an Evelyn Wood alumnus who reportedly went from 362.5 to 5,024 words per minute with a 20% increase in comprehension, said he didn't feel he was seeing every word he was supposed to be reading at the faster speeds. What you get from the speed reading, he said, is the basic theme, the characters, and the plot of a book.

Tunon was one of thousands of people who have been drawn to the reading system's free mini-lessons by advertising that features students flipping through texts as if they were looking through picture books.

Once at the mini-session, an instructor tells the student that anyone can learn the necessary skills, that all it takes is practice, that if you break the bad habits you learned as a child, you'll be reading six times faster. It's a 15-minute buildup that ends with a passing reference to the $395 price tag ($295 if another member of your family enrolls).

The students are told if they stop subvocalizing—reading the individual word to yourself—and regressing—rereading a line—they'll save 40% of reading time.

They also show a 15-minute film on the reading method. The highlight is a 1975 "Tonight Show" segment of an interview with Elizabeth Jaffee, then a 13-year-old wunderkind of speed reading, who reads 30 pages of a highly technical book in one minute.

What they don't tell you is that Jaffee, now a college freshman, isn't really a speed reader anymore. That the Evelyn Wood alumna sued and received a $25,000 out-of-court settlement because she claimed that the technique works only for certain kinds of reading.

Levy attempted in her own experiments to suppress subvocalization by requiring that subjects repeatedly count from one to ten as they read a short paragraph. They were told to count quickly and continuously in a soft voice while reading the sentences and to try to remember all the sentences in the paragraph. You may want to try this as you read the two paragraphs in Table 4.2. When they finished reading the paragraph, people were shown one of the sentences in the paragraph or a slight variation and were asked to judge whether the test sentence was identical to the one presented earlier.

Since the altered sentences were only slightly changed, people had to remember the details to do well on this task. The first two sentences following each paragraph in Table 4.2 are examples of altered sentences. The lexical alteration changes a single word but preserves the meaning of the sentence—the word *mother* is changed to *woman* for the first paragraph and the word *child* to *youngster* for the second paragraph. The semantic alteration changes the meaning of the sentence by switching the order of two nouns—for the first paragraph, the order of *mother* and *physician*. The results of this study revealed that people performed more poorly when they had to count while reading. They were not as accurate in identifying when changes occurred, regardless of whether there were lexical changes or semantic changes.

Suppressing subvocalization did not interfere with performance when people listened to the sentence, however. The fact that counting while listening did not

Table 4.2 Examples of lexical, semantic, and paraphrase tests

1. **An emergency**
   The hospital staff paged the busy doctor.
   The solemn physician distressed the anxious mother.
   The sobbing woman held her unconscious son.
   A speeding truck had crossed the mid-line.
   Her oncoming car was hit and damaged.
   Her child had plunged through the windshield.
   The medical team strove to save him.

   The solemn physician distressed the anxious *woman*. (lexical)

   The solemn *mother* distressed the anxious *physician*. (semantic)

   The solemn *doctor upset* the anxious mother. (paraphrase—yes)

   The solemn *officer helped* the anxious mother. (paraphrase—no)

2. **A lost boy**
   The lost boy searched the crowded street.
   His careless mother had forgotten about him.
   The concerned policeman approached the worried child.
   The kindly man dried the boy's tears.
   The young lad gave his home address.
   And the police cruiser escorted him home.
   In future his mother was more careful.

   The concerned policeman approached the worried *youngster*. (lexical)

   The concerned *child* approached the worried *policeman*. (semantic)

   The concerned *officer* approached the *upset* child. (paraphrase—yes)

   The concerned *woman* approached the *carefree* child. (paraphrase—no) affect performance shows that suppression interfered specifically with reading, not with language comprehension in general. The difference between listening and reading is that the listener receives an acoustic code rather than a visual code. The fact that counting interfered only with recall following reading suggests that translating visual material into an acoustic code helps preserve detailed information in the text.

Although the acoustic code improved recall of detailed information, it was not necessary to preserve the gist of the paragraph (Levy, 1978). Support for this claim comes from a second experiment, in which subjects made paraphrase judgments. These subjects were not encouraged to maintain the exact wording of sentences, because word changes occurred in all the test sentences. However, positive examples preserved the general meaning of an original sentence and negative examples altered the meaning. In the paraphrase changes, unlike the semantic changes, the meaning was altered by replacing two words in the sentences rather than changing the order of words (see Table 4.2). Therefore, less information was required to distinguish between positive and negative examples in the paraphrase task than to judge correctly in the lexical or semantic task. People could do well on the paraphrase if they remembered the general ideas expressed in the paragraph. Since the counting task did not interfere with performance, Levy concluded that acoustic coding was not required to remember the more important ideas.

Levy's findings are consistent with my own experiences in preventing subvocalization. When the material is relatively simple and detailed recall is not required, people can recall the major ideas without subvocalization. However, subvocalization did facilitate the detection of more subtle changes, such as changing the order of two words or replacing a word with a semantically similar word. Additional evidence also supports this conclusion. Hardyck and Petrinovich (1970) measured subvocalization by recording the muscle activity of the larynx. Subjects in the experimental group were trained to keep their muscle activity at nonreading relaxation levels. Any increases in activity during reading activated an audio signal to remind them to suppress subvocalization. A control group read the same material but were allowed to subvocalize as they read. A comprehension test revealed that the two groups did not differ in recall of easy material, but the subvocalization group recalled more of the difficult material than the suppression group.

The studies on speech processing during reading suggest that although subvocalization is not necessary for comprehension, it does facilitate retention of detailed or complex information. A popular explanation of these findings is that subvocalization makes it easier to retain words in STM until they can be integrated with other words in the sentence or paragraph (Conrad, 1972; Kleiman, 1975). We would be able to evaluate this suggestion more accurately if we had a better understanding of the role of STM in reading. Fortunately, considerable progress has been made over the past several years in understanding the psychological processes involved in text comprehension. Chapter 11 summarizes this progress and indicates how STM is used in reading.

Recognition of Items in STM

Searching STM

Our discussion of STM up to this point has emphasized the *recall* of material, as shown in the experiments asking for recall of three consonants, a string of letters or digits, a chessboard, or a circuit diagram after a short delay. Psychologists have also been interested in how people try to "recognize" whether a given item is contained in STM. First, they present a sequence of items, which the subject stores in STM. The sequence is usually six items or fewer so that all the items can be easily maintained. Then a test item occurs, and the subject must decide whether that item is one of the items in the sequence.

This procedure was invented by Saul Sternberg at Bell Laboratories in order to study how people encode a pattern and compare it with other patterns stored in STM. Sternberg first showed a sequence of digits (the memory set), which the subject stored in STM. Then he presented a test digit, and the subject quickly decided whether the test digit was a member of the memory set. When Sternberg (1966) varied the size of the memory set from one to six digits, he discovered that the time required to make the decision increased as a linear function of the number of digits in STM. Whenever the size of the memory set was increased by one additional digit, the response time was lengthened by 38 msec. Sternberg proposed that the test digit was sequentially compared with each item stored in STM and that it required about 38 msec to make each comparison.

In one of the early applications of the paradigm, Sternberg (1967) varied the quality of the test digit in addition to the size of the memory set. The memory set consisted of one, two, or four digits, and the test digit was either intact or degraded to make it difficult to recognize. Sternberg suggested that two operations were needed to perform the task. First, the observer had to encode the test digit in order to compare it with other digits stored in STM. The subject then had to scan the memory set to determine whether any of the digits matched the test digit.

Sternberg showed how it would be possible to determine whether a degraded pattern would influence the encoding time or the memory scan time. The slope of the function relating reaction time (RT) to memory-set size indicates the amount of time needed to compare the test digit with a digit stored in STM: it is the amount of additional time needed whenever another digit is added to the memory set. If a degraded digit slows down the rate of comparison, the slope should increase. Figure 4.9a shows this prediction. Notice that the more items in the memory set, the greater the difference in RT. The encoding of the test digit occurs only once, however, and should be independent of the number of items in the memory set. If the degraded digit lengthens the encoding time, the reaction time should increase by a constant amount (the additional time needed for encoding), which is independent of the number of items in the memory set. Figure 4.9b shows this prediction.

Figure 4.10 shows the results Sternberg actually obtained over two sessions. Degradation greatly affected the encoding time in both sessions. The data for degraded and intact digits form nearly parallel lines, similar to those shown in Figure

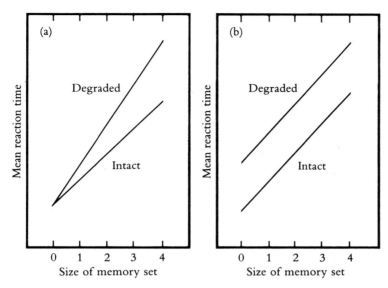

Figure 4.9 Predicted reaction time functions if degrading affects the memory comparison time (a) or the encoding time (b)

4.9b. The effect on the memory comparison time (as measured by differences in slopes) was minimal. Degrading the test digit primarily affected the time needed to encode the pattern and had little effect on the time required to compare the test digit with other digits stored in STM. This finding implies that a visually degraded digit was not directly compared with the other digits, since this would have slowed down the comparisons. The longer encoding time suggests that the effect of degradation was compensated for during the encoding stage. The subject may have changed the degraded image into a normal image and matched the normal image against the visual images stored in STM. Or the subject may have named the test digit and compared it with the names of digits stored in STM. The latter explanation is particularly attractive because acoustic codes are usually used to maintain information in STM. It should take longer to name a degraded digit, and hence the encoding time would be slowed down. However, once named, the degraded image would no longer be used, so the rate of comparison would be relatively unaffected.

Some Determinants of the Memory Comparison Rate

Although degradation of the test digit had very little effect on the comparison rate, use of qualitatively different kinds of stimuli does influence the comparison rate. Furthermore, there is a very orderly relation between the memory span and the rate of searching STM. Cavanagh (1972) found seven classes of stimuli in which measures were available for both the number of stimuli that could be recalled in a memory span test and the comparison rate of stimuli in a Sternberg task. Both measures were

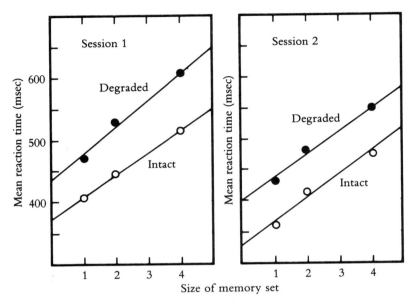

Figure 4.10   Mean reaction time for intact and degraded test stimuli

available for the digits 0 through 9; colors; the letters of the alphabet; familiar words; geometrical shapes such as squares, circles, and triangles; random forms; and nonsense syllables composed of a vowel between two consonants.

The average comparison rate ranged from 33 msec for digits to 73 msec for nonsense syllables. The average memory span ranged from 3.4 items for nonsense syllables to 7.7 items for digits. Figure 4.11 shows the almost perfect inverse relation between the two measures: the greater the memory span, the faster the processing rate. An interesting implication of the results shown in Figure 4.11 is that the same amount of time is always required to search STM when it is filled to its capacity. The average capacity of STM is 3.4 nonsense syllables, 3.8 random forms, 5.3 geometrical shapes, 5.5 words, 6.4 letters, 7.1 colors, and 7.7 digits. It takes about one-quarter second to search STM in each of these cases. When there are more items to search, the rate of search is faster, so the total search time remains constant.

We still don't know the cause of this inverse relation, but Cavanagh suggests several possible explanations. One of the simplest is that the items are represented in memory by a list of features. Short-term memory has a constant, limited amount of "space," which can hold only a fixed number of features. Since nonsense syllables, random forms, and geometrical shapes are more complex than letters, colors, and digits, they would have more features, and each item would take up more space in STM. The feature explanation of the comparison rate would assume that the time it takes to compare a test item with an item in the memory set is determined by how many features have to be compared. The complexity of the stimulus, as defined by number of features, would therefore affect both how many items could be stored in

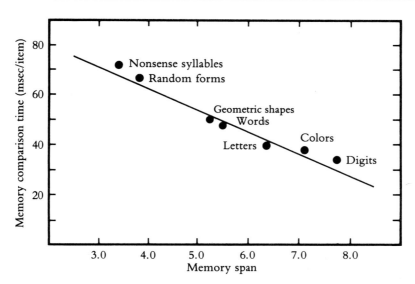

Figure 4.11 Relation between the memory comparison rate and the memory span

STM and the time required to compare two items. The feature explanation is consistent with many of the ideas about pattern recognition discussed in Chapter 2; however, further research is necessary in order to determine whether it is the best explanation.

Although the stimuli studied by Cavanagh differed in their rate of comparison, they all caused the typical increase in response time as the size of the memory set increased. Is it possible to find cases in which the size of the memory set does not influence response time? There are a few such interesting cases, one of which was revealed by DeRosa and Tkacz (1976). The subjects in their experiment were shown a series of three, four, or five pictures. The pictures were part of an ordered sequence of pictures shown in Figure 4.12. If the pictures were randomly selected from the sequence, response time increased as a linear function of the number of items in the memory set. For example, if people were shown the five birds numbered 3, 7, 6, 9, and 1 in Figure 4.12, it would take them longer to search STM than if they were shown only birds 3, 7, and 9. However, the size of the memory set did not make any difference when they were shown sequences of adjacent items. They could search memory as fast for the sequence 3, 4, 5, 6, and 7 as they could for the sequence 3, 4, and 5. Furthermore, the sequence did not have to be presented in an ascending order to obtain this result. People who were shown items 3 to 7 in order 5, 3, 7, 4, 6 could also search a five-item sequence as fast as they could search a three-item sequence.

The results indicate that people can represent a sequence of adjacent items as a single, unified whole rather than as separate items. The finding that the order of presentation within the sequence did not make a difference suggests that we are able

Stimulus type   Ordinal position

Figure 4.12   Five organized sequences of visual stimuli

to rapidly reorganize items to make a unified whole. Perhaps we quickly establish the two boundaries of the sequence and examine whether the test item falls within the boundaries. This interpretation is supported by the fact that the speed of negative responses is determined by how far the test item is from the nearest boundary of the sequence. If the memory set consisted of items 2, 3, 4, and 5, it would take much longer to reject the sixth item than the ninth item in the sequence. The finding that organization facilitates the search of information in STM is but one example of how organization can improve performance.

I have attempted in this chapter to discuss some of the major characteristics of STM. We use STM in so many different cognitive tasks that it would be impossible to confine this discussion to a single chapter. The next chapter focuses on LTM but also emphasizes the interaction between STM and LTM. If we are interested in learning information, rather than simply maintaining it over a short period of time, we must attempt to enter that information into a more permanent store. We will begin our study of learning by looking at a model that represents learning as the transfer of information from STM into LTM.

Summary

Short-term memory has several limitations that distinguish it from long-term memory. First of all, STM results in rapid forgetting. Items that are not actively rehearsed can be lost in 20 to 30 seconds. Evidence suggests that interference, rather than

Know difference btwn Recognition + Recall

decay, is the primary cause of forgetting. Interference can result from items presented either before (proactive interference) or after (retroactive interference) the tested item. Release from proactive interference illustrates how the reduction of interference improves memory.

Another limitation of STM is its capacity. After reviewing a large number of findings on absolute judgment and memory span, George Miller identified the capacity limitation as consisting of about seven chunks. A chunk is a group of items that is stored as a unit in LTM. For instance, the sequence *F B I T W A C I A I BM* is easy to recall when grouped as *FBI–TWA–CIA–IBM* because the 12 letters have been grouped as four chunks. De Groot argued that the superior ability of a master player to reproduce a chessboard is a result of the ability to group the pieces into familiar configurations. Using pauses as a measure of chunk boundaries, Chase and Simon concluded that master chess players have both more chunks and larger chunks stored in LTM than less experienced players. Success in reproducing other configurations, such as circuit diagrams, also depends on the availability of chunks.

The use of verbal rehearsal to maintain information in STM is confirmed by acoustic confusions—errors that sound like the correct response. Laughery's simulation model accounts for acoustic confusions by assuming that acoustic codes consist of phonemes, and phonemes can be independently forgotten. Although we usually rely on an acoustic code when we read, we can remember the general ideas from our reading without subvocalizing. However, subvocalization improves our ability to recall details and complex material.

A recognition task consists of showing an item and asking the subject to verify whether the item is contained in a set of items stored in STM. The finding that the time required to make this decision increases as a linear function of the number of items stored in STM suggests that people search the items one at a time. Degrading the test item has relatively little effect on the rate of search, but it does lengthen the time needed to encode the test item before comparing it with the other items in STM. However, the comparison rate is influenced by whether the items are simple, such as letters or digits, or more complex, such as random forms or nonsense syllables. There is an inverse relation between search rate and memory span: the faster the search rate, the greater the number of items that can be stored in STM. A possible explanation is that both findings are influenced by the number of features composing each item. There are a few cases in which time is uninfluenced by the number of items in STM, one example being items that can be sequentially organized.

Recommended Reading

Baddeley and Hitch (1974; Hitch & Baddeley, 1976) have been actively involved in exploring the properties of STM as a working memory (see also Klapp, Marshburn, & Lester, 1983). Slowiaczek and Clifton (1980) investigated the role of subvocalization in reading and found that subvocalization is useful when people have to combine ideas expressed in different sentences. There are several good books on memory, including Baddeley (1976), Crowder (1976), Klatzky (1980), and Zechmeister and Nyberg (1982). A book edited by Gruneberg, Morris, and Sykes (1978) contains articles on practical aspects of memory. Reviews of memory research frequently appear in the *Annual Review of Psychology* (for example, Horton and Mills, 1984; Johnson and Hasher, in press) and provide a summary of research over the past several years. Arguments against the importance of STM have been presented by Crowder (1982).

5

Long-Term Memory

Memory is that part of the brain that reminds us on Friday what we should have done the previous Monday.

POPULAR SAYING

Most of us at one time or another have envied someone who has a very good memory and wished that we could improve our own memory. It's questionable whether we would all be more successful if we had better memories, but at least some people attribute their success to their ability to remember a lot of details. One such person is Isaac Asimov, the author of more than 200 books, 1300 articles, and 250 short stories. In an article titled " 'Computer' Memory Helps Him Write a Book a Month," Asimov claimed that he is able to write on such a wide variety of topics because of his talent for retention: "I read, and I have read a lot. I've heard a lot. And I remember it all and have it on tap. I can recall instantly from the files in my head so I never take notes. My memory is my staunch and unfailing support" (*The Oakland Tribune*, 1979).

The storage of all this information obviously does not occur in STM, so psychologists have proposed a more permanent store, called long-term memory (LTM). The first section of this chapter describes some ways in which information can be transferred from a temporary to a more permanent store. We start by considering the basic characteristics of LTM, including learning strategies. Much of what was known about this topic was summarized in an important paper by Atkinson and Shiffrin published in 1968. The authors discussed several strategies that could facilitate learning, but they studied primarily verbal rehearsal. They assumed that each time an item was rehearsed, information about that item was entered into LTM.

The selection of a learning strategy such as verbal rehearsal helps us transfer information into LTM, but are such strategies always required? You can certainly recall many events that happened during the day even though you did not try to "memorize" these events. The concept of *automatic processing*, introduced in Chapter 3, can be applied to remembering, as well as other cognitive skills. Remembering some kinds of information may require little conscious effort, and one of the tasks facing cognitive psychologists has been to determine the kind of information that people can remember as a result of automatic processing.

Psychologists have also been interested in discovering how people retrieve information after it is stored in LTM. An initial step is to decide whether the information is in LTM. If we decide that it is, our next step is to select a plan for retrieving the information if we cannot immediately recall it. Recalling relevant information is usually important even in recognition tasks because recognizing an event or a person as familiar is often insufficient—we usually need to know additional information. After discussing some theoretical aspects of recall and recognition, I will conclude the chapter with an example of how the two combine to determine the accuracy of eyewitness identification. But let us first return to the basics, as represented by the Atkinson-Shiffrin model that was shown in Figure 4.1.

The Atkinson-Shiffrin Model

Structural Components and Control Processes

The theory proposed by Atkinson and Shiffrin (1968, 1971) emphasizes the interaction between STM and LTM. In their theory the structural components consist of a sensory store, a short-term memory, and a long-term memory. The sensory store preserves information for a few hundred milliseconds; its characteristics were identified by George Sperling (1960) for the storage of visual information. STM, the second basic component of Atkinson and Shiffrin's system, is regarded as a person's working memory. Information is lost from STM within 15 to 30 seconds if it is not rehearsed.

The third component, LTM, differs from the other two components because it contains information that is relatively permanent. Some psychologists have suggested that information is never lost from LTM, although we lose the ability to retrieve it. Whether information is lost or impossible to recover may not be of much practical significance, but if we knew that it was still in memory, we might hope to recover it eventually.

The rate of forgetting from LTM varies from a few minutes to many years. Ideally, we would like to have a single forgetting rate for STM and a single forgetting rate for LTM. The fact that there is a wide range of forgetting rates is one of the criticisms that have been directed at theories about the distinction between STM and LTM. In order to be more specific about the rate of forgetting, we have to know how information is coded, a topic we will study in Chapter 6.

Another difference between STM and LTM is that LTM is unlimited in its capacity. We never reach the point where we cannot learn new information because LTM is filled. Nevertheless, it is not always easy to enter new information into LTM.

Atkinson and Shiffrin proposed several control processes that could be used in an attempt to learn new information. The control processes are strategies that a person uses to facilitate learning; they include rehearsal, coding, and imaging.

Rehearsal is the repetition of information—either aloud or silently—over and over until it is learned.

Coding attempts to place the information to be remembered in the context of additional, easily retrievable information, such as a mnemonic phrase or sentence. For example, many of us learned that the lines of a treble clef are E, G, B, D, F by remembering the sentence "Every good boy does fine."

Imaging is creating visual images to remember verbal information. This is an old memory trick—it was even recommended by Cicero for learning long lists or speeches.

The list of control processes could be further expanded, but rehearsal, coding, and imaging are three of the primary ways of learning. Because there are so many control processes to study, Atkinson and Shiffrin (1968) decided to focus their research on only one—verbal rehearsal. More recent work by psychologists has emphasized coding, organizational strategies, and imagery; these strategies are discussed in the second part of this book.

Verbal Rehearsal and Learning

Verbal rehearsal is usually considered a form of "rote learning" because it involves simply repeating information over and over until we think we have learned it. It can be useful when the material seems rather abstract, making it difficult to use strategies such as coding or imaging. The task designed by Atkinson and Shiffrin (1968) required the learning of abstract, meaningless material and therefore encouraged the use of rehearsal.

The undergraduates in their experiment tried to learn associations between a two-digit number (the stimulus) and a letter (the response). The paired associates included items such as 31–Q, 42–B, and 53–A. Each pair was shown for three seconds, followed by three seconds before the next trial. Interspersed throughout these study trials were test trials, in which only the two-digit number was presented and the subject was asked to supply the letter that had accompanied it earlier. One of the variables in the experiment was the number of trials that occurred between the study and test trials. Some associates were tested on the very next trial and others after a delay that could last as long as 17 trials.

Atkinson and Shiffrin interpreted the data on this experiment by proposing a model in which verbal rehearsal was used to learn the associates. They assumed that the students maintained a fixed number of items in STM and that these items were rehearsed whenever the student was not viewing a new item or responding during a test trial. The effect of rehearsal was to transfer information about that item into LTM. The extent of learning depended on how long a particular pair was maintained in the rehearsal set. Atkinson and Shiffrin proposed that learning increased as a linear function of the number of trials over which the item was rehearsed. Once the item was no longer rehearsed, information about that particular item decreased as each succeeding item was presented for study. The predicted probability of a correct response therefore depended on both the number of trials in which the item was rehearsed and the number of intervening trials that occurred between the time the item left the rehearsal set and the test trial. Figure 5.1 shows how both factors influenced the predictions.

The prediction shown in Figure 5.1 is the probability of retrieving the correct response from LTM. If an item has been kept active in STM through rehearsal, it will be responded to correctly if it is still in STM at the time of the test. If the subject has been rehearsing 31–Q right up until the time of the test on 31, it is easy to respond Q. If the item had been rehearsed but is no longer in STM, the answer has to be retrieved from LTM. A third possibility exists when an item is not rehearsed at all. Since the model assumes that only a limited number of items can be maintained in the rehearsal set, rehearsing a new item will be done at the expense of eliminating one of the items already in the set. Atkinson and Shiffrin proposed that an item that is not rehearsed can be responded to correctly only if it is tested on the trial immediately following its presentation.

Rehearsal and the Serial Position Effect

An easy way to test the proposal that verbal rehearsal results in learning is to ask someone to rehearse out loud. The experimenter can then count the times each item was rehearsed and determine whether the probability of recalling an item is related to the number of rehearsals. A task designed by Rundus (1971) was exactly of this type. He presented lists of 20 nouns to undergraduates at Stanford. The words were presented one at a time for a period of five seconds each. Rundus instructed the

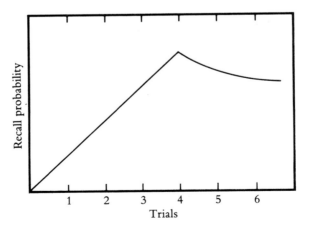

Figure 5.1   Predicted recall probability of an item that was rehearsed for four trials and tested two trials after it left the rehearsal set

students to study by repeating aloud words on the list during each five-second interval. They were free to rehearse any word on the list as long as their rehearsal filled the intervals. After presentation of the list, the students tried to recall the words in any order.

Figure 5.2 shows the results of the experiment. The probability of recalling a word depended on its position in the list. Words at the beginning and words at the end of the list were easier to recall than words in the middle of the list. The U shape of the recall curve, which is called a *serial position effect*, is often obtained in recall experiments. The better recall of words at the beginning of the list is called a *primacy effect*, and the better recall of words at the end of the list is called a *recency effect*.

The curve showing the number of times each word was rehearsed illustrates that words at the beginning of the list were rehearsed more often than the other words. Because a person does not have much choice in what to rehearse at the beginning of the list, these words are rehearsed more often, as is illustrated by the example shown

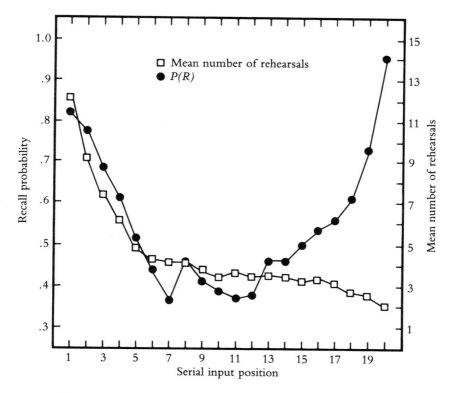

Figure 5.2   Relation between the average probability of recall—
P(R)—and the average number of rehearsals as a function of serial
position

in Table 5.1. The relation between the rehearsal and recall curves reveals that the primacy effect can be explained by Atkinson and Shiffrin's theory. Since early words were rehearsed more often than the other words, they should have a higher probability of being retrieved from LTM. This explanation implies that the primacy effect should be eliminated if all the words on the list are rehearsed equally often. In fact, when subjects were instructed to rehearse each word equally often by rehearsing only the displayed word, the primacy effect disappeared (Fischler, Rundus, & Atkinson, 1970).

Although the number of rehearsals can predict the primacy effect, it does not predict the recency effect. People were very good at recalling the words at the end of the list even though they did not rehearse them any more than the words in the middle of the list. The recency effect is often explained by the proposal that the words at the end of the list are still in STM when a person begins the recall. The students in Rundus's experiment recalled the words immediately after the last item was presented; it is therefore reasonable to assume that the words they had just seen were still available in STM.

We learned from the Peterson and Peterson experiment discussed in Chapter 4 that information is rapidly lost from STM if people have to perform another task. If the recency effect is caused by retrieving the most recent items from STM, it should be eliminated if a person has to perform another task before recalling the items. Subjects in an experiment designed by Postman and Phillips (1965) had to perform an arithmetic task for 30 seconds before they tried to recall a list of words. The arithmetic task was successful in eliminating the recency effect, implying that the words at the end of the list had decayed from STM.

It is only fair to point out that there have been other explanations of the recency effect, which have been reviewed by Greene (1986). One such explanation is that the recency effect occurs because the positions at the end of the list are more distinctive than those in the middle. In the next chapter we will see that distinctive items are easier to recall, but I would now like to return to the topic of how people can use rehearsal to learn new information.

Table 5.1   A partial listing of items rehearsed by one of the subjects

Item presented	Items rehearsed (rehearsal set)
1. Reaction	Reaction, reaction, reaction, reaction
2. Hoof	Hoof, reaction, hoof, reaction
3. Blessing	Blessing, hoof, reaction
4. Research	Research, reaction, hoof, research
5. Candy	Candy, hoof, research, reaction
6. Hardship	Hardship, hoof, hardship, hoof
7. Kindness	Kindness, candy, hardship, hoof
8. Nonsense	Nonsense, kindness, candy, hardship
.	.
.	.
.	.
20. Cellar	Cellar, alcohol, misery, cellar

Deciding What to Rehearse

Rehearsal is a rather obvious learning strategy, and we have all used it at one time or another. What to rehearse is a little less obvious, but we could probably agree that we should rehearse material we haven't already learned.

Imagine that you have to learn some foreign vocabulary words. You will want to be able to recall the translations not only during the time you study the words but also on subsequent days. To succeed, you must be able to tell when you have really learned the translation and are not simply retrieving it from STM. My own experience has been that I sometimes find it difficult to judge when I have really learned what I was studying. Although the information appeared easy to recall shortly after I read or heard about it, it was gone the next day.

There are many tasks that a computer can do much better than people can, so why not let the computer decide when we have really learned an item? Since a computer can only follow the instructions of a programmer, it must be given instructions derived from a good model of learning. The advantage of using a formal model of learning and a computer to improve recall was demonstrated in a study by Atkinson (1972a, 1972b). The task required that undergraduates learn the English translation of 84 German words. The words were divided into seven lists, each containing 12 words. One of the lists was displayed on each trial of an instructional session, and either the student or the computer selected one of the items for test and study. After the student attempted to provide the English translation, the correct translation was presented. The computer then displayed the next list, and the procedure repeated for a total of 336 trials. Figure 5.3 shows a typical list and the design of the instructional session.

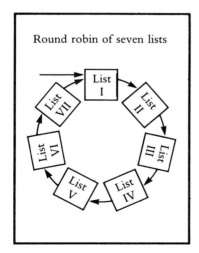

Round robin of seven lists

Typical list

1. das   Rad
2. die   Seite
3. das   Kino
4. die   Gans
5. der   Fluss
6. die   Gegend
7. die   Kamera
8. der   Anzug
9. das   Geld
10. der   Gipfel
11. das   Bein
12. die   Ecke

Figure 5.3   Illustration of the language-learning task designed by Atkinson

Atkinson designed the experiment to compare the learning of three groups of students. Students in one group were allowed to pick which words they wanted to study. They were told that they should try to learn all the vocabulary words, and the best way to proceed was to test and study words that they did not already know. Students in a second group received items to study that were selected according to a learning model. Atkinson formulated the model in an attempt to optimize learning by presenting those words that the students most needed to study. The words were selected on the basis of a response-sensitive strategy that carefully kept track of a student's previous responses. Students in a third group received words that were randomly selected. Random selection, of course, is not a very good procedure, because it would include words that a student had already learned. The performance of this third group is of interest because it provides a standard against which to compare the other two groups.

The learning model assumes that an item can be in one of three states:

1. An *unlearned* state. Items in this state have not yet been learned, so the learner will respond incorrectly.
2. A *temporary* state. Items in this state have been temporarily learned. The student will initially give the correct answer but will forget the translation as she attempts to learn other items. We might think of these items as being stored in STM.
3. A *permanent* state. The translations of items in this state are relatively permanent in the sense that the learning of other vocabulary items will not interfere with them. We might think of these items as being stored in LTM.

The goal of the learning model is to select for study those items that are not yet in LTM in order to maximize the number of items in LTM at the end of the session. Items in the unlearned state are easy to identify because the student will be unable to provide the correct translation. Clearly, these items need further study, and on the basis of the research discussed previously, we might expect that students would study them. Items in the temporary state are more difficult to identify because the student will be able to provide the correct answer on some of the trials. Let's consider the case in which a student receives two tests on the same item and responds correctly on both occasions. Is that item in a permanent state, implying that it wouldn't have to be presented again? We don't know for certain, but our decision should be influenced by the number of trials that occurred between the two tests. The greater the number of intervening trials, the greater the probability that the item is in the permanent state, because studying other items should cause the student to forget the translation if it had been only temporarily learned.

The advantage of a computer is that it can record and remember exactly how a student responded on each of the items. When this information is used in a model that attempts to optimize learning, it is possible that the model could select items for study better than the student could. The results of Atkinson's experiment demonstrated that this possibility can be realized. Figure 5.4 shows the performance of each of the three groups during a delayed test given one week later. It is apparent that the worse the students did during instruction, the better they did on the test.

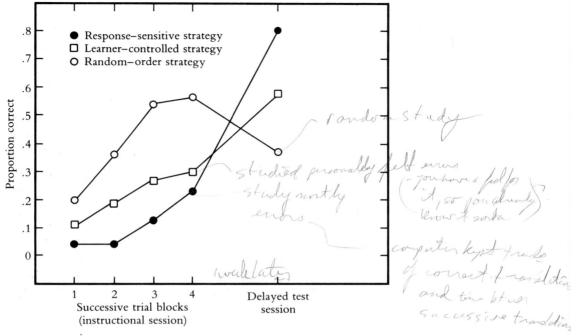

Figure 5.4   Proportion of correct responses during the instructional session and during the delayed test given one week later

The reason is that successful instruction requires identifying and presenting the unlearned words, resulting in many errors during the instruction. The response-sensitive strategy based on the learning model was the most successful in identifying unlearned items. Those students who could select their own items for study (the learner-controlled strategy) did much better on the test than when the items were randomly selected, but they did much worse than the model. Performance on the test indicated that the learner-controlled strategy yielded a gain of 53% over the random procedure, but the computer-controlled strategy yielded a gain of 108%.

The results provide a clear demonstration of the usefulness of a good learning model that can be carried out by a computer. Although learner-controlled instruction was better than random selection, it was worse than selection of items by the learning model. It seems clear that serious consideration should be given to using the model on a wide scale. The declining cost of computers should make instructional programs like the one developed by Atkinson a possibility in more situations.

Automatic Encoding

Learning a foreign vocabulary usually requires considerable effort and the use of deliberate learning strategies such as verbal rehearsal. But we can also recall many events that we did not consciously attempt to learn. For example, we can recall our activities at the end of the day even though we did not set out to learn or rehearse a list of activities. Learning that occurs without intention is called *incidental learning.*

Control processes such as verbal rehearsal can help us learn difficult material, as the previous section showed. But control processes do not account for incidental learning, because we do not consciously select learning strategies during incidental learning. A better account is provided by the concept of automatic processing that was introduced in the chapter on attention. As you may recall, one criterion of automatic processing was that it occurs without intention (Posner & Snyder, 1975), and this is what happens during incidental learning. A complete account of how we encode information for storage in memory should include not only encoding that occurs during deliberate learning but also encoding that occurs automatically.

Hasher and Zacks's Theory

Hasher and Zacks (1979) have proposed a theory of automatic encoding. They distinguished between two kinds of memory activities—those that require considerable effort, or capacity, and those that require very little or none. The former, or *effortful processes,* include various strategies to improve memory, such as visual imagery, elaboration, organization, and verbal rehearsal. The latter, or *automatic processes,* support incidental learning when we are not consciously trying to learn. Hasher and Zacks proposed that we can automatically record frequency, spatial, and temporal information without consciously intending to keep track of this information.

Frequency information is information about how frequently different stimuli occur. An experimenter might vary the number of times people see different pictures during an experiment and then ask them to estimate how many times each picture appeared. Spatial information is information about where objects occur in the environment. The experimenter could present pictures in different locations and then ask people to recall the locations. Temporal information is information about when or for how long objects occur. The experimenter might ask people about the relative recency or the relative duration of events that occurred during the experiment.

The claim that all three kinds of information can be automatically recorded in memory cannot be tested unless we specify the implications of automatic processing. Hasher and Zacks proposed five criteria that distinguish between automatic and effortful processing. Table 5.2 summarizes the criteria and their predicted effects. The predictions are:

1. *Intentional versus incidental learning.* Intentional learning occurs when we are deliberately trying to learn; incidental learning occurs when we are not. Incidental learning is as effective as intentional learning for automatic processes but is less effective for effortful processing. People should therefore have knowledge of frequency, spatial, and temporal information even when they are not trying to learn this information.

2. *Effects of instructions and practice.* Instructions on how to perform a task and practice on the task should not affect automatic processes, because they can

Table 5.2   Predicted effects for automatic and effortful processing

	Automatic processing	Effortful processing
Intentional versus incidental learning	No difference	Intentional better
Effect of instructions and practice	No effects	Both improve performance
Task interference	No interference	Interference
Depression or high arousal	No effects	Decreased performance
Developmental trends	None	Decreased performance in young children or elderly

already be carried out very efficiently. Both instructions and practice should improve performance on effortful processes.

3. *Task interference.* Automatic processes should not interfere with each other, because they require little or no capacity. Effortful processes require considerable capacity and should interfere with each other when they exceed the amount of available capacity.

4. *Depression or high arousal.* Emotional states such as depression or high arousal can reduce the effectiveness of effortful processes. Automatic processes should not be affected by emotional states.

5. *Developmental trends.* Automatic processes show little change with age. They are acquired early and do not decline in old age. Effortful processes show developmental changes; they are not performed as well by young children or the elderly.

Evaluation of the Predictions

Hasher and Zacks (1979) predicted that memory for frequency, temporal, and spatial information should not be affected by intentional versus incidental learning, practice, task interference, depression or high arousal, and developmental trends. Recent evidence suggests that these predictions are more accurate for frequency information than they are for temporal information.

If temporal information is encoded automatically, then students should not improve with practice and there should not be substantial individual differences among students, as suggested by the criterion about developmental trends. Neither of these two predictions was supported in a study that measured students' ability to determine the order in which words had occurred on a list (Zacks, Hasher, Alba, Sanft, & Rose, 1984). Students were shown a list of 30 words and later had to reconstruct the original order when the words were presented in a different order.

In contrast to the predictions of Hasher and Zacks's theory, both practice and individual differences influenced students' success in remembering the temporal order of the words. Students did better with practice, and students with high SAT scores did better than students with low SAT scores.

But there is a substantial amount of evidence to support the claim that the frequency of events is automatically encoded (Hasher & Zacks, 1984). Neither practice nor individual differences, including changes in development, have much influence on people's ability to judge the relative frequency of events. There is also considerable incidental learning of event frequencies. People were very good at judging the relative frequency of events, even when they did not know they would be tested on their knowledge of frequencies. The automatic encoding of this information is useful because knowledge of frequencies allows us to develop expectations about the world. We will see specific examples of how people make use of this information in the chapters on categorization and decision making.

The work on automatic encoding is a valuable supplement to the work on the selection of learning strategies. Incidental learning seems to occur through automatic processing, whereas intentional learning seems to occur through the use of learning strategies such as verbal rehearsal. We will see further instances of incidental and intentional learning in the next two chapters. But our immediate goal is to study how people retrieve information from memory.

Memory Retrieval

Although memory retrieval often requires little effort, we occasionally need to use strategies to aid recall. For example, if asked a difficult question, we may have to decide whether we have the relevant information in memory. Glucksberg and McCloskey (1981) proposed that people first conduct a preliminary search of memory to decide whether they have stored any information that is relevant to the question. Most people would not find any relevant information if asked "Does Margaret Thatcher use an electric toothbrush?," so they could quickly respond that they didn't know. If potentially relevant facts were retrieved, however (as could occur for a question like "Is Kiev in the Ukraine?"), a person should then search LTM for confirming or disconfirming evidence.

After deciding that it is worthwhile to search LTM, a person must decide how to conduct the search. Atkinson and Shiffrin proposed that people develop plans for searching LTM. For example, if asked to recall the names of all 50 states, we could organize our search by either alphabetical order or geographical location. Searching memory is clearly important when we must recall information, but is it necessary for recognition? The role of search in retrieving information during recognition and recall tasks is the topic of this last section.

Recall

Recalling information from LTM sometimes occurs so rapidly that psychologists have little opportunity to study how people retrieve the information. However, occasionally retrieval succeeds only after a slow search of LTM, such as occurs in the "tip of the tongue" phenomenon. A word is on the tip of your tongue when you know it is stored in LTM but are momentarily blocked from retrieving it. Successful retrieval is often helped by using partial information, such as the length of the word or its initial letter, to limit the search of LTM (Brown & McNeill, 1966).

Read and Bruce (1982) studied the tip-of-the-tongue phenomenon by giving subjects pictures or verbal descriptions of entertainers. For example, the verbal description of Ray Bolger was "On Broadway he created the role of Charley in *Charley's Aunt,* but is perhaps best remembered as the scarecrow in the Judy Garland movie *The Wizard of Oz.*" Students were intensively tested in 11 sessions over a three-week period, during which time the experimenters obtained nearly 500 cases in which students thought they knew the answer but could not immediately retrieve the name. These names were tested again in the following sessions until they were remembered, sometimes with the help of additional information. When a name was recalled, subjects answered questions about how they had retrieved the answer.

Subjects were fairly accurate in judging whether they would be able to retrieve a name. The average delay in retrieval was 1.9 days for names that were judged to be on the tip of the tongue, 2.7 days for names that were judged to require some thought, and 7.2 days for names that were judged to have little chance of being recalled. The most frequently reported strategy for recalling names was to make use of partial information, as reported initially by Brown and McNeill (1966). Partial information includes information about the length of a name or letters or sounds within a name. Two other popular strategies were to generate plausible names and to use contextual information. The generation of plausible names was often guided by partial information to limit the search. Contextual information is information associated with the person, such as movie and television roles or ethnic origin. Only infrequently did subjects report that they spontaneously recalled the name without thinking about the target person. Successful retrievals, therefore, usually occurred as a result of a planned search of memory.

In the previous chapter, on STM, I made the distinction between recall and recognition. Recognition in LTM is usually studied by showing students many items and later asking them to select items that they had previously seen in the experiment. Current theories of recognition memory emphasize that there are two components of recognition, one based on judging the familiarity of the item and one based on recalling information about the item (Mandler, 1980; Humphreys & Bain, 1983).

Part of the problem in deciding whether we recognize someone or something is to recall the context in which a previous encounter might have occurred. Mandler (1980) gives an example of a person who sees someone on a bus who looks familiar but is unsure why the person looks familiar. It is only after a suitable context is recalled—the person works in the butcher shop—that recognition seems complete. Thus the recall of contextual information is valuable in both recall and recognition experiments.

The final section of this chapter is concerned with an important application of how both judged familiarity and the recall of contextual information are needed for eyewitness identification. But before considering this application, I want to show you how familiarity is modeled by cognitive psychologists. The model was borrowed from psychologists who were interested in a seemingly simple act of perception.

A Signal Detection Theory of Recognition

The theory we're about to consider was originally developed to describe performance in signal detection experiments. The signal detection task requires that an observer report whether a signal occurred—for instance, whether a tone occurred in a background of noise. The listener can make two kinds of errors. First, he can respond negatively when a signal did occur. This kind of error is called a *miss* because the subject failed to detect the signal. Second, the listener can respond positively when a signal did not occur. This kind of error is called a *false alarm.*

James Egan (1958) showed that the theory developed to describe performance on a signal detection task could also be used to describe performance on a recognition memory test. There are two kinds of items on the memory test—old items that occurred before in the experiment and new items that did not occur. Although the task requires distinguishing between old and new items rather than between signals and noise, the same kinds of errors can occur when people try to identify old items. A person can respond negatively to an old item by failing to remember that it occurred before. This error is called a *miss,* as when a person misses a signal. Or a person can respond positively to a new item that hasn't occurred before. This error is called a *false alarm,* as when a person incorrectly states that a signal occurred.

The signal detection theory assumes that items vary along a continuous dimension, which is labeled *memory strength* or *familiarity.* The effect of presenting an item during the experiment is to increase its familiarity in the experiment. Since old items were previously presented in the experiment, they will generally have higher familiarity values than new items. This situation is represented in Figure 5.5 by the placement of the two distributions (representing new items and old items) along the continuum. The height of the distribution on the left shows how many new items have that particular familiarity value. The average value for new items is represented by the vertical line labeled *Ave(N).* The height of the distribution on the right shows how many old items have that particular familiarity value. The average value for old items is represented by the vertical line labeled *Ave(O).*

Notice that the two distributions overlap and that some new items actually have higher familiarity values than old items. Why should this be? First, we must remember that the term *familiarity* is being used to define how familiar an item seems to be within the context of the experiment. You are very familiar with your name, but if it didn't occur in the experiment, it would have a low familiarity value. Since the familiarity values reflect how confident you are that an item occurred in the experiment, your name should have a very low familiarity value because you should be very confident that it was not one of the old items. Other new items, however, would be more difficult to judge. For example, if the word *boat* were presented and you were later tested on the word *ship,* you might respond positively because the two words

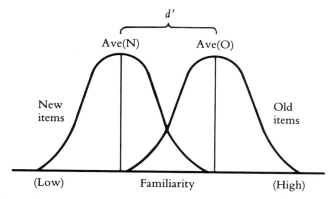

Figure 5.5   A signal detection representation of old and new items along a familiarity continuum. Ave(N) is the average familiarity value for new items, and Ave(O) is the average familiarity value for old items.

have similar meanings. The word *ship* would seem familiar even though it did not occur.

A measure called d' is used to represent how much the two distributions overlap or how well a person performs on a recognition test. It is a measure of the difference in the means of the two distributions—that is, Ave(O) − Ave(N)—relative to the variance of the new-item distribution. A low value of d' implies that there is a considerable overlap of the two distributions because a person makes many mistakes. The extreme case is $d' = 0$, which indicates that the average familiarity value is the same for old and new items. A d' of 0 would occur if a person couldn't remember any of the items in the experiment and simply guessed when given the memory test.

Since d' is a measure of how well a person performs on a recognition memory test, it reflects the probability of making an error on the test. It does not, however, tell us the kinds of errors that occur. In order to know the kinds of errors, we have to know how a person distinguishes new items from old items. Since old items generally have higher values on the continuum than new items, a person should respond that familiar items were previously presented and unfamiliar items were not previously presented. This sounds simple enough, but exactly where should the cutoff be placed separating familiar from unfamiliar items if familiarity varies along a continuum? The placement of the dividing line differs across people and tasks, so it is necessary to calculate the location of the boundary. The vertical line labeled β in Figure 5.6 shows two possible locations. Signal detection theory assumes that people respond that an item was not previously presented if its familiarity value is less than β and that it was previously presented if its familiarity value is greater than β.

The location of β determines how a person's errors are divided into misses and false alarms. Notice in Figure 5.6 that part of each distribution is on the wrong side of the dividing line. The familiarity values of most new items are less than β, so they will be correctly labeled as new items. But a few new items have familiarity

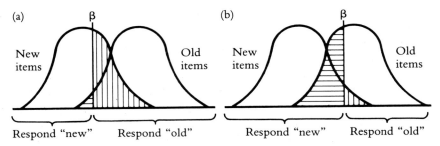

Figure 5.6   Influence of the response criterion (β) on the probability of a miss (horizontal lines) and a false alarm (vertical lines)

value greater than β, so they will be incorrectly identified as having previously occurred, resulting in a false alarm. The probability of a false alarm is represented by the proportion of new items that have familiarity values greater than β, the areas of vertical lines in Figure 5.6. The probability of a miss is represented by the proportion of old items that have familarity values less than β, the areas shaded with horizontal lines. Since the latter do not seem very familiar, they will be classified as new items.

Notice in Figure 5.6 that there is a trade-off between misses and false alarms as the criterion is moved either to the left or to the right. Moving the criterion to the left (Figure 5.6a) implies that a person responds positively more often. This causes a decline in the number of misses but an increase in the number of false alarms. Moving the criterion to the right (Figure 5.6b) implies that a person responds positively less often. This causes an increase in the number of misses but a decline in the number of false alarms. The exact placement of the criterion can be calculated by making use of this trade-off between the proportion of false alarms and misses.

The application of signal detection theory to recognition memory therefore provides two measures of performance. The first measure—d'—is a measure of accuracy. It indicates how well a person can distinguish between old items and new items. Accuracy is determined by such factors as individual differences in memory, length of the retention interval, and degree of similarity between old and new items. The second measure—β—indicates the response criterion selected by an individual. It is a value on the familiarity continuum that the individual uses for deciding whether an item was presented before. Items with familiarity values greater than the criterion are classified as old, and items with familiarity values less than the criterion are classified as new. The location of the criterion determines whether the errors are primarily misses or false alarms.

Eyewitness Identification

The discussion of recognition memory has been rather abstract so far. Let's see how it is used in a particular task. Recognition memory is studied in the laboratory by showing people a sequence of items and then asking them whether a test item was a member of the sequence. The subjects have to remember not only that they saw that item before but that they saw it during the experiment. In other words, they have to remember the context in which they saw the item. Recalling the correct context is often useful in everyday situations. For instance, you may recognize someone as a person you met before but may not be able to remember where the meeting took place. Remembering the appropriate context might help you recall additional information about that person.

Eyewitness identification is a situation in which recalling the context of information is important. Accurate identification depends not only on being able to recognize a face as someone familiar but on recalling that the person was seen performing a crime rather than seen in a newspaper, on television, or in police mug shots. The possibility that the witness might be able to recognize a face without being able to recall the correct context was addressed by the U.S. Supreme Court in *Simmons v. United States* 390 U.S. 377 (1968) (cited in Brown, Deffenbacher, & Sturgill, 1977). The court noted the potential biasing effect caused by showing a witness a single mug shot or showing mug shots that emphasized a particular suspect. They held that the biasing effects would be particularly misleading if the witness originally had only a brief glimpse of the suspect or saw him under poor conditions (Buckhout, 1974).

The possible biasing effects that can occur during eyewitness identification were investigated in two experiments by Brown, Deffenbacher, and Sturgill (1977). In one experiment students in a large introductory psychology class were asked to view ten "criminals" (graduate and upper-class undergraduate white males) for 25 seconds each. The experimenter told the class to observe them carefully because they would have to pick them out from mug shots later that evening and from a lineup the following week. One and one-half hours later, the students looked at 15 mug shots consisting of color slides showing a front and a side view. They were asked to indicate, for each mug shot, whether that person had appeared earlier in front of the class. Five of the 15 mug shots were of people who had actually appeared. The five criminals were correctly identified as criminals 72% of the time; however, the ten noncriminals were also identified as criminals 45% of the time. The value of d' calculated from these percentages is significantly above 0, but it is not very large. This finding implies that although the accuracy of identification was significantly above chance, it was not very good. Furthermore, the high false-alarm rate (45%) indicates that many people in the mug shots were falsely accused.

A major goal of this experiment was to determine whether presenting a mug shot would cause a bias toward identifying the person in the photograph as a criminal. Notice that the students saw the mug shots of only five of the ten criminals. Would they be more likely later to identify these five as criminals than the five criminals whose mug shots were not presented? One week later students saw a lineup and were asked to indicate whether each person in the lineup was one of the original criminals who had appeared in front of the class. The criminals whose mug shots had been shown were identified on 65% of the occasions, compared with 51% for criminals whose mug shots had not been shown. Showing a mug shot made it significantly more likely that a person would be identified as a criminal, perhaps because the "witnesses" could not recall whether they had previously seen the person or the photograph.

At this point we might say "So what? They were all guilty anyway." But what about innocent people? Would showing their mug shots make it more likely that they would be identified as criminals during the lineup? This was the issue that concerned the Supreme Court in the *Simmons v. United States* decision. In the Brown, Deffenbacher, and Sturgill experiment, nine of the persons included in the lineup had not initially appeared in front of the class, but pictures of four of the nine were included among the mug shots. If showing a mug shot of an innocent person biases the witnesses to label that person as a criminal, these four should be identified as criminals more often than the other five. The results support this hypothesis. The four persons whose pictures had been included in the mug-shot session were incorrectly identified as criminals on 20% of the occasions, compared with 8% for persons whose pictures had not appeared. The greater tendency to identify a person as a criminal after seeing a mug shot affected the "innocent" as well as the "guilty."

One objection to this experiment is that students were initially asked to remember what ten persons looked like rather than only one or two, a more typical situation in a real crime. Brown and his colleagues eliminated this objection in a second experiment, in which a different class of students was asked to identify only two persons. The two persons handed out the first midterm exam in the class; members of the class were not told that they would later be asked to identify the two persons. The design of the experiment was similar to the one described above except that the mug shots were shown two or three days after the exam and the lineup occurred four or five days after the students viewed the mug shots. The same pattern of results occurred as in the previous experiment: presenting a mug shot of a person made it more likely that the person would be identified in the lineup.

The false identification occurred because the person identified looked very familiar as a result of having his picture included among the mug shots. However, as stated earlier, successful recognition often depends on the recall of a specific context in addition to a judgment of familiarity. Although these experiments do not pretend to duplicate what an actual witness is confronted with during a crime, they do raise serious questions about our ability to identify the context in which a person is perceived. The findings suggest that great care should be taken in what material is shown to a witness who must make the final identification of a suspected criminal.

Summary

Learning can be represented as the transfer of information from STM to LTM. The decay rate for information in LTM is slow compared with the rapid decay rate from STM. Furthermore, LTM does not suffer from a capacity limitation; that is, it is not limited in the amount of information it can store. The distinction between STM and LTM, as well as the role of rehearsal in transferring information into LTM, was emphasized in a model proposed by Atkinson and Shiffrin. One of the findings that their model accounts for is the serial position effect: the better recall of words at the beginning of a list can be explained by their storage in LTM, and the better recall of words at the end of the list can be explained by their storage in STM. In other situations it may be difficult to decide whether successfully retrieved new information came from STM or LTM. The ability to make this distinction is useful because the student should concentrate on items that are not yet stored in LTM. A learning model used this distinction to determine which items should be presented during an instructional session in order for students to recall them during a test given one week later.

Incidental learning differs from intentional learning because it occurs without intention to learn. The concept of automatic processing, introduced in Chapter 3, can be applied to incidental learning. Hasher and Zacks proposed that automatic processing occurs during incidental learning, does not benefit from instruction or practice, does not interfere with other processes, is not influenced by emotional states, and shows little change with development. Although Hasher and Zacks initially claimed that temporal, spatial, and frequency information are encoded automatically, their recent work supports their claim for frequency, but not temporal, information.

In order to retrieve information from LTM, we must initially decide whether the information is stored in LTM. The "tip of the tongue" phenomenon occurs when a person knows information is stored in LTM but cannot immediately retrieve it. Strategies for searching LTM include using partial information such as word length or sounds, generating plausible names, and using contextual information associated with a name.

A recognition task differs from a recall task in that it tests judgment of whether an item was previously presented, usually within a specified context. A model of recognition memory derived from signal detection theory assumes that items vary in familiarity along a continuum. Items that were presented before (old items) generally have higher familiarity values than items that were not presented before (new items), but the two distributions overlap. A person must select a criterion value along this continuum in order to decide whether an item is old or new. The location of the criterion determines whether the errors are primarily misses or false alarms. False alarms in eyewitness identification are increased by showing mug shots to a witness. The witness may falsely identify a person because of a failure to recall the context in which that person was seen.

Recommended Reading

The general references on memory cited at the end of Chapter 4 discuss LTM as well as STM. Bahrick (1979) studied very long-term memory by asking alumni to recall various kinds of information (such as street and building names) about their college town. Herrmann and Neisser (1978) designed an *Inventory of Everyday Memory Experiences* that contained 48 questions about everyday forgetting and 24 questions about memory for events from early childhood. Readers interested in eyewitness testimony should consult Goldstein (1977) and Yarmey (1979)—both authors emphasize the limitations of evidence based on eyewitness testimony. Articles by Burke and Light (1981), Craik and Rabinowitz (1983), and Guttentag (1985) discuss how memory is affected by aging.

6

Levels of Processing

It is abundantly clear that what determines the level of recall or recognition of a word event is not intention to learn, the amount of effort involved, the difficulty of the orienting task, the amount of time spent making judgments about the items, or even the amount of rehearsal the items receive; rather it is the qualitative nature of the task, the kind of operations carried out on the items, that determines retention.

F. I. M. CRAIK AND ENDEL TULVING (1975)

The preceding two chapters developed a theory of memory as consisting of a short-term store and a long-term store. This theory provides a beginning, but it leaves us with many questions. Why are there many different decay rates in LTM? Does verbal rehearsal always cause learning? What other control processes can we use to enter information into LTM? How is memory organized? And what about visual knowledge?

In the next four chapters I will try to provide some answers to these questions about the representation and organization of knowledge. Our immediate objective is to learn the ways memory codes differ and the implications of these differences for learning and retrieval. When people try to learn, they most likely form several kinds of memory codes, and psychologists have little control over what people do. So instead of asking people to learn, we often ask them to make judgments about words without telling them they will have to recall the words after the judgment task. The purpose of the judgment task (often called an *orienting task*) is to try to control the kind of memory code formed by requesting that a person make decisions about a particular aspect of the word, such as its pronunciation or its meaning. We can then examine how well that person can recall the word as a function of the aspect emphasized.

The first section of this chapter examines a theory of memory called *levels of processing*, proposed by Craik and Lockhart (1972), which proposes that success in recalling a word depends on the kinds of operations carried out while encoding the word. That is, retention is determined by the characteristics that are emphasized during initial perception or rehearsal. Evidence supporting the theory is reviewed in the second section. The third section seeks to explain why semantic codes are better than structural codes. The argument that memory for an event is improved by making the code more elaborate and distinctive is used to explain how coding influences retention. The final section considers the principle of encoding specificity, which states that the effectiveness of a retrieval cue depends on how well its characteristics correspond to the characteristics of the stored event.

The Levels-of-Processing Theory

Emphasis on Coding Strategies

The paper by Craik and Lockhart (1972) had three objectives: to examine the reasons for proposing multistore models, to question the adequacy of such models, and to propose an alternative framework in terms of levels of processing. We have already considered some of the major characteristics of the three memory stores (sensory store, STM, and LTM) in the previous chapter. Craik and Lockhart summarized the commonly accepted differences among these stores as shown in Table 6.1.

The sensory store is preattentive in the sense that it occurs before perceptual recognition. Attention influences what observers recognize, as when they attend to a particular row of letters after hearing a tone. The sensory store provides a literal copy of the stimulus input but rapidly decays away. It isn't possible to use a control process or strategy to maintain the store, so information must be read out using pattern recognition in order to preserve it in a more permanent store.

In order to enter STM, the information must be attended to and described. It can be maintained in STM by continued attendance to it or by use of verbal rehearsal.

Table 6.1   Commonly accepted differences among the three stages of verbal memory

Feature	Sensory store	Short-term memory	Long-term memory
Entry of information	Preattentive	Requires attention	Rehearsal
Maintenance of information	Not possible	Continued attention Rehearsal	Repetition Organization
Format of information	Literal copy of input	Phonemic Probably visual Probably semantic	Largely semantic Some auditory and visual
Capacity	Large	Small	No known limit
Information loss	Decay	Displacement Possibly decay	Possibly no loss Loss of accessibility or discriminability by interference
Trace duration	¼ –2 seconds	Up to 30 seconds	Minutes to years
Retrieval	Readout	Probably automatic Items in consciousness Temporal/phonemic cues	Retrieval cues Possibly search process

Since verbal rehearsal is often used, the format is primarily phonemic, but it can also be visual or semantic. STM is limited by its small capacity and fast decay rate, but retrieval is easy because so few items have to be searched.

Information is entered into LTM mainly through verbal rehearsal. Long-term memory is largely semantic; that is, it is organized according to meaning. It has no known limits in capacity, and its contents, if lost at all, are lost through interference. The ability to retrieve information from LTM can last from minutes to years. Cues are very useful in retrieving information from LTM, as we will see later in this chapter, but retrieval may require a lengthy search and a considerable amount of time.

Although most psychologists had accepted the characterization of memory represented in Table 6.1, Craik and Lockhart believed that the evidence for a distinction between STM and LTM was not as clear as it should be. They argued, first, that the capacity of STM was really more variable than Miller's estimate of from five to nine chunks. For example, people can reproduce strings of up to 20 words if the words form a sentence. One might reasonably argue that the words in a sentence form chunks and that it should be easy to recall 20 words from STM if there are about three words in each chunk. But this argument requires objective evidence that such chunks exist. Second, although the format is mainly phonemic in STM and semantic in LTM, there is evidence for visual and semantic codes in STM (see Shulman, 1971) and visual and phonemic codes in LTM. Third, as we have already seen, decay rates vary considerably depending on the material being learned. Ideally, we would like to see a single, fast rate of decay for STM and a single, slow rate of decay for LTM.

The distinction among the three memory stores summarized in Table 6.1 is therefore an idealized view of how the stores differ. Although I believe there is much experimental support for this view, we must remember that most theories, including the theory that proposes three separate memory stores, are oversimplified. The part of the theory that seems the weakest to me is the variety of decay rates. Where do all these decay rates come from? The strength of the levels-of-processing theory is its attempt to answer this question.

The levels-of-processing theory proposes that there are different ways to code material and that memory codes are qualitatively different. Preliminary processing is concerned with the analysis of physical features such as lines, angles, brightness, pitch, and loudness. Later stages of analysis are concerned with pattern recognition and identification of meaning. After the stimulus is recognized, it may be further elaborated—a word, sight, or smell may trigger associations, images, or stories on the basis of the individual's past experience with that particular stimulus. The levels-of-processing theory claims that analysis proceeds through a series of sensory states to levels associated with pattern recognition to semantic-associative stages.

Each level of analysis results in a different memory trace—but a memory trace that varies in its decay rate. The memory code and its persistence are therefore both by-products of perceptual processing. When only the physical features of a stimulus have been analyzed, the memory trace is fragile and quickly decays. When the stimulus has been identified and named, the memory trace is stronger and can be represented by an intermediate decay rate. Memory is best when a person elaborates the meaning of the stimulus.

The levels-of-processing theory is a theory of how we analyze the stimulus and of the memory codes that result from different levels of analysis. Unlike the Atkinson-Shiffrin (1968) theory, it is not concerned with the structural components or stages of memory; the two theories, therefore, can coexist. Craik (1979b) has recently stated that the point of most levels-of-processing studies has been to gain a fuller understanding of memory codes operating in LTM, not to deny the distinction between STM and LTM. When viewed from this perspective, the work on levels of processing extends rather than replaces a stage analysis by showing how control processes can influence the retention of material.

Implications for Verbal Rehearsal

We saw in the previous chapter that the Atkinson-Shiffrin model emphasized verbal rehearsal as a means of transferring information from STM to LTM. Since most of us have used this method to learn material, the role of rehearsal in learning seems intuitively attractive. But rehearsal does not automatically result in learning, according to Craik and Lockhart. The effectiveness of rehearsal, like other methods of study, depends on the level at which material is processed. The reason rehearsal often results in learning is that people usually attend to the meaning of the material during rehearsal.

Nor is rehearsal always used for learning. Sometimes it is used to maintain information in STM, as when we dial a telephone number. Would rehearsal result in learning if people used it simply to maintain items in STM? Does rehearsal automatically result in learning, or are there different kinds of rehearsal, only some of which promote learning? To answer these questions, Craik and Watkins (1973) asked people to perform a fairly simple task. Students were told to listen to a series of word lists and, at the end of each list, to report the last word beginning with a particular letter. The experimenter told them the critical letter before each list and assumed that they would maintain a word starting with that letter in STM until they heard another word beginning with that letter or the list ended. The task was quite easy, and students almost always gave the correct answer at the end of the list.

The purpose of the experiment was to vary the length of time a word would have to be maintained in STM. For example, if *g* were the critical letter and the list contained, in order, the words *daughter, oil, rifle, garden, grain, table, football, anchor,* and *giraffe,* the word *garden* would be immediately replaced by *grain,* which would eventually be replaced by *giraffe.* Since there are no intervening words between *garden* and *grain* but three intervening words between *grain* and *giraffe, grain* would have to be maintained in STM for a longer time than *garden.* The word *grain* should therefore be rehearsed more often than *garden.* Craik and Watkins controlled the amount of time a word would have to be maintained in STM by varying the number of intervening (noncritical) words from 0 to 12. If maintenance rehearsal results in learning, the probability of recalling a word at the end of the experiment should be a function of the length of time it was maintained in STM.

After hearing 27 lists of words, the students were asked to recall as many words as they could from all the lists. Craik and Watkins found that the probability of recalling a word was independent of the length of time it was maintained in STM. To consider the two extreme cases, students recalled 12% of the words that were immediately replaced in STM by the next word on the list and 15% of the words that were maintained over 12 intervening words.

The small difference between 12% and 15% shows that rehearsal does not automatically cause learning. According to the levels-of-processing view of memory, the students did not try to form a lasting memory code, because they thought they would have to remember the word for only a very short time. In particular, they did not emphasize the meaning of the words. A good analogue might be reading the words in a book without thinking about what you are reading. You would be rehearsing the words in the sense that you would be covertly pronouncing them, but your thoughts might be on yesterday's football game or tonight's party. Suddenly you realize that you can't remember what you just read because you weren't thinking about what it meant. Let's look now at the evidence that the way material is processed determines what kind of memory code is formed, which, in turn, determines how well the material is remembered.

Supporting Evidence

The Hyde-Jenkins Experiment

The influence of levels of processing on retention was nicely demonstrated in a study by Hyde and Jenkins (1969) at the University of Minnesota. Their results were published several years before Craik and Lockhart's theory and most likely influenced its development. Like most of the studies used later to test the levels-of-processing theory, Hyde and Jenkins's study used an incidental learning paradigm. In an incidental learning task people are given some material but are not told that they have to learn it. The experimenter then later gives them a recall or recognition test on the items presented during the experiment. In an intentional learning task, by contrast, the subjects are explicitly told to learn the material.

The first experiment in Hyde and Jenkins's study compared seven groups of subjects, but we will consider only four to simplify the discussion. One of the four groups was given an intentional learning task in which the subjects were asked to try to remember 24 words. The words consisted of 12 pairs of primary associates—words that are highly associated. For example, the word *red* is highly associated with the word *green*, and *table* is highly associated with *chair*. The 24 words were presented in a random order, with the restriction that primary associates could not occur together in the list. After the subjects in the "intentional" group had listened to a tape recording of the 24 words, they tried to recall as many as they could, in any order.

The other three groups were incidental learning groups who were not informed that they should try to remember the words. They heard the same recording of 24 words but were asked to make a judgment about each item on the list. One group simply rated the words as pleasant or unpleasant, another group judged whether each word contained the letter *e,* and a third group estimated the number of letters in each word. The purpose of using three judgment groups was to try to create different levels of processing. The first group would have to consider the meaning of the words. The latter two groups would have to consider the spelling of the words; the meaning of the words would be irrelevant to them. Since, according to the levels-of-processing theory, semantic processing should result in better recall than nonsemantic processing, the undergraduates who rated the pleasantness of the words should show better recall than those who considered the spelling of the words.

The results supported the prediction. The average number of words recalled was 16.3 for those students who rated pleasantness, 9.9 for those who estimated the number of letters, and 9.4 for those who judged the presence of the letter *e.* The most striking aspect of the results is that students in the pleasant/unpleasant group recalled virtually as many words as those who were told to try to learn the words (16.3 versus 16.1). In other words, incidental learning was as effective as intentional learning when the students considered the meaning of the words.

We have been assuming, along with Hyde and Jenkins, that differences in recall among the three incidental groups were caused by the possibility that the students in the pleasant/unpleasant group were more likely to attend to the meaning of the words than students in the other two groups. Do we have any direct evidence for this assumption? The fact that the list consisted of pairs of words that are semantically related provides a clue. Recognizing that words are related in meaning can make it easier to recall them. For example, the recall of *green* may remind a person that *red* was also on the list. One indication that people were attending to the meaning of words would be if they recalled the primary associates together—*red* followed by *green* or vice versa.

Hyde and Jenkins defined the percentage of clustering as the number of associated pairs recalled together, divided by the total number of words recalled. The amount of clustering was 26% for the group that made judgments about the letter *e,* 31% for the group that estimated the number of letters, 64% for the group that was told to study words, and 68% for the group that judged the pleasantness of the words. These results support the assumption that groups differed in how much they used meaning to aid recall. Those groups that were the most sensitive to the meaning recalled the most words.

Structural, Phonemic, and Semantic Processing

Tests of the levels-of-processing theory have generally focused on three levels in which the depth of processing increases from structural to phonemic to semantic coding. Table 6.2 shows examples of questions that have been asked in order to emphasize different levels of coding. The structural question asks whether the word is in capital letters. Coding at the phonemic level is encouraged by asking whether a word rhymes with another word—the question emphasizes pronunciation. Questions about whether a word is a member of a certain category or whether it fits into a

Table 6.2   Typical questions used in levels-of-processing studies

Level of processing	Question	Yes	No
Structural	Is the word in capital letters?	TABLE	table
Phonemic	Does the word rhyme with WEIGHT?	crate	MARKET
Category	Is the word a type of fish?	SHARK	heaven
Sentence	Would the word fit the sentence		
	"He met a _____ in the street"?	FRIEND	cloud

sentence encourage coding at the semantic level—a person must evaluate the meaning in order to answer correctly.

In a series of experiments conducted by Craik and Tulving (1975) one of the questions preceded each brief exposure of a word. Participants were informed that the experiment concerned perception and speed of reaction. After a series of question-and-answer trials, the subject was unexpectedly given a retention test for the exposed words. Craik and Tulving expected that memory would vary systematically with depth of processing.

Figure 6.1 shows the results from one of Craik and Tulving's experiments that used a recognition test. When students were asked which words had been presented during the initial judgment task, they recognized the most words when they had initially judged whether the word fit into a sentence and the fewest words when they had initially judged whether the letters were upper- or lower-case. Recognition accuracy was at an intermediate level when the students had been asked whether one word rhymed with another. The findings supported the prediction that retention would increase as processing proceeded from the structural to the phonemic to the semantic level. The same pattern of results occurred when Craik and Tulving used a recall, rather than a recognition, test. Questions about a word's meaning resulted in better memory than those about a word's sound or the physical characteristics of its letters.

The left half of Figure 6.1 shows the average response time required to answer the three kinds of questions. The "case" questions could be answered most quickly, followed by the "rhyme" questions, followed by the "sentence" questions. Although the recognition results on the right can be predicted from the response times on the left, it is not always true that slower responses lead to better memory. It is possible to design a structural decision task that results in slow responses and poor retention.

Imagine that an experimenter shows you a card with a five-letter word such as *stoop* or *black*. Your task is to respond positively if the word consists of two consonants followed by two vowels followed by a consonant and negatively for any other sequence of consonants and vowels. As you might guess, your response times would be relatively slow. In fact, it takes about twice as long to make this kind of structural decision as to make a semantic decision about whether a word fits into a sentence. If good retention is caused by long response times, the structural processing should now result in better retention than the semantic processing. However, recognition is still much better after semantic processing, proving that the level of processing, not the time spent processing, is the best determinant of retention.

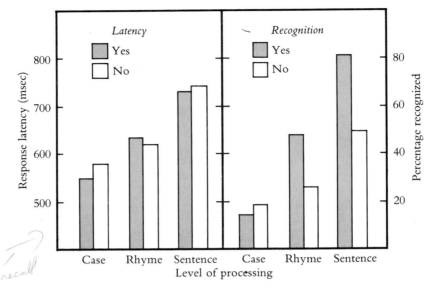

Figure 6.1   Initial decision latency and recognition performance for words as a function of the initial task

Criticisms and Modifications

Criticisms

The levels-of-processing theory has had a major impact on memory research: many investigators designed studies to explicitly test its implications; others found it a convenient framework in which to discuss their results. As much of this research was quite supportive of the theory, it wasn't until about five years after the Craik and Lockhart paper that psychologists began to seriously question the usefulness of the theory (Baddeley, 1978; Eysenck, 1978; Nelson, 1977). One of the main criticisms was that it was too easy to account for differential rates of forgetting by appealing to the theory. An investigator might claim that differences in rates of forgetting were caused by differences in level of processing, without measuring the level of processing.

In order to avoid this criticism, it is necessary to be able to measure depth of processing independently of retention. The argument that depth increases from structural to phonemic to semantic processing appealed to most psychologists because it is consistent with the ordering of the information-processing stages shown in Figure 1.1 (Chapter 1). Analyzing the physical structure of a pattern leads to retrieving its name, which, in turn, leads to considering its meaning by retrieving stored associations from LTM. One problem with this assumption is that although this sequence provides a reasonable account of how information is analyzed, it is not a *necessary* sequence (Baddeley, 1978; Craik, 1979b). Although Craik and Lockhart originally hoped that encoding time would provide an independent measure of depth of processing, we have seen that this measure has its limitations (Craik & Tulving, 1975).

Another difficulty with the concept of depth of processing is that even if we had an objective ordering of the "depth" of different memory codes, it still would not tell us why some codes are more effective than others. Why are semantic codes better than phonemic codes and phonemic codes better than structural codes? Psychologists have suggested two possible answers. One is that memory codes differ in how elaborate they are, and more elaborate codes result in better memory. The other is that memory codes differ in distinctiveness, and more distinctive codes result in better memory.

Elaboration

One explanation of how memory codes differ proposes that they differ in the number and types of elaborations stored in memory (Anderson & Reder, 1979). This view assumes that people store much more than simply the items presented to them by forming additional associations to help them remember the items. Anderson and Reder have proposed that although it is very easy to elaborate material at the semantic level, it is difficult to construct elaborations at the structural or phonemic level. Most of the associations we have are concerned with meaning rather than with the physical structure of letters, spelling, or pronunciation. Anderson and Reder suggest that the reason for this difference is that people usually try to remember the meaning of what they read rather than such details as what the letters looked like. As a consequence, people have learned to elaborate on the semantic content because it is generally more useful than elaborating on nonsemantic content.

One virtue of the elaboration hypothesis is that it provides a possible explanation of how differences can occur within a particular level of processing (Craik, 1979b). Although the original levels-of-processing proposal predicted that semantic processing should be superior to nonsemantic processing, it could not account for differences in retention for two different semantic tasks. The elaboration hypothesis predicts that such differences should occur if the two tasks differ in the extent of semantic elaboration.

One method for increasing semantic elaboration is to provide a richer, more elaborate context. This approach is illustrated by one of the experiments in the Craik and Tulving (1975) study. The experiment tested for the recall of words after a semantic judgment task in which people determined whether a word would fit into a sentence frame. There were three levels of sentence complexity—simple, medium, and complex. For example:

Simple. She cooked the _____ .
Medium. The ripe _____ tasted delicious.
Complex. The small lady angrily picked up the red _____ .

After completing 60 judgments, subjects were asked to recall as many words as they could from the initial phase of the experiment. They were then shown the original sentence frames and asked to recall the word associated with each sentence. The first part of the recall task is called *noncued recall* and the second part is called *cued recall* because students could use the sentence frames as retrieval cues. Figure 6.2 shows the proportion of words recalled as a function of sentence complexity. Sentence complexity had a significant effect on recalling words that did fit the sentence. This was true for both cued recall (CR–yes) and noncued recall (NCR–yes), although the effect was greater for cued recall. The effect of sentence complexity supported Craik and Tulving's hypothesis that more complex sentence frames would produce a more elaborate memory code and improve recall.

The more elaborate code was ineffective, however, if the word did not fit the sentence. This finding suggests that the elaboration must be consistent with the meaning of the word in order to be effective. Even when elaboration is generally consistent with the meaning of a word, it can vary in effectiveness depending on how precisely it relates to the word's meaning. Imagine that you read the sentence *The fat man read the sign*. Some time later someone shows you the same sentence with the word *fat* replaced by a blank and asks you to recall the missing word. If elaboration is effective, you might do better if you read an elaborated sentence such as

1. The fat man read the sign that was 2 feet high.
   or
2. The fat man read the sign warning about thin ice.

Although both sentences provide additional information, there is an important distinction between the two elaborations. The first is an *imprecise elaboration* because there is no apparent relation between the adjective *fat* and the height of the sign. The second is a *precise elaboration* because the degree of danger of thin ice depends on a person's weight.

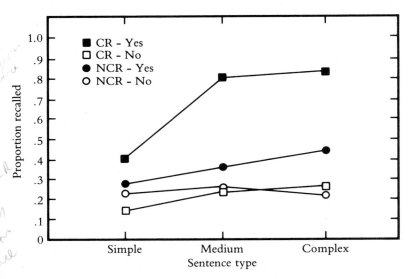

Figure 6.2   Proportion of words recalled as a function of sentence complexity. CR = cued recall; NCR = noncued recall.

Stein and Bransford (1979) tested the effectiveness of precise and imprecise elaboration by comparing four groups of students in an incidental learning task. Students in the control group read ten short sentences and were told that the purpose of the experiment was to measure sentence comprehensibility. The second and third groups of students were told the same thing. They read the same ten sentences elaborated by an additional phrase that was either precisely or imprecisely related to a target word in the sentence. A fourth group of students were told to generate their own elaborations so the experimenters could measure the probability that certain phrases would be generated. At the end of the experiment everyone was shown the unelaborated sentences and asked to recall a missing target word.

Students in the control group recalled an average of 4.2 words, compared with 2.2 words for the imprecise elaboration group, 7.4 words for the precise elaboration group, and 5.8 words for the self-generation group. The results show that elaboration is not always effective in recall, since imprecise elaboration actually caused a decline in performance relative to the control group. In order to be effective, the elaboration should clarify the significance or relevance of a concept (such as fat man) relative to the context (thin ice) in which it occurs.

The fact that recall following self-generation was intermediate between that for precise and imprecise elaboration suggests that the students' elaborations contained a mixture of the two types. Two judges therefore divided the subject-generated elaborations into two groups (precise and imprecise), depending on whether the information clarified the relevance of the target words in the sentence. Students were able to recall 91% of the target words when they generated precise elaborations and 49% when they generated imprecise elaborations. A second experiment revealed that instructions were effective in encouraging subjects to generate precise elaborations. Subjects in the imprecise elaboration group were asked to elaborate with the question "What else might happen in this context?" Subjects in the precise elaboration group were prompted to elaborate with the question "Why might this man be engaged in this particular type of activity?" Students in the latter group recalled significantly more target words, indicating that elaboration is particularly effective when it is directed toward understanding the potential relevance of the information presented.

Distinctiveness

Memory codes can differ in distinctiveness as well as in the extent of elaboration. The term *distinctive* refers to how easy it is to distinguish one item from another. In order to remember something, we would like to make it really stand out from other items that could interfere with our memory. Elaboration is one possible strategy to make an item more distinctive, but the elaboration should emphasize characteristics that differentiate that item from other items (Eysenck, 1979).

You can probably think of events that are easy to recall because they were particularly distinctive. I once played a game of "cootie" with my two sons, who were then 3 and 4 years old. One threw the die and it landed in the toilet, an event that both thought was very funny. I was surprised when, a week later, they could both recall the number that they were trying to get at that time and the number they actually got. That particular event was different enough from all the other rolls of the die that the numbers before and after it did not interfere with their memory.

Release from proactive interference, discussed in Chapter 4, illustrates another means of improving recall in a memory task—shifting to a new semantic category. People recalled more items when the material changed from words to numbers or from numbers to words than when the material stayed the same. Recall also improved when the items changed from sports events to political events or from political events to sports events. All the changes made the material more distinct from preceding items.

Recall of nonsemantic material is also facilitated when the material is made more distinct. The nonsemantic tasks studied by Hyde and Jenkins (1969) required that people make judgments about the spelling of a word, such as estimating its length or indicating whether it contains the letter *e*. Another characteristic of a word's spelling is called *orthographic distinctiveness*. A word is orthographically distinctive when it has an unusual shape—that is, sequencing of short and tall letters. Orthographically distinctive words include *lymph*, *khaki*, and *afghan*. Examples of orthographically common words are *leaky*, *kennel*, and *airway*. The first three words have unusual shapes, and the last three have more typical shapes.

When people are asked to recall a list of words, half of which are orthographically distinctive and half of which are orthographically common, they recall significantly more of the distinctive words (Hunt & Elliott, 1980). It is clear that the shape of the words, rather than some other factor, causes the results. When the same list is presented auditorily, rather than visually, there is no difference in recall. There is also no difference in recall when the words are typed in capital letters—people do not recall LYMPH, KHAKI, and AFGHAN any better than LEAKY, KENNEL, and AIRWAY. Apparently the different heights of lower-case letters contribute to the effect, since all letters are the same height when they are capitalized.

Release from proactive interference and the effect of orthographic distinctiveness show that distinctiveness can account for different amounts of recall at a single level of processing. Can distinctiveness account for different levels of recall between levels of processing? In order to demonstrate that distinctiveness can account for the levels-of-processing effect, it would be necessary to show that semantic codes are more distinct than phonemic codes and phonemic codes are more distinct than physical codes. Some research has already been directed toward the first comparison.

Several psychologists (Eysenck, 1979; Moscovitch & Craik, 1976) have argued that semantic codes result in better retention than phonemic codes because semantic codes are much more distinctive than phonemic codes. They base their argument on the fact that there is a relatively small number of phonemes, so that phonemic codes necessarily overlap with each other, whereas the domain of possible meanings is essentially limitless.

The experimental study of elaboration and distinctiveness has modified the original conception of levels of processing (Craik, 1979b). Some of the original ideas have survived, however. The central idea that there are qualitative differences in memory codes, that different orienting tasks can determine which codes are emphasized, and that memory codes differ in their decay rate remains a useful conception of memory. The major shift in emphasis has been the attempt to provide a theoretical basis for these findings by determining how structural, phonemic, and semantic codes can differ in distinctiveness and elaboration.

Encoding Specificity and Retrieval

The Encoding Specificity Principle

The change in emphasis from "levels" to "elaboration" and "distinctiveness" was accompanied by another refinement in the theory. The original theory (Craik & Lockhart, 1972) had much to say about how words were coded but little about how they were retrieved. The usefulness of providing an appropriate context for facilitating retrieval is illustrated by the difference between positive and negative responses in Figure 6.1. Words that resulted in positive responses, because they either formed a rhyme or fit the context of a sentence, were recalled more often than words that resulted in negative responses. We have also seen that the use of more complex, elaborate sentence frames facilitated recall for positive responses but not for negative responses (Figure 6.2). This effect was particularly evident when the context was provided as a retrieval cue. Craik and Tulving (1975) interpreted this finding as support for their view that a more elaborate context is beneficial only when the test word is compatible with the context and forms an integrated unit. A complex sentence like *The small lady angrily picked up the red* _____ makes it easier to retrieve a positive response (*tomato*) but does not make it easier to retrieve a negative response (*walking*).

These results show that, under certain conditions, some retrieval cues are more effective than others. A general answer to the question of what makes a retrieval cue effective is provided by the *encoding specificity principle*, which has been stated as follows: "Specific encoding operations performed on what is perceived determine what is stored, and what is stored determines what retrieval cues are effective in providing access to what is stored" (Tulving & Thomson, 1973, p. 369).

Let's dissect this definition into two parts. The first part states that memory traces differ not only in their durability but also in the kind of information they contain. The second part states that the information memory traces contain determines what kind of retrieval information should facilitate their recovery. The first part is essentially equivalent to the levels-of-processing framework; the second part forces us to take a closer look at retrieval. The second part implies that it is possible to hold constant the encoding conditions of an item and still observe large differences in its recall, depending on the retrieval conditions. The encoding and retrieval conditions can interact in the sense that a cue effective in one situation may or may not be effective in another.

Interaction between Encoding and Retrieval Operations

A study by Thomson and Tulving (1970) provided some initial support for the encoding specificity principle. It seems intuitively obvious that the effectiveness of a retrieval cue should depend on how closely the cue is associated with a test item. The following are good retrieval cues: *white* for BLACK, *meat* for STEAK, *dumb* for STUPID, *woman* for MAN, *ice* for COLD, and *dark* for LIGHT. People who are asked to remember BLACK, STEAK, STUPID, MAN, COLD, and LIGHT can recall more of these words if they are given the retrieval cues during the recall test. It is also intuitively obvious that weakly associated words do not make good retrieval cues—for example, *train* for BLACK, *knife* for STEAK, *lamb* for STUPID, *hand* for MAN, *blow* for COLD, and *head* for LIGHT. When people were given the weakly associated cues during the recall test, they recalled fewer words than subjects who were given no retrieval cues.

Tulving and Thomson demonstrated, however, that even ineffective retrieval cues can become effective if they are presented with the test words during the study session. When a weak associate was paired with a test word, it became a more effective retrieval cue than a strong associate. If people studied *train* and BLACK together, then the presentation of *train* during the recall test would more likely lead to the recall of BLACK than would the presentation of *white*. The effectiveness of a retrieval cue therefore depends on what occurs during the initial encoding of a word, as the encoding specificity hypothesis predicts.

A somewhat similar finding was reported by Light and Carter-Sobell (1970), using a recognition test. Subjects in their experiment were shown sentences that contained an adjective and a noun printed in capital letters. For example, subjects might see the sentence *The CHIP DIP tasted delicious.* They were informed that there would be a memory test on the adjective-noun phrases after they had read all the sentences. The recognition test required that they decide whether a noun had appeared in the previous sentences. Some nouns on the recognition test were preceded by the same adjective (CHIP DIP), some were preceded by a different adjective (SKINNY DIP), and some were preceded by no adjective (DIP). Presenting the same adjective resulted in better recognition of the noun than presenting no adjective, but presenting a different adjective resulted in worse recognition.

Perhaps one reason a different adjective produces a decline in performance is that the different adjective was consistent with an alternative meaning of the noun—*skinny dip* as opposed to *chip dip*. The experimenters argued that the adjective determines which semantic features of a noun are stored in memory. If their hypothesis is correct, then a different adjective that is consistent with the encoded meaning should be a more effective retrieval cue than a different adjective that is inconsistent with the encoded meaning. *Raspberry jam* should be a more effective retrieval cue than *traffic jam* if the original phrase was *strawberry jam*. The results supported the hypothesis, although the most accurate performance was still the condition in which the same adjective occurred during the study and test sessions.

The studies by Thomson and Tulving (1970) and Light and Carter-Sobell (1970) both investigated encoding specificity within the semantic domain. The first study showed that an ineffective retrieval cue—a weak semantic associate—can become an effective retrieval cue if it is associated with a test item during the study session. The second study showed that an adjective that preserved the semantic encoding of a word is more effective than an adjective that changes the semantic encoding.

Let us now consider how the encoding specificity principle applies when there are two different processing levels—semantic and phonemic. Imagine that you are in an experiment and have to answer yes or no to the question *associated with sleet?* You then see the word *hail* and answer yes. After making a series of judgments about rhymes and associations, you are given one of the following retrieval cues:

1. Associated with *sleet*
2. Associated with *snow*
3. Rhymes with *bail*

Which of the three retrieval cues do you think would be most helpful for retrieving the word *hail?*

We would probably agree that the first cue would be most effective because it is identical to the question asked during the encoding trials. But what about cues 2 and 3? The second cue is similar to the original context in that, like the initial question, it emphasizes semantic associations. The third cue, by contrast, emphasizes the phonemic code and is therefore different from the original context. The encoding specificity principle predicts that the original context is the best retrieval cue, a similar context is the next best cue, and a different context is the least effective cue. The results shown in Table 6.3 support this prediction (Fisher & Craik, 1977).

Now consider what might have happened if the word *hail* had been preceded by the question *Rhymes with pail?* The same principle applies. Reproducing the exact context is the best cue, and providing a different context—a semantic association in this case—is the worst cue (see Table 6.3). The interaction between encoding and retrieval is illustrated by the fact that the effectiveness of a retrieval cue depends on how a word was coded. When its semantic characteristics were emphasized, a semantic cue was more effective than a phonemic cue. When its phonemic characteristics were emphasized, a phonemic cue was more effective than a semantic cue. In other words, the specific encoding of an item determines which retrieval cues are most effective for gaining access to what is stored—the encoding specificity principle.

Table 6.3   Proportions of words recalled as a function of similarity between encoding context and retrieval cue

	Rhyme	*Associate*
Encoding context		
Example: *hail*	Rhymes with *pail*	Associated with *sleet*
Retrieval context		
Identical	Rhymes with *pail* .24	Associated with *sleet* .54
Similar	Rhymes with *bail* .18	Associated with *snow* .36
Different	Associated with *sleet* .16	Rhymes with *bail* .22

A recent study (Hertel, Anooshian, & Ashbrook, 1986) found that people were unable to accurately predict the relative effectiveness of retrieval cues. Subjects rated the pleasantness of 40 words in a semantic-orienting task, predicted the number of words they could recall, and then tried to recall the words. One group received semantic retrieval cues, another group retrieved phonemic retrieval cues, and a control group received no retrieval cues. We would expect from Fisher and Craik's findings that the semantic retrieval cues would be more effective than phonemic cues—an expectation that was confirmed. Only those subjects who received semantic cues recalled significantly more words than the control group.

But the superiority of the semantic cues was not anticipated by subjects in the experiment, who predicted that the semantic and phonemic cues would be equally effective. The faulty predictions seemed to be based on overgeneralization from past experiences in which phonemic cues had been effective. For example, when our search has already been limited to a particular category, such as the names of songs, phonemic information is likely to be helpful. What subjects failed to realize was that the effectiveness of a retrieval cue depends on the context in which the word was coded. The context, in this case, emphasized the semantic characteristics of the words.

Improving Eyewitness Recall

The principle that reproducing the context improves recall has some practical implications. Let us again consider the memory of the eyewitness. Hypnosis has been extensively used to improve witnesses' ability to retrieve information about a crime. This use of hypnosis is based on a videotape model of memory in which the witness tries to "replay" a videotape of the event. An important component of this technique is that the hypnotist attempts to reinstate the context by telling the witness to imagine, for example, that he is once again at the scene of the crime.

Although there have been many reports of cases in which hypnosis helped witnesses recall additional details about a crime, there are problems associated with its use (Smith, 1983). A major concern is that encouragement by the hypnotist may induce witnesses to report inaccurately. For example, in one study, 90% of the hypnotized witnesses tried to recall the number on a shirt in a simulated crime, compared with only 20% of the subjects in a control group (Buckhout, Eugenio, Licitra, Oliver, & Kramer, 1981). None of the witnesses was able to recall the number correctly. The possibility that recall may be inaccurate has caused the courts to question the reliability of recall during hypnosis.

There is also a problem with evaluating the effectiveness of hypnosis because successful recall during hypnosis may not have been caused by hypnosis. Smith (1983) identifies other possible causes, such as repeated testing and the reinstatement of context. As indicated by the findings of Read and Bruce (1982), discussed in the previous chapter, repeated testing can cause additional recall. Improved recall attributed to hypnosis may simply result from the fact that witnesses are attempting a second or a third recall that would have resulted in retrieval of more details without hypnosis. Or improved recall could result from some aspect of the procedure such as encouraging witnesses to try to reinstate the context of the crime.

To determine whether encouraging nonhypnotized subjects to reinstate the context would improve recall, Malpass and Devine (1981) asked an actor to vandalize some equipment during a demonstration before a large class of unsuspecting students. Five months after the staged vandalism, witnesses viewed a lineup of five individuals and were asked to identify the vandal if he was in the lineup. Half the witnesses were to reinstate the context of the crime before they made their choice. The interviewer asked them to try to visualize the events of that evening, including the lecture room, the equipment, the vandal, and their own feelings.

Witnesses who were told to reinstate the context before making a decision were correct 60% of the time. Those who did not receive special instruction were correct 40% of the time. Thus guided retrieval that emphasizes the reinstatement of context can lead to improved recall. But how does guided retrieval without hypnosis compare with guided retrieval with hypnosis?

To answer this question, Geiselman, Fisher, MacKinnon, and Holland (1985) asked both hypnotized and nonhypnotized subjects to recall information about a simulated crime. Subjects saw a four-minute film of a violent crime and were interviewed two days later by law-enforcement personnel. Subjects were randomly assigned to one of three interview conditions. The *standard* interview followed questioning procedures that law-enforcement personnel would normally use. The *hypnosis* interview involved asking hypnotized subjects to restate what they remembered from the film. The *cognitive* interview involved the use of four memory retrieval techniques that encouraged subjects to reinstate the context of the incident, report everything, recall the events in different orders, and recall the incidents from different perspectives.

Both the cognitive and hypnosis procedures resulted in the recall of a significantly greater number of correct items of information than did the standard interview. The investigators attributed this finding to the memory guidance techniques that are common to these two procedures. Although the cognitive interview did not result in better recall than the use of hypnosis, it is easier to learn and to administer. The cognitive interview technique could be learned and applied with little training. It also required less time to instruct the witness on the use of the retrieval strategies than placing the witness under hypnosis.

In conclusion, memory retrieval techniques have proved effective in increasing witnesses' ability to recognize participants in a crime and to recall details about the crime. Reinstatement of context, as implied in the encoding specificity principle, is an important component of these techniques. Although reinstatement of context is also encouraged during hypnosis, this technique is more difficult to learn and apply. It may also encourage witnesses to recall inaccurate information.

Our discussion of different kinds of memory codes continues in the next chapter. So far the emphasis has been on verbal material, and I have said very little about visual knowledge. The next chapter examines the important role of visual imagery in performing many cognitive tasks.

Summary

The levels-of-processing theory proposes that how an item is encoded determines how long it can be remembered. Qualitatively different memory codes are established by asking people in an incidental learning task to make decisions about a word's physical structure, pronunciation, or meaning. When people are unexpectedly asked to recall the words, they recall the most words following semantic processing and the fewest words following structural processing. Further support for the theory is the finding that rehearsal does not necessarily result in learning, presumably because subjects do not attend to the meaning of words they only want to keep active in STM.

Although the theory originally proposed that retention is determined by the depth of processing (with physical, phonemic, and semantic processing, respectively, representing increasing depth), the failure to find an independent measure of depth resulted in an increasing emphasis on the elaborateness and distinctiveness of memory codes. The elaboration hypothesis claims that it is easier to retrieve more elaborate codes and easier to provide associations at the semantic level. The distinctiveness hypothesis claims that it is easier to retrieve distinctive codes and that semantic codes are more distinctive than phonemic codes. Studies of elaborateness and distinctiveness using semantic material have found that increasing either one will improve recall. Making the semantic context more elaborate (by using complex sentences) or making words more distinctive (by shifting to a new semantic category) increases the number of words recalled.

The encoding specificity principle states that the effectiveness of a retrieval cue is determined by how well it corresponds to the characteristics of the memory trace. When the memory trace emphasizes semantic characteristics, a semantic cue is the most effective; when the memory trace emphasizes phonemic information, a phonemic cue is most effective. The best retrieval cue is one that exactly duplicates the original context, and for the cue to be at all effective, the item should fit the context.

An attempt to reinstate the original context is an important component of memory retrieval techniques developed by cognitive psychologists to improve the recall of eyewitnesses. The techniques have proved effective in increasing witnesses' ability to recognize participants in a crime and recall details about the crime.

Recommended Reading

The book edited by Cermak and Craik (1979) contains many excellent chapters on how the levels-of-processing concept evolved during the 1970s. Eich (1985) has recently developed a holographic recall model to account for many of these findings. Although elaborative rehearsal is clearly more effective than maintenance rehearsal, students are not always aware of this difference (Shaughnessy, 1981). A general implication of the encoding specificity principle is the use of transfer-appropriate processing, which emphasizes that the value of a particular learning strategy is relative to a particular goal (Morris, Bransford, & Franks, 1977). For example, d'Ydewalle and Rosselle (1978) showed that students do more poorly if they receive a test that differs in format (either multiple-choice or essay) from the format they expect. Other applied areas that can be related to the concepts of levels of processing and encoding specificity are context-dependent memory in deep-sea divers, the enhancement of face recognition, and attempts to understand certain aspects of amnesia and aphasia (Baddeley, 1982). Johnson (1983) has proposed a memory model in which events can create multiple entries in a sensory, perceptual, and reflection system. The similarities—and differences—between her theory and the levels-of-processing theory are evident in her chapter. Brewer and Pani's (1983) chapter in the same book contains a more complex taxonomy of memory. Blaney's (1986) review of research on affect and memory includes a discussion of issues on encoding specificity.

7

Visual Images

Mental imagery has long played a central role in psychologists' and philosophers' accounts of cognitive processes and the representation of knowledge in the mind. The construct of the image, however, has never been operationalized well enough to satisfy most psychologists, and so it is not surprising that imagery has disappeared periodically from the mainstream of Western psychology. Nevertheless, the concept has such magnetism that it has never stayed away for long, and it is currently enjoying remarkable popularity.

STEPHEN KOSSLYN AND JAMES POMERANTZ (1977)

The discussion in the preceding chapters emphasized verbal knowledge. The stimuli studied usually consisted of items that could be easily assigned a verbal label, such as words, letters, digits, or even nonsense syllables. We may question, however, whether we assign verbal labels to everything we perceive. Some events may be hard to describe verbally, and others simply may be easier to remember as an image. Although images can exist for each of the sensory modalities, psychologists have been interested mainly in visual images. This chapter considers how visual images contribute to knowledge.

A distinction between verbal knowledge and visual or spatial knowledge is often made on intelligence tests. Verbal knowledge is usually measured by vocabulary questions or questions that test comprehension of written material. Spatial knowledge is usually measured by performance of such operations as mentally folding connected squares into a cube or mentally rotating an object to determine whether it matches another object. Although most tests place a much greater emphasis on verbal knowledge than on spatial knowledge, some specialized tests contain rather difficult questions on spatial transformations. One example is the Dental Admissions Test, used to help select applicants to dental schools. Since spatial skills are very useful in dentistry, the test includes some challenging problems on spatial relations. People

Figure 7.1   A sample question from the Dental Admissions Test. Students must select the opening through which the object at the far left could pass.

would presumably answer the question illustrated in Figure 7.1 by forming a visual image of the object and rotating the image to align it with the openings.

The study of visual imagery has been one of the main contributions of cognitive psychology. However, psychologists ignored imagery for many years because of the influence of John B. Watson's *Behaviorism* (1924), which was dedicated to wiping out the study of mental events. Watson argued that only behavior could be objectively studied, an argument that certainly had some merit but almost completely eliminated the study of mental processes such as visual imagery. It wasn't until the 1960s that psychologists once again began to try to understand the role of visual images in the acquisition of knowledge. Visual imagery is still difficult to study because it cannot be directly observed, but research over the past two decades has provided strong evidence that visual images are used in performing many tasks.

The first section of this chapter presents some evidence for visual images. The results of the experiments would be difficult to explain if we believed that all knowledge was verbal. The second section argues that forming visual images is an effective method for remembering information. However, formation of a visual image is much easier for concrete material than for abstract material, and we will examine the implications of this finding. For many centuries people have recognized the usefulness of imagery in aiding memory, and many mnemonic strategies are based on visual imagery. The third section describes several memory strategies and shows how they can be used to learn names of people, foreign languages, and lists of items. The final section shows that even visual images have limitations. Fortunately, their lack of detail usually doesn't restrict their usefulness.

Evidence for Images

Although psychologists have seldom questioned that images exist, some have questioned the usefulness of images as explanatory constructs. The most influential paper challenging the usefulness of images in psychological theories was written by Pylyshyn (1973). Pylyshyn argued that it was misleading to think of images as uninterpreted photographs, analogous to pictures in the head. He supported the alternative view that an image is much closer to being a description of a scene than a picture of it. The emphasis on the descriptive characteristics of images, rather than their sensory characteristics, is the central theme of a *propositional theory*.

Kosslyn and Pomerantz (1977) agreed with Pylyshyn that images are interpreted and organized, but they argued that we often process images in the same way that we process perceptual information. In response to Pylyshyn's paper, they summarized five experimental findings that they thought could be better explained on the basis of imagery than nonsensory information. Two of the five findings were concerned with scanning visual images, a task studied by Kosslyn and his associates. We will look first at one variable influencing scanning time—the effect of distance between objects. We will then examine the other three findings on visual matching, mental rotation, and selective interference.

Scanning Visual Images

Many explanations of performance based on visual imagery assume that an image is a spatial representation analogous to the experience of seeing an object during visual perception. Furthermore, many of the operators that are used in analyzing visual patterns are also used to analyze visual images (Kosslyn & Pomerantz, 1977). One such operator is visual scanning. The analogy between pictures and images suggests that the time it takes to scan between two objects in an image should be a function of their distance from each other. Evidence obtained by Kosslyn, Ball, and Reiser (1978) supports this prediction.

Figure 7.2   A fictional map used to study the effect of distances on mental scanning time

One of their experiments required that undergraduates at Johns Hopkins University learn the exact locations of the objects shown in Figure 7.2. The map was then removed, and the students were given a series of trials that began with the name of an object. The task required that they form a mental image of the entire map and focus on the named object. Subjects then heard the name of a second object and scanned the map in the way they had been instructed—by imagining a black speck moving in a straight line from the first object to the second. When they reached the second object they pushed a button that stopped a clock. There are 21 possible distances among the seven objects, and the longest distance is nine times as great as the shortest distance. If distance determines the scanning time, as predicted, reaction time should be a linear function of the distance between two locations. Figure 7.3 shows how closely the prediction was supported.

These results suggest that we can mentally scan visual images in the same way that we can scan pictures. But an alternative view is that subjects in imagery tasks may be able to respond appropriately without actually using visual images (Pylyshyn, 1981; Intons-Peterson, 1983). According to this view, subjects may guess what the experimenter expects and respond so as to please the experimenter. A study by Mitchell and Richman (1980) showed that people can accurately predict how distance should influence scanning time. When the experimenters asked subjects to predict their scanning time for the different pairs of objects in Figure 7.2, predicted scanning times also increased as a linear function of distance. It is therefore possible

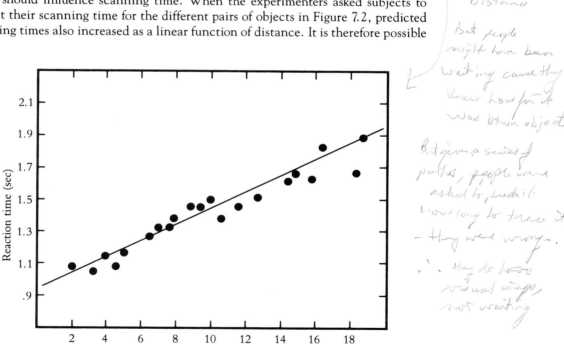

Figure 7.3   Scanning time between all pairs of locations on the imaged map

that subjects did not actually mentally scan their visual images but simply waited longer before pushing the button as the distance increased between two objects.

This criticism can be avoided if the outcome of the experiment cannot be predicted. Reed, Hock, and Lockhead (1983) hypothesized that people may not be able to predict how the shape of patterns will influence their scanning time. For example, one of their patterns was a straight line and another was a spiral. The rate at which people scanned a visual image of the pattern depended on its shape. An image of a straight line was scanned more quickly than an image of a spiral. However, people were unsuccessful in predicting how the different shapes would influence their scanning time. Because they couldn't predict the outcome of the experiment, their scanning times must have been produced by their actually scanning the different patterns rather than by their predictions.

Although the data of some imagery experiments may have been generated without subjects' using imagery, it is highly unlikely that people could perform many spatial tasks without using imagery. Finke (1980) cites specific examples of tasks in which the expected outcome would not be obvious to subjects, usually because they were doing the task for the first time. Let us now consider some other tasks that allow us to distinguish between visual and verbal memory codes.

Sequential versus Parallel Processing

One difference between information maintained in a visual image and information maintained as a verbal code is that a visual image makes it possible to match information in parallel. When you look at the schematic faces in Figure 7.4, you can perceive many features of the faces simultaneously. However, when you describe these same features verbally, you do not have access to all the features at the same time, because language is sequential. You have to decide the order in which you describe the features.

The parallel representation of spatial information and the sequential representation of verbal information influence how quickly a person can determine whether a perceived pattern matches a memorized pattern. If the memorized pattern is stored as a visual image, the match should occur quickly and should be relatively uninfluenced by the number of features that have to be matched. If a pattern is stored as a verbal description, the match should occur more slowly and should be influenced by the number of features that have to be compared.

Nielsen and Smith (1973) tested these predictions by showing students either a picture of a schematic face or its verbal description. There were five features of the face—ears, eyebrows, eyes, nose, and mouth—that varied in size. Each of the features could assume one of three values—large, medium, or small (see Figure 7.4 for an example). After students studied either the description or the picture for four seconds, the stimulus was removed. After a retention interval that lasted either four or ten seconds, the experimenters presented a test face, and the students decided whether it matched the face or description presented earlier.

Figure 7.4 Three sample faces illustrating size differences of feature values

In order to test the prediction that the number of features would influence reaction time only when people compared the test face with a verbal description, Nielsen and Smith varied the number of relevant features from three to five. The students knew that they could ignore the ears and eyebrows when there were three relevant features because these features never changed, and they could ignore the ears when there were four relevant features. But they had to compare all five features when all five were relevant. Figure 7.5 shows the amount of time needed to respond that either the initial face (task FF) or description (task DF) matched the test face. The data are from the four-second delay, but the same pattern of results occurred for the ten-second delay. The response times indicate that matching was relatively fast and independent of the number of relevant features only when the initial item was a visual pattern.

The results imply that when a person can maintain a visual image of a pattern in STM, a second visual pattern can be compared with it very quickly. It's almost as if the person were superimposing the two patterns and comparing all the features simultaneously. When the features are described verbally, a match requires sequentially retrieving information from the description, such as large ears, small eyebrows, small eyes, medium nose, and large mouth. Each feature on the list is individually compared with the corresponding feature on the test face. The response time therefore increases as a function of the number of relevant features on the list. The reaction time functions for the DF task in Figure 7.5 may remind you of the reaction time functions found in the Sternberg memory scanning task (Figure 4.10, Chapter 4). The similarity is not surprising, since both tasks require that people sequentially scan a list of items in STM. Maintenance of an image in the FF task avoids a list of separate items by combining the individual features on the list into a single integrated pattern. The efficiency with which this integrated pattern can be compared with other visual patterns is an important difference between a visual image and a verbal description.

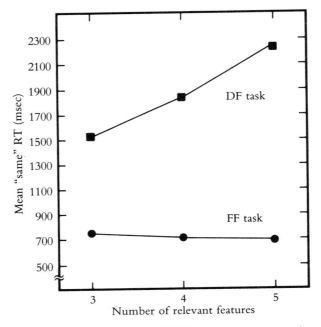

Figure 7.5   Mean reaction time (RT) for correct responses when stimuli were the same, as a function of the task and number of relevant features

Mental Rotation

Deciding whether two patterns match is considerably more difficult if they differ in orientation. The task shown in Figure 7.6 requires judging whether the two patterns in each pair are the same object (Shepard & Metzler, 1971). Pairs A and B are different orientations of the same pattern, but pair C consists of two different patterns. One method for determining whether two patterns are identical is to rotate one pattern mentally until it has the same orientation as the other pattern. When the patterns have the same orientation, it is easier to determine whether they match.

The pairs used by Shepard and Metzler differed in orientation from 0 degrees to 180 degrees in 20-degree steps. Half of the pairs could be rotated to match each other, and half of the pairs were mirror images that did not match. Figure 7.7 shows that the time required to decide that two patterns were identical increased linearly with an increase in the number of degrees they differed in orientation, suggesting that the subjects were rotating a visual image of one of the forms until it had the same orientation as the other form. Self-reports were consistent with this interpretation: subjects reported that they imagined one object rotating until it had the same orientation as the other and that they could rotate an image only up to a certain speed without losing its structure.

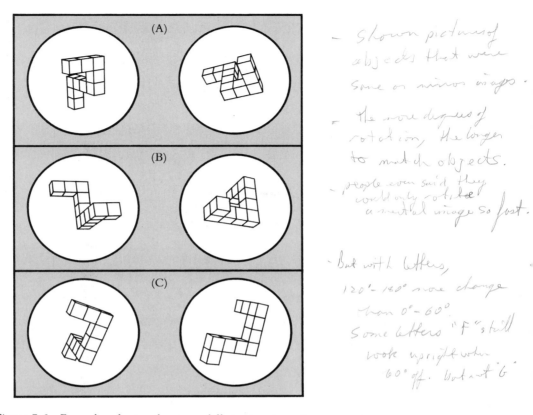

Figure 7.6 Examples of pairs of patterns differing in orientation

Similar results occur when people have to make judgments about familiar patterns. Cooper and Shepard (1973) showed subjects letters of the alphabet and asked them to indicate whether the pattern was a normal letter (R) or its mirror image (Я). Response times depended on how much the pattern was rotated from its normal upright position. Response times were shortest when the pattern was upright and longest when the pattern was upside down, or rotated 180 degrees. However, response times were not a linear function of the angle of rotation, as they were for the block patterns. A 60-degree increase in rotation increased response time more between 120 degrees and 180 degrees than between 0 degrees and 60 degrees.

A plausible explanation of why letters are less affected by small degrees of rotation than block patterns are is that letters may appear to be upright even when they are slightly rotated (Hock & Tromley, 1978). Some letters (such as F) can be rotated more than others (such as G) and still appear upright. Hock and Tromley used the physical characteristics of letters to classify them into sets that should appear either tilted or upright when slightly rotated. The "tilted" letters produced results

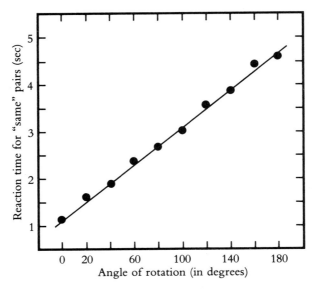

Figure 7.7   Reaction time to judge that two patterns have the same three-dimensional shape

that were similar to those obtained for block patterns. Since these letters are very sensitive to orientation, response time to decide whether the letter was normal or reversed increased as a linear function of rotation. The "upright" letters produced results similar to those obtained by Cooper and Shepard. Since these letters were less affected by small changes in orientation, decision time changed very little for small angles of rotation.

The ability to imagine movement is valued in sports training programs that use mental rehearsal as a training technique. Box 7.1 describes some of these programs. A key feature of mental rehearsal is the transformation of a list of instructions into an image of continuous movement. There is a need, however, for additional research to evaluate the success of this technique. A chapter by Suinn (1983) provides a good summary of the experimental study of imagery in sports.

Interference

We have seen in earlier discussions that a major cause of forgetting is interference. The research on release from proactive interference (Wickens, 1972) demonstrated that interference can be reduced by shifting semantic categories. Interference can also be reduced by shifting between visual and verbal material, as was shown in a study by Lee Brooks (1968).

In the visual task in this study, subjects were shown a block diagram of a letter (see Figure 7.8). The letter was then removed, and the subjects had to use their memory of the letter to respond *yes* to each corner that was on the extreme top or

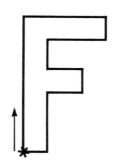

Figure 7.8   A block diagram of a letter

(handwritten margin notes)
- go around corners + say yes if outer edge corner, no if else
- or listen to sentence say yes for nouns, no else
- if answer for visual is visual ie point to answer, then performance goes down.
- same for verbal.
- but if response of different modality, better response time

bottom and *no* to each corner that was in between. The correct answers for the example, starting at the asterisk at the lower left and proceeding in the direction of the arrow, are *yes, yes, yes, no, no, no, no, no, no, yes.*

The verbal task in Brooks's experiment required that people respond positively to each word in a sentence that was a noun. For example, people listened to the sentence *A bird in the hand is not in the bush* and then classified each word as a noun or a nonnoun. The correct answers for the example are *no, yes, no, no, yes, no, no, no, no, yes.*

Brooks assumed that his subjects would rely on a verbal code to maintain the sentence in memory and a visual image to maintain the block diagram in memory. If his assumption is correct, it should be possible to interfere selectively with performance by using two different methods of responding. One method required that the answers be given verbally, by overtly responding *yes* or *no*. A verbal response should cause a greater conflict when classifying the words of a sentence than when classifying the corners of a block diagram. Another method required that a subject point to a *Y* for each positive response and an *N* for each negative response, using a diagram like the one in Figure 7.9. The diagram shows the correct answers for classifying the words in the sample sentence. Pointing to the correct letter requires close visual monitoring and should interfere more with the block task than with the sentence task.

The selective nature of interference is revealed by the average response time required to complete each task. Classifying the words in a sentence took longer when people gave a verbal response; classifying the corners of a letter took longer when people pointed to the correct response. In other words, giving a verbal response interfered more with memory for verbal material (a sentence) than with memory for visual material (a block diagram), and vice versa.

The selective nature of interference within a modality has implications for the number of items that can be maintained in STM. When we reviewed the evidence on STM capacity in Chapter 4, we looked at research that presented items from the same modality, such as a string of letters in a memory span task or different levels of brightness in an absolute judgment task. What would happen if we designed a memory span task in which some items could be retained by using a verbal code and other

Box 7.1   Mental images help athletes train their bodies
CHARLES GARFIELD

"I never hit a shot, not even in practice, without having a very sharp, in-focus picture of it in my head."

—golfer Jack Nicklaus

If you learn mental rehearsal techniques by using your imagination to create mental images of yourself performing, you can perform at optimal levels. This technique is the single most powerful tool in the Soviet mental training arsenal. It enables you to build confidence, accelerate reaction times and improve physical coordination and accuracy, and it allows you to work out complex strategies before executing them.

Mental rehearsal is by no means unknown to most athletes. But the formalization of the technique and its systematic use in athletic training programs, as has been done in the Soviet Union, is quite new to us. And whereas the Russians and East Germans use the technique in routine "mental workouts" as a way to perform their best, mental rehearsal has been applied in the United States largely to correct, rather than prevent, problems.

What exactly is mental rehearsal? Soviet psychologist Gregory Raiport, who worked with Russian national teams from 1972 to 1976, has explained how mental rehearsal is used to help train athletes at the National Research Institute of Physical Culture in Moscow: In their mental rehearsal sessions, the Russian athletes are taught to "imagine or visualize themselves performing the different stages of the event," and by doing so they actually provide themselves with invaluable neuromuscular practice.

In mental rehearsal, the mental images must include movement.

In his study on the effects of mental rehearsal on 53 Alpine skiers, Swedish sports psychologist Lars-Eric Unestahl found the most positive results were obtained when athletes created mental images of actions rather than of static postures.

The temptation for many people just starting out with mental rehearsal is to create "still shots" of positions that they know, in principle, are correct. This has the effect of freezing the mental image, a little like what happens when film gets stuck in a motion picture projector. But because motion is the essence of sports, movement and one's response to the changing circumstances created by movement must be included in the rehearsal.

items could be retained by using a visual code? If such variety reduces interference, people should be able to recall more items.

An experiment by two Dutch psychologists (Sanders & Schroots, 1969) revealed that a person's memory span can, in fact, be increased by using material from two different modalities. One modality was the typical verbal modality, created by showing a string of consonants. The other modality was a visual or spatial modality, created by showing a random sequence of lights on a two-dimensional light board.

Box 7.1 *(continued)*

Thus, Unestahl instructed his athletes: "Tell your body what to do by thinking through the run—that is, imagining yourself skiing down. Then start your body and let it do the rest. The task while you are skiing down will be to sing, hum or whistle a melody."

According to Unestahl, the highest number of negative results came when athletes created mental images that focused on specific postures, and so subconsciously directed their bodies to remain set in particular positions—even when they were performing complex actions that required constant change in response to changing circumstances.

The mental images that athletes create are what Stanford University researcher Karl Pribram has called mental holograms, three-dimensional mental images that direct nerve impulses to all the muscles of the body that will be involved in executing a task. As long as we allow these holograms to direct our movements—and the word "movements" is the key here—those moves in real life will be smooth, confident and precise.

The following is the example Unestahl presents of a mental rehearsal that hurts performance: "Concentrate on the following things while you are skiing down: a) arms forward, easily bent, the underarms parallel to the ground; b) initiate the turn: Sink down and put your poles down during the raising up; c) the vertical work: Turn the skis when you are in the highest position; d) the turn: Bring your hip in toward the hill and compensate with your upper body down while sinking down."

Unestahl's point is subtle, but if you imagine how you would feel if you were to ski while trying to remember this long list of static instructions, you will probably clutch up just thinking about it.

With movement and change programmed into the mental image, athletes can then let the mind and body take over. Once the action begins, the athletes turn their attention away from deliberate mental activity by whistling or humming. Conscious, deliberate thought ceases and the images of action take over automatically.

From the *Sun-Sentinel*, Fort Lauderdale, July 23, 1984. © 1984 Charles Garfield.

In the second condition subjects responded by pointing to the lights on the board in the correct order of their appearance.

The lack of interference between modalities suggests that people should be able to increase their memory span by storing the consonants as a verbal code and the light sequence as a visual code. Recall was, in fact, better when a sequence consisted of both visual and verbal items. For example, when people were asked to recall a string of 11 consonants, they correctly recalled an average of 5.4 items. When they

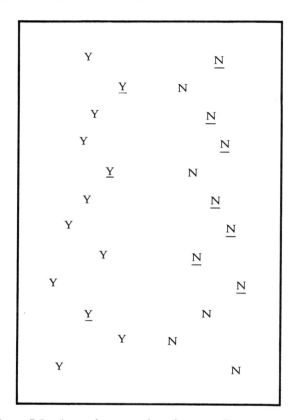

Figure 7.9   A sample answer sheet for responding *yes* or *no* in classifying words in the sample sentence. Correct responses are underscored.

were asked to recall a string of 6 consonants followed by a string of 5 spatial positions, they correctly recalled an average of 8.3 items. The improvement in recall was not due to the possibility that spatial positions were easier to recall than consonants, as previous research had shown that recalling spatial positions was actually more difficult. Rather, the findings were caused by the relative lack of interference between the visual and verbal codes. These results, along with those obtained by Brooks and many other psychologists, show that using two different modalities can reduce interference and improve performance.

This research illustrates how visual images can be used to improve performance on many cognitive tasks, including preserving the spatial relations among different parts of a picture, lowering reaction time for processing spatial information, and reducing interference between visual and verbal codes. We will now look more closely at additional evidence that visual codes can be used effectively to improve recognition and recall.

Visual Imagery and Learning

You may be able to recall times when you relied on visual imagery to learn material. When I moved to Cleveland some years ago to begin my academic career at Case Western Reserve University, my home telephone number was 283-9157. I decided to learn the number by verbal rehearsal. I wrote it down and rehearsed it several times before I was confident that I had learned it. After two days of unsuccessful practice, I decided to look for a different learning strategy.

My choice was influenced by the old "sing along with Mitch" routine, in which a bouncing ball appears over the words of a song. Where would the ball go if I pictured it bouncing over a sequence of numbers—1 2 3 4 5 6 7 8 9? If you try it for the sequence 283-9157, your will see that it has a rather nice pendulum motion, swinging back and forth and ending up in the middle. Once I discovered this relationship, I immediately learned the number, and I have been able to reconstruct it even though it ceased being my number quite a few years ago.

This may be an unusual example of how creation of an image can facilitate learning. But there are many other ways that imagery is used in learning, as we will see in the next two sections. The most obvious example is when we try to remember pictures without having to translate the entire picture into words.

Memory for Pictures

One indication that visual imagery might provide an effective memory code is that people usually find it easier to recognize pictures than to recognize words. Roger Shepard (1967) was one of the first to show that recognition accuracy for visual material is very high. Subjects in his experiment viewed 612 pictures at a self-paced rate and were later given a recognition memory test on pairs of pictures. Each pair consisted of a picture they had previously seen and a novel picture. When they were tested two hours later, the participants were virtually perfect in identifying which member of the pair they had seen. Another group of participants, tested one week later, was still able to identify the correct picture in 87% of the pairs.

One reason they did so well is that the test was easy. We could remember very little about a picture itself and still be able to tell which of two possibilities had been presented. But when the same test was repeated using words instead of pictures, recognition accuracy wasn't as high. Subjects tested immediately after seeing the words could identify which of two words had been presented in only 88% of the pairs (Shepard, 1967). Their performance was about the same as when pictures were tested after a week's delay.

An experiment by Standing (1973) provided further evidence that it is easier to remember pictures than words. One group of dedicated subjects viewed 10,000 pictures over a five-day period. Immediately after the learning session on the fifth day, the participants were given a recognition memory test similar to the one designed by Shepard. Standing estimated the number of items they must have retained in memory in order to reach the level of performance they attained on the test (taking into account the probability of guessing correctly). His estimate was that the participants must have remembered 6600 pictures. This estimate does not imply that the participants remembered all the details of a picture—but they did remember enough details to distinguish that picture from a novel picture.

Subjects in Standing's experiment were not shown 10,000 words for comparison, but other groups were shown 1000 words, 1000 ordinary pictures (such as a dog), or 1000 vivid pictures (such as a dog holding a pipe in its mouth). Two days later subjects were asked which of two possibilities had occurred in the experiment. Standing estimated that the participants had retained enough information about 880 vivid pictures, 770 ordinary pictures, and 615 words to make the correct choice without guessing. The finding that recognition memory is better for pictures than for words replicates Shepard's results.

Images and Advertising

The finding that people are better at recognizing pictures than words should have important implications for a number of applied fields. Let's consider advertising as an example. Advertisers often spend a lot of money trying to convince people that they should buy a product. Part of their task, particularly for a new or little-known product, is to help people remember the product's name. An ad may seem very interesting and even enjoyable, but it would not be effective if the potential buyer couldn't remember the name of the product that was advertised.

When I was a graduate student in Los Angeles, I participated in a marketing study that tested an audience's response to two new television shows scheduled to appear the following September. We were asked to rate the shows and a series of commercials that occurred between them. When the second show finished, the staff asked us to recall the names of the products advertised 30 minutes earlier. This was a surprisingly difficult task.

Lutz and Lutz (1977) studied the role that imagery can play in advertising. Learning the names of products is an example of paired-associate learning, in which the advertiser wants us to associate the brand name with the product being advertised. Research on memory for pictures suggests that combining the product and brand name into a single interactive picture should facilitate recall of the brand. When people shop for that particular product, they may remember the picture of the product and the associated brand name.

Lutz and Lutz searched the Yellow Pages of a telephone directory to collect samples of two kinds of pictures: (1) an *interactive* illustration, which integrates the brand and product into a single illustration, and (2) a *noninteractive* illustration, which shows either the brand or the product by itself. The second type of illustration is more common and usually includes a picture of the product with the brand name next to it. Figure 7.10 shows two examples of interactive illustrations and two examples of noninteractive illustrations. Interactive illustrations combine the brand and product into a single picture, either by including an illustration of each (picture interaction) or by combining the illustration of a product and a letter of the brand name

Figure 7.10   Interactive and noninteractive advertisements

(letter accentuation). Noninteractive pictures contain either an illustration of the brand name or an illustration of the product.

The students' task was to learn to associate the company's brand name with its product or service. Each student was assigned to one of four groups, consisting of two imagery groups (interactive and noninteractive) and their corresponding control groups. Students in each group studied 24 brand/product pairs for ten seconds each. Members of the interactive imagery group were shown pictures like the ones at the top of Figure 7.10. The control group had to learn the same pairs (such as Rocket Messenger Service or Dixon Crane Company) but saw only the words without the pictures. The noninteractive group saw a picture of either the product or the brand name, but the pictures were not shown to its control group.

In the recall test participants were given a list of the 24 products and asked to supply the appropriate brand name for each. The results indicated that only the interactive pictures facilitated recall of the brand names. People in the interactive group recalled significantly more names than people who had tried to learn the same pairs without the pictures. However, this finding was based almost entirely on the picture interaction condition; the letter accentuation condition was much less effective. People in the noninteractive group did not learn more pairs than the people in their control group.

The experimenters interpreted the results as supporting the use of pictures in ads—if the pictures form interactive images. Picture interaction is the most effective type of imagery, but it requires that both the product and the brand name be portrayable as pictures. This constraint is usually easy to satisfy for products but is more difficult for brand names unless the company has a name like Lincoln National Life or Bell Telephone. The fact that words vary in how easy they are to translate into images implies that the successful use of imagery depends on the nature of the material to be learned.

Effect of Material on Image Formation

The work of Alan Paivio at the University of Western Ontario established how the effectiveness of visual and verbal codes is influenced by the abstractness of material. After an extensive series of studies, Paivio (1969) argued that there were two major ways a person could elaborate on material in a learning experiment. One form of elaboration emphasizes verbal associations. A word like *poetry* may result in many associations that could help you distinguish it from other words. You might think of different styles of poetry, particular poems, or experiences in an English class. We saw in the previous chapter that verbal associations helped people recall words in the Hyde and Jenkins (1969) experiment. People who considered the meaning of the words recalled primary associates together because recalling one word reminded them of its associate.

The other form of elaboration is creation of a visual image to represent a word. If I asked you to remember the word *juggler,* you might form an image of a person juggling three balls. If I asked you to remember the word *truth,* however, you would probably have difficulty forming an image. The first word refers to a concrete object, the second to an abstract concept. It is easy to form an image to represent a concrete object but difficult to form an image for an abstract concept. Paivio (1969) argued that the concrete/abstract dimension is the most important determinant of ease in forming an image. At the concrete end of the continuum are pictures, because the picture itself can be remembered as a visual image, and the person doesn't have to create an image. Pictures often result in better memory than concrete words, which usually result in better memory than abstract words.

If visual images and verbal associations are the two major forms of elaboration, is one more effective than the other? To answer this question, we have to know how easy it is to form either an image or a verbal association to a word. The imagery potential of words is usually measured by asking people to rate on a scale how easy it is to form an image for a given word. As we might expect, concrete words are rated high on imagery and abstract words rated low. The association value of a word is usually measured by asking people to give as many associations as they can over a one-minute interval. Paivio and his colleagues have found that the imagery potential of words is a more reliable predictor of learning than the association potential of words. High-imagery words are easier to learn than low-imagery words, but high-association words are not necessarily easier to learn than low-association words (Paivio, 1969).

A study by Paivio, Smythe, and Yuille (1968) reveals the beneficial effect of imagery on learning. Students at the University of Western Ontario were asked to learn a list of paired associates consisting of 16 pairs of words. The words were equally divided between high-imagery (H) words, such as *juggler, dress, letter,* and *hotel,* and low-imagery (L) words, such as *effort, duty, quality,* and *necessity.* The list contained four pairs each that were high–high, high–low, low–high, and low–low, where the first term refers to the imagery value of the stimulus and the second term refers to the imagery value of the response. Examples include *juggler–dress* (H–H), *letter–effort* (H–L), *duty–hotel* (L–H), and *quality–necessity* (L–L).

Figure 7.11 shows how well the students could recall the response when given the stimulus. The powerful effect of imagery is quite evident. The H–H pairs resulted in the best recall and the L–L pairs the worst. When only one member of the pair had a high imagery value, recall was better when that word was used as the stimulus (H–L). The fact that H–H pairs were easiest to learn is consistent with the previously mentioned finding that interactive pictures improve the recall of brand names. When images can be created for both members of a word pair, the images can be combined to form an interactive image. For example, one can associate the word *dress* with *juggler* by forming an image of a juggler wearing a dress.

It is interesting to note that high-imagery words were easier to recall than low-imagery words even though the learners were not told to use visual imagery. Perhaps the participants spontaneously generated images whenever they could. Support for

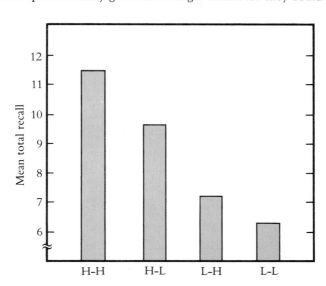

Figure 7.11 Mean total recall over four trials as a function of high (H) and low (L) imagery values

this hypothesis was obtained in a questionnaire completed after the learning task. The students indicated, for each of the 16 pairs on the list, which one of five strategies they had used in trying to learn that pair. Their options were *none, repetition* (rehearsal), *verbal* (a phrase or rhyme connecting two words), *imagery* (mental pictures that include the items), and *other.* The *none* and *other* options were reported infrequently. The distribution of the other three responses depended on whether the pairs consisted of high- or low-imagery words (see Figure 7.12). The reported use of imagery was highest for the H–H pairs and lowest for the L–L pairs. The striking resemblance between learning (Figure 7.11) and the reported use of imagery (Figure 7.12) suggests that imagery is an effective learning strategy.

The reason images are effective, according to Paivio (1975), is that an image provides a second kind of memory code that is independent of the verbal code. Paivio's theory is called a *dual-coding* theory because it proposes two independent memory codes, either of which can result in recall. A person who has stored both the word *cat* and an image of a cat can remember the item if she retrieves either the image or the word. Evidence suggests that the two memory codes are independent in the sense that a person can forget one code without forgetting the other code (Paivio, 1975). Having two memory codes to represent an item therefore provides a better chance of remembering that item than having only a single code. Since images facilitate recall, it is only natural that they should play a key role in suggestions for improving memory.

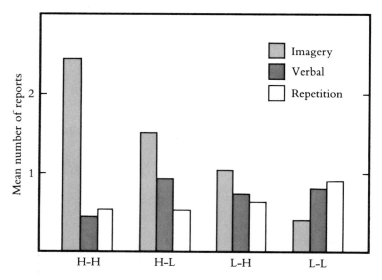

Figure 7.12   Mean number of pairs for which imagery, verbal, and repetition strategies were reported as a function of high (H) and low (L) imagery values

Mnemonic Strategies

Every so often a book appears on how to improve memory. Such a book is usually written by a person who not only has practiced mnemonic (memory) techniques but can successfully apply them to demonstrate rather remarkable acts of recall. One example, *The Memory Book* by Lorayne and Lucas (1974), was on the best-seller list for weeks.

Although memory books always discuss several techniques for improving memory, they usually emphasize visual imagery. The author presents a mnemonic strategy, in which imagery usually plays a key role, and claims that use of the strategy will improve recall. The claim, however, is seldom supported by experimental data. Is there proof that the proposed strategy works? Fortunately, supportive data exist in the psychology journals. We will now consider some of those data.

Comparison of Association Learning Strategies

The results obtained by Paivio et al. (1968) suggested that visual imagery is a particularly good strategy to use when images can be generated to represent words. Their study, however, was not designed to teach people to use a particular strategy, unlike an experiment conducted by Bower and Winzenz (1970). Subjects in the latter experiment were asked to learn paired associates consisting of concrete nouns. Each participant was assigned to one of four groups given different instructions on how to learn the associations. Students in the "repetition" condition were asked to rehearse each pair silently. Students in the "sentence reading" condition read aloud a sentence in which the two words of a pair were capitalized as the subject and object of the sentence. The experimenters told the members of this group to use the sentence to associate the two critical nouns. Students in the "sentence generation" condition made up their own sentence to relate the two words in a sensible way. Students in the "imagery" condition formed a mental image that combined the two words in a vivid interaction. They were encouraged to make their image as elaborate or as bizarre as they wished.

After a single study trial on each of 30 word pairs, the students were given a recall test on 15 pairs and a recognition test on the other 15. Recognition of the correct response was easy, and all four study strategies resulted in a high level of performance. Recall of the correct response was more difficult, however, and here the differential effectiveness of the strategies was apparent. The average number of correct recalls was 5.6 for the repetition group, 8.2 for the sentence-reading group, 11.5 for the sentence-generation group, and 13.1 for the imagery group. The data dramatically illustrate that although verbal rehearsal does result in some learning, it is less effective than the elaboration strategies. Comparison of the imagery and sentence-generation conditions shows that visual elaboration was more effective than semantic elaboration. Although the use of concrete nouns made visual elaboration possible, the fact that sentence generation was also an effective strategy suggests that this technique could be used when it is necessary to learn abstract words.

A specific application of the imagery strategy in paired-associate learning is learning to associate a name to a face. I would guess that just about everyone has had difficulty learning names at one time or another. Many authors of memory books can perform a very impressive demonstration in which they repeat back the names of all the members of an audience after hearing them only once. The method used by Lorayne involves first converting the name into a visual image and then linking the image to a prominent feature of the person's face. For example, if Mr. Gordon has a large nose, the image might be a garden (*garden* sounds like *Gordon*) growing out of his nose. Although the method may seem rather bizarre, it has experimental support.

A group of British psychologists found that people who were taught this strategy learned significantly more names than a control group that was not taught the strategy (Morris, Jones, & Hampson, 1978). The learning task required associating a different name (randomly selected from a telephone directory) to each of 13 photographs of male adults. After a study period of ten seconds for each item, the imagery group could correctly name ten of the photographs, compared with five for the control group. The authors admit that the use of mnemonic strategies requires some effort, and not everyone will be willing to make that effort to learn names. However, their results should provide encouragement to those who wonder whether the effort will be worthwhile.

Although research has shown that the use of visual imagery is effective for learning associations, it has also shown that bizarre images are not always more effective than plausible images. Rather, the degree of interaction in the image is a better predictor of its effectiveness (Kroll, Schepeler, & Angin, 1986). Bizarre imagery is more effective than plausible imagery only in limited situations, such as when the greater distinctiveness of bizarre images can enhance memory (McDaniel & Einstein, 1986).

The Mnemonic Keyword Method and Vocabulary Learning

The use of imagery to remember names obviously depends on how easy it is to form an image from a name. Some names should be fairly easy, such as Smith (form an image of a blacksmith) or Green (form an image of the color). Other names, such as Gordon or Detterman, may require associating a concrete word to the name and then forming an image of the associated word. The associated word, called a *keyword*, should sound like the name that is being learned. The association of *garden* with *Gordon* is an example of the keyword method. *Garden* is a keyword that can be used to form an image. The words *debtor-man* might be a good keyword for Detterman if one formed an image of Mr. Detterman dressed in ragged clothes.

You may have some reservations at this point about the keyword method. It is certainly more complicated than simply forming an image, because you have to remember not only the image but also the association between the keyword and the name in order to remember the original name correctly. Mr. Gordon might not appreciate being called Mr. Garden, and Mr. Detterman would certainly not like being called Mr. Debtorman.

Even though the keyword method requires two stages—learning the association between the name and the keyword and forming an image of the keyword—the method is still very effective. A striking demonstration of its effectiveness is illustrated in a study by Atkinson and Raugh (1975) on the acquisition of a Russian vocabulary. The keyword method divides the study of a vocabulary word into two stages. The first stage is to associate the foreign word with an English word, the keyword, that sounds approximately like some part of the foreign word. The second stage is to form a mental image of the keyword interacting with the English translation. For example, the Russian word for *building* (*zdanie*) is pronounced somewhat like *zdawn-yeh*, with the emphasis on the first syllable. Using *dawn* as the keyword, one could imagine the pink light of dawn being reflected in the windows of a building.

Appropriate selection of keywords is an important aspect of the method. A good keyword should satisfy the following criteria: it should (1) sound as much as possible like a part of the foreign word, (2) be different from the other keywords, and (3) easily form an interactive image with the English translation. Table 7.1 shows a sample of 20 Russian words and their associated keywords. As an exercise in using the method, you can try to create an image linking the first pair of words.

Students in Atkinson and Raugh's study tried to learn the English translations of 120 Russian words over a three-day period. The students were divided into two

Table 7.1   A sample of 20 items from the Russian vocabulary with related keywords

Russian	Keyword	Translation
VNIMÁNIE	[pneumonia]	ATTENTION
DÉLO	[jello]	AFFAIR
ZÁPAD	[zap it]	WEST
STRANÁ	[straw man]	COUNTRY
TOLPÁ	[tell pa]	CROWD
LINKÓR	[Lincoln]	BATTLESHIP
ROT	[rut]	MOUTH
GORÁ	[garage]	MOUNTAIN
DURÁK	[two rocks]	FOOL
ÓSEN	[ocean]	AUTUMN
SÉVER	[saviour]	NORTH
DYM	[dim]	SMOKE
SELÓ	[seal law]	VILLAGE
GOLOVÁ	[Gulliver]	HEAD
USLÓVIE	[Yugoslavia]	CONDITION
DÉVUSHKA	[dear vooshka]	GIRL
TJÓTJA	[Churchill]	AUNT
PÓEZD	[poised]	TRAIN
KROVÁT	[cravat]	BED
CHELOVÉK	[chilly back]	PERSON

groups—the "keyword" group and a control group. Subjects in the keyword group were taught how to use the keyword method. After the pronunciation of each foreign word, they were shown both a keyword and the English translation. The instructions said that the students should try to picture an interactive image linking the keyword and the English translation or should generate a sentence incorporating both words if they could not form an image. The keywords were not shown to students in the control group, who were told to learn the translations in whatever manner they wished. The control group did not receive instructions on the use of keywords or mental imagery.

On the day after the three study sessions, students in both groups were tested on the entire 120-word vocabulary. Students in the keyword group provided the correct translation for 72% of the Russian words; students in the control group did so for 46% of the words. This difference is particularly impressive considering that Russian was selected as a special challenge to the keyword method because the pronunciation of most Russian words is quite different from English pronunciation. Since many people find the Russian vocabulary harder to learn than the vocabularies of other foreign languages, it is valuable to have a method that can facilitate learning. Atkinson and Raugh planned to use the keyword method in a computerized vocabulary-learning program designed to supplement a college course on Russian. Students would be free to study the words in any way they wished but would have the option of requesting a keyword by pressing an appropriate button on the terminal.

The Method of Loci

The mnemonic methods we have reviewed so far have been applied to paired-associate learning such as associating a name with a face or an English word with a Russian word. Another kind of memory task is *serial learning*, which means memorizing a sequence of items in their correct order. For example, if you are going shopping, you may want to remember a list of items in the order in which you plan to purchase them.

A long list of items can be memorized by using the *method of loci*, a technique invented many centuries ago. The need for a good memory was particularly important in the ancient world, which lacked printing and even paper for notes. The classical art of memory was taught mainly as a technique for delivering long speeches (Yates, 1966). An unknown teacher of rhetoric recorded the principles in *Ad Herennium*, a book written about 86–82 B.C. The first step was to commit to memory a series of loci, or places—usually parts of a building, such as the forecourt, living room, bedrooms, and parlors, including statues and other ornaments in the rooms. The topics of the speech were then translated into images that were placed at the various locations in the order in which they would be discussed. The orator imagined walking through the building in a specified order, retrieving each image as he came to the next location. The method assures that the topics are remembered in their correct order, since the order is determined by the sequence of locations in the building.

The memory section of *Ad Herennium* did more than simply describe the method of loci; it gave a detailed set of rules for how the method should be used. For instance, there were rules for selecting locations:

> Memory loci should not be too much like one another, for instance too many intercolumnar spaces are not good, for their resemblance will be confusing. They should be of moderate size, not too large, for that renders the images placed on them vague, and not too small for then an arrangement of images will be overcrowded. They must not be too brightly lighted for then the images placed on them will glitter and dazzle; nor must they be too dark or the shadows will obscure the images [Yates, 1966, p. 23].

And rules for creating images:

> We ought, then, to set up images of a kind that can adhere longest in memory. And we shall do so if we establish similitudes as striking as possible; if we set up images that are not many or vague but active; if we assign to them exceptional beauty or singular ugliness; if we ornament some of them, as with crowns or purple cloaks, so that the similitude may be more distinct to us; or if we somehow disfigure them, as by introducing one stained with blood or soiled with mud or smeared with red paint, so that its form is more striking, or by assigning certain comic effects to our images, for that, too, will ensure our remembering them more readily [Yates, 1966, p. 25].

Two aspects of these rules are rather striking. The first is the concern with the visual precision of images. The recommendation that images be of a certain size to be most effective is consistent with current research on imagery (Kosslyn, 1975; Kosslyn, Ball, & Reiser, 1978). However, the recommendation that the loci not be too bright or too dark seems unusual to me. Do our images so closely reflect reality that we have to be concerned about lighting? Perhaps people who relied extensively on imagery had images that were so detailed and accurate that lighting was a concern. My own belief is that the images of most people are highly schematic and not very detailed, a belief I will try to support in the next section.

The second significant aspect of the rules is their attempt to reduce interference by creating loci and images that are highly distinctive. The importance of distinctiveness is still emphasized in current theories of memory, as we saw in the previous chapter. The author of *Ad Herennium* recommended that the loci should be different enough from one another that they would not be confused. One implication of this rule is that storing more than one image in a single location interferes with retrieval.

Crovitz (1971) tested this implication by asking undergraduates at Duke University to learn a set of 32 English words. Another set of 32 items (such as pet store, zoo, fire station, hospital) were selected as memory loci. The locations were typed individually on cards, which were placed on the experimenter's table. The number of cards or locations varied across groups. The control group was given no memory instructions and no cards. Six other groups received 1, 2, 4, 8, 16, or 32 locations, along with instructions to picture each word on the list vividly at the successive locations. The instructions indicated that subjects would hear 32 words and would have to store more than one word at a location if there were fewer than 32 cards.

Figure 7.13 shows the percentage of words that were recalled in their correct order as a function of the number of locations. The group that was asked to associate all the words to a single location did not do significantly better than the control group (0 locations), which tried to learn the words without using the method of loci. However, performance improved rapidly as the number of locations increased to 16, suggesting that two images could be stored at each location without producing interference. Storing more than two images at a location made it hard to remember the words, particularly in their correct order. It is important to note, however, that even a few locations led to better recall than the control group produced, and using many locations produced a substantial improvement in recall.

Limitations of Images

The usefulness of visual images as memory codes may seem surprising. If you are like me, you may feel that you cannot create very vivid images and perhaps even question whether you use any images at all. Let me give you a chance to form an image by asking: Does the Star of David contain a parallelogram (a four-sided figure whose opposite sides are parallel)? Try to form an image of the Star of David and examine it to answer the question. Many people have difficulty using images to identify the parts of a pattern, even after they have just seen the pattern (Reed & Johnson, 1975). Since we have seen many results that show the usefulness of images, it is only fair to discuss a few of their limitations before leaving the topic.

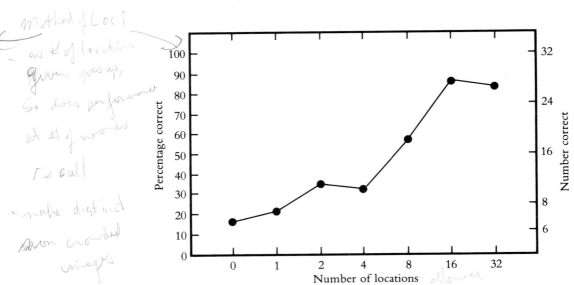

Figure 7.13   Recall of items in their correct order as a function of number of locations

Figure 7.14   Fifteen drawings of a penny that were used in a recognition memory test

Memory for Details

Our discussion so far has focused on the successful use of visual images to improve memory. We learned that memory for pictures is better than memory for words and memory for concrete words better than memory for abstract words. Both these findings are related to the ease with which an image can be created to represent a concrete word or picture. We also saw how instructions to form interactive images facilitated the learning of people's names, vocabulary words, and lists of items. If images can do all this, how are they limited?

One answer is that the tests that showed good memory for visual material were not very challenging. For example, the experiments by Shepard (1967) and Standing (1973) used a recognition memory test in which a person decided which one of two pictures had occurred in the experiment. Although the results of these studies suggest that visual memory contains an abundance of information, in reality the results do not allow us to conclude how much information is stored. All we know is that people retained enough information to distinguish the "old" picture from the new one.

Nickerson and Adams (1979) investigated how completely and accurately people remember visual details by asking them to recognize a very common object, a U.S. penny. Figure 7.14 shows 15 drawings of a penny, only one of which is correct. If you can identify the correct choice, you did better than the majority of subjects in the experiment, who selected incorrectly. Although we have seen a penny many times, most of us have never learned its details, probably because they are not very useful in everyday life. Attributes such as color and size allow us to distinguish quickly between a penny and other coins, making the learning of additional details unnecessary. When a new coin is introduced (such as the Susan B. Anthony dollar) that requires more attention to details to distinguish it from another coin, there is considerable resistance to its acceptance.

Retention of details is usually unnecessary when we use images to remember words. Your image of a penny would not have to be detailed or accurate to help you remember the word *penny*; it would only have to be detailed enough to allow you to recall the correct word when you retrieved your image. Experimental results have shown that people who were good at recalling the names of pictures they had seen two weeks earlier did not have more detailed images than people who could not recall as many names (Bahrick & Boucher, 1968). For example, people who could recall that they had seen a cup did not necessarily remember many details of the cup in a recognition test similar to the one illustrated by Figure 7.14. The evidence suggested that people were using visual images to aid their recall, but it was necessary to remember only enough details about an object to recall its name. Visual images can therefore be incomplete if the task does not require memory for details.

Studies showing the limitations of visual images provide both good news and bad news. The bad news is that using visual images is not a universal solution for improving memory performance. The good news is that even if people believe they have poor images, their images may still be sufficient for performing the many tasks that do not require great detail.

Reality Monitoring — *ability to define btwn real images and imagined one u external a internal. Stories.*

If our images of objects or events were as accurate and detailed as the actual events, then our ability to distinguish between actual and imagined events would be impaired. People can remember information from two basic sources—external sources, derived from perception, and internal sources, derived from imagination or thought. The ability to distinguish between these two sources has been called *reality monitoring* by Johnson and Raye (1981).

In order to study how well people can distinguish between actual and imagined events, Johnson, Raye, Wang, and Taylor (1979) showed subjects pictures of common objects. Subjects saw the picture of each object either two, five, or eight times and the name of each object either two, five or eight times. They were instructed to generate an image of an object each time its name occurred. At the end of the session, they received an unexpected test in which they had to estimate how often they had seen each of the pictures.

If people are very good at discriminating between seeing and imagining pictures, then their estimates of seeing should not be influenced by the number of times they imagined each picture. Note that although the ability to form accurate images is an asset for performing most spatial tasks, good imagery would be a liability for this particular discrimination task. Because people with good imagery might find it hard to discriminate between what they imagined and what they saw, the experimenters also gave subjects an imagery test to measure their imagery ability.

Figure 7.15 shows the results. The left panel contains the average estimates of the good imagers, and the right panel contains the average estimates of the poor imagers. The labels 8, 5, and 2 on the lines that show the estimates refer to the number of times the pictures had been shown. Notice that subjects were quite good at estimating how many times they had seen each picture, even when they had to distinguish between seeing and imagining the pictures. But the image trials did influence their judgments: the estimates of presentation frequency increased as the number of image trials increased. A comparison of the left and right panels of Figure 7.15 reveals that the number of image trials had a greater effect on the good imagers than on the poor imagers. As expected, people with good imagery distinguished less accurately between seeing and imagining.

Johnson and her colleagues' findings show that although the number of image trials did influence subjects' judgments of presentation frequency, their judgments were nonetheless fairly accurate. In general, people are able to remember the origin of information (internal versus external) remarkably well. What kind of cues help us make this distinction?

Johnson and Raye (1981) have proposed that several kinds of cues are helpful. First, there is *sensory* information. Perceptual events have more spatial detail than imagined events, although the amount of sensory information varies among individuals, as shown by the difference between good and poor imagers. Second, there is *contextual* information. Perceptual events occur in an external context that contains other information. We have seen in previous chapters that contextual information is important in recalling information, and it is also important in helping us distinguish between whether an event was internally or externally generated.

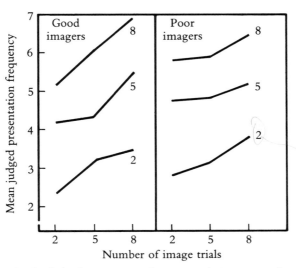

Figure 7.15   Judged presentation frequency of pictures as a function of the number of image trials. The number next to each line indicates whether a picture was presented two, five, or eight times.

A third cue for making this distinction is memory for the *cognitive operations* that are required to generate the image. If we can generate an image automatically without much conscious awareness, we will have poor memory for the cognitive operations used to generate the image. Dreams that occur during sleep are of this type. They often seem very real because we are not aware of generating them. In contrast, daydreams seem much less real because they are more influenced by our conscious control.

Reality monitoring is an interesting topic because it concerns issues that are important to people interested in clinical problems. Confusion between real and imagined events is particularly important in making a diagnosis of schizophrenia. Continuation of the theoretical and empirical work reported by Johnson and Raye (1981) should therefore provide a bridge between the study of imagery in clinical and cognitive psychology.

Summary

A variety of evidence suggests that visual images are important to our ability to perform many cognitive tasks. Visual images preserve the spatial relations among the objects of a scene or the features of a pattern. The time it takes to mentally scan between two objects in an image is therefore a function of the distance between them. Visual images also make it possible to compare all the features of two patterns simultaneously when we try to match a visual pattern with an image of another pattern. In contrast, features described verbally must be compared one at a time because of the sequential nature of language. When we are comparing two patterns that are in different orientations, a visual image makes it possible to rotate one of them mentally until the two patterns have the same orientation. The distinction between visual and verbal codes is also suggested by selective interference between the two codes. Experiments have revealed, for instance, that circling responses on an answer sheet interfered more with classifying the corners of a block diagram, whereas responding verbally interfered more with classifying the words in a sentence.

The usefulness of visual images in memory is supported by research showing that people usually remember pictures better than concrete words and concrete words better than abstract words. These results correspond to the fact that images are easiest to form from pictures and hardest to form from abstract words. Learning pairs of items is facilitated by forming an interactive image that combines the members of the pair. For example, recall of advertisements was best when people saw an illustration that combined a picture of the brand name with a picture of the product. The dual-coding theory explains the usefulness of visual imagery in recall by proposing that a visual image provides an extra memory code that is independent of the verbal code. A person therefore has two chances to recall the item rather than only one.

The knowledge that visual imagery improves memory has existed for centuries and has resulted in the use of imagery in many mnemonic strategies. A study that compared four strategies—verbal rehearsal, sentence reading, sentence generation, and imagery—found that people who used the imagery strategy recalled the most words. However, the two sentence elaboration strategies produced much better recall than simple rehearsal, suggesting that the former strategies could facilitate learning abstract words. Visual images can also be used to learn people's names and a foreign vocabulary, although it is often necessary to translate a name or foreign word into a similar-sounding concrete keyword first. An interactive image is then formed to link the keyword with a face or the English translation of the foreign word. The method of loci is a mnemonic strategy that can be used to learn a sequence of items, such as the major topics in a speech. A person selects a familiar physical structure, such as a building, and produces an interactive image linking a word or topic with each location in the building. The order of the topics is preserved by locating the topics in the order in which one would encounter them while walking through the building. Experiments evaluating the effectiveness of mnemonic strategies have usually found a dramatic improvement in performance.

Although the use of visual images often produces a dramatic improvement in recognition or recall, the images of most people seem to be limited in clarity and detail. An experiment that asked people to select the correct drawing of a penny from a set of similar alternatives found that most people made the wrong choice. A likely explanation is that we do not need to remember the details of a penny. This is also true for the images used to represent words in a memory task: it is only necessary to remember enough about the image to recall the word. An advantage of the lack of detailed sensory information in images is that it helps us distinguish between perceived and imagined events (reality monitoring).

Recommended Reading

Paivio's *Imagery and Verbal Processes* (1971) discusses the experimental work during the 1960s that helped restore imagery as a major topic in experimental psychology. Kosslyn's (1983) book *Ghosts in the Mind's Machine* provides a very readable introduction to the research on creating and using images. *Imagery: Current Theory, Research, and Application* (Sheikh, 1983) contains chapters on a wide variety of topics, including clinical implications of imagery. Individual differences in the use of imagery have been studied by MacLeod, Hunt, and Mathews (1978). Articles by Anderson (1978), Finke (1985), Kosslyn (1981), Pylyshyn (1981), and Shepard and Podgorny (1978) discuss the representation of information in images and the relation between imagery and perception. Research by Posner, Boies, Eichelman, and Taylor (1969) provided evidence on the maintenance of visual codes in STM. However, their conclusion that visual codes are quickly replaced by verbal codes has been challenged by Kroll and Parks (1978). Psychologists continue to study the practical implications of imagery, including its use as a mnemonic (McCarty, 1980; Pressley, Levin, Hall, Miller, & Berry, 1980) and its role in the acquisition of spatial knowledge (Thorndyke & Stasz, 1980). In addition, research continues on issues related to reality monitoring (Anderson, 1984).

8

Categorization

We begin with what seems to be a paradox. The world of experience of any normal man is composed of a tremendous array of discriminably different objects, events, people, impressions. But were we to utilize fully our capacity for registering the differences in things and to respond to each event encountered as unique, we would soon be overwhelmed by the complexity of our environment. The resolution of this seeming paradox—the existence of discrimination capacities which, if fully used, would make us slaves to the particular—is achieved by man's capacity to categorize. To categorize is to render discriminably different things equivalent, to group the objects and events around us into classes, and to respond to them in terms of their class membership rather than their uniqueness.

J. S. BRUNER, J. J. GOODNOW, AND G. A. AUSTIN (1956)

This chapter and the next one discuss ways in which people organize knowledge. One way to organize knowledge is to form categories. Categories consist of objects or events that we have grouped together because we feel they are somehow related. The ability to categorize enables us to interact with our environment without becoming overwhelmed by its complexity. Bruner, Goodnow, and Austin, in their influential book *A Study of Thinking* (1956), listed five benefits of forming categories.

1. Categorizing objects "reduces the complexity of the environment." Scientists have estimated that there are more than 7 million discriminable colors. If we responded to all of these as unique, we could spend our entire lifetime just trying to learn the names of colors. When we classify discriminably different objects as being equivalent, we respond to them in terms of their class membership rather than as unique items.

152

2. Categorizing is "the means by which objects of the world are identified." We usually feel that we have recognized a pattern when we can classify it into a familiar category such as *dog, chair,* or the letter A.

3. The third achievement is a consequence of the first two: the establishment of categories "reduces the need for constant learning." We do not have to be taught about novel objects if we can classify them; we can use our knowledge of items in the category to respond to the novel object.

4. Categorizing allows us to "decide what constitutes an appropriate action." A person who eats wild mushrooms must be able to distinguish between poisonous and nonpoisonous varieties. Eating a poisonous variety is clearly not an appropriate action.

5. Categorizing "enables us to order and relate classes of objects and events." Although classification is by itself a useful way to organize knowledge, classes can be further organized into subordinate and superordinate relations. The category *chair,* for example, has *high chair* as a subordinate class and *furniture* as a superordinate class. The three categories form a hierarchy in which *furniture* contains *chair* as a member, and *chair* contains *high chair* as a member.

Psychologists have used several experimental procedures to study how people make classifications. The first section of this chapter describes a procedure called *concept identification.* The categories in concept identification tasks typically contain geometric patterns that vary along several obvious dimensions—for example, shape, size, and color. The experimenter selects a rule to define the concept, and the task requires discovering the rule through learning which patterns are examples of the concept. The rule might be relatively simple, such as "All red patterns are examples," or it might be more complex, such as "Either red patterns or small patterns are examples."

One limitation of this approach is that many categories cannot be distinguished on the basis of a simple rule. We can usually distinguish a dog from a cat, but it is questionable whether we use a simple rule to make this distinction. The second section discusses some characteristics of natural, or real-world, categories and emphasizes how we use these characteristics to organize knowledge. In order to recognize objects and reduce the need for constant learning, we have to be able to classify novel objects into a familiar category. The final section discusses how people do this.

Concept Identification

Discovering Logical Rules

The most basic distinction between two categories occurs when they can be distinguished by the values of a single dimension. For example, a rule for sorting objects could state that large objects belong to one category and small objects belong to another category. Experimenters do not always use such simple concepts, however, and they have often studied how people learn concepts defined by logical rules typically requiring two dimensions, such as shape and color. Figure 8.1 shows how four logical rules divide stimuli into two categories. Notice that each dimension has three attributes—*red* (cross-hatched), *black,* and *white* for color; and *square, triangle,* and *circle* for shape. The attributes *red* and *square* specify the concept in the example.

The rule that is usually the easiest to learn is the *conjunctive rule.* Since the conjunctive rule uses the logical relation *and,* the concept in this case is *red and square.* A stimulus is a member of the category only if both attributes are present. The red square is the only stimulus that satisfies this criterion.

The *disjunctive rule* uses the logical relation *or.* A stimulus is an example of the concept if it is red or if it is a square. The three red stimuli and the three squares are now all examples of the concept.

The *conditional rule* makes use of the *if, then* relation—for example, if the stimulus is red, then it must be a square to be an example. One characteristic of the conditional rule that may seem strange is that all stimuli that are not red are positive examples. An analogue would be if you worked in a fancy restaurant and had to enforce the rule that if a person is a man, he must wear a tie. All people who were not men would be admitted under this restriction.

The *biconditional rule* is so called because the conditional rule applies in both directions. The biconditional rule includes the previous rule—if a stimulus is red, then it must be a square. But it also applies in the reverse direction—if a stimulus is a square, then it must be red. You should notice in Figure 8.1 that the biconditional

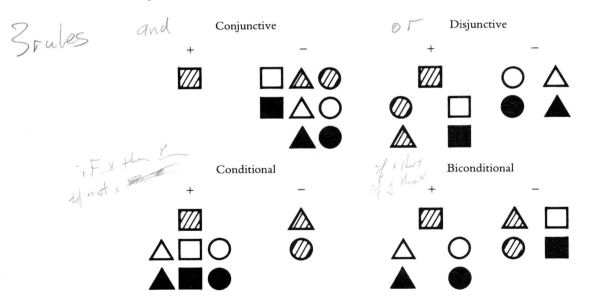

Figure 8.1　Positive and negative examples for four logical rules— conjunctive, disjunctive, conditional, and biconditional. The relevant attributes are *red* and *square.*

rule excludes two squares from the positive category that were not excluded by the conditional rule. Since the biconditional rule applies in both directions, a square is not an example of the category unless it is red. The greater exclusiveness of the biconditional rule is also illustrated by the previous analogue. In addition to excluding men who were *not* wearing ties, the biconditional rule would exclude women who *were* wearing ties. The reverse of the *if man, then tie* rule is *if wearing a tie, then man.*

As you can imagine, learning the correct conceptual rule can be difficult. One way to simplify the task would be to tell subjects the relevant attributes. This task is called *rule learning* because people have to learn only the correct logical rule when they are told the relevant attributes (Haygood & Bourne, 1965).

Bourne (1970) tested the comparative difficulty of the four rules by designing an experiment in which subjects solved a series of nine successive rule-learning problems. The stimuli varied on four dimensions—color, shape, number, and size— but the experimenter always specified the two relevant attributes before each problem. Each problem required that a person learn to classify the stimuli as either positive or negative examples of the concept. Subjects received one stimulus at a time, made their classification, and were told whether they were correct. They were considered to have solved a problem when they could state the rule or make a certain number of correct responses in a row.

Figure 8.2 shows the results. There are large initial differences in the difficulty of the four rules. The conditional rule requires over twice as many trials to learn on the first problem as the conjunctive and disjunctive rules, and the biconditional rule requires over three times as many trials to learn. However, with practice people become very good at applying the biconditional and conditional rules and eventually perform as well on these problems as on the conjunctive and disjunctive problems. After solving six problems using the same rule, all subjects solved the remaining problems without errors, no matter how difficult the rule was at the outset.

Discovering Relevant Attributes

In the rule-learning problems, the experimenter told the subjects what the two relevant attributes were but did not tell them the appropriate rule. A variation of the procedure—called *attribute learning*—is to tell people the rule and let them discover the appropriate attributes (Haygood & Bourne, 1965). The problem is solved when people can consistently identify stimuli as either positive or negative instances of the concept.

Studies of attribute learning generally reveal that efficiency in identifying the relevant attributes depends on which rule specifies the concept. The order of difficulty of the four rules is the same as in rule-learning tasks: attribute problems based on the conjunctive rule are the easiest, followed by the disjunctive rule, the conditional rule, and the biconditional rule (Bourne et al., 1976).

Why should the choice of rule influence task difficulty when participants are told the rule before each problem? Bourne and his colleagues proposed a frequency

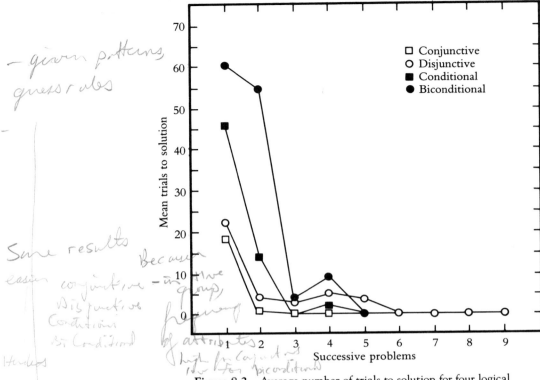

(Handwritten margin notes:)
- given patterns, guess rules
- Same results easier conjunctive — Disjunctive Conditional Bi-Conditional
- Harder
- Also, given rules, guess attributes

Figure 8.2   Average number of trials to solution for four logical rules—conjunctive, disjunctive, conditional, and biconditional

theory to account for these results. The frequency theory can apply to stimuli in both the positive and negative categories, but the results indicate that the positive category is more important (Bourne et al., 1976). Let's return to the categories shown in Figure 8.1 to see how the frequency theory works when applied to the stimuli in the positive category.

It is easy to identify the relevant attributes for a conjunctive rule because irrelevant attributes (*black* and *white* or *circle* and *triangle*) never appear in the positive category. The relevant attributes therefore appear 100% of the time because all positive stimuli are red and square. It is not quite so easy for the disjunctive rule. Figure 8.1 shows that three of the five positive stimuli are red and three of the five positive stimuli are square. The relevant attributes therefore appear 60% of the time in the positive category. For the conditional rule, only one of the seven positive stimuli is red, and three of the seven are square. The two relevant attributes therefore occur 29% of the time (the average of 1/7 and 3/7). The lowest percentage occurs for the biconditional rule. Only one of the five positive stimuli is red, and only one is square. The two relevant attributes occur only 20% of the time.

You should notice that the ordering of these percentages corresponds to the ordering of the difficulty of attribute identification tasks. The results suggest that people form frequency differences among the values of each dimension. When the relevant values (such as *red* and *square*) frequently occur in the positive category, it is fairly easy to identify these values as relevant. When the relevant values seldom occur in the positive category, it is much harder to identify them as relevant. The attribute frequency theory is consistent with several other findings in the concept identification literature. We will return to one of these findings later in the chapter when we discuss a feature frequency theory of categorization.

Critique of the Concept Identification Paradigm

Not all cognitive psychologists are satisfied with the concept identification task; some have criticized it as highly artificial and unrelated to the cognitive tasks we usually encounter in the real world. This criticism does not mean that we are unable to draw any analogy between skills needed in concept identification tasks and skills needed in other tasks. For example, to learn the correct rule in a concept identification task, subjects must evaluate a number of hypotheses. Our inability to evaluate a large number of hypotheses simultaneously is found not only in concept identification tasks (Levine, 1966) but also in real-world tasks such as medical diagnosis (Elstein, Shulman, & Sprafka, 1978). Yet real-world tasks are often different enough from concept identification tasks that we must be very careful in making generalizations.

The predominant criticism of the concept identification paradigm is that real-world categories are unlike the categories studied in the laboratory. This is not a new argument. Bruner, Goodnow, and Austin (1956) recognized that most real-world categories cannot be distinguished by the different values along a single dimension or by logical rules. One of the chapters in their book discussed categorizing with probabilistic cues in which the values of a dimension did not uniquely specify a category. For example, 67% of the airplanes in one category may have a straight tail, and 67% of the planes in another category may have a curved tail. The tail is a probabilistic cue because it tells us only the most likely category of a plane, not its definite category.

Although Bruner, Goodnow, and Austin reported some experiments on categorizing with probabilistic cues, their work is remembered mainly for research using the standard concept identification paradigm. A dramatic change in how psychologists viewed real-world categories had to wait until the 1970s, when Eleanor Rosch and her students at the University of California, Berkeley, began to study the characteristics of natural categories (Rosch, 1973). One of the characteristics of concept identification tasks that bothered Rosch is that all members of the concept are equally good members. Consider the five examples in Figure 8.1 that satisfy the conjunctive rule *red* or *square*. All of the five positive instances are equally good members because they all satisfy the rule. In contrast, natural categories are not composed of equally good members. If we gave people different variations of the color red, they would agree that some variations were more representative of the color than others (a "good" red versus an "off" red).

Another characteristic of natural categories is that they may be composed of continuous dimensions rather than discrete dimensions. Colors, for example, vary along a continuum in which red gradually becomes orange, and orange gradually becomes yellow. Natural categories are also hierarchically organized—larger categories often contain smaller categories. These characteristics of natural categories have important implications for how we make use of categories to organize knowledge. The next section discusses these implications.

Natural Categories

As we saw, one characteristic of real-world, or natural, categories is that they are hierarchical—some categories contain other categories. For example, the category *furniture* contains chairs, and the category *chairs* contains living-room chairs. Each of these levels contains a variety of objects, but the variety decreases as the category becomes smaller. There are many kinds of furniture (beds, sofas, tables, chairs), fewer kinds of chairs (living-room chairs, dining-room chairs, high chairs), and still fewer kinds of living-room chairs. The first part of this section looks at how the hierarchical organization of categories influences our behavior.

Another characteristic of natural categories is that some members seem to be better representatives of the category than others. We could all agree that chairs are furniture, but what about a piano? Shirts are certainly a good example of clothing, but what about a necklace? The second part of this section examines the implications of the fact that the members of categories are not all equally good members.

The Hierarchical Organization of Categories

Rosch and her colleagues studied the hierarchical organization of categories by using the three levels shown in Table 8.1 (Rosch, Mervis, Gray, Johnsen, & Boyes-Braem, 1976). The largest categories are the superordinate categories, such as *musical instruments*. They contain the basic-level categories (such as *drum*), which in turn contain the subordinate categories (such as *bass drum*). The most important of the three levels, according to Rosch, is the basic level, because basic-level categories are the most differentiated from one another, and they are therefore the first categories we learn and the most important in language.

The differentiation of categories can be measured by determining how much the members of a category share attributes with one another but have different attributes than the members of other categories have. At the superordinate level, the difficulty is that members share few attributes. Examples of furniture—such as table, lamp, and chair—have few attributes in common. At the subordinate level, the difficulty is that the members share many attributes with members of similar subordinate categories. For example, a kitchen table has many of the same attributes as a dining-

Table 8.1   Examples of subordinate, basic, and superordinate categories

Superordinate	Basic level	Subordinates	
Musical instrument	Guitar	Folk guitar	Classical guitar
	Piano	Grand piano	Upright piano
	Drum	Kettle drum	Bass drum
Fruit	Apple	Delicious apple	Mackintosh apple
	Peach	Freestone peach	Cling peach
	Grapes	Concord grapes	Green seedless grapes
Tool	Hammer	Ball-peen hammer	Claw hammer
	Saw	Hack handsaw	Cross-cutting handsaw
	Screwdriver	Phillips screwdriver	Regular screwdriver
Clothing	Pants	Levi's	Double-knit pants
	Socks	Knee socks	Ankle socks
	Shirt	Dress shirt	Knit shirt
Furniture	Table	Kitchen table	Dining-room table
	Lamp	Floor lamp	Desk lamp
	Chair	Kitchen chair	Living-room chair
Vehicle	Car	Sports car	Four-door sedan car
	Bus	City bus	Cross-country bus
	Truck	Pickup truck	Tractor-trailor truck

room table. The intermediate level of categorization—the basic level—avoids the two extremes. Members of a basic-level category, such as chair, not only share many attributes but have attributes that differ from those of items in other basic-level categories, such as lamp and table.

Evidence for the differentiation of categories comes from a study in which people were asked to list the attributes of objects at different levels in the hierarchy (Rosch et al., 1976). Some people listed the attributes of superordinate objects (such as musical instruments, fruit, tools, clothing); others listed the attributes of basic-level objects (guitar, apple, hammer, pants); and still others listed the attributes of subordinate objects (classical guitar, Mackintosh apple, claw hammer, Levi's).

The experimenters analyzed the data by identifying attributes that people seemed to agree were associated with the specified category. Table 8.2 shows the average number of shared attributes at each level in the hierarchy. The number of shared attributes increases from the superordinate to the subordinate level. The members of a superordinate category have very few attributes compared with the basic level. However, the increase in shared attributes from the basic level to the subordinate level is very small. The differences between levels can be illustrated by the three examples shown in Table 8.3. Only two attributes were listed for the superordinate category *clothing*—you wear it and it keeps you warm. These same two attributes plus an additional six were listed for the basic-level category *pants*. Pants have legs, buttons, belt loops, pockets, and two legs and are made of cloth. One additional attribute was listed for the subordinate category *Levi's*—blue—and two additional attributes were listed for double-knit pants—comfortable and stretchy. Notice that

Table 8.2   Number of attributes in common at each hierarchical level

	Raw tallies			Judge-amended tallies		
Category	Super-ordinate	Basic level	Sub-ordinate	Super-ordinate	Basic level	Sub-ordinate
Musical instrument	1	6.0	8.5	1	8.3	8.7
Fruit	7	12.3	14.7	3	8.3	9.5
Tool	3	8.3	9.7	3	8.7	9.2
Clothing	3	10.0	12.0	2	8.3	9.7
Furniture	3	9.0	10.3	0	7.0	7.8
Vehicle	4	8.7	11.2	1	11.7	16.8

although the items in subordinate categories share slightly more attributes than those in basic-level categories, there is a considerable overlap of attributes for subordinate categories. Although Levi's and double-knit pants differ on a few attributes, they also share many attributes, making it easier to distinguish between pants and shirts than to distinguish between Levi's and double-knit pants.

The same argument can be extended to the bodily movements we use in dealing with different objects at a particular level in the hierarchy of categories. There are very few movements in common at the superordinate level: the movements entailed in working with a tool or getting dressed depend on which tool or which article of clothing is involved. Motor movements at the basic level are more standard. We put on pants the same way whether they are Levi's or double-knit pants. The result is a large increase in common motor movements going from the superordinate to the

Table 8.3   Examples of shared attributes at different hierarchical levels

Tool	Clothing	Furniture
make things	you wear it	no attributes
fix things	keeps you warm	**Chair**
metal	**Pants**	legs
Saw	legs	seat
handle	buttons	back
teeth	belt loops	arms
blade	pockets	comfortable
sharp	cloth	four legs
cuts	two legs	wood
edge	**Levi's**	holds people—
wooden handle	blue	you sit on it
Cross-cutting handsaw	**Double-knit pants**	**Kitchen chair**
used in construction	comfortable	no additional
Hack handsaw	stretchy	**Living-room chair**
no additional		large
		soft
		cushion

basic level but a very small increase going from the basic to the subordinate level. We therefore say "He puts on his pants one leg at a time" rather than "He puts on his clothing one leg at a time" or "He puts on his double-knit pants one leg at a time." The reference to clothing is too general because motor movements differ for different kinds of clothes, and the reference to double-knit pants is too specific because the same motor movements apply to pants in general.

Another characteristic of categories is particularly important for prototype theories—the shape of objects within the category. The prototype of a category is usually defined as the "average" of the patterns in the category. It represents the central tendency of the category. But is it meaningful to talk about the average shape of real-world categories? The answer depends on which hierarchical level we are talking about.

The objects in Figure 8.3 represent basic-level categories, and the four objects in each row belong to the same superordinate category. Rosch and her colleagues found that people were not very good at identifying the average shape of two different basic-level objects belonging to the same superordinate category. For example, the average shape of a table and a chair together would look like neither a table nor a chair but something in between that would be difficult to identify. These results are not surprising if we try to think of what an "average" object would look like for superordinate categories such as furniture, clothing, vehicles, and animals. We can think of good examples of each category, but this is not the same as forming an average of all the examples.

The concept of an average example becomes meaningful if we think of objects from the same basic level. Although the average shape of furniture is unreasonable, the average shape of a chair is a more reasonable concept. In fact, people were quite

Figure 8.3   Examples of outlines of pictures representing basic-level categories. The pictures in each row belong to the same superordinate category.

accurate in identifying the average shape of two objects from the same basic-level category—for example, the average of two chairs still looks reasonably like a chair, and the average of two shirts still looks reasonably like a shirt. Basic-level objects are sufficiently similar to each other that the average shape is identifiable. Creation of an average pattern to represent a category is therefore possible at the basic level (and at the subordinate level, where the shapes of objects in the same category are even more similar) but is not possible at the superordinate level.

Family Resemblances

So far we have emphasized comparing categories at different levels of generality. Rosch and her colleagues argued that the intermediate level of generality—the basic level—is the most important. It is the most general level at which a prototype, or concrete image, can be formed to represent the category as a whole. It is also the level at which categories are the most differentiated from one another, because the members of basic-level categories share many attributes with one another but do not share many attributes with members of other categories.

We will now shift our emphasis to comparing the members within a category. Psychologists use the term *typicality* to refer to differences in how well members of a category represent that category. For instance, people agree that chairs, sofas, and tables are good examples of furniture; cars, trucks, and buses are good examples of vehicles; and oranges, apples, and bananas are good examples of fruit. Table 8.4 lists

Table 8.4   Typicality of members in six superordinate categories

Item	Furniture	Vehicle	Fruit	Weapon	Vegetable	Clothing
1	Chair	Car	Orange	Gun	Peas	Pants
2	Sofa	Truck	Apple	Knife	Carrots	Shirt
3	Table	Bus	Banana	Sword	String beans	Dress
4	Dresser	Motorcycle	Peach	Bomb	Spinach	Skirt
5	Desk	Train	Pear	Hand grenade	Broccoli	Jacket
6	Bed	Trolley car	Apricot	Spear	Asparagus	Coat
7	Bookcase	Bicycle	Plum	Cannon	Corn	Sweater
8	Footstool	Airplane	Grapes	Bow and arrow	Cauliflower	Underpants
9	Lamp	Boat	Strawberry	Club	Brussels sprouts	Socks
10	Piano	Tractor	Grapefruit	Tank	Lettuce	Pajamas
11	Cushion	Cart	Pineapple	Teargas	Beets	Bathing suit
12	Mirror	Wheelchair	Blueberry	Whip	Tomato	Shoes
13	Rug	Tank	Lemon	Icepick	Lima beans	Vest
14	Radio	Raft	Watermelon	Fists	Eggplant	Tie
15	Stove	Sled	Honeydew	Rocket	Onion	Mittens
16	Clock	Horse	Pomegranate	Poison	Potato	Hat
17	Picture	Blimp	Date	Scissors	Yam	Apron
18	Closet	Skates	Coconut	Words	Mushroom	Purse
19	Vase	Wheelbarrow	Tomato	Foot	Pumpkin	Wristwatch
20	Telephone	Elevator	Olive	Screwdriver	Rice	Necklace

20 members for each of six superordinate categories, ranked from the most typical to the least typical, based on people's ratings.

Although the rank order may seem fairly obvious to us, it isn't obvious *why* the order exists. Why is a car a good example and an elevator a poor example of a vehicle? Both can transport people and materials. Rosch and Mervis (1975) hypothesized that good members will share many attributes with other members of the category and few attributes with members of other categories. Notice that Rosch is applying the same hypothesis she used to compare superordinate, basic, and subordinate categories to compare the typicality of members within a category.

Rosch and Mervis tested their hypothesis by asking people to list the attributes of each of the category members shown in Table 8.4. For example, for a bicycle, people might list that it has two wheels, pedals, and handlebars; you ride on it; and it doesn't use fuel. To test the hypothesis that the good examples of categories should share many attributes with other members of the category, it is necessary to calculate a measure of *family resemblance* for each item by considering how many other members share each attribute of the item. Let's take a specific example. Since a car has wheels as one of its attributes, we would count the vehicles that also have wheels. Since a car has a windshield, we would count the members that have a windshield. The numerical score for each attribute can vary from 1 to 20, depending on how many of the 20 members in Table 8.4 possess that attribute. The family resemblance score for each member is obtained by adding together the numerical scores of all attributes possessed by that member. If 14 members of the category have wheels and 11 have windshields, the family resemblance score would be 25 for a car if it had only those two attributes. The actual score, of course, is much higher, since we also have to add the numerical scores for all the other attributes listed for a car. The results revealed that good representatives of a category had high family resemblance scores. The correlations between the two variables were between .84 (for vegetable) and .94 (for weapon) for the six superordinate categories listed in Table 8.4.

Another way of viewing these results is to compare how many attributes are shared by the five most typical and five least typical examples in each category. The five most typical vehicles are car, truck, bus, motorcycle, and train. The five share many attributes, since they possess many common parts—the subjects in the experiment were able to identify 36 attributes that belonged to all five members. The five least typical examples are horse, blimp, skates, wheelbarrow, and elevator—the subjects identified only two attributes that belong to all five of the least typical members (perhaps that they carry people and move). The results were similar for the other five superordinate categories.

The fact that typical members of categories tend to share attributes with other members is also true for basic-level categories. You may have noticed that the examples of the superordinate categories shown in Table 8.4 are basic-level categories. Rosch and Mervis (1975) selected six of these examples (car, truck, airplane, chair, table, lamp) to test the same hypothesis—that the most typical members of basic-level categories should share more attributes with other members than the least typical members. For each of the six categories the experimenters selected 15 pictures, varying from good to poor examples. Rosch and Mervis then asked groups of under-graduates to rate how well each picture represented their idea of the category. As was found for the members of superordinate categories, there was a high correlation between the typicality of a member and the number of shared attributes.

Although family resemblance scores are useful for predicting the typicality of members in common taxonomic categories like those listed in Table 8.4, they are not useful in predicting typicality for goal-derived categories (Barsalou, 1985). Goal-derived categories consist of examples that satisfy a goal such as "make people happy when you give a birthday present." According to subjects' ratings, good examples of birthday presents include clothing, party, jewelry, dinner, watch, cake, and card. Notice that these examples are dissimilar to one another and do not share many attributes. Barsalou calculated family resemblance scores for members of goal-derived categories and found that family resemblance scores did not predict the typicality of the examples.

The reason is that members of goal-derived categories are selected on the basis of some underlying principle, rather than on the basis of shared attributes (Murphy & Medin, 1985). Thus, when we select weekend activities, we consider events that we enjoy; when we select things we would take from our home during a fire, we consider things that are valuable and irreplaceable, such as children and important papers. Although similarity of attributes determines how we form many categories and judge the typicality of category members, Murphy and Medin (1985) argue that we will need to learn more about underlying principles in order to have a more complete understanding of categorization.

Person Perception

The structure of natural categories, such as hierarchical organization and typicality, is also relevant for how we classify people (Cantor & Mischel, 1979). An example of a superordinate category might be people who have a strong commitment to a particular belief or cause. This category can be subdivided into religious devotees and social activists. Religious devotees can be further classified according to their particular religions, and social activists can be classified according to their particular causes. Cantor and Mischel's work parallels the work of Rosch by examining such issues as the number of shared attributes at different levels in the person hierarchy.

Typicality differences also apply to person perception, as has been recognized in current views about psychiatric diagnosis. Examples of diagnostic categories include functional psychosis, paranoid schizophrenia, and manic-depressive disorder. Attributes associated with each of these categories are used in diagnosis. For example, attributes that characterize paranoid schizophrenia include delusions of persecution, hostility, suspicion, associative disturbance, delusions of grandeur, hallucinations, autism, affective disturbance, projection, and rigidity in coping with stress. Differences in typicality occur because more typical patients have most of the attributes associated with a particular diagnostic category, whereas less typical patients have only some of those attributes (Cantor, Smith, French, & Mezzich, 1980).

The diagnostic manual of the American Psychiatric Association distinguishes among different categories by listing a large number of features, some of which appear in more than one category (Cantor et al., 1980). This approach to classification has several implications. In contrast to the approach in which each category is defined by several unique features, the recommended approach allows treatment of the patient to take into account the overlap in symptoms across disorders. It also encourages clinicians to expect diversity among patients who have the same diagnosis and to react appropriately to individual differences.

The procedures people use to classify objects or other people is a pervasive topic in cognitive psychology. The young child who is trying to decide whether an animal is a dog or a cat and a trained clinician who is trying to decide whether a patient is a paranoid schizophrenic or a chronic undifferentiated schizophrenic are both faced with categorization problems. In the next section we will examine different models of how people make these decisions. We will first consider perceptual patterns such as schematic faces and will later consider person perception in which the attributes are more abstract (educational level, marital status).

Categorizing Novel Patterns

At the beginning of this chapter we learned that one advantage of categories is that they enable us to recognize novel objects. A young child who encounters a new dog for the first time can use previous knowledge of dogs to recognize the new dog. Lacking this ability to classify novel objects, the child would have to be told the identity of every new object.

People are quite good at making perceptual classifications, and psychologists are naturally interested in how they do it. The characteristics of natural categories may provide a clue. One characteristic is that some category members are more prototypical, or better representatives, of the category than other members. People might therefore create a pattern, or prototype, that they feel is a very good representative of the category and use it to classify other patterns. A model based on this strategy is called a *prototype model.* Another characteristic of category members is that they share features, or attributes. People might therefore classify a novel pattern by determining how many of its feature values match the feature values of category patterns. A model based on this strategy is called a *feature frequency model.*

The two models can be illustrated by referring to the examples in Figure 8.4, taken from one of my experiments (Reed, 1972). If you were a subject in this experiment, I would first tell you that the upper row of faces represents one category, and the bottom row represents another category. I would then ask you to study the two categories because you would have to classify novel faces as members of one of the two categories. Students in my experiments classified from 20 to 25 novel faces (faces that didn't match any of the faces shown in Figure 8.4). Figure 8.5 shows three novel faces.

The feature frequency model proposes that people match the feature values of the novel pattern to the feature values of the patterns in the two categories. For example, the four features of each novel face (forehead, eyes, nose, and mouth) would be compared with the features of the five faces in each category. The novel pattern is then classified into the category that results in the most feature matches.

The prototype model proposes that people create a pattern that best represents each category. This prototype is usually a pattern that is the average of all the other patterns in the category. The prototype for either row of faces in Figure 8.4 is the pattern that is created by finding the average feature values of the five patterns in that category. It has the average forehead height, average eye separation, average nose length, and average mouth height. The middle pattern in Figure 8.5 is the prototype for the top row of faces, and the right pattern is the prototype for the bottom row of faces. We will now review evidence that supports each of these two models, beginning with the prototype model.

The Prototype Model

The prototype model proposes that the perceiver creates a prototype to represent each category and classifies a novel pattern by comparing it with the category prototypes, finding which prototype it most closely resembles, and selecting that category. For example, if the novel pattern is more similar to the Category 1 prototype than to the prototype for any other category, it will be classified into Category 1.

The prototype rule has the advantage that it doesn't require many comparisons in order to classify a pattern. Instead of comparing a novel pattern with every pattern

Figure 8.4 Example of a perceptual categorization task. The upper five faces represent Category 1, and the lower five faces represent Category 2.

Figure 8.5   Examples of novel faces for Figure 8.4. The middle face is the Category 1 prototype, and the right face is the Category 2 prototype.

in the category, a person has to compare a novel pattern with only a single pattern in each category—the pattern that is the best representative of that category. As we encounter more patterns in a category, it would become harder to compare a novel pattern with all of them. The prototype strategy is therefore an economical strategy because only a single comparison is required for each category regardless of how many patterns are in it.

Initial support for the use of a prototype strategy in classifying patterns came from a study by Posner and Keele (1968). The investigators created four prototype patterns—a triangle, the letters M and F, and a random pattern. Each prototype was made up of nine dots and could be distorted by varying the dots. Figure 8.6 shows different amounts of distortion for one of the prototypes. The numbers show how much the dots were allowed to vary, larger numbers implying greater distortions. Posner and Keele constructed distortions of each prototype at each of three levels of variability: low variability (level 1), moderate variability (level 5), and high variability (level 7.7). Undergraduates at the University of Oregon learned a list of 12 patterns, 3 from each prototype (triangle, M, F, and random). Group 1 subjects learned to classify three low-variability distortions of each prototype, and Group 5 subjects learned to classify three moderate-variability distortions of each prototype. You will notice in Figure 8.6 that the prototype is fairly obvious for level 1 distortions but is not so obvious for level 5 distortions. Group 1 subjects should therefore have a much better idea than Group 5 subjects of what the prototype looks like.

After the undergraduates could correctly classify all 12 patterns into the four categories, they were asked to classify high-variability patterns they had never seen before. The crucial comparison in this experiment is whether Group 1 subjects or Group 5 subjects would be better in classifying the novel patterns. Group 1 subjects should have a better idea of what the prototype looked like, but Group 5 subjects should have a better idea of how patterns could vary within a category, since they had trained on more variable patterns. It turned out that Group 5 subjects were significantly better than Group 1 subjects in classifying the highly distorted, novel patterns. In other words, subjects were more able to recognize highly distorted patterns when they had trained on moderately distorted patterns than when they had trained on slightly distorted patterns. The implication is that making the prototype very obvious by using low-distortion patterns is not sufficient when people have to

[Handwritten margin notes:]

2 groups. 4 classes △, M, F, other = 9 dots

#1 training level 1 distortion those on level 5 distortion

#2's did better at guessing level 7.7 distortions

— suggests they learned about the variabilities of classes better

— they could also do level 1 distortion the same as group 1

— suggest they also formed prototypes.

Distortion level

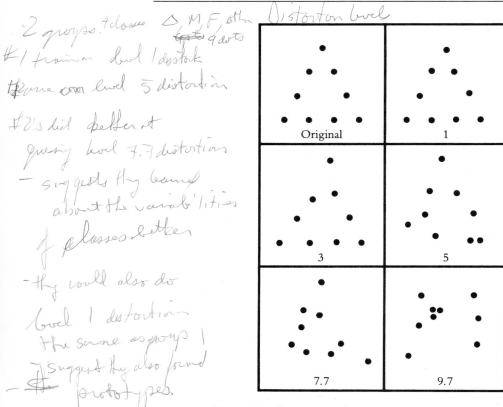

Figure 8.6 Distortions of a prototype (original) pattern at different levels of variability

classify highly distorted patterns. It is also necessary to learn how patterns can vary within a category.

Although the superiority of the Group 5 subjects suggested that learning about category variability may be more important than learning the category prototypes, Posner and Keele also obtained results that supported the use of a prototype strategy. First, they found that ability to correctly classify a novel pattern depended on the degree of similarity between the novel pattern and the category prototype. The more similar a novel pattern was to one of the category prototypes, the easier it was to classify correctly. This result would be expected if people had created a prototype to represent each category. Second, undergraduates who had trained on the moderately distorted patterns could later classify the category prototypes as well as they could classify the patterns they studied during the training session. Remember that they had not seen the prototypes previously because all the training patterns were distortions of the prototype. This finding suggests that even Group 5 subjects could create a prototype from the training patterns.

The results of this study suggested that people could create prototypes to represent categories and use them to classify novel patterns. However, there was also evidence that people learned more than simply the category prototypes, since the variability of the patterns within a category also influenced their performance on classifying novel patterns. Posner and Keele's findings were an important contribution to the study of how people classify patterns. Subsequent research by other investigators has focused largely on directly comparing the prototype model with other categorization models.

Comparing Alternative Models

The results obtained by Posner and Keele (1968) were certainly consistent with a prototype model, but how would a prototype model compare with alternative models? I became interested in this question as a graduate student and decided to devote my dissertation to it. It seemed to me that people classify a pattern into a category because that pattern is similar to other patterns in the category. One method of measuring similarity is simply to show people pairs of patterns and ask them to rate the similarity of the two patterns in each pair. The use of similarity to categorize patterns can be illustrated by considering a simple classification rule called the *nearest-neighbor rule.* The nearest-neighbor rule states that a person should classify a novel pattern by comparing it with all the patterns in each category in order to find the single category pattern that is most similar to the novel pattern. The novel pattern is then classified into the category that produces the best match. The problem with the nearest-neighbor rule is that it requires that a person compare the test pattern with all the category patterns but uses only a single pattern (the one most similar to the test pattern) as the basis for decision. If the most similar pattern is not very representative of its category, the decision could easily be wrong. For example, a young child who had a Pekingese dog as a pet might classify a long-haired cat as a dog because the cat looks more like the Pekingese than like other cats. The error would occur because, although a Pekingese is a dog, it is not a very good representative of the category.

A better rule, called the *average distance rule,* states that a person should compare the novel pattern with all the patterns in each category in order to determine the average similarity between the novel pattern and the patterns in each category. If the average similarity is greater for Category 1 patterns, Category 1 should be selected; otherwise Category 2 should be selected. The average distance rule has the advantage over the nearest-neighbor rule that it uses all category patterns as the basis for the decision instead of only one pattern. It has the disadvantage that a person must compute the average similarity in addition to comparing the novel pattern to all category patterns.

Both these disadvantages are eliminated by the *prototype rule.* If a person can create a prototype to represent each category, a novel pattern has to be compared only with this single pattern. According to the prototype rule, a person should select Category 1 whenever a novel pattern is more similar to the Category 1 prototype and Category 2 whenever a novel pattern is more similar to the Category 2 prototype.

add up number of objects in a class that have the same feature for

– do for all features

– highest class wins

← heavy computational

The final model we will consider is different from the first three in that it uses features in making predictions. The *feature frequency rule* is concerned with matching features rather than measuring the similarity between patterns. It looks at the features on the novel pattern and compares how many times they exactly match features of the category patterns. Consider the left pattern shown in Figure 8.5. It has a large forehead, closely spaced eyes, a short nose, and a high mouth. Inspection of the two categories in Figure 8.4 reveals that four faces in Category 1 have a large forehead, one has closely spaced eyes, and one has a high mouth. Therefore, the total number of feature matches with the novel face is six. By contrast, four faces in Category 2 have closely spaced eyes, three have short noses, and two have high mouths. Since the number of matches is higher for Category 2, the pattern should be classified into Category 2, according to the feature frequency rule.

You may have noticed that each of the four models—nearest neighbor, average distance, prototype, and feature frequency—states how a pattern should be classified. Since the models use different information, they sometimes differ in their selection of categories. Therefore, the models could be used to make predictions about how people would classify the patterns. If the prototype model, for example, were more successful than the other models in predicting how people classified novel patterns, this would imply that they used a prototype strategy. In fact, the results of my studies did support the prototype model.

The results do not prove that everyone used the prototype strategy, but they suggest that it was the predominant strategy used. This suggestion was confirmed by asking people which strategy of the four listed in Table 8.5 they had used. The majority selected the prototype strategy, and very few selected the two strategies that required comparing the novel patterns (projected faces) with all the category patterns. These particular results are from an experiment in which UCLA undergraduates had to classify novel patterns after learning the two categories shown in Figure 8.4. Comparing a novel pattern with all the category patterns should be particularly difficult when the category patterns are stored in memory rather than physically present. However, the data supported the prototype model even when all the patterns were simultaneously present, as they are in Figure 8.4 (Reed, 1972).

One qualification of these results is necessary before we consider other research. The best-predicting model was a prototype model in which the dimensions were differentially weighted, or emphasized, to account for the fact that some dimensions are more useful than others in distinguishing between categories. For the two categories shown in Figure 8.4, the weights calculated to reflect the usefulness of the dimensions were .46 for forehead (eye height), .24 for eye separation, .24 for nose length, and .06 for mouth height. The weights indicate that the forehead is a good dimension for distinguishing between the two categories and the mouth is a poor dimension. The results suggest that the most popular strategy was to compare the similarity of the novel pattern to the two category prototypes but to emphasize some dimensions more than others when making the comparison. The finding that people emphasized some dimensions more than others is consistent with our discussion of

Table 8.5   Percentage of subjects who reported using each classification strategy after learning the category patterns

Strategy	Percentage
1. **Prototype**	
I formed an abstract image of what a face in Category 1 should look like and an abstract image of what a face in Category 2 should look like. I then compared the projected face with the two abstract images and chose the category that gave the closest match.	58
2. **Nearest neighbor**	
I compared the projected face with all the faces in the two categories, looking for a single face that best matched the projected face. I then chose the category in which that face appeared.	10
3. **Feature frequency**	
I looked at each feature on the projected face and compared how many times it exactly matched a feature in each of the two categories. I then chose the category that gave the highest number of matches.	28
4. **Average distance**	
I compared the projected face with each of the five faces in Category 1 and with each of the five faces in Category 2. I then chose the category in which the faces were more like the projected face, basing my decision on all faces in the two categories.	4

pattern recognition (Chapter 2), where we saw that difficulty in discriminating pairs of letters could be analyzed in terms of the relative importance of feature dimensions.

The Feature Frequency Model

Although the prototype model was much more successful than the feature frequency model in predicting how people would classify schematic faces (Reed, 1972), there are situations in which a feature frequency model is more appropriate. Schematic faces consist of features that vary along continuous dimensions such as eye separation or mouth height, so it is possible to create an average pattern, or prototype, to represent the category. Not all items consist of features that vary along a continuous dimension, however. Consider the following task, designed by Hayes-Roth and Hayes-Roth (1977).

The task was to classify people as belonging to Club 1, Club 2, or neither club. The variation of three features affected the classification: age, education, and marital status. Each feature had one of four values. The age of a person was 30, 40, 50, or 60; the educational level was junior high, high school, trade school, or college; and the marital status was single, married, divorced, or widowed. People would have considerable difficulty creating an average person to represent each of the two clubs. It would be easy to compute the average age, but computing an average for education or marital status is more problematic. We might translate educational level into years of education, but this would blur the distinction between trade school and college. Forming an average marital status is even more difficult.

The point of this example is simply that the kind of stimuli being classified places constraints on which strategies are the easiest to use. Hayes-Roth and Hayes-Roth found that a version of the feature frequency model was a good predictor of how students would classify people into clubs. The most successful model compared combinations of features in addition to individual features. For example, if a person were 30 years old and divorced, the model would examine how many people in each club were *both* 30 and divorced in addition to matching the two individual features. Neumann (1974) also tested a feature frequency model that matched both individual features and combinations of features. Once again, the model was successful in predicting how people would classify patterns that did not consist of continuous dimensions. The only problem with feature frequency models is that they may require a great number of comparisons if they match combinations of features in addition to the individual features (see Reitman & Bower, 1973).

Medin and Schaffer (1978) avoided this problem by proposing a model in which feature combinations are important but are not directly stored as frequency counts. According to their model, people store examples of category patterns in memory and classify new patterns by comparing them with retrieved examples. The greater the similarity of the new pattern to an example stored in memory, the greater the probability that the example will be retrieved. But unlike the nearest-neighbor and average distance models, Medin and Schaffer's model uses combinations of features to measure similarity. In a test of how subjects would use symptoms to diagnose fictitious diseases, Medin and his colleagues found that subjects' decisions were influenced by feature combinations (Medin, Altom, Edelson, & Freko, 1982).

Our current knowledge about categorization models suggests that the success of a model in predicting classifications depends on the features of the items to be classified. When the stimuli consisted of dot patterns or schematic faces that had continuous dimensions, people used a prototype strategy (Posner & Keele, 1968; Reed, 1972). The possibility that the prototype could have been retained as a visual image might also have encouraged the construction of a prototype. When the items did not have continuous dimensions, variations of the feature frequency model were successful in predicting classifications (Neumann, 1974; Hayes-Roth & Hayes-Roth, 1977; Medin et al., 1982). Since items in the real world possess many kinds of features, it is fortunate that we have some flexibility in our classification strategies.

Box 8.1 shows how both feature frequencies and category averages were used to predict the composite Miss America. The average values of previous winners were used to determine height, weight, and measurements. Other data—such as the fact that winners typically have green eyes, major in communications, and sing classical music—were determined by how frequently previous winners possessed these particular characteristics. By using a combination of category averages and feature frequencies, a statistical analyst successfully predicted the winner of the pageant.

Box 8.1   Computer didn't miss in selecting Miss Mississippi
SUN-SENTINEL WIRE SERVICES

SEATTLE—A retired statistics professor said Sunday he never doubted Susan Akin of Mississippi would walk down the runway as Miss America.

"No one in all my eight years of forecasting Miss America has ever come so close as to the composite Miss America," George Miller said. "She deviated the least."

Akins' only possible drawbacks to winning the crown were her blue eyes, which over the years have been less popular than green or brown, said Miller, who taught statistics and forecasting at Northern Illinois University before moving to the Northwest where last year he taught at Seattle University.

Miller, 62, has correctly picked the winner ahead of the judges four times out of seven—beginning with the 1979 pageant when he chose another Miss Mississippi. He also accurately forecast the 1980 and 1983 winners.

Miller doesn't compute hair color or the contestants' overall appearance into his statistical study. What he uses are facts and figures that can be correlated—such as talent, weight, height, education level and major, and physical measurements.

"I don't consider hair color because one-third of the contestants are blonds and one-third of the winners over the years have been blond," he said. "And I don't look at their pictures because a photographer can pose them or doctor the photos."

Miller said the "ideal Miss America" would be 5 feet 7 inches tall, weigh 115 pounds, have measurements of 35-23-35, be 21 years old, have green eyes, be a college junior majoring in communications, and sing classical music.

From the *Sun-Sentinel*, Fort Lauderdale, September 16, 1985.

Summary

One way we organize knowledge is through categories and hierarchies made up of categories. Categories reduce the complexity of the environment and the need for constant learning and enable us to recognize objects, respond appropriately, and order and relate classes of events.

The concept identification paradigm is one approach to the study of categorization. People try to learn a conceptual rule by receiving feedback on positive and negative instances of the concept. Concepts that are defined by logical rules are easiest to learn for a conjunctive rule, followed by the disjunctive, conditional, and biconditional rules. The same order of difficulty occurs when people are told the rule and have to identify the relevant attributes.

Real-world, or natural, categories generally cannot be distinguished by a simple rule. Frequently they are hierarchically organized—for example, double-knit pants are included in the category *pants,* and pants are included in the category *clothes.* Rosch has argued that most classifications are made at the intermediate, or basic level—the most general level at which a prototype can be constructed and the level at which categories are most differentiated. The members of natural categories vary in how well they represent the category. Oranges and apples are considered good examples of fruit, whereas coconuts and olives are considered poor examples. The attributes of good members are shared with other members of the category and are not shared by members of alternative categories. The concepts of hierarchical organization and category typicality also apply to person perception.

The two most popular theories of classifying novel patterns are the prototype model and the feature frequency model. The prototype model proposed that people create patterns that best represent the categories and then classify novel patterns by comparing them with the category prototypes. The prototype is usually the central tendency of the category, formed by calculating the average of all the patterns in the category. Prototype theories have been most successful in predicting how people will classify perceptual patterns consisting of feature values that vary continuously along a dimension. By contrast, the feature frequency model proposes that people classify patterns by comparing how frequently their feature values match the feature values of the category patterns and then selecting the category that results in the greatest number of feature matches. Predictions are often improved by considering feature combinations. The feature frequency theory has been most successful in predicting how people classify patterns consisting of feature values that do not vary continuously along a dimension.

Recommended Reading

Medin and Smith (1984) provide a recent overview of the literature on categorization, supplementing an earlier review by Mervis and Rosch (1981). Taylor and Crocker (1981) discuss the role of categorization in social information processing. Martin and Caramazza (1980) investigated whether subjects would use logical rules or similarity relations to classify schematic faces. Kemler Nelson (1984) found that the incidental learning of categories favors learning based on overall similarity, whereas intentional learning favors the learning of criterial attributes. Some limitations of similarity-based models are discussed by Murphy and Medin (1985). Homa (1984) also reviews categorization models and discusses how variables such as category size, distortion, and feedback influence classification. Strauss (1979) studied prototype abstraction in infants and adults to determine whether the prototype or the feature frequency theory could best account for the findings. Although both theories seek to explain how people abstract information, some investigators (Brooks, 1978; Jacoby & Brooks, 1984) have argued that people use specific examples rather than abstracted information.

9

Semantic Organization

A scientist must organize. One makes a science with facts in the same way that one makes a house with stones; but an accumulation of facts is no more a science than a pile of stones is a house.

HENRI POINCARÉ

The need to organize knowledge is universal—it applies as much to the arts and humanities as to the sciences. Imagine that you wrote every fact you knew on a separate card and someone mixed all the cards and put them in a gigantic pile. Now imagine that someone asked you in which city the Declaration of Independence was signed and you had to retrieve the right card in order to answer the question. How would you find the card? Even worse, what if you had to write an essay on the Declaration of Independence? Since all the cards are mixed up, finding one card would provide no clues about the location of other cards on the same topic.

In order to retrieve related information from LTM, we must be able to organize our memory. Much of this organization is semantic—that is, it is based on the meaning of the information. Ericsson (1985) has argued that people who have exceptional memories are not genetically endowed with a superior memory. Rather, they have acquired very efficient encoding and retrieval skills through extensive practice. A particularly effective way to organize information is to form hierarchies. The first section of this chapter illustrates how hierarchical organization facilitates recall and includes an example of how a person's memory span can be dramatically increased through extensive practice (Chase & Ericsson, 1979).

A popular procedure for studying the organization of semantic memory is to ask people to respond *true* or *false* to statements such as *A robin is a bird* or *A canary is a building.* In order to answer the question *Is a robin a bird?* we have to consider the meaning of both *robin* and *bird.* The time needed to respond provides psychologists with a clue about the organization of semantic information in LTM. The second section of this chapter describes how psychologists have followed this approach to construct models of semantic memory. Two major classes of models are used. One model assumes that people compare the features of two categories to determine their relationship. For example, we could decide whether a robin is a bird by determining whether a robin possesses the features of a bird. This model is somewhat similar to the categorization models discussed in the previous chapter. The other model assumes that the relation between two categories is stored directly in memory in a semantic network, which consists of concepts joined to other concepts by links that specify the relation between them.

The third section illustrates how semantic networks can be applied to a variety of tasks. A key assumption here is the idea of *spreading activation*. Spreading activation means that the activation of a concept can lead to the activation of related concepts as the activation spreads along the paths of the network. This is a very general assumption that allows us to apply semantic network models to many tasks. Since semantic network models might possibly provide a general theory, we will consider their strengths and limitations carefully.

Hierarchical Organization

We have seen examples in the previous chapter of how some information is hierarchically organized and how a hierarchical organization can influence our performance on cognitive tasks such as classifying visual patterns. Hierarchical organization can also influence performance by facilitating the recall of semantic information.

Recall of Hierarchical Information

One advantage of a well-organized memory is that it helps us to retrieve information in a systematic way. I began this chapter by asking you to imagine that you had to retrieve information by searching a gigantic pile of cards. If the information on the cards were organized in some systematic way, this would be a manageable task. If the information were not systematically organized, the task would be very difficult and your level of achievement would not be very impressive.

An experimental analogue of this task was created to study the effects of hierarchical organization on recall (Bower, Clark, Winzenz, & Lesgold, 1969). The material consisted of conceptual hierarchies of words like the one shown in Figure 9.1. Participants in the experiment saw four different hierarchies, each containing 28 words. One group of subjects, in the "organized" condition, studied the four hierarchies for approximately one minute each. They then tried to recall all 112 words in whatever order they wished. The study and recall trial was repeated three more times. The upper curve in Figure 9.2 shows how well this group performed: they recalled 73 words after the first study trial and all 112 words after three study trials.

Level

1

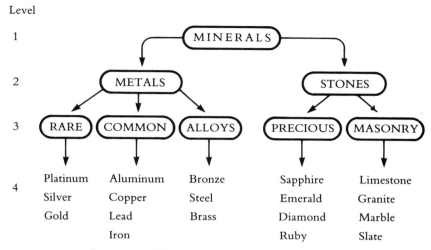

Figure 9.1   Hierarchical organization of minerals

Another group of subjects, in the "random" condition, saw the same 112 words inserted randomly in the four hierarchies. For example, if the four hierarchies consisted of plants, instruments, body parts, and minerals, each set of 28 words would contain words from all four hierarchies inserted randomly into a spatial tree like the one shown in Figure 9.1. The high level of performance of subjects in the organized condition is particularly impressive when compared with performance in the random condition. After four study trials the random group was still recalling fewer words than the organized group recalled on the very first trial (see Figure 9.2).

Figure 9.2   Average number of words recalled by subjects in the "organized" and "random" conditions

We should note at this point that the effects of organization are not limited to hierarchical organization. In another experiment Bower presented people with associated words linked together. For example, the words *bread, mouse,* and *yellow* were linked to *cheese;* the words *cat* and *trap* were linked to *mouse;* and *sun* and *butterfly* were linked to *yellow.* When the associated words were linked together, people recalled many more words than when the same words were randomly linked together (for example, when *cat* and *bread* were linked to *yellow*). Semantic organization of the material improved recall, even though the organization did not consist of a hierarchy. The difference between the organized and random conditions was more striking for hierarchical organization, however, suggesting that hierarchical organization is particularly effective.

Category Size

Figure 9.1 shows that each category in the hierarchy is divided into several smaller categories. The division of a category into subcategories raises the question of how big the groups should be. The advantage of grouping items might be reduced if the groups were too small. However, information might be difficult to remember or retrieve if the groups were too large.

In Chapter 4 we learned that the capacity of STM can be increased by forming chunks consisting of several items stored as a group in LTM. The grouping of chess pieces (Chase & Simon, 1973) is an example of how chunking improves recall in an STM task—the average size of a chunk for an expert chess player was 2.5 pieces. We know from both research (Charness, 1976) and demonstrations (Box 9.1) that chess experts also have a very good LTM for chess positions. In order for such a good LTM to exist, it is likely that the smaller chunks are part of a very large hierarchy of board positions.

Psychologists have used several techniques to study how people group information. The estimated size of the groups depends on the experimental procedure, but it generally ranges from two to five items. Chase and Ericsson (1979) demonstrated how groupings can improve recall by testing a single subject over a one-year period. The subject began with a typical digit span of seven digits. After one year of practice he could recall a string of 70 digits. Pauses in his recall indicated that he organized the digits into groups of three or four and never formed groups larger than five digits. Since the subject was a long-distance runner, he initially tried to encode many of the groups as running times. For instance, he encoded 3492 as 3.492, a near world-record time for running a mile. He also showed evidence of using hierarchical organization: he combined digits into larger groups that usually consisted of three smaller groups. After recalling the first three groups of four digits each, he would pause longer before recalling the next three groups of four digits each. One interesting finding is that the subject's ability to recall groups of digits didn't generalize to letters. When he was tested on recalling letters, his memory span immediately fell back to about six consonants.

Box 9.1   At age 75, chess master is still a blindfolded whiz

Chess master George Koltanowski set a world's record Saturday in San Francisco—at age 75—by playing and beating four opponents at once without looking at the boards.

Koltanowski, the chess editor of The Chronicle, thus became the oldest player to hold what chess players call a blindfold simultaneous exhibition.

His four opponents had full use of chessmen and boards as they called their moves out in turn to the master, who sat in a corner of his apartment with his eyes shut and his arm propped on a television.

The first player was checkmated in 13 moves and the other three resigned shortly thereafter. Mike Duncan of San Mateo lasted 26 moves before moving his rook to the wrong square and falling into a trap.

"I knew I'd lose," said Duncan, "but it's fascinating to find out just when the blow is going to come."

Koltanowski said he was nervous before the exhibition began, but, as his opponents began to slip up, he sat back, cracked an occasional joke and nibbled cookies.

"It was like the good old days," said the master, who, in 1937, took on 34 opponents in a simultaneous blindfold exhibition in Scotland, winning 24 games and drawing ten.

"I'm back on the warpath," he added. "Next month I'm going to play six at once."

His wife, Leah, who witnessed the exhibition but who does not know how to play chess, smiled when asked if Koltanowski remembers such things as bringing home items from the market.

"George remembers what he wants to remember," she said.

From the *San Francisco Chronicle*, February 26, 1979. © *San Francisco Chronicle*, 1979. Reprinted by permission.

Broadbent (1975) also studied pauses in recall to determine how people store categorized information in LTM. He asked people to name television programs, the countries of Europe, the seven dwarfs, and the colors of the rainbow. On the basis of pauses in their recall and other experimental findings, he argued that people usually form groups consisting of about three items. One of the experiments he cited was a study by Wickelgren (1964) that investigated the size of rehearsal groups. Wickelgren asked people to rehearse a string of digits and instructed them on how to group the digits in the string. The instructions varied both the number and the size of the groups. Recall was best when the digits were divided into groups consisting of either three or four digits. Telephone numbers, of course, are grouped in this way, which presumably makes them easier to rehearse. And we use commas to divide long strings of digits into three-digit groups.

A good example of how small groups can form a very large hierarchy is the organization of information contained in a book or newspaper. Detterman and Ramig (1978) collected paragraphs from a wide variety of newspapers, novels, and upper-division textbooks. They found that the average number of sentences in a paragraph was about two for newspapers, three for novels, and five for textbooks. They then gave people examples of the sentences and asked them to divide each sentence into its major parts. The instructions did not specify the meaning of "major parts," nor did they suggest how many major parts should be in a sentence. People identified an average of 2.4 parts per sentence. They were then instructed to break the major parts into smaller parts if they could. They divided the major parts into an average of 3.6 smaller parts, each containing an average of 2.2 words. Each of the words contained an average of 2.3 syllables, and each syllable contained an average of 2.6 phonemes. The data illustrate how a paragraph can be partitioned into smaller and smaller categories, each consisting of two to four items.

The paragraph hierarchy contained a mixture of subjective and objective units. The objective units—sentences, words, syllables, and phonemes—are well defined and can be measured simply by counting how frequently they occur. The other two levels—the parts and subparts of sentences—were measured by asking people to break up a sentence into its parts. Of course, it is likely that objective grammatical units—noun phrases, verb phrases, and prepositional phrases—influenced the way people partitioned a sentence. We will encounter some of these units in the next chapter, on language, when we learn how the rules of a grammar can provide a hierarchical description of sentences.

Hierarchical organization could be extended even further if we had started with an entire book rather than a single paragraph. For example, I wrote this book on a hierarchical plan. The book is divided into three major parts on (1) information-processing stages, (2) the representation and organization of knowledge, and (3) cognitive skills. Each part contains four or five chapters, and each chapter contains three or four sections, which are divided into two to four subsections. I'm not certain whether this kind of organization is beneficial to readers, but it is consistent with experimental findings on hierarchical organization and category size. It also makes a very large hierarchy if we connect it to the paragraph hierarchy investigated by Detterman and Ramig.

Verification of Semantic Statements

In addition to influencing the amount of recall, hierarchical organization influences the time required to retrieve information from LTM. A popular procedure for studying the organization of semantic knowledge is to ask people to verify semantic statements. The experimenter might present a statement such as *A bird is an animal* and ask the subject to respond *true* or *false* as quickly as possible. The time it takes to respond to different kinds of statements provides some clues about the organization of semantic memory. As you might expect, hierarchical organization influences the time required to verify semantic statements.

Figure 9.3 shows a three-level hierarchy in which the most general category, *animal,* is divided into two subcategories—*bird* and *fish.* At the bottom of the hierarchy are specific instances of birds and fish, such as canary and shark. Hierarchical organization influences classification time in that people can generally verify that an instance is a member of a basic-level category faster than they can verify that it is a member of a superordinate category. For instance, they can more quickly determine that a canary is a bird than that a canary is an animal. People can also classify more typical instances faster than less typical instances. It is easier to verify that a canary is a bird than that an ostrich is a bird.

A number of theories have been proposed to account for these findings. The two most popular are the hierarchical network model of Collins and Quillian (1969, 1970) and the feature comparison model of Smith, Shoben, and Rips (1974). The distinction between the two models can be summarized briefly with the aid of the diagram in Figure 9.4. The *feature comparison model* assumes that instances are classified by comparing the features, or attributes, of the two nouns representing the member and the category. To verify that a robin is a bird, a person would compare the features of robin with the features of bird. In contrast, the *hierarchical network*

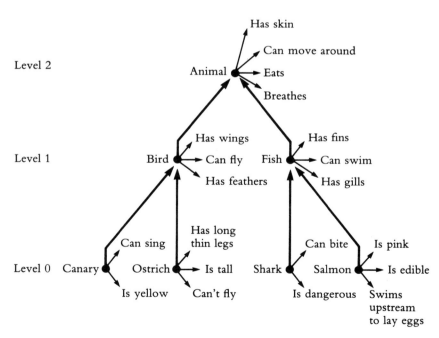

Figure 9.3   Example of a hierarchically organized memory structure

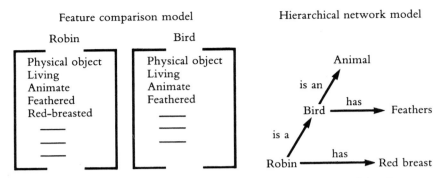

Figure 9.4   Distinction between the feature comparison model and the hierarchical network model

model assumes that category information is stored directly in memory by means of associations. The right half of Figure 9.4 shows that *robin* is associated with *bird* and *bird* is associated with *animal*. In order to make predictions, both theories require more specific assumptions. We will now examine the strengths and weaknesses of these assumptions.

The Hierarchical Network Model

Figure 9.3 shows how information is stored in the hierarchical network model. Each word in the network is stored with pointers (arrows) showing how it is related to other words in the network. By following the pointers, we know that ostrich and canary are examples of birds, and birds and fish are examples of animals. We also know that a canary, an ostrich, a shark, and a salmon are animals, because the pointers connect these instances with the superordinate category *animal*.

The pointers also show how features are stored at different levels in the hierarchy. Features that are true of all animals—such as eating and breathing—are stored at the highest level. Features that apply to basic-level categories—such as that birds have wings, can fly, and have feathers—are stored at an intermediate level. Properties stored at the lowest level are true for that particular member but not for all members of the category. It is at this level that we know that a canary is yellow and can sing.

One advantage of this kind of network is that it provides an economical way to store information because the information does not have to be repeated at each of the three levels. It isn't necessary to specify that eating and breathing are features of birds, fish, canaries, ostriches, sharks, and salmon, because the network tells us that all are examples of animals, which eat and breathe. This economy of storage comes at a cost, however: retrieval of the fact that a canary eats requires two inferences—first, that a canary is a bird and, second, that a bird is an animal. In other words, it is necessary to go to the appropriate level in the hierarchy before retrieving the features stored at that level.

Although the network model was originally developed as an efficient means of storing information in a computer, it provides a number of interesting predictions if we use it as a model of human memory. Collins and Quillian (1969), in fact, used the model for that purpose by making two primary assumptions: that it takes time to move from one level in the hierarchy to another and that additional time is required if it is necessary to retrieve the features stored at one of the levels.

Collins and Quillian tested the model by asking people to respond *true* or *false* as quickly as they could to sentences like *An elm is a plant* or *A spruce has branches*. The first sentence is an example of a question about set relations—it asks whether one category is a member of another. The second question is a question about properties—it asks about the features of a category member.

The average reaction times to six kinds of true sentences are shown in Figure 9.5. A specific example illustrates the different points on the graph. The three lower points—the response times to questions about set relations—support the prediction that it takes time to move between levels in the network. To verify that *A canary is a canary* requires no change in level; *A canary is a bird* requires a one-level change; and *A canary is an animal* requires a two-level change. The graph shows that response times depend on the number of changes.

The upper three points show that it takes longer to respond to property questions. This finding is consistent with the assumption that response time should increase if

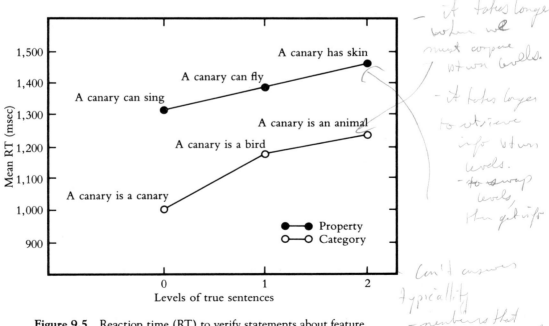

Figure 9.5   Reaction time (RT) to verify statements about feature attributes and category membership

it is necessary to retrieve the features stored at one of the levels in the hierarchy. Furthermore, the level in the network where the properties are stored influences response times. The network model proposes that information about singing is stored at the lowest level, information about flying is stored at the intermediate level, and information about skin is stored at the highest level. The data support this assumption and suggest that this is how property information is stored in human memory.

Another interesting prediction based on the network model concerns facilitating retrieval from memory (Collins & Quillian, 1970). Facilitation occurs when the retrieval of information is made easier because the previous question required retrieval of similar information. For example, it should be easier to verify a property of a canary if the previous question was also about a canary. The network model, however, allows us to make a more specific prediction. Collins and Quillian proposed that the degree of facilitation should depend on whether one follows the same path in the network to answer the two questions. This concept can be illustrated by considering whether it would be easier to verify that A canary is a bird after A canary can fly or after A canary can sing. The answer isn't intuitively obvious, but the network model predicts that A canary can fly should cause greater facilitation because the property fly is stored at the bird level and sing is stored at the canary level. The same path is followed only when both questions require retrieving information from the bird level. The data were quite supportive of the prediction that the extent of semantic facilitation should depend on using the same path as the previous question (Collins & Quillian, 1970).

The successful predictions of the reaction time data in Figure 9.5 and the predictions about semantic facilitation are impressive accomplishments of the network model. There are two findings, however, that the model does not account for without additional assumptions. The first is that it is possible to find instances in which verification time is not a function of levels in the hierarchy. For example, it takes longer to verify that a chimpanzee is a primate than that a chimpanzee is an animal. The network model should predict the opposite because primate, like bird and fish, is at a lower level in the hierarchy than animal. The second finding is that the network model does not account for the typicality effect—the fact that more typical members of categories are easier to classify than less typical ones. It is easier to verify that a canary is a bird than that an ostrich is a bird. However, since both are one level from bird, as is illustrated in Figure 9.3, the model does not predict differences in response time. The feature comparison model attempted to correct these deficiencies by offering an alternative formulation.

The Feature Comparison Model

The feature comparison model proposed by Smith, Shoben, and Rips (1974) seeks to account for classification times in somewhat the same way as the prototype model accounts for classifications. This model assumes that the meaning of words can be represented in memory by a list of features. The features can be used to define categories, but they vary in the extent to which they are associated with a category. Smith, Shoben, and Rips considered the most essential features to be *defining* features and the remainder to be *characteristic* features. Defining features are features that an entity must have in order to be a member of a category, whereas characteristic features are usually possessed by category members but are not necessary. The defining features for birds might include being alive and having feathers and wings; the characteristic features might include being able to fly and being within a certain size range. Since the defining features are more essential, they should play a more important role in how people make classifications.

The feature comparison model has two stages. The first stage compares all the features of two concepts to determine how similar one concept is to the other. For example, to determine whether a robin is a bird, we would compare the features of robin with the features of bird. If the comparison reveals that the two concepts are either very similar or very dissimilar, we can respond *true* or *false* immediately. The second stage is necessary when the degree of similarity is between the two extremes. The answer isn't obvious in this case, so the model proposes that we examine only the defining features to determine whether the example has the necessary features of the category. The distinction between the two stages corresponds to our experience that sometimes we make classifications very quickly on the basis of the close similarity between two concepts, and sometimes we make classifications more slowly after we evaluate the criteria for category membership.

Examples that are similar to the concept should usually be classified immediately without consideration of their defining features during the second stage. The probability that the second stage is necessary increases as the similarity between the category concept and the example decreases. The model therefore predicts that the more typical members of a category (such as robin, sparrow, bluejay) should be classified more rapidly than the less typical members (chicken, goose, duck) because evaluating the defining features during the second stage slows down the classification. Smith et al. (1974) found that people could, in fact, classify instances that are typical of the category faster than they could classify instances that are not typical of the category. The ability to account for the typicality effect is one advantage of the feature comparison model over the network model.

The other advantage of the feature comparison model is that, unlike the network model, it can account for the reversal of the category size effect. The *category size effect* refers to the fact that people are usually able to classify a member into a smaller category faster than into a larger category—for example, verifying that a collie is a dog more quickly than that a collie is an animal. The network model is consistent with the category size effect because the smaller category (*dog*) requires fewer inferences than the larger category (*animal*). Since the smaller category is a part of the larger category, it appears lower in the hierarchy and will therefore be reached sooner. There are cases, however, that violate the category size effect because the classification times are faster for the larger category. For example, people were able to verify more quickly that Scotch is a drink than that Scotch is a liquor, even though *drink* is a larger category than *liquor*.

The feature comparison model can account for violations of the category size effect because its predictions are based on similarity rather than category size. The reason it is usually easier to verify that an example belongs to a smaller category is that the similarity between the example and one's concept of the smaller category is greater than the similarity between the example and the larger category. However, there are exceptions to this rule. Sometimes—as Smith, Shoben, and Rips showed—there is a greater similarity between the example and a larger category. The feature comparison model predicts that in this case people should be able to classify into the larger category more quickly than into the smaller category. Experimental results support this prediction (Smith et al., 1974).

Although the feature comparison model accounts for both typicality and category size effects, the model has some weaknesses. Let's now listen to what the critics have to say about its limitations.

Limitations of the Feature Comparison Model

One of the problems with the feature comparison model, as one of its developers pointed out (Smith, 1978), is that it relies on ratings to make most of its predictions. It's not very surprising that if people rate an example as highly similar to their concept of a category, they will be fast to verify that it belongs to that category. The predictions about both typicality and category size reflect the degree of similarity between a member and its category. The predictions made by the feature comparison model are therefore rather weak predictions. Its principal asset is that the major alternative—the network model—does not make even these predictions unless it uses so many additional assumptions that it can predict almost anything.

A second criticism of the feature comparison model is its proposal that all our classifications require computations—we use the features of concepts to compute their degree of similarity. Computation is an essential part of the categorization models discussed in the previous chapter, where the emphasis was on classifying novel patterns. But once we have learned to associate examples with categories, is it still necessary to use features to compare the similarity of two concepts? Couldn't we use the associations among concepts, as suggested by the proponents of the network model (Collins & Loftus, 1975)? If we have learned that a robin is a bird, it would seem easier to use this information directly rather than to compute the similarity between robin and bird. What information is stored directly in memory and what is computed is a very important issue that is discussed by Smith (1978).

A third criticism of the feature comparison model is the argument against necessary, or defining, features (Collins & Loftus, 1975; Rosch & Mervis, 1975; McCloskey & Glucksberg, 1979). The feature comparison model avoids this criticism to some extent by proposing that features are more or less defining, and only the more defining features are evaluated during the second stage. This implies, however, that people can identify the more defining features of categories, and we have little direct support for this assumption. Rosch and Mervis's (1975) results, in fact, suggest the opposite—that the structure of categories is based not on defining features possessed by all members of the category but on a large number of features that are true of only some category members.

In order to avoid entirely the problem of defining features, McCloskey and Glucksberg (1979) modified the feature comparison model to consist of only a single stage. Their model proposes that decision time is determined by the number of features that have to be compared before the evidence is strong enough to make a classification. Each category is represented by features that include the values of typical members of that category. For example, the color of fruit might include the values *red, yellow, orange,* and *green,* and the height of a man might include the values *between 5 feet and 6½ feet.* The assumption that only the most typical values of a category are stored implies that some members of the category may have feature values that are not specified. Some men are taller than 6½ feet, and some fruits have a color different from those mentioned. The stored values represent the values of only the typical members.

Category membership is verified by comparing the feature values of an example with the feature values that represent the category. The comparison of each feature yields either positive or negative evidence that the example belongs in that category. The color of a banana, an orange, or an apple would yield positive evidence that these examples are fruit because their color matches one of the four representative colors of that category. McCloskey and Glucksberg propose that a person continues to compare the different features of an example until the proportion of positive evidence or negative evidence exceeds some criterion. Their model predicts that people will verify the more typical members of a category relatively quickly, since positive evidence accumulates at a faster rate for these members.

Semantic Network Models

The preceding discussion reflected both the strengths and the weaknesses of the hierarchical network model and the feature comparison model. Each provided an explanation for some aspects of the data but could not explain other aspects. We should remember that thus far we have emphasized only hierarchical relations, and there are other kinds of semantic relations. Even if we limit our study to only hierarchical relations, we would have to allow for the fact that a word is actually stored in many hierarchies. The word *salmon,* for example, is part of a *food* hierarchy and a *fishing* hierarchy in addition to being part of an *animal* hierarchy.

In order to represent a greater variety of semantic relations, psychologists have proposed more general semantic network models. We will look at two models that share some of the assumptions of the hierarchical network model but are not limited to specifying only hierarchical relations. The first is the spreading activation theory proposed by Collins and Loftus (1975). The model is particularly interesting because it is an attempt to correct some of the limitations of the hierarchical network model proposed by Collins and Quillian (1969). The second model, called ACT, was proposed by John Anderson (1976) in his book *Language, Memory, and Thought.*

ACT attempts to formulate a very general model that is capable of integrating many of the topics studied by cognitive psychologists.

A Spreading Activation Theory

The *spreading activation model* (Collins & Loftus, 1975) is representative of semantic network models in its emphasis on concepts joined together by links that show relationships. Figure 9.6 shows how a part of human memory can be represented in the network. The length of each link represents the degree of semantic relatedness between two concepts. Thus the concept *red* is closely related to other colors and less closely related to red objects. Notice that the model can also account for the typicality effect, because the links represent different degrees of semantic relatedness. The shorter links reveal that *car* and *bus* are more closely related to *vehicle* than is *ambulance* or *fire engine*.

The spreading activation model assumes that when a concept is processed, activation spreads out along the paths of a network, but its effectiveness is decreased as it travels outward. For example, presentation of the word *red* should strongly activate closely related concepts like *orange* and *fire* and should cause less activation

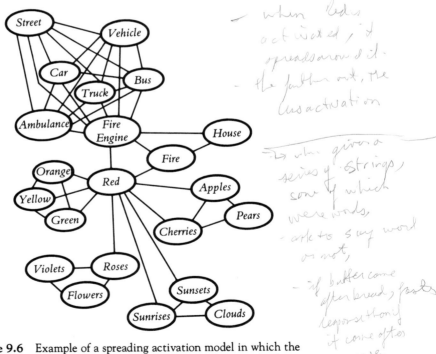

Figure 9.6   Example of a spreading activation model in which the length of each line (link) represents the degree of association between two concepts

of concepts like *sunsets* and *roses*. The model therefore predicts the typicality effect because more typical members will activate the superordinate category sooner than less typical members—for instance, *car* and *bus* will activate *vehicle* sooner than *fire engine* or *ambulance* will.

The idea of activation spreading throughout a semantic network of interconnected concepts provides a clear picture of the semantic relations among concepts. It is easy to imagine activation decreasing in strength as it travels outward. The model also assumes that activation decreases over time or intervening activity. This assumption places a constraint on the amount of activation that can occur, because the activation of a second concept will decrease the activation of the first concept.

Although the model provides a convenient metaphor, its success will depend on how well it can account for experimental results. One such result is the effect of *semantic priming*. Priming occurs when a decision about one concept makes it easier to decide about another concept. An example of priming can be found in the lexical decision task studied by Meyer and Schvaneveldt (1976), which required that people judge whether a string of letters formed a word. Some of the letters did (*BUTTER*), and some did not (*NART*). Each trial consisted of a pair of strings, and the second string was presented immediately after subjects made their decision about the first string. The most interesting results occurred when both strings were words. If the two words were semantically related, people were faster in verifying that the second string was a word than if the two words were unrelated. For example, people verified faster that the string *BUTTER* was a word when it was preceded by *BREAD* than when it was preceded by *NURSE*.

The spreading activation model can account for these results, because it proposes that the presentation of a word activates related words. *BUTTER* will be activated by *BREAD* but will not be activated by *NURSE*. The activation of the word makes it easier to identify, resulting in faster response times.

In addition to the direct representation of semantic relations in a network, the spreading activation model allows for the use of feature matching in verification of semantic statements. It therefore includes the assumptions of both the hierarchical network model and the feature comparison model. One way we can decide that a mallard is a bird is to find superordinate links between *mallard* and *duck* and between *duck* and *bird*. Another way is to find that there are common properties in our concept of *mallard* and our concept of *bird*. Collins and Loftus suggest that we consider the evidence obtained from both feature comparisons and superordinate links when we make a decision.

Thus the model has considerable flexibility, but it makes predictions with difficulty. Critics of the model (for instance, Smith, 1978; McCloskey & Glucksberg, 1979) have argued that, with so many assumptions, it is not surprising that the model accounts for many empirical findings. They find its main weaknesses to be both the number of assumptions it makes and its failure to make many clear-cut predictions. In fact, the model was developed primarily to show how its assumptions are consistent with existing data rather than to make interesting predictions. It remains to be seen whether psychologists can design experiments to seriously test the model.

Another possible limitation of the spreading activation model is that it does not account for the spontaneous recall of a word after an initial failure to recall it. We have all sometimes failed to recall a word and then later recalled it spontaneously. Perhaps the spontaneous recall was actually triggered by the spreading activation from another word, but my own experience is that I am usually unaware of any associations between the word and current stimuli. Box 9.2 describes several examples of recall failure and a suggested remedy. Although the suggestion may save us time by curtailing search, it does not solve the problem of why momentary failures of recall occur.

ACT

In spite of their limitations, semantic network models appeal to many people because they are sufficiently general to provide a common framework for many of the issues studied by cognitive psychologists. The generality of the network models is nicely illustrated by ACT. Anderson (1976) designed ACT to apply to a wide variety of cognitive tasks, ranging from scanning STM to making complex inferences. The basic assumptions of ACT are similar to those of the spreading activation model: knowledge is stored in a semantic network consisting of interconnected nodes, and activation can spread down network paths from active nodes to activate new nodes and paths. Although the basic assumptions of the two models are the same, Anderson applies ACT to many tasks not considered by Collins and Loftus (1975).

Many aspects of ACT are too technical to discuss in an introductory book, but we will consider how Anderson applied the model to predict how quickly people can retrieve stored knowledge. The stored knowledge in this case was information that people learned in a fact retrieval experiment. The purpose of asking them to learn information was to control experimentally the number of relations among the concepts. The experimental material consisted of 26 sentences of the form A [person] is in the [location] (see Table 9.1 for some examples). A particular individual and a particular location occurred in one, two, or three sentences; for example, a hippie occurred in three sentences, and a debutante occurred in one sentence. After the subjects had learned all the information in the sentences, they were given test sentences and instructed to respond true to test sentences that they had previously learned and false to any other sentences. Anderson was interested in how quickly people could respond true or false to each test sentence.

Table 9.1 shows examples of the test sentences, each preceded by a two-digit number. The first digit shows the number of times the person appeared in the study material, and the second digit shows the number of times the location appeared in the study material. Thus the sentence A hippie is in the park is marked 3–3 because both hippie and park appeared three times in the study material. Anderson found that reaction time increased as a function of the number of times a person or a location occurred in the study sentences. Subjects were relatively slow in verifying a sentence like A hippie is in the park because hippie and park both occurred three times.

Table 9.1 Sample sentences used in Anderson's (1976) fact retrieval study

Subject studies	True test probes
1. A hippie is in the park.	3–3 A hippie is in the park.
2. A hippie is in the church.	1–1 A lawyer is in the cave.
3. A hippie is in the bank.	1–2 A debutante is in the bank.
4. A captain is in the park.	
5. A captain is in the church.	
6. A debutante is in the bank.	
7. A fireman is in the park.	False test probes
.	3–1 A hippie is in the cave.
.	1–2 A lawyer is in the park.
.	1–1 A debutante is in the cave.
26. A lawyer is in the cave.	2–2 A captain is in the bank.
	.
	.
	.

[Handwritten margin notes: "Act — Spreading activation through a semantic network." "— given 26 sentence to learn." "— the more times place or person was used, the longer to answer the question" "this is because activation spreads along many paths, not just one."]

[Handwritten annotations within table: "# of trip place was used" and "# of times person was used."]

In contrast, they were relatively fast in verifying a sentence like *A lawyer is in the cave* because both *lawyer* and *cave* occurred only once in the study material.

Figure 9.7 shows how information about the sentences is represented by ACT. In order to verify *A hippie is in the park*, it is necessary to find a path in the network that joins *hippie* and *park*. Since the experiment measured response times, the theoretical question is how quickly the path can be found. Presentation of the test sentence *A hippie is in the park* causes the activation of both *hippie* and *park*. The time it takes to find the path that links *hippie* and *park* depends on (1) the rate at which activation spreads from the two concepts, (2) the length of the path joining the two concepts, and (3) the possible alternative paths the activation can take.

When a concept is activated, the rate of spread down the appropriate path (the links joining *hippie* and *park*) is determined by the strength of the appropriate link relative to the strength of the other links that join the concepts. The other links include both preexperimental links that were a part of the subject's semantic network before the experiment and experimental links learned in the experiment. The preexperimental links include various associations that a person has to concepts like *hippie* and *park*. In Anderson's predictions the preexperimental links do not vary. The parameter that does vary is the number of experimental links. Since the word *hippie* occurred three times in the study material, it is linked to three locations (*park*, *church*, and *bank*). The word *park* is linked to three persons (*hippie*, *captain*, and *fireman*). Increasing the number of experimental links increases the time to find an intersecting path joining two concepts because it slows the spread of activation along the appropriate path. The activation of *hippie* and *park* is divided among three experimental links, whereas the words *lawyer* and *cave* have only a single experimental link. ACT therefore predicts that verification time should increase with an increase in the number of experimental links to either the person or the location.

There are two other parameters in ACT that determine how quickly an intersecting path can be found between two concepts. Neither of the two parameters was

Box 9.2   Total recall? Forget it!
Goodman Ace

Listen. I'm going to share with you my discovery of the secret for a long and joyous life as you reach the later years. Briefly, all you have to do is what I have done: give up trying futilely to recall totally something that's on the tip of your brain—an elusive date or a happening or a quotation—when your memory is out to lunch.

After years of gradual self-destruction at this typewriter, desperately attempting to bring into focus a recollection without scurrying to lift a heavy dictionary or an encyclopedia, I've come to the medical conclusion that hours can be added to the life span by accepting my principle that total recall is for the birds.

In my case I accidentally happened upon a cartoon in *The New Yorker* some months ago. It showed a handsome, bemused young caveman, nattily attired in the latest bearskin, obviously on his way to woo his cavewoman, his fingers at his lips as if he were trying to recall some line he could hand her. The caption was "Roses are red, violets are blue, something, something, and so are you."

Now, quickly. If you are unable to supply that missing "something, something" without a peek at the end of this piece,* welcome aboard the Happy World of Non-recall. I say "happy" because after spending ten anguished minutes trying to verbalize that line, I decided to forget ever having stared at that cartoon.

As I settled back in my chair I was overcome by a warm, overwhelming, euphoric calm. In that lovely stupor, I began to realize that I had discovered the secret scientific formula for a carefree, tolerable life: ICR equals FI. Translated into lay language for your convenience, "If You Can't Recall It, Forget It." So, as have many of my fellow discoverers before me, I whispered, "Eureka."

However, before announcing this new panacea to the world or, more important, to the Food and Drug Administration, I decided, in the interest of saving myself a malpractice suit, to self-test it. Now, in the August years of my life, I can do no less than to give unstintingly to mankind what remains of myself.

It was that same afternoon of my discovery—or was it the following week?—that I sat at my typewriter composing a column for *SR* in which I was describing a man as being "as handsome as Cary Grant." But I couldn't recall Mr. Grant's first name. Ulysses S. first came to mind, then Lou Grant, the name of Mary Tyler Moore's TV boss. Also Lee Grant, one of my favorite actresses, and Grant Withers who sneaked in somehow or other.

But when the name of the governor of New York, Hugh Carey, flashed across my screen, and I found myself thinking, *Hugh Grant,* I realized that I was on my way to being caught up in another total-recall trap. I stopped cold turkey. The withdrawal pains, I admit, were severe. But I got hold of myself and settled for non-recall. And, very simply, I changed the line to read, "The man was as handsome as Paul Newman." Eureka again. And *voilà!*

* (Sugar is sweet.)

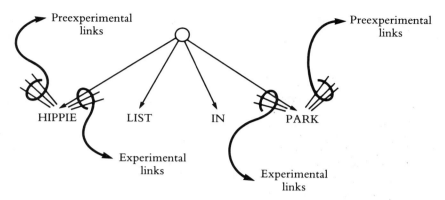

Figure 9.7 Representation of semantic information in ACT

varied in this experiment, but they are useful in predicting the results of other experiments. One parameter is the number of links that must be activated along the intersecting path. Figure 9.7 shows that in this example only two links are involved. Yet you may recall that the number of links is a very important parameter in the hierarchical network model because it is used to predict verification times at different hierarchical levels. The other parameter is the number of irrelevant paths that exist along the relevant path. Figure 9.7 shows two irrelevant paths. One indicates that *A hippie is in the park* was contained in the list of study sentences. The other indicates that the relation between *hippie* and *park* is that the hippie is "in" the park. The irrelevant paths have the same effect as the irrelevant links joined directly to the concept: they tend to reduce the spread of activation along the relevant path by dividing the activation among the paths.

In conclusion, ACT is an example of a spreading activation model in which the activation spreads throughout a semantic network. At each point in the network, the activation is divided among alternative links according to their relative strengths. Although only the number of experimental links varied in the experiment we considered, the other parameters give the model considerable generality and facilitate its application to other experiments.

Integration of Knowledge

Psychologists' reactions to semantic network models have ranged from the belief that they are totally useless to the belief that they are the only hope of achieving a general theory in cognitive psychology. The reason for such divided opinion is that, like most other theories, semantic network models have both advantages and disadvantages. The advantage is that semantic network models are extremely flexible. It is very easy to introduce many assumptions into the model to make it consistent with many kinds of data. However, the price of this advantage is that it is very hard to test the model. If a model becomes so flexible that it is consistent with almost any experimental finding, it loses its predictive power. A model has predictive power only if it predicts that certain events should not occur. One can then evaluate the model by determining which events do in fact occur.

The challenge for the developers of semantic network models is not only to take advantage of their flexibility but also to place some constraints on the models in order to make some interesting predictions. Now, when a network model fails to make a correct prediction, the developers usually create additional assumptions to give the model greater flexibility. Consequently, the revised model usually succeeds where the original failed, but many psychologists find the revision less satisfactory. Collins and Loftus's (1975) revision of the hierarchical network model corrected the limitations of the former but sacrificed the precise predictions that made the hierarchical network model one of the more interesting semantic network theories.

Other network models, such as ACT, also require revision to accommodate new experimental findings. Consider ACT's prediction that increasing the number of links to a concept will slow down retrieval time because the spreading activation will be divided among the alternative paths. Smith, Adams, and Schorr (1978) argued that the model implies that increasing knowledge about a topic should lead to increasing difficulty in answering questions about it. In order to resolve this counterintuitive prediction, they investigated whether the integration of new knowledge could reduce the interference caused by additional links.

Their procedure was similar to Anderson's. Subjects learned either two or three facts about a person—for example, that *Marty broke a bottle* and *Marty did not delay the trip*. The third fact either provided a common theme for the first two facts or was unrelated. *Marty was chosen to christen the ship* provides a theme for *Marty broke the bottle* and *Marty did not delay the trip*, whereas *Marty was asked to address the crowd* is not obviously related to the first two facts. The test required that people then make rapid judgments about whether test sentences had appeared in the study set. When the facts were unrelated, people required more time to recognize a statement if they had learned three facts than if they had learned two. This finding replicated Anderson's results and is consistent with the predictions of ACT. When the third fact integrated the first two, people could recognize any one of the three facts as quickly as they could when there were only two facts. In other words, integration allows one to overcome the potential interference of learning new information.

This experiment shows that increasing the number of links at a concept node does not necessarily slow down recognition time. Does this result seriously challenge ACT? In the final chapter of *Language, Memory, and Thought*, Anderson provides the following answer:

> Another remark that needs to be made about the empirical accountability of ACT is that one cannot seriously expect to perform a single experiment and slay ACT. If ACT makes a prediction that proves wrong, that exact version of ACT will have to be abandoned but I am obviously going to propose a slight variant of the theory with slightly changed assumptions that is compatible with those data. It would be nice if the theory could be reduced to a few critical assumptions that could be subject to simple experimental tests. However, things just do not work that way. ACT is only going to be rejected by repeated attacks that keep forcing reformulations until the point comes when the theory becomes unmanageable with its patches and bandages [Anderson, 1976, p. 532].

Anderson has kept his promise by formulating a slight variation of the theory to meet the challenge raised by Smith, Adams, and Schorr. His modified version of ACT uses subnodes to integrate related material (Reder & Anderson, 1980). In Figure 9.8a, the original ACT representation, all four facts are linked directly to Marty. In Figure 9.8b, the modified ACT representation using subnodes, only two facts are linked directly to Marty—that he cooked spaghetti and that he participated in a ship christening. The three facts about the ship christening are all linked to the same subnode.

Reder and Anderson propose that, under certain conditions, people can evaluate a fact by making a consistency judgment rather than by trying to retrieve the fact. When given the test statement *Marty broke the bottle*, people respond positively because this information is consistent with the theme that Marty christened the

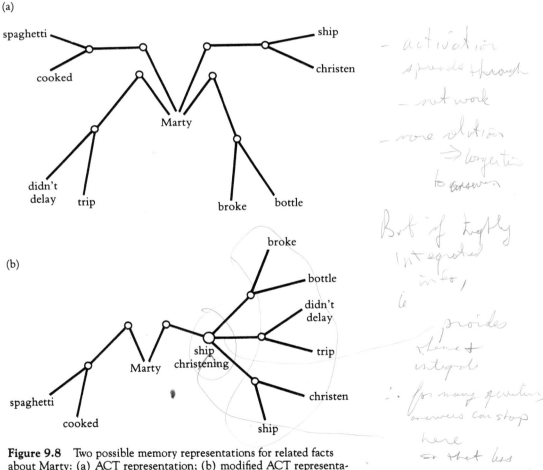

Figure 9.8   Two possible memory representations for related facts about Marty: (a) ACT representation; (b) modified ACT representation using subnodes

ship. In this case, they would respond as soon as activation reached the *ship christening* subnode and then would not attempt to retrieve the facts connected to the subnode. Response times would therefore not be influenced by the number of facts connected to the subnode, as Smith et al. (1978) found.

However, the integration of facts at a common subnode does not always eliminate interference. The number of facts influences response time when a person must examine the specific facts at that subnode. Imagine that you read statements about a ship christening, but some of the statements described Marty's activities and other statements described James's activities. If you now had to evaluate the statement *Marty broke the bottle,* you might have difficulty, since both were involved in the christening. Evaluating the statement therefore requires retrieving the specific facts associated with Marty. The data collected by Reder and Anderson revealed that even integrated facts can interfere with each other when the subject is forced to examine the specific facts and cannot make a general consistency judgment.

Their findings suggest that integration results in faster decisions when examining only the subnode is sufficient for making the decision. This conclusion is also supported by the influence of irrelevant information on response times. The fact *Marty cooked spaghetti* is irrelevant to his activities associated with ship christening. Inclusion of this statement delays the evaluation of statements about ship christening because activation also spreads down irrelevant paths. However, additional statements about cooking spaghetti do not further delay decisions about ship christening, because these statements can be integrated at a *cooking spaghetti* subnode, and activation will stop once this irrelevant subnode is reached.

The subnode model is an example of a successful revision of ACT to incorporate new findings. The basic assumption of ACT remains the same: activation spreads along the paths of a semantic network. The revision is simply that activation can stop at a subnode rather than spread to the integrated facts linked to that subnode.

More recent research has shown that increasing the amount of information about an event can even result in faster response times if that information is very well integrated. Myers, O'Brien, Balota, and Toyofuku (1984) followed the general procedure used by Reder and Anderson (1980) but, in a high-integration condition, used facts that were causally linked. The facts were presented in four pairs of stories. Each pair of stories shared a common theme—going to either a baseball game, a restaurant, a saloon, or a racetrack.

Each story had three variations, as shown in Table 9.2 for the baseball pair. Notice that although the Fan 3 condition contained three facts and the Fan 6 condition contained six facts, the two test sentences were identical for each condition. For the high-integration condition, the two test sentences were preceded by statements that were causally related. For example, the banker had to wait in line *because* he found a crowd buying tickets, and he cheered loudly *because* his team scored. In the low-integration condition, the additional facts were not causally related to the test statements.

Myers and his colleagues found that students were usually faster in deciding whether test sentences were true or false if they had studied six highly integrated

Table 9.2 Sample sentences used in integration study by Myers, O'Brien, Balota, and Toyofuku (1984)

Fan 3	
The banker	The actor
arrived at the ball park.	went to the ball game.
waited in line. *	saw the start of the ball game. *
cheered loudly. *	went home early. *
Fan 6: High integration	
The banker	The actor
decided to see a baseball game.	had a ticket for a Red Sox game.
arrived at the ball park.	went to the ball game.
found a crowd buying tickets.	sat down as the umpire yelled play ball.
waited in line. *	saw the start of the ball game. *
entered to see his team score.	found the first few innings boring.
cheered loudly. *	went home early. *
Fan 6: Low integration	
The banker	The actor
decided to see a baseball game.	had a ticket for a Red Sox game.
arrived at the ball park.	went to the ball game.
bought a souvenir pennant.	bought a hot dog from a vendor.
waited in line. *	saw the start of the ball game. *
sat near the first-base dugout.	looked at his program.
cheered loudly. *	went home early. *

Note: The Fan 3 examples contain three facts and the Fan 6 examples contain six facts. The test sentences are marked by asterisks.

statements than if they had studied three statements. Providing the additional causal statements therefore facilitated memory retrieval. However, the fan effect usually occurred for the six low-integrated statements—that is, in the low-integration condition, students responded more slowly if they had learned six facts than if they had learned three.

These findings provide an impressive demonstration of how integration can facilitate memory retrieval. The investigators proposed two possible explanations for this facilitation. One explanation is similar to the judged-plausibilities explanation offered by Reder and Anderson (1980). According to this explanation, people judge whether a test statement is plausible on the basis of propositions encountered as activation spreads through the network. Encountering the statement that the actor found the first few innings boring would make it plausible that he went home early (a true statement) and implausible that he cheered loudly (a false statement). A second explanation is similar to that offered by Smith et al. (1978). According to their elaborative network explanation, highly integrated statements may become directly connected to each other. For example, finding the first few innings boring and going home early would be connected not only to the actor but to each other, providing a "shortcut" in the semantic network. This explanation proposes that integration helps people locate information in the semantic network, rather than simply judge whether it is plausible.

An important component of the highly integrated material shown in Table 9.2 is the causal relations that exist among the statements in the story. We will see in

Chapter 11 that comprehension and recall of information from stories is also greatly influenced by causal relations.

Summary

Psychologists have studied semantic memory to learn how people use meaning to organize information in LTM. One effective way to organize material is to use hierarchical organization by partitioning a large category into smaller and smaller categories. Experiments have shown that people can learn hierarchical information quickly, but they have considerable difficulty learning the same information when it is presented randomly. The study of how people retrieve information reveals that they typically group from two to five items together. Groups of this size can form the basis for a large hierarchy—for instance, a paragraph: the paragraph can be divided into sentences, sentences into major ideas, major ideas into smaller word groups, word groups into words, words into syllables, and syllables into phonemes.

The hierarchical organization of categories influences the amount of time it takes to verify sentences about the members of categories. It usually takes less time to verify category membership at the basic level than at the superordinate level. For example, it is easier to verify that a canary is a bird than that a canary is an animal. The hierarchical network model predicts this result by assuming that semantic information is organized in a hierarchy and that it takes time to change levels in the hierarchy. The network model also predicts that the time it takes to verify a property of an object will depend on the level in the hierarchy where the property is stored. This assumption implies that it should take longer to verify that a canary eats than that a canary can fly, because eating is stored at the animal level and flying is stored at the bird level. In contrast, the feature comparison model assumes that statements are verified by using features to compute the similarity of two concepts. When there is an intermediate amount of similarity, people must evaluate only the most necessary, or defining, features of the category. The feature comparison model correctly predicts that classification time depends more on similarity than on category size and also depends on whether the example is a typical member of its category. Critics of the feature comparison model question its reliance on ratings to make predictions, its failure to make direct use of learned associations in memory, and its somewhat artificial distinction between characteristic and defining features.

The hierarchical network model is an example of a semantic network model in which concepts are represented by nodes in a network and relations are represented by links joining the concepts. The spreading activation model was proposed to correct some limitations of the hierarchical network model. Its main assumption is that activation of a concept results in activation of related concepts spreading along the paths of the network. Another network model, ACT, uses the same assumption to provide a theoretical account of many experimental findings, including the differences in reaction time for retrieving facts. The typical increase in reaction time caused by increasing the number of unrelated facts (the fan effect) can be avoided if the facts are well integrated. The advantage of semantic network models is that they are general enough to provide a broad theoretical framework for incorporating a large variety of findings. Their major disadvantage is that they often make so many assumptions that they lose their ability to make predictions.

Recommended Reading

Bower (1970) reviewed research on organizational factors in memory in the first issue of the journal *Cognitive Psychology*. Rosch (1975) used the priming technique to investigate the organization of semantic categories. Mandler (1967), one of the first psychologists to study the hierarchical organization of memory, proposed that each level in the hierarchy contained about five categories. Nelson and Smith (1972) studied the acquisition and forgetting of hierarchically organized information, whereas Goldberg (1986) used rating procedures to measure hierarchical level. Stevens and Coupe (1978) argue that spatial knowledge is also hierarchically organized—for example, most people wrongly infer that San Diego, California, is west of Reno, Nevada, because most of California is west of Nevada. Additional research on semantic integration is reported by Reder and Ross (1983). Anderson's (1983) book *The Architecture of Cognition* describes a recent version of ACT, and an article by Chang (1986) evaluates alternative models of semantic memory.

PART 3

Complex
Cognitive Skills

10

Language

Words differently arranged have a different meaning, and meanings differently arranged have different effects.

PASCAL

The discussion of semantic memory in the previous chapter emphasized associations among words. We are now ready to consider how words can be combined to form sentences. One possible theory is that this combination occurs by associations. We could argue that just as *robin* is associated with *bird*, the words in a sentence can be associated with each other. The problem with this view of language is that there are so many ways words can be combined that we would have to learn an infinite number of associations in order to form sentences. An alternative theory is that we learn a *grammar*—a system of rules that is capable of producing sentences. Ideally, the rules of a grammar should generate all the sentences of a language without generating any strings of words that are not sentences. The first section of this chapter provides a brief description of two kinds of grammatical rules—phrase structure rules and transformation rules.

The second section deals with the comprehension of sentences. The comprehension of ambiguous sentences is a particularly interesting study because we must resolve the ambiguity in order to understand the sentence. The final section considers the distinction between asserted and implied statements. Findings on how well people can make this distinction offer some applications of research on the understanding of language, particularly in relation to the evaluation of courtroom testimony and advertising claims.

Psychology and Grammar

One of the important influences on the development of cognitive psychology during the 1960s was the work of the linguist Noam Chomsky. Prior to Chomsky's influence on psycholinguistics (the psychological study of language), psychologists had explored the possibility that people could learn language by learning the associations between adjacent words in a sentence. According to this view, we learn to speak correctly through paired-associate learning: each word in a sentence serves as a stimulus for the word that follows it. In the sentence *The boy hit the ball*, the word *the* is a stimulus for the response *boy*, and the word *boy* is a stimulus for the word *hit*. The speaker of a language would therefore have to learn which words could follow any other word in a sentence.

Chomsky (1957) argued that there are several problems with the association view of language. First of all, there are an infinite number of sentences in a language. It is therefore unreasonable to expect that people could learn a language by learning associations between all adjacent words. Consider simply a word like *the*. There are many, many words that could follow *the*, and a person might never learn all of them. When you consider all the possible words that can occur in a sentence and all the words that could possibly follow each word, you can see that this would be a very inefficient way to learn a language. Another problem with the association view is that it does not account for the relations among nonadjacent words. For example, in the sentence *Anyone who says that is lying*, the pronoun *anyone* is grammatically related to the verb *is lying*, but this relation is not revealed if we consider only the relation between adjacent words. The association view, in fact, ignores the hierarchical structure of sentences in proposing how people learn to speak grammatically correct sentences.

The hierarchical structure of sentences is revealed in the diagrams that you may have constructed in school. Many of us were taught how to break down a sentence into parts. We might begin by dividing a sentence into a noun phrase and a verb phrase and then divide the noun phrase into an adjective and a noun and the verb phrase into an adverb and a verb. Division into smaller units produces a hierarchical organization that reveals the grammar of the sentence. The diagram, which is based on a set of rules, provides a picture of the grammatical organization. The rules are part of what we call a *phrase structure grammar* because they reveal how we can form phrases consisting of groups of words.

Phrase Structure Grammar

An alternative to representing language as a string of words is representing it as a rule system. This approach can be illustrated by considering a very simple set of rules taken from a phrase structure grammar (Table 10.1). The rules are expressed by using an arrow that means *can be rewritten as*. The symbols refer to sentences (S), noun phrases (NP), verb phrases (VP), and determiners (Det). The first rule states that a

Table 10.1 **Examples of phrase structure rules**

1. S→NP + VP	4. Det→a, the
2. NP→Det + Noun	5. Noun→boy, ball, stick
3. VP→Verb + NP	6. Verb→hit

sentence can be rewritten as a noun phrase followed by a verb phrase. The second rule states that a noun phrase can be rewritten as a determiner followed by a noun. The third rule states that a verb phrase can be rewritten as a verb followed by a noun phrase. The last three rules give examples of words that can be substituted for a determiner, a noun, and a verb.

The rules may seem more familiar to you if they are expressed visually. Figure 10.1 shows how they can be used to reveal the grammatical structure of a sentence. The sentence is first rewritten as a noun phrase followed by a verb phrase (Rule 1). Rule 2 then allows us to rewrite the noun phrase, and Rule 3 allows us to rewrite the verb phrase. Since the application of Rule 3 produces another noun phrase, it is necessary to apply Rule 2 again to rewrite the second noun phrase. Using the vocabulary rules to substitute words for the determiners, nouns, and verbs, we can now produce a small number of sentences—for instance:

The boy hit a ball.
The stick hit the boy.
A ball hit a ball.

Although the number of sentences we can produce using this particular grammar is quite limited, the grammar illustrates how sentences can be produced through the application of rules. Creation of additional rules, such as including adjectives in a noun phrase, would allow us to generate a greater variety of sentences.

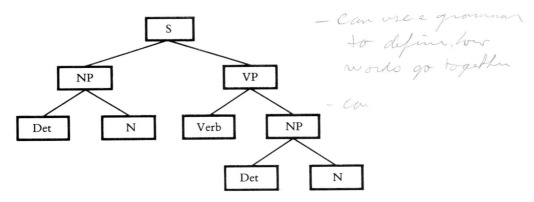

Figure 10.1 A sentence diagram based on the phrase structure rules in Table 10.1

Transformational Grammar

Chomsky (1957) argued that one limitation of a phrase structure grammar is that it does not reveal how a sentence can be modified to form a similar sentence. For example, how can we change (1) an active statement into a passive statement, (2) a positive statement into a negative statement, or (3) an assertion into a question? Given the sentence *The boy hit the ball*, the first change produces *The ball was hit by the boy*; the second change produces *The boy did not hit the ball*; and the third change produces *Did the boy hit the ball?* The modification in each case transforms an entire sentence into a closely related sentence. Transformation rules therefore serve a different function than phrase structure rules, which reveal the grammatical structure of a sentence. Chomsky, however, made use of the phrase structure rules in developing his transformational grammar, because the transformations are based on the grammatical structure of a sentence.

Consider the transformation of *The boy hit the ball* into *The ball was hit by the boy*. The transformation rule in this case is

$$NP1 + V + NP2 \rightarrow NP2 + was + V + by + NP1$$

The transformation changes the position of the two noun phrases and inserts additional words into the passive sentence. The passive sentence begins with the second noun phrase (*the ball*) and ends with the first noun phrase (*the boy*). It is also necessary to add the words *was* and *by*. Notice that the transformation rule shows how a phrase structure description of a passive sentence can be formed from a phrase structure description of an active sentence.

The transformational grammar proposed by Chomsky in 1957 was an advance over a phrase structure grammar because, in addition to revealing grammatical structure, it showed how sentences could be transformed. Chomsky was not entirely satisfied with the transformational grammar, however, and in 1965 he wrote a second book to correct some of its limitations. The changes that he made were concerned mainly with allowing meaning to play a more important role in the grammar.

One problem with the 1957 grammar was that it could generate sentences that seemed grammatical but did not express meaningful ideas. This point can be illustrated by adding another verb—*took*—to the rules shown in Figure 10.1. This addition allows us to produce new sentences like *The boy took the ball* and *The ball took the boy*. Although both sentences appear to be grammatical, the second sentence doesn't make much sense. The reason is that the verb *took* usually requires an animate subject—someone who is alive and therefore capable of taking something. Chomsky tried to correct this deficiency by placing constraints on which words could be substituted into a sentence. Instead of treating all verbs the same, he argued that some verbs require animate subjects. This restriction is based on the meaning of words.

Another problem with the earlier version of the transformational grammar was that it could not always distinguish between different meanings of an ambiguous sentence, although it was sometimes successful because some ambiguous sentences can be distinguished by the use of phrase structure rules. Consider the sentence *They are flying planes.* One interpretation considers *flying* to be part of the verb phrase *are flying,* whereas the other interpretation considers *flying* to be an adjective in the noun phrase *flying planes.* In the first interpretation *they* refers to someone who is flying planes; in the second interpretation *they* refers to the planes. A phrase structure grammar can make this distinction because each interpretation has a different derivation (see Figure 10.2).

There are other ambiguous sentences, however, that cannot be distinguished by phrase structure rules because both interpretations of the sentence produce the same derivation. Consider the sentence *Flying planes can be dangerous.* The sentence has the same ambiguity as the previous sentence. The two interpretations can be revealed by rephrasing the sentence as either *Flying planes is dangerous* or *Flying planes are dangerous.* The first interpretation means that flying is dangerous to the pilot; the second means that the planes themselves are dangerous. In both interpretations, however, *flying planes* is the subject of the sentence, so the ambiguity cannot be resolved by appealing to different phrase structure rules.

Chomsky (1965) proposed that, in order to resolve the ambiguity, it is necessary to postulate a level of analysis that directly represents the meaning of a sentence. He therefore modified the transformational grammar to consist of two levels: the surface level, directly related to the sentence as it is heard, and the deep level, directly related to the meaning of the sentence. The only way to resolve the ambiguity of a sentence like *Flying planes can be dangerous* is to know which of the two deep levels is intended—flying is dangerous to the pilot or the planes themselves are dangerous.

The concepts Chomsky introduced had a major impact on the emerging field of psycholinguistics. Psychologists who were interested in language studied the implications of a transformational grammar for theories of how people comprehend and remember sentences. The following study of ambiguous sentences illustrates the kind of research that resulted from Chomsky's ideas.

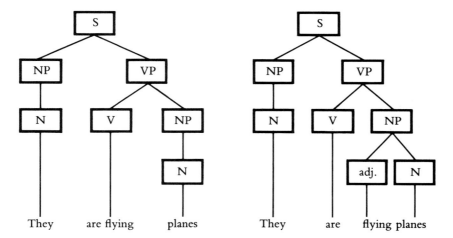

Figure 10.2   Two alternative derivations of an ambiguous sentence

— but, grammars can produce sentences that have no meaning

— also ambiguity to be proposed a structural level that removes ambiguities

Ambiguous Sentences

Comprehension of sentences, like recognition of patterns, is a complex skill that we perform very well. Ambiguous sentences afford us some insight into how difficulties in comprehension might arise. One technique for studying comprehension is to measure how quickly people can complete a sentence. Try to finish the following three sentences as quickly as you can.

1. Although he was continually bothered by the cold . . .
2. Although Hannibal sent troops over a week ago . . .
3. Knowing that visiting relatives could be bothersome . . .

Each of the three sentences represents a different kind of ambiguity studied by MacKay (1966). The first example represents *lexical* (word) *ambiguity* because the word *cold* can refer either to the temperature of the environment or to an illness. The second example represents *surface ambiguity* because it concerns the grouping of words. The word *over* can be either part of the verb phrase (*sent troops over*) or part of the prepositional phrase (*over a week ago*). Linguistically, this distinction can be represented by the phrase structure rules because each interpretation would have a different derivation. The third example represents an *underlying ambiguity* because the ambiguity can be resolved only if we know the underlying meaning (deep structure) of the sentence. Notice that the phrase *visiting relatives* is ambiguous in the same sense that *flying planes* was ambiguous in the example given earlier. It is unclear who are the visitors—and this ambiguity cannot be resolved at the phrase structure level.

It is possible, of course, that people may never notice these ambiguities and therefore find it as easy to complete these sentences as to complete closely related unambiguous sentences. The following three sentences show unambiguous variations of each of the three examples. The italicized word is the only change.

4. Although he was continually bothered by the *headache* . . .
5. Although Hannibal sent troops *almost* a week ago . . .
6. Knowing that visiting *some* relatives could be bothersome . . .

MacKay studied the effect of ambiguity on sentence completion times by giving people either ambiguous sentences or unambiguous variations of the same sentences. Their task was to finish each sentence as quickly as they could. The completions had to be short, grammatical, and related to the beginning of the sentence.

Figure 10.3 shows the average amount of time required to complete each class of sentences. There was no difference among the unambiguous control sentences, but there were differences among the three kinds of ambiguous sentences—all of which took more time to complete than the control sentences. Participants had the least difficulty with lexical ambiguities, more difficulty with surface ambiguities, and still more difficulty with underlying ambiguities. Sentences that contained more than one ambiguity (multiple ambiguities) were the most difficult to complete. It is interesting that very few of the participants reported that they noticed the ambiguities, although they took significantly longer to complete the ambiguous sentences.

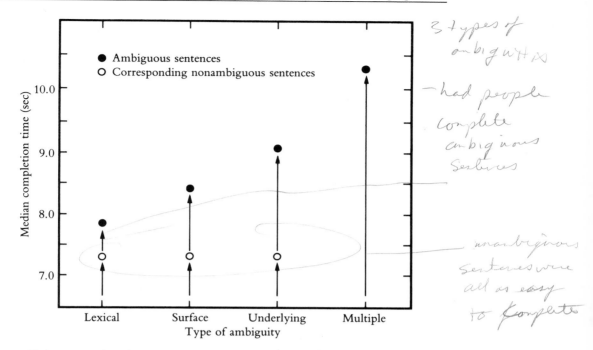

Handwritten margin notes:
3 types of ambiguity
– had people complete ambiguous sentences
– unambiguous sentences were all as easy to complete

Figure 10.3   Completion times for ambiguous and nonambiguous sentences

Although Chomsky's ideas had a major impact on the emerging field of psycholinguistics, current research on language is more concerned with meaning than with grammar (see Lachman et al., 1979, for a detailed account of this shift in emphasis). For example, ambiguous words and noun phrases often do not seem ambiguous to us when we read them in a sentence, because their meaning is made clear by the meaning of the words that preceded them. The sentence provides a context for interpreting words. In the next section we will learn how this context influences comprehension.

Effect of Context on Comprehension

Context and Ambiguity

The reason many potentially ambiguous sentences do not seem ambiguous in our everyday use of language is that the intended meaning is usually clear from the context. If I say that I am bothered by the cold, the preceding sentences should reveal the intended meaning. We might therefore expect that context should make it as easy to comprehend ambiguous sentences as unambiguous sentences. An experiment by Swinney and Hakes (1976) supports this hypothesis.

The subjects in their experiment performed two tasks simultaneously while they listened to pairs of sentences. One task asked them to judge how closely they felt the two sentences of each pair were related. This task required comprehension of the

Handwritten margin note:
– context can get rid of ambiguities

sentences. The second task required that they press a button as soon as they heard a word beginning with a specified sound (phoneme). The rationale of this experiment is that people should be slower in responding to the phoneme whenever they are having difficulty in comprehending the sentence. The following pair of sentences is a typical example:

> Rumor had it that, for years, the government building had been plagued with problems. The man was not surprised when he found several "bugs" in the corner of his room [Swinney & Hakes, 1976, p. 686].

The target phoneme in this example occurs at the beginning of the word *corner*, shortly after the ambiguous word *bugs*. To determine whether the ambiguous word would delay comprehension and therefore detection of the phoneme, Swinney and Hakes compared performance on the ambiguous sentences with performance on unambiguous control sentences. The unambiguous version of the example contained the word *insects* in place of the word *bugs*. Swinney and Hakes found that subjects took significantly more time to detect the phoneme when it followed an ambiguous word than when it followed an unambiguous word. The findings were consistent with MacKay's (1966) results in suggesting that an ambiguity can delay comprehension.

However, sometimes the ambiguous word occurred in a context that made it clear which meaning of the word was intended. For example:

> Rumor had it that, for years, the government building had been plagued with problems. The man was not surprised when he found several spiders, roaches, and other "bugs" in the corner of his room [Swinney & Hakes, 1976, p. 686].

When the context clarified the meaning of the ambiguous word, people could comprehend the ambiguous word *bug* as quickly as they could comprehend the unambiguous word *insect*. There was no longer any difference in response times to the target phoneme.

We could interpret these results by arguing that only a single meaning of the ambiguous word is activated when the context indicates the intended meaning. This argument has considerable intuitive appeal, but recent findings suggest that it is wrong. In the previous chapter we saw that when people are asked to decide whether a string of letters is a word, their decision is faster when a word is preceded by a semantically related word, such as *bread* preceded by *butter*. If people consider only a single meaning of an ambiguous word, a word like *bug* should facilitate the recognition of either *ant* or *spy*, depending on which meaning is activated.

Swinney (1979) tested this prediction by replacing the phoneme-monitoring task with a lexical decision task. He explained to the subjects that a string of letters would appear on a screen as they listened to some of the sentences, and they were to decide as quickly as possible whether or not each letter string formed a word. He did not mention that some of the sentences and words were related. The letter string appeared on the screen immediately after subjects heard the ambiguous word and was contextually appropriate, contextually inappropriate, or unrelated to the meaning of the ambiguous word. A contextually appropriate word appearing on the screen, such as *ant*, was consistent with the meaning of the ambiguous word that was suggested by the context. A contextually inappropriate word, such as *spy*, was consistent with the meaning that was not suggested by the context. An unrelated word, such as *sew*, was consistent with neither of the two meanings.

If the context causes the activation of only a single meaning, it should be easier to recognize only the contextually appropriate word (*ant*). But if both meanings of the ambiguous word are activated, the contextually inappropriate word (*spy*) should also be easier to recognize than the unrelated word (*sew*). The results showed that when the visual test word immediately followed the ambiguous word, both the contextually appropriate and the contextually inappropriate words were easier to recognize than the unrelated words. But when the test word occurred four syllables (about 750–1000 msec) after the ambiguous word, recognition of only the contextually appropriate word was facilitated.

Swinney's findings suggest that more than one meaning of an ambiguous word is activated even when a prior context indicates which meaning is appropriate. If only one meaning of *bugs* were activated by the phrase *He found several spiders, roaches, and other bugs,* it is not clear why it would be as easy to respond to *spy* as to *ant*. However, when the test word occurred four syllables after the ambiguous word, recognition of only the word *ant* was facilitated. It therefore appears that although both meanings of an ambiguous word are momentarily activated, the context allows the listener to select the appropriate meaning quickly. Selection of the appropriate meaning occurred quickly enough to prevent interference in the phoneme detection task. As you may recall, there was a slight delay between the ambiguous word and the target phoneme. This was sufficient time to resolve the ambiguity when there was an appropriate context. An appropriate context therefore seems to allow the listener to select the appropriate meaning of a word quickly rather than to prevent more than one meaning from being activated.

Contextual Facilitation and Interference

Carpenter and Daneman (1981) have proposed a model of how context influences the interpretation of a word. Figure 10.4 shows their model. The first step is to fixate on and encode each word in the sentence. The encoding of a word will activate one or more concepts, which are retrieved into STM if the activation reaches some threshold level. When at least one concept reaches threshold, the reader tries to integrate it with the previous text. If the concept is compatible with the context, such as the interpretation of *bug* as an insect, it will be used in further processing. If the concept is not compatible with the context, such as the interpretation of *bug* as a monitoring device, its activation level will quickly decay. When the reader successfully integrates the word with its context, he or she is ready to fixate and encode the next word in the sentence.

Occasionally a successful integration does not occur, and it is necessary to use the error recovery heuristics. Consider the following passage:

Cinderella was sad because she couldn't go to the dance that night. There were big tears in her brown dress.

· how people
bevelop sentences,
following concepts,
and chick when errors
occur

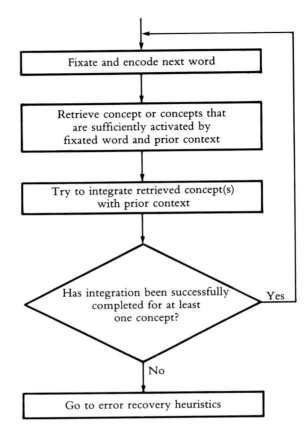

Figure 10.4   A flow chart showing the encoding, activation, integration, and error recovery stages of reading

Because the context indicated that Cinderella was sad, the readers may interpret the word *tears* to mean crying. This interpretation fits the context, so the reader continues to encode the rest of the sentence. But the word *dress* suggests that a misinterpretation occurred, requiring the reader to recover from his or her error. Examples of error recovery heuristics include trying to reinterpret the inconsistent word, checking previous words that may have caused the difficulty, reading on for further information, and elaborating the apparent inconsistency to make it consistent.

The sentences studied by Carpenter and Daneman represent extreme cases in which a misleading context caused readers to incorrectly interpret an ambiguous word. However, a context can cause interference in a more subtle way, as illustrated by the following two sentences: (1) *John kept his gym clothes in a locker.* (2) *John kept his gym clothes in a closet.* The words *locker* and *closet* are both preceded by a suitable context, but the context creates a strong expectation for the word *locker.* Sentences that create a high expectation for a particular word are called "high-constraint sentences."

Schwanenflugel and Shoben (1985) studied the effect of high-constraint sentences on the processing of expected words (*locker*) and unexpected words (*closet*) by using the lexical decision task. After reading either a high-constraint context or a neutral context, readers had to decide whether a string of letters was a word. The high-constraint context facilitated recognition of the expected word but interfered with recognition of the unexpected word. People were faster at deciding *locker* was a word when they received the high-constraint context but were faster in deciding that *closet* was a word when they received the neutral context, consisting of a string of Xs.

The high-constraint sentence caused interference in the latter case because people were expecting a particular word which did not occur. What would happen if our expectations for a particular word were not as strong? Schwanenflugel and Shoben tried to answer this question by including low-constraint sentences in their study. The following two sentences are examples: (1) *The lady was a competent cook.* (2) *The lady was a competent chef.* The sentences are low-constraint because a lady could be competent in performing many different tasks. However, the first sentence contains an expected word and the second sentence contains an unexpected word because a lady is more likely to be called a cook than a chef. The results of several experiments indicated that the low-constraint context caused facilitation for both the expected and the unexpected words. In contrast to the high-constraint sentences, in which a large facilitation effect occurred for the expected word and a large interference effect occurred for the unexpected word, the low-constraint sentences caused a moderate amount of facilitation for both the expected and the unexpected words.

Schwanenflugel and Shoben account for this finding by proposing an explanation based on semantic features. They argue that changes in the scope of facilitation due to sentence constraint may occur because subjects generate fewer and more general features for low-constraint than for high-constraint sentences. For the low-constraint example, *The lady was a competent _____* , the missing word is constrained only by features such as [skilled activity] and [something humans can be]. Facilitation could occur for any concepts that possess these two features. In contrast, high-constraint sentences may cause an expectation for concepts that satisfy a more detailed set of features. The sentence *John kept his gym clothes in a _____* may cause readers to generate nearly the complete set of features for *locker*, such as [small], [rectangular], [associated with gyms], [holds clothes], and [shuttable]. If facilitation is restricted to those concepts that completely match the feature description, low-constraint sentences will facilitate recognition of many more words than high-constraint sentences. Thus the word *chef* would satisfy the two semantic features generated from the low-constraint sentence, but the word *closet* would not satisfy the more extensive set of specific features generated from the high-constraint sentence.

The studies by Carpenter and Daneman (1981) and Schwanenflugel and Shoben (1985) show that contexts may occasionally have negative, as well as positive, effects.

A misleading context can cause an incorrect interpretation of a word, and a high-constraint context can slow down lexical decisions for unexpected words. One caution, however, in evaluating such studies is that finding contextual interference is affected by the research methodology used to study contextual effects. Another frequently used procedure, instead of lexical decision, is to measure how quickly subjects can *name* a word that follows a context. Studies that have used both procedures have revealed that interference effects are more likely to be found in lexical decision tasks than in naming tasks (Stanovich & West, 1983). An important challenge for cognitive psychologists is therefore to show how performance on such tasks as naming and lexical decision is related to the comprehension that occurs during normal reading (Seidenberg, Waters, Sanders, & Langer, 1984).

Understanding Noun Phrases

The preceding discussion emphasized how context influences the understanding of a single word. Let us now consider a larger unit such as a noun phrase consisting of an adjective and a noun. Noun phrases may also be sources of ambiguity if it is not clear which word is the adjective and which word is the noun. An extreme case is the title of the article in Box 10.1: "Adjective Substitution Demonstration: Noun String Findings Analysis." The title of the article is particularly awkward because each adjective looks like a potential noun. The reader therefore has to decide whether each word in the title is an adjective or a noun, and this decision delays comprehension.

An important issue in studying how people understand groups of words such as noun phrases is whether the meaning of the noun is influenced by the meaning of the adjective. When we hear a noun phrase such as *the burning house*, do we select the meaning of *burning* and the meaning of *house* independently and then combine the two meanings? Or is the meaning of *house* directly influenced by the adjective that precedes it? Since it is not obvious which words are adjectives in a noun string, it is unlikely that the adjectives would immediately influence the meaning of the noun. On encountering a noun string like the examples in Box 10.1, a reader probably retrieves the meaning of each word and then tries to combine the individual meanings. Comprehension would be facilitated, however, if the meaning of an adjective directly influenced the meaning of the noun. The evidence suggests that there is a direct influence for noun phrases such as *the burning house*.

Potter and Faulconer (1979) used a picture probe task to investigate how people understand noun phrases. (Figure 10.5 shows examples of sentences and pictures used in the experiment.) Subjects listened to sentences such as *It was already getting late when the man first saw the burning house ahead of him.* Immediately after the noun *house*, a picture appeared illustrating either the noun alone (*house*) or the noun

**Box 10.1   Adjective substitution demonstration:
Noun string findings analysis**

What's this article about? A careful look at the words in the title shows that they are all nouns that are commonly used in government, business, and academe. Moreover, they are often used in "strings" like this, especially in the titles of projects, programs, agencies, and processes. These "noun strings" are one of the hallmarks of stilted, incomprehensible bureaucratic prose.

Short noun strings are everywhere in our written and spoken language. Doublets are especially common and well accepted: *day care, form letter, pressure cooker, case study, career choice, grant application, life style.* Strings of three or more nouns are not common in everyday speech or writing, but are very common in professional jargon: *health service provider, management information requirement, system level specification, Document Design Center, human factors engineering support, video training system application, U.S. Army weapons systems.* These all may seem reasonable and familiar to you, even if you don't know exactly what they mean. But excesses are also quite common, particularly in the Federal government: just what exactly is a *host area crisis shelter production planning workbook?*

Why are noun strings so difficult to understand? Why do we usually spend some time poring over a new one we encounter, trying to decipher it? It cannot be because of the words themselves; they are usually fairly common and nontechnical. It must be because of the way that they are used together and the complex process we must go through to decode them.

Let's look at the structure of a noun string first. A noun string is a sequence of nouns that function as a unit: the final noun of the string is the "head noun"; all the other nouns preceding it (and any adjacent or intervening adjectives) function as adjectives that modify this head noun. If we understand only one thing about a phrase like *ozone probability target,* we know that it is about some kind of target. The head noun in a noun string is easy to identify: it's always at the end of the string.

But how does a reader find the end of a noun string? Nouns still look like nouns, even though they may be functioning as adjectives. As a reader progresses through a noun string, each noun is a potential candidate for the head noun of that string or phrase—unless another noun follows. Everything in a noun string is therefore ambiguous until all the nouns have been identified. Consider *management information system plan.* The reader does not know whether it refers to information, a system, or a plan until the end of the string, but in the meantime the reader has been forming and abandoning false hypotheses about the meaning of the phrase. . . .

From the May 1980 issue of *Fine Print* (now called *Simply Stated*). Reproduced with permission from the Document Design Center, American Institutes for Research.

It was already $\left\{\begin{array}{l}\text{burning}\\ \text{getting late}\end{array}\right\}$ when the man first saw the {burning} house ahead of him.

"It's {dripping} on the table," Sally said, gesturing at the {dripping} candle that she had made.

Seeing it {drooping} in the yard, the boyscout wondered how many years the {drooping} flag had been used.

Although it was $\left\{\begin{array}{l}\text{low}\\ \text{borrowed}\end{array}\right\}$, Jill thought that the {low} table would be adequate.

Figure 10.5   Examples of sentences and typical versus modified picture probes

phrase (*burning house*). The subject's task was to decide whether the pictured object had been named in the sentence. When the adjective was not included in the noun phrase, subjects were faster in verifying the more typical pictures shown on the left in Figure 10.5. For example, when the subjects heard the sentence *It was already getting late when the man first saw the house,* they could verify the picture of a typical house faster than a picture of a burning house. This finding is analogous to the typicality effects discussed in the chapter on categorization (Chapter 8). Since the typical pictures are more representative of their category than the modified pictures, they can be verified more quickly.

[handwritten marginal notes:]
listened to sentences, then given picture:
if burning was in front of wood house, this was quicker response:
if no burning this was quicker
if burning in sentence, but not near house, this is still quicker.

≠ meaning of adj preceding noun affects comprehension
≠ context affects meaning

A more interesting question is what happens when the noun is preceded by the adjective. If the meaning of the noun is selected independently of the meaning of the adjective, then we would expect that the more typical picture should still be verified more rapidly. However, if the meaning of the noun is influenced by the adjective, the modified picture should be verified more quickly. The results supported the second of the two alternatives: the subjects verified the modified picture more quickly than the typical picture when the noun was preceded by the adjective. These results occurred even though the task required only verification of the noun, so participants could have ignored the meaning of the adjective when they made their decisions. The magnitude of the effect was related to the familiarity of the noun phrase: the modified picture was verified faster for familiar noun phrases (for example, *roasted turkey*) than for unfamiliar noun phrases (for example, *broken screwdriver*).

In another version of this experiment, the information conveyed by the adjective came at the beginning of the sentence rather than just before the noun. For example, people heard the sentence *It was already burning when the man first saw the house ahead of him*. People's verification times for this condition were similar to their verification times when the adjective was not presented: they were faster at verifying the typical picture than the modified picture. The results imply that selecting the meaning of a noun can be influenced by an immediately preceding adjective but is not likely to be influenced when the same information occurs earlier in a sentence.

In conclusion, context has an important influence on which meaning of a word will be selected. The selected meaning allows the reader to integrate the word with the text that has preceded it. Although the context usually facilitates comprehension, it can interfere with comprehension if it is misleading or creates an expectation for a particular word that does not occur.

Our study of comprehension has thus far been limited to considering how people understand sentences in which information is directly asserted. However, we can also use language to imply something without directly asserting it. An important aspect of comprehension then becomes the ability to distinguish between asserted and implied statements. This distinction is the topic of the next section.

Implications of Sentences

Studies have shown that language can have an impact on behavior without making direct assertions. It is often sufficient for a message simply to imply an action to convince a listener that the action actually occurred. For example, the sentence *The hungry python caught the mouse* may convince the listener that the python ate the mouse, even though that action is not explicitly stated. The fact that people may not distinguish implications and direct statements can have important consequences. For example, a consumer could be misled by the implications of an advertisement, or a jury could be misled by the implications of testimony. We will first consider the effect of implications on courtroom testimony.

Courtroom Testimony

(handwritten margin note: This provides more yes answers)

The asking of leading questions is one way implications can influence a person's responses. Elizabeth Loftus designed a procedure to simulate what might occur during eyewitness testimony (for example, Loftus, 1975). The procedure consists in showing people a short film of a car accident and, immediately afterward, asking them questions about what occurred in the film. One experimental variation involved phrasing a question as either *Did you see a broken headlight?* or *Did you see the broken headlight?* The word *the* implies that there was a broken headlight, whereas the word *a* does not. The results showed that people who were asked questions containing the word *the* were more likely to report having seen something, whether or not it had actually appeared in the film, than those who were asked questions containing the word *a*.

(handwritten margin note: this provides faster speed answers)

Another experiment revealed that the wording of a question can affect a numerical estimate. The question *About how fast were the two cars going when they smashed into each other?* consistently yielded a higher estimate of speed than when *smashed* was replaced by *collided, bumped, contacted,* or *hit.* These results, when combined with similar findings from other experiments conducted by Loftus and her associates, show that leading questions can influence eyewitness testimony.

Implications can influence not only how a witness responds to questions but what a jury remembers about the testimony of a witness. In another experiment (Harris, 1978) subjects listened to simulated courtroom testimony and then rated statements about information in the testimony as true, false, or of indeterminate truth value. Half of the test statements were directly asserted (for instance, *The intruder walked away without taking any money*) and half were only implied (*The intruder was able to walk away without taking any money*). The test item that the intruder did not take any money would be true for the asserted statement but of indeterminate truth value for the implied statement.

Harris found that people were more likely to indicate that asserted statements were true than that implied statements were true. There was, however, a disturbing tendency to accept implied statements—subjects responded *true* to 64% of the statements that were only implied. Furthermore, instructions warning people to be careful to distinguish between asserted and implied statements did not significantly reduce the acceptance of implied statements.

The work of Loftus and Harris should be of interest to people in the legal professions. A judge can immediately rule a leading question out of order, but not before the members of the jury have heard the question. Instructions from the judge to disregard certain evidence may not prevent the jurors from considering that evidence when making their decision. More subtle uses of language, such as use of the word *crash* rather than the word *hit,* may not even be identified as potentially misleading.

Harris has speculated that the distinction between asserted and implied statements may be even harder to make in a real courtroom than in an experimental situation. People in his experiment made their judgments immediately after hearing a five-minute segment of simulated trial testimony. Members of a jury make their final decision after a much longer delay and after they have heard much more information. It is therefore important to clarify immediately any courtroom statements that are ambiguous regarding whether information was asserted or implied. If the witness is unwilling to assert the information directly—and thus become liable for perjury—the jury should be made aware of the questionable value of the information.

Advertising Claims

The acceptance of implied statements is as important an issue in advertising as it is in courtroom testimony. The Federal Trade Commission makes decisions about deceptive advertising, but deciding what constitutes deceptive advertising is a complex question. The decision may be particularly difficult if a claim is only implied. Consider the following commercial:

> Aren't you tired of sniffles and runny noses all winter? Tired of always feeling less than your best? Get through the whole winter without colds. Take Eradicold Pills as directed.

This doesn't say that these pills prevent colds.

Notice that the commercial does not directly assert that Eradicold Pills will get you through the whole winter without colds—it is only implied. To test whether people can distinguish between asserted and implied claims, Harris (1977) gave people a series of 20 fictitious commercials, half of which asserted claims and half of which implied claims. The subjects were instructed to rate the claims as true, false, or of indeterminate truth value on the basis of the information presented. Some of the people made their judgments immediately after hearing each commercial, and others made their judgments after hearing all 20 commercials. In addition, half the people were given instructions that warned them not to interpret implied claims as asserted and were shown an example of a commercial that made an implied claim.

The results showed that subjects responded *true* significantly more often to assertions than to implications. Furthermore, instructions were helpful in reducing the number of implications accepted as true. Although these results are encouraging, however, they are not unqualifiedly positive. First, even in the condition that was most favorable to rejecting implications—the group that had been warned and that gave an immediate judgment after hearing each commercial—people accepted about half the implied statements as true. When the judgments were delayed until all 20 commercials were presented, people accepted as true about as many implied statements as direct statements—even when they had been explicitly warned about implied statements.

Acceptance of implied statements is a problem that exists outside the psychology laboratory. In fact, one of the most frequently accepted implied statements in Harris's (1977) study was a verbatim statement from a real commercial. Another real commercial, created after Harris's study, was changed because competitors complained that it made unfair implications about their product (see Box 10.2). Their complaints resulted in a modification of the commercial.

Box 10.2 American Express ads challenged

NEW YORK—Those "Don't-leave-home-without-them" television commercials for American Express Travelers Cheques are under attack, and American Express reportedly plans to re-do them.

Competitors say the ads unfairly imply that people who lose travelers checks may not be able to get a refund unless the checks were issued by American Express.

NBC News reported that American Express has agreed to change its commercials. Actor Karl Malden will reshoot the endings, NBC said, and make it clear that all travelers checks are refundable, not just American Express checks.

Collot Guerard of the division of advertising practices in the Federal Trade Commission's Bureau of Consumer Protection said the agency "probably will take a look at the American Express ad."

Deciding whether it is deceptive, she said, will depend on the answers to a number of questions, including: "How easy is it to get refunds for the other companies' travelers checks?"

The American Express TV campaign introduced in June shows people in a variety of situations. They lose their travelers checks. Panic. A plea for help. But the checks were not American Express. What is to be done? The question is unanswered. At the end, comes the voice of Malden: "American Express Travelers Cheques. Don't leave home without them."

From the *San Francisco Chronicle*, August 17, 1979. © Associated Press Newsfeatures. Reprinted by permission.

Logical Implications

In the examples we have been looking at so far, people often were unable to distinguish between assertions and statements with fairly obvious implications. Attempts to comprehend many logical statements, however, often reveal the opposite problem—the logical implications are not very obvious. Imagine that you are shown four cards, each containing a *D*, a *K*, a 3, or a 7 (see Figure 10.6). The experimenter tells you that each card has a letter on one side and a number on the other side and then asks which cards you would have to turn over to determine the truth of the sentence *Every card that has a D on one side has a 3 on the other side*. Try to answer this question before reading further.

The experiment, known as the four-card selection problem, has been analyzed by Wason and Johnson-Laird (1972). It is an example of a conditional reasoning task. The correct answer is that you would have to turn over the cards containing a *D* and a 7. The selection of a *D* is fairly obvious—the rule would be false if the other side of the card did not contain a 3. The rule would also be false if you turned over the card containing the 7 and found a *D* on the other side. It is not necessary to turn over the

Drink   Drink   16 yrs   22 years
Coke   beer   old   old

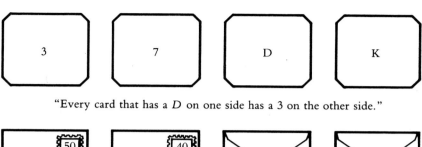

"Every card that has a *D* on one side has a 3 on the other side."

"If a letter is sealed, then it has a 50-lira stamp on it."

Figure 10.6   The four-card selection problem

card containing the 3, although this is a common mistake. The rule does not specify what should be on the opposite side of a 3; it only specifies what should be on the opposite side of a *D*. For example, finding a *K* on one side of the card and a 3 on the other side would not make the rule false.

Experiments using this task reveal that the implications of a conditional rule are not very clear to most people. The combined results of four experiments indicated that only 5 of 128 subjects correctly turned over only the two correct cards (Wason & Shapiro, 1971). The most popular choice was to turn over the two cards mentioned in the rule—the letter *D* and the number 3 for the above example.

Wason and Johnson-Laird (1972) argued that people make mistakes because they seek information that would verify the rule rather than information that would falsify it. Only the latter information is necessary. Turning over the card containing the 3 would verify the rule if a *D* were found on the other side, but it's not logically necessary to turn over this card, since the rule does not specify what should be on the other side. It is necessary to turn over the 7, but people usually overlook this card because they are not seeking ways to disprove the rule.

Wason and Shapiro (1971) hypothesized that the poor performance in this task was due in part to the abstract material. They predicted that using more realistic materials related to everyday knowledge would make the task significantly easier. The realistic rules were of the general form *Every time I go to Manchester I travel by car.* The four cards contained two destinations (Manchester and Leeds) and two modes of transport (car and train). One side of the card specified the destination and the other side the transportation. Of 16 British subjects 10 selected the two correct cards (Manchester and train) when realistic material was used, compared with only 2 of 16 subjects when abstract material was used.

A problem with even greater appeal as a realistic task is the letter-sorting task used by Johnson-Laird, Legrenzi, and Legrenzi (1972). Italian subjects in the realistic condition were asked to imagine that they worked at a post office, and their job was to make sure that the letters conformed to each of the following rules: (1) if a letter is sealed, then it has a 50-lira stamp on it, and (2) a letter is sealed only if it has a 50-lira stamp on it. Two letters were face down, revealing either a sealed or an unsealed envelope, and two letters were face up, revealing either a 40-lira or a 50-lira stamp (see Figure 10.6). Subjects in the symbolic condition were asked to test two abstract rules involving letters with an *A* or a *D* on one side and a 3 or a 5 on the other side. Seventeen of the 24 subjects in the realistic condition were correct on both rules, compared with none of the 24 subjects in the symbolic condition.

A question raised by these findings is why people improve when they are given realistic information. Do they become better reasoners, or do they recall specific experiences from memory that eliminate the need to reason? Research by Griggs and Cox (1982) suggest that the latter explanation is more appropriate. Griggs and Cox tested 24 undergraduates at the University of Florida on a variation of Johnson-Laird's letter task and found that students did as poorly on the realistic task as on the abstract task. Griggs and Cox suggested that the good performance reported by Johnson-Laird et al. could be explained by their Italian subjects' personal knowledge about the postal rule and its counterexamples. The American subjects, in contrast, lacked personal experience that they could retrieve from memory, because the United States rates were the same for sealed and unsealed letters.

To test the memory retrieval explanation for the superiority of realistic materials, Griggs and Cox (1982) gave their subjects a rule that was familiar: If a person is drinking beer, then the person must be over 19 years of age. This rule was the law in the state of Florida when the study was conducted. Furthermore, 76% of the subjects later reported that they had personally violated the rule more than once, and 97% of the subjects could remember specific instances of someone other than themselves violating the drinking-age rule. When given the four cards, DRINKING A BEER, DRINKING A COKE, 16 YEARS OF AGE, and 22 YEARS OF AGE, 29 of 40 subjects made the correct selection for detecting violations of the drinking-age rule (DRINKING A BEER, 16 YEARS OF AGE), while none of the 40 subjects did so for the abstract version of the task (If a card has an A on one side, then it has a 3 on the other side).

These studies show that people perform better when the conditional statement contains familiar information. The semantic content of the statement is thus an important determinant of performance. Investigations of how semantic content influences performance currently make up the majority of psychological studies of comprehension (Lachman et al., 1979). This emphasis on semantic variables rather than syntactic variables represents a shift from the early studies in psycholinguistics—today psychologists are less interested in the syntactic issues discussed by Chomsky (1957). This may be due partly to the greater emphasis Chomsky himself placed on semantics in the revision of his theory (Chomsky, 1965). But it is also due to the realization that the semantic knowledge of the listener or reader plays a major role in comprehension. The interaction between the comprehender's knowledge and the semantic nature of the material is particularly evident in studies of text comprehension. The next chapter, on text comprehension, expands the unit of analysis from the sentence to the paragraph. Just as comprehension of a word usually depends on its context in a sentence, comprehension of a sentence often depends on the context of the paragraph.

Summary

One of the major questions that have fascinated psychologists interested in language is how people learn to speak in grammatically correct sentences. An early view suggested that children learn to associate the adjacent words in a sentence. According to this view, each word serves as a stimulus for the word that follows it. There are several problems with this theory, the major one being that a person would have to learn an infinite number of associations. The alternative view is that a child learns a grammar consisting of rules for generating sentences. The transformational grammar proposed by Chomsky stimulated much research as psychologists investigated how well it could account for the results of language experiments. The grammar consisted of both phrase structure rules for describing the parts of a sentence (such as noun phrase and verb phrase) and transformation rules for changing a sentence into a closely related sentence (such as an active sentence into a passive sentence).

Psychologists have occasionally used ambiguous sentences to study comprehension and have found that it takes longer to complete an ambiguous sentence than an unambiguous one. A clarifying context apparently allows the listener to quickly select the appropriate meaning of an ambiguous word, although both meanings have been activated. However, a context can also cause interference if it is misleading or if a strongly expected word does not occur. The study of how people comprehend noun phrases indicates that the meaning of a noun is immediately influenced by the adjective that precedes it. The research on comprehension seeks to identify how context influences the meaning of words and raises the question of how different experimental tasks relate to the comprehension that occurs during ordinary reading.

An aspect of language that has direct practical applications is the distinction between assertions and implications. A sentence that only implies some event may have as great an impact as a sentence that directly asserts this event. Making people aware of the distinction between an asserted and an implied statement is particularly important in courtroom testimony. Research using simulated testimony has found that people often do not distinguish or do not remember what information was only implied and what was asserted. Similar results have been found for advertising claims. In contrast to these studies—in which people easily accepted the implications— studies on logical reasoning show that the implications of logical statements are not very apparent. People are seldom correct when abstract material is used but improve when they can relate the statement to their own experiences.

Recommended Reading

An easy introduction to the theoretical contributions of Chomsky is a book by Lyons (1970). Jenkins (1969) discusses the influence of grammatical theories on the way psychologists have thought about language acquisition. Lachman, Lachman, and Butterfield (1979) review the shift in psycholinguistics from a preoccupation with syntax to a preoccupation with semantics. The consistent use of either syntactic or semantic information creates parallel structure and facilitates comprehension (Frazier, Taft, Roeper, Clifton, & Ehrlich, 1984). Schvaneveldt, Meyer, and Becker (1976) used their lexical decision task to study the effect of semantic context on visual word recognition. Blank and Foss (1978) studied how an appropriate semantic context facilitates comprehension of sentences. Examples of how knowledge sources interact to determine comprehension are discussed by Bock (1982) and Salasoo and Pisoni (1985).

There have been many studies on memory for sentences. Jarvella (1979) reviews studies on immediate memory for the exact words of a sentence. Bransford and Franks (1971) performed a classic study on the integration of ideas in sentences, in which they showed that people have difficulty recognizing the exact words in a sentence because they combine the ideas in related sentences. Kintsch and Bates (1977) studied recognition memory outside the laboratory by testing students' memory for statements made during a classroom lecture. Keenan, MacWhinney, and Mayhew (1977) found that their colleagues often could remember the exact words of statements that had high emotional content, but usually only the general meaning of sentences is remembered (Sachs, 1967).

11

Comprehension and Memory for Text

Reading a book should be a conversation between you and the author.

MORTIMER ADLER AND CHARLES VAN DOREN

It may be difficult to single out any one cognitive skill as more important than the others, but if we had to make a choice, comprehension would be a prime contender for the honor. Much of what we learn depends on our ability to understand written material. The comprehension of written material has attracted considerable interest.

This interest in comprehension has resulted in attempts to rewrite regulations and instructions to make them easier to understand. For instance, President Jimmy Carter issued an order requiring that each federal regulation be written in plain English and be understandable to those who had to comply with it. One example of the attempt to improve instructions is the study conducted by Charrow and Charrow (1979). The goal of the study was to make it easier to understand jury instructions by identifying difficulties in comprehension. Box 11.1 shows two versions of instructions to a jury. The first version is the original; the second version is a modification designed to be easier to understand.

Charrow and Charrow tested the success of their modifications by asking prospective jury members to paraphrase the instructions. After the members heard the instructions, they tried to recall them in their own words. The jury members who listened to the modified instructions were more successful than the members who listened to the original instructions. For the example show in Box 11.1, ability to recall the instructions improved by about 50%.

Box 11.1   Making legal language understandable

Original

You must not consider as evidence any statement of counsel made during the trial; however, if counsel for the parties have stipulated to any fact, or any fact has been admitted by counsel, you will regard that fact as being conclusively proved as to the party or parties making the stipulation or admission.

As to any question to which an objection was sustained, you must not speculate as to what the answer might have been or as to the reason for the objection.

You must not consider for any purpose any offer of evidence that was rejected, or any evidence that was stricken out by the court; such matter is to be treated as though you had never known of it.

You must never speculate to be true any insinuation suggested by a question asked a witness. A question is not evidence and may be considered only as it supplies meaning to the answer.

Modified

As I mentioned earlier, it is your job to decide from the evidence what the facts are. Here are five rules that will help you decide what is, and what is not, evidence.

1. *Lawyers' Statements.* Ordinarily, any statement made by the lawyers in this case is not evidence. However, if all the lawyers agree that some particular thing is true, you must accept it as the truth.

2. *Rejected Evidence.* At times during this trial, items or testimony were offered as evidence, but I did not allow them to become evidence. Since they never became evidence, you must not consider them.

3. *Stricken Evidence.* At times, I ordered some piece of evidence to be stricken, or thrown out. Since that is no longer evidence, you must ignore it, also.

4. *Questions to a Witness.* By itself, a question is not evidence. A question can only be used to give meaning to a witness's answer. Furthermore, if a lawyer's question to a witness contained any insinuations, you must ignore those insinuations. And

5. *Objections to Questions.* If a lawyer objected to a question, and I did not allow the witness to answer the question, you must not try to guess what the answer might have been. You must also not try to guess the reason why the lawyer objected to the question.

From "Making Legal Language Understandable: A Psycholinguistic Study of Jury Instructions," by R. P. Charrow and V. R. Charrow. In *Columbia Law Review*, 1979, 79, 1306–1374. Reprinted by permission of the authors.

Psychologists have used primarily two measures of comprehension, and we will encounter examples of each in this chapter. One is a subjective measure of understanding. Psychologists ask people to rate on a scale how easy various texts were to understand, or they might ask people to press a button as soon as they think they understand a sentence. The second measure is the number of ideas that people can recall from a text. This measure assumes that someone who has really understood the ideas should be able to recall more ideas than someone who didn't understand the ideas.

Two important components influence comprehension—the reader and the text. The reader comes equipped with prior knowledge that can help her understand the text by relating what she reads to what she already knows. The quotation at the beginning of this chapter—"Reading a book should be a conversation between you and the author"—reflects this interaction between the reader and the author. But unlike a real conversation, the conversation proceeds in only one direction. This places an added burden on the author to anticipate how the reader might respond— to foresee difficulties and answer questions that the reader might have.

The three sections of this chapter emphasize the reader, the text, and the interaction between the reader and the text. The first section looks at how the reader's knowledge influences the comprehension and recall of ideas in a text. The second section is about the organization of ideas in a text. The final section discusses a specific model of how comprehension occurs. Although the model is not completed, it is already successful in predicting how easy it is to read different paragraphs.

Prior Knowledge of the Reader

Effect of Prior Knowledge on Comprehension

A central issue for psychologists interested in studying comprehension is specifying how people use their knowledge to understand new or abstract ideas. The influence of prior knowledge on the comprehension and recall of ideas was dramatically illustrated in a study by Bransford and Johnson (1973). They asked people to listen to a paragraph and try to comprehend and remember it. After listening to the paragraph, subjects rated how easy it was to comprehend and then tried to recall as many ideas as they could. You can get some feeling for the task by reading the following passage once and then trying to recall as much as you can.

> If the balloons popped, the sound wouldn't be able to carry, since everything would be too far away from the correct floor. A closed window would also prevent the sound from carrying, since most buildings tend to be well insulated. Since the whole operation depends on a steady flow of electricity, a break in the middle of the wire would also cause problems. Of course, the fellow could shout, but the human voice is not loud enough to carry that far. An additional problem is that a string could break on the instrument. Then there could be no accompaniment to the message. It is clear that the best situation would involve less distance. Then there would be fewer potential problems. With face to face contact, the least number of things could go wrong [p. 392].

Bransford and Johnson intentionally designed the passage to consist of abstract, unfamiliar statements. If you found it difficult to recall the ideas, your experience was similar to the experience of the people who participated in the experiment. They recalled only 3.6 ideas from a maximum of 14. The ideas can be made less abstract by showing people an appropriate context, as is illustrated in Figure 11.1. Does the picture help you recall any more ideas?

- context helps comprehension ideas only if context is presented before passage

- test was by # of facts remembered.

Figure 11.1   Appropriate context for the balloon passage

Bransford and Johnson (1973) tested the effect of context by comparing a "no context" group with two other groups. The "context before" group saw the picture before they read the passage. They recalled an average of 8.0 ideas, a substantial improvement over the no-context group. The "context after" group saw the picture immediately after reading the passage. They recalled only 3.6 ideas—the same number as the no-context group. The effect of context was useful, but only if people were aware of the context before reading the passage.

The results suggest that context does much more than simply provide hints about what might have occurred in the passage. If the picture provided useful retrieval cues, the people who saw the picture after reading the passage should have recalled more ideas than the group who didn't see the picture. Since recall was improved only when people saw the picture before reading the passage, the experiment suggests that the context improved comprehension, which, in turn, improved recall. People in the context-before group rated the passage as easy to comprehend, in contrast to the context-after group. When the abstract ideas were difficult to comprehend, they were quickly forgotten, and providing the context after the passage had no effect on recall.

The balloon passage is an example of a novel context, since most of us have never encountered this particular situation. But even a familiar context is useful only if we know when it is appropriate. Consider the following passage:

> The procedure is actually quite simple. First you arrange things into different groups. Of course, one pile may be sufficient depending on how much there is to do. If you have to go somewhere else due to lack of facilities, that is the next step; otherwise you are pretty well set. It is important not to overdo things. That is, it is better to do too few things at once than too many. In the short run this may not seem important, but complications can easily arise. A mistake can be expensive as well. At first the whole procedure will seem complicated. Soon, however, it will become just another facet of life. It is difficult to foresee any end to the necessity for this task in the immediate future, but then one never can tell. After the procedure is completed, one arranges the materials into different groups again. Then they can be put into their appropriate places. Eventually they will be used once more, and the whole cycle will then have to be repeated. However, that is part of life [Bransford & Johnson, 1973, p. 400].

The paragraph actually describes a very familiar procedure, but the ideas are presented so abstractly that the procedure is difficult to recognize. People who read the passage had as much trouble recalling ideas as the people who read the balloon passage—they recalled only 2.8 ideas from a maximum of 18. A different group of subjects, who were informed after reading the passage that it referred to washing clothes, didn't do any better; they recalled only 2.7 ideas. But subjects who were told before they read the passage that it described washing clothes recalled 5.8 ideas. The results are consistent with the results on the balloon passage and indicate that background knowledge isn't sufficient if people don't recognize the appropriate context. Although everyone is familiar with the procedure used to wash clothes, people didn't recognize the procedure because the passage was so abstract. Providing the appropriate context before the passage therefore increased both comprehension and recall, as it did for the balloon passage.

Effect of Prior Knowledge on Retrieval

The failure of the context-after group to recall more ideas than the no-context group was caused by the difficulty in comprehending material when there was not an obvious context. The results might have been different, however, if the material had been easier to understand as presented. Bransford and Johnson, in fact, suggest that if people initially understand a text and are then encouraged to think of the ideas in a new perspective, they might recall additional ideas that they failed to recall under the old perspective.

A study by Anderson and Pichert (1978) supports the hypothesis that a shift in perspective may result in the recall of additional ideas. The participants in their study read about two boys who played hooky from school. The story told that they went to one of the boys' homes because no one was there on Thursdays. It was a very nice home on attractive grounds, set back from the road. But because it was an older home, it had some defects—a leaky roof and a damp basement. The family was quite wealthy and owned a lot of valuable possessions, such as ten-speed bikes, a color television, and a rare coin collection. The entire story contained 72 ideas, which had previously been rated for their importance to a prospective burglar or to a prospective homebuyer. For example, a leaky roof and damp basement would be important to a homebuyer, whereas valuable possessions and the fact that no one was usually home on Thursday would be important to a burglar.

The subjects read the story from one of the two perspectives and, after a short delay, were asked to write down as much of the exact story as they could remember. After another short delay they again attempted to recall ideas from the story. Half did so from the same perspective and half from a new perspective. The experimenters told the subjects in the "same perspective" condition that the purpose of the study was to determine whether people could remember things they thought they had forgotten if they were given a second chance. Subjects in the "new perspective" condition were told that the purpose of the study was to determine whether people could remember things they thought they had forgotten if they were given a new perspective.

As might be expected, the perspective influenced the kind of information people recalled during the first recall period. The group that had the burglar perspective recalled more burglar information, and the group that had the homebuyer perspective recalled more homebuyer information. The results during the second recall attempt supported the hypothesis that a change in perspective can result in recall of additional information. The group that shifted perspectives recalled additional ideas that were important to the new perspective—7% more ideas in one experiment and 10% more in another. In contrast, the group that did not shift perspective recalled slightly less information on its second attempt than on its first attempt.

Notice that these findings differ from the findings of Bransford and Johnson (1973) in that the shift to a new perspective aided the retrieval, rather than the comprehension, of ideas. Since the story was easy to comprehend, comprehension wasn't a problem; the problem was being able to recall all the ideas. Anderson and Pichert proposed three possible explanations for why changing perspectives aided recall. One possibility is that people simply guessed ideas that they didn't really remember but that were consistent with the new perspective. The chance of guessing correctly, however, is rather low. A second alternative is that people did not recall all they could remember because they thought it was not important to the original perspective. The instructions, however, were to recall all the information. The third possibility was the one favored by Anderson and Pichert because it was the most consistent with what the participants reported during interviews that followed their recall. Many subjects reported that the new perspective provided them with a plan for searching memory. They used their knowledge about what would interest a homebuyer or a burglar to retrieve new information that was not suggested by the original perspective.

Effect of Prior Knowledge on False Recognitions

The previous studies support the idea that prior knowledge influences either the comprehension or the retrieval of information in a text. People who could interpret abstract ideas as related to a serenade or to washing clothes had an advantage in comprehending and recalling the ideas. In addition, adopting a particular perspective enabled people to retrieve more concrete ideas that they had initially been able to comprehend.

Although background knowledge usually makes comprehension and recall easier, it can also be the source of errors. When we already know something about the given topic and then read more about it, we may have difficulty distinguishing between what we read and what we already know. This can create a problem if we are asked to recall the source of the information. Consider the following biographical passage:

> Gerald Martin strove to undermine the existing government to satisfy his political ambitions. Many of the people of his country supported his efforts. Current political problems made it relatively easy for Martin to take over. Certain groups remained loyal to the old government and caused Martin trouble. He confronted these groups directly and so silenced them. He became a ruthless, uncontrollable dictator. The ultimate effect of his rule was the downfall of his country [Sulin & Dooling, 1974, p. 256].

People who read this passage should not associate it with their knowledge of famous people, since Gerald Martin is a fictitious person. It would be easy, however, to modify the passage by changing the name of the dictator. In an experiment designed by Sulin and Dooling (1974) half the subjects read the Gerald Martin passage, and half the subjects read the same passage with the name changed to Adolf Hitler. Either five minutes or one week after reading the passage, the subjects were given a recognition memory test consisting of seven sentences from the passage randomly mixed with seven sentences that were not in the passage. Subjects were asked to identify the sentences that occurred in the passage.

Four of the sentences not in the passage were completely unrelated (neutral), and the other three varied in their relatedness to the Hitler theme. The low-related sentence was *He was an intelligent man but had no sense of human kindness.* The medium-related sentence was *He was obsessed by the desire to conquer the world.* The high-related sentence was *He hated the Jews particularly and so persecuted them.* Figure 11.2 shows the recognition of sentences for the two retention intervals. At the short retention interval there were few false recognitions, and the results were uninfluenced by whether the passage was about a famous person (Hitler) or a fictitious person (Martin). After one week, however, it was more difficult for people who read the Hitler passage to distinguish between what was in the passage and what they knew about Hitler. People were likely to recognize a sentence incorrectly as having occurred in the passage if it described Hitler. False recognitions also increased with the retention interval for people who read the Gerald Martin (fictitious) passage, but to a lesser degree.

In conclusion, prior knowledge can influence the comprehension and recall of text in a variety of ways. Prior knowledge can make abstract ideas seem less abstract and easier to comprehend. It can also determine what we emphasize in a text and provide a framework for recalling ideas. The price we pay for these benefits is that it may be more difficult to locate the source of our knowledge if what we read is integrated with what we know. In most cases the price is fairly small relative to the benefits.

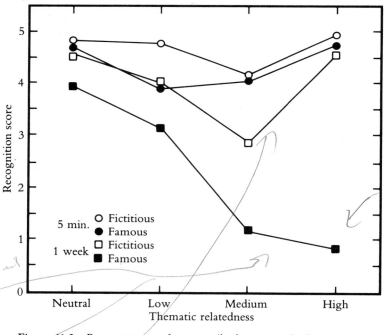

Figure 11.2   Recognition performance (high score = high performance) on new information as a function of main character, retention interval, and thematic relatedness

Organization of Events

A large component of text comprehension is concerned with reading stories that describe a sequence of events. Our prior knowledge about events determines what we are likely to emphasize and remember when we read a story. In order to make predictions about what aspects of a story are considered important, psychologists have had to develop theories about how people organize events. Let us begin by considering routine activities that are familiar to most of us.

Scripts: Representing Events

Schank and Abelson (1977) proposed that our knowledge is organized around many kinds of routine activities—for example, going to a restaurant, visiting a dentist, or riding a bus. They used the term *script* to refer to what we know about each of these situations. For example, a restaurant script would specify what we know about going to a restaurant. At a very general level, a restaurant script consists of standard roles, props or objects, conditions, and results. The conditions for going to a restaurant are that a customer is hungry and is able to pay for the meal. The props are tables and chairs, a menu, food, a bill, and money or a credit card. Supporting actors include waiters or waitresses and sometimes other personnel such as bartenders or busboys. The results are that the customer has less money but is no longer hungry, while the owner has more money. Between the times that a customer enters and leaves, there is a fairly standard sequence of events that include selecting a table, looking at the menu, ordering the food, eating, and paying the bill.

Since the sequence of events is quite standard, if someone asks us about our visit to a particular restaurant, there is no need to mention all the actions that took place. Instead we would mention events that are not standard—such as the quality of the food, the service, the decor, and perhaps the cost. The advantage of all the standard information stored in a script is that it enables the listener to fill in the missing details without having to recapitulate everything.

A study by Bower, Black, and Turner (1979) used the concept of scripts to investigate how people's knowledge of routine activities helps them understand and remember information. The first question they asked is to what extent people agree about the events that occur in standard activities such as going to a restaurant, attending a lecture, getting up in the morning, grocery shopping, or visiting a doctor. They asked people to list about 20 actions or events that occur during each of these activities. Table 11.1 presents the lists in the order in which the events were usually mentioned. All the events listed in Table 11.1 were mentioned by at least 25% of subjects. The lists show that there is considerable agreement on the actions that occur during routine activities.

What effect does knowledge of script-related activities have on memory for text? One effect is that scripts determine what is emphasized as we read a text. The typical events in a script provide a framework for comprehension but are themselves uninteresting because we already know about them. What is usually interesting is the

Table 11.1   Actions associated with different events

Going to a restaurant	Attending a lecture	Getting up	Grocery shopping	Visiting a doctor
Open door	ENTER DOOR	Wake up	ENTER STORE	Enter office
Enter	Look for friends	Turn off alarm	GET CART	CHECK IN WITH RECEPTIONIST
Give reservation name	FIND SEAT	Lie in bed	Take out list	SIT DOWN
Wait to be seated	SIT DOWN	Stretch	Look at list	Wait
Go to table	Settle belongings	GET UP	Go to first aisle	Look at other people
BE SEATED	TAKE OUT NOTEBOOK	Make bed	Go up and down aisles	READ MAGAZINE
Order drinks	Look at other students	Go to bathroom	PICK OUT ITEMS	Name called
Put napkins on lap	Talk	Use toilet	Compare prices	Follow nurse
LOOK AT MENU	Look at professor	Take shower	Put items in cart	Enter exam room
Discuss menu	LISTEN TO PROFESSOR	Wash face	Get meat	Undress
ORDER MEAL	TAKE NOTES	Shave	Look for items forgotten	Sit on table
Talk	CHECK TIME	DRESS	Talk to other shoppers	Talk to nurse
Drink water	Ask questions	Go to kitchen	Go to checkout counters	NURSE TESTS
Eat salad or soup	Change position in seat	Fix breakfast	Find fastest line	Wait
Meal arrives	Daydream	EAT BREAKFAST	WAIT IN LINE	Doctor enters
EAT FOOD	Look at other students	BRUSH TEETH	Put food on belt	Doctor greets
Finish meal	Take more notes	Read paper	Read magazines	Talk to doctor about problem
Order dessert	Close notebook	Comb hair	WATCH CASHIER RING UP	Doctor asks questions
Eat dessert	Gather belongings	Get books	PAY CASHIER	DOCTOR EXAMINES
Ask for bill	Stand up	Look in mirror	Watch bag boy	Get dressed
Bill arrives	Talk	Get coat	Cart bags out	Get medicine
PAY BILL	LEAVE	LEAVE HOUSE	Load bags into car	Make another appointment
Leave tip			LEAVE STORE	LEAVE OFFICE
Get coats				
LEAVE				

Items in all capital letters were mentioned by most subjects, items in italics by fewer subjects, and items in lower-case letters by the fewest subjects.

occurrence of an event that is related to the script but unexpected. For example, a customer may need help translating a menu because it is in French, or the waiter may spill soup on the customer. Schank and Abelson (1977) refer to such events as *obstacles* or *distractions* because they interrupt the major goals of the script, such as ordering and eating.

Bower and his colleagues (1979) hypothesized that such interruptions should be remembered better than the routine events in the scripts listed in Table 11.1. From the viewpoint of the reader, they are the only "point" of the story. Bower also hypothesized that events that are irrelevant to the goals of the script should be remembered less well than the routine events in the script. For example, the type of print on the menu or the color of the waitress's hair is irrelevant to the goals of the script.

Bower and his colleagues tested this hypothesis by asking subjects to read six script-based stories about making coffee, attending a lecture, getting up in the morning, attending a movie, visiting a doctor, and dining at a restaurant. After reading all six stories and then completing an intervening task for ten minutes, subjects attempted to recall the stories in writing. The results supported the predictions—subjects recalled 53% of the interruptions, 38% of the script actions, and 32% of the irrelevant information.

Goal-Directed Events

The finding that people recalled statements that interrupted goals suggests that scripts are very goal-oriented. This goal-oriented characteristic of scripts gives us a clue about their internal organization. Imagine that you have a flat tire and you need to put on the spare. Changing a tire consists of a sequence of activities that might be organized in memory according to either the centrality or the temporal order of the activities.

Figure 11.3a shows an organization in which some activities (such as removing the bad tire) are more central than others (such as putting away the jack). The more central activities are those activities that are particularly important in accomplishing the goal. If activities are organized according to their centrality, then people should be faster in verifying that the more central activities are included in a script. You may have noticed that the representation in Figure 11.3a is analogous to the semantic network proposed by Collins and Loftus (see Figure 9.6), but the shorter links represent a strong association between an activity and a script instead of a strong association between an exemplar and its category. An alternative representation, shown in Figure 11.3b, consists of activities organized according to their sequential order. If activities are reconstructed in the order in which they are performed, people should be faster in verifying that earlier activities are included in the script.

Galambos and Rips (1982) tested which theory was more appropriate by asking students to rank-order the activities of different scripts according to both their temporal order and their centrality. They then showed another group of subjects pairs of items that consisted of the name of a script (changing a flat) and an activity (take

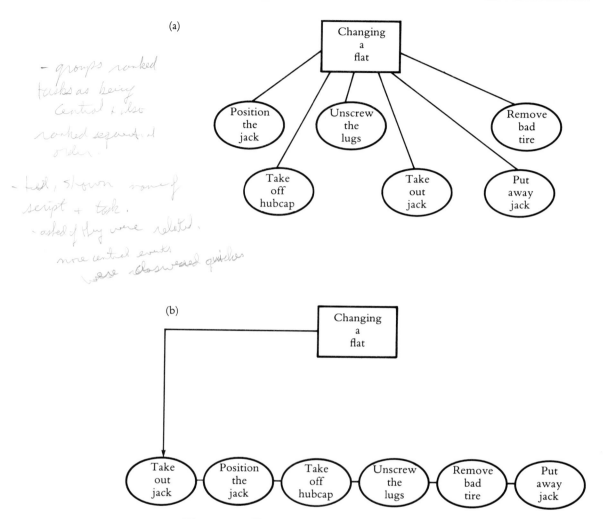

handwritten notes in left margin:
- groups ranked tasks as being central + also ranked sequential order.
- told, shown name of script + task.
- asked if they were related.
more central events were answered quicker

Figure 11.3 Two representations of a routine: (a) according to the centrality of component activities and (b) according to their sequential order

out jack). Students were asked to respond as quickly as possible whether the activity was included in the script. More central events were verified more quickly than less central events, but earlier events were not verified more quickly than later events. The results therefore supported the organization shown in Figure 11.3a.

The more central events in Figure 11.3a are presumably more central because they closely relate to the goal structure of the script. Brewer and Dupree (1983) obtained direct support for the importance of goal-directed actions. They proposed that goal-directed actions are linked together by the *in-order-to* relation. An example of this relation occurs if your goal is to get into your house. You take out your keys in order to unlock the door, in order to open the door, in order to walk into your house. Other actions such as putting the keys back and closing the door are less goal-oriented because they are not necessary to get into your house.

Brewer and Dupree tested people's memory for goal-directed actions by making a videotape of an actress carrying out a series of actions. In one version of the videotape a particular action was goal-directed and in another version the same action was not goal-directed. An example of a goal-directed action is taking out a ruler from between two books in order to set the hands on a wall clock. An example of an action that is not goal-directed is taking out a ruler from between two books and placing it on the desk, without using it to achieve a goal. The results showed that actions that were part of a goal-directed plan were recalled 70% of the time, whereas the same actions not embedded in a plan were recalled only 30% of the time.

In conclusion, these studies demonstrate that our knowledge about sequences of actions determines what we retrieve from memory and how quickly we can retrieve it. Such sequences are goal-oriented, and actions that either disrupt the goal or are important for achieving the goal are more likely to be recalled than actions that are irrelevant to the goal. Many stories contain actions that are goal-oriented, and these actions are also important, even if they are part of an unfamiliar event. In the next section we will look at the structure of stories to see how story structure influences recall.

Story Structure

One characteristic of simple narrative stories is that the structure determines how the events in the story are organized. We can study this structure at a very general level by representing a story as consisting of a setting, a theme, a plot, and a resolution (Thorndyke, 1977). The *setting* describes time, location, and major characters. The *theme* provides the general focus of the story, often a goal that the main character is trying to achieve. The *plot* consists of a series of actions attempting to achieve the goal. There may be several subgoals or intermediate goals that have to be accomplished before the main goal is reached. The *resolution*—the final outcome of the story—often describes whether the main character was successful in achieving the goal. Each of the components is evident in the following story. (Statements are numbered for the purpose of the discussion below.)

(1) Circle Island is located in the middle of the Atlantic Ocean (2) north of Ronald Island. (3) The main occupations on the island are farming and ranching. (4) Circle Island has good soil but (5) few rivers and (6) hence a shortage of water. (7) The island is run democratically. (8) All issues are decided by a majority vote of the islanders. (9) The governing body is a senate (10) whose job is to carry out the will of the majority. (11) Recently, an island scientist discovered a cheap method (12) of converting salt water into fresh water. (13) As a result, the island farmers wanted (14) to build a canal across the island, (15) so that they could use water from the canal (16) to cultivate the

island's central region. (17) Therefore, the farmers formed a procanal association (18) and persuaded a few senators (19) to join. (20) The procanal association brought the construction idea to a vote. (21) All the islanders voted. (22) The majority voted in favor of construction. (23) The senate, however, decided that (24) the farmers' proposed canal was ecologically unsound. (25) The senators agreed (26) to build a smaller canal (27) that was 2 feet wide and 1 foot deep. (28) After starting construction on the smaller canal, (29) the islanders discovered that (30) no water would flow into it. (31) Thus the project was abandoned. (32) The farmers were angry (33) because of the failure of the canal project. (34) Civil war appeared inevitable [Thorndyke, 1977, p. 80].

The setting is described in the first ten statements, which inform us about the location and central characters. The next six statements establish the theme and introduce the goal of building a canal across the island. Statements 17–31 contain the plot, which describes how the islanders attempted to accomplish the goal but were overruled by the senate. The last three statements describe the final resolution, or outcome.

The structure of this simple narrative is very apparent. It proceeds from the setting to the theme, plot, and resolution. To evaluate how useful the goal structure of a story is in facilitating comprehension, Thorndyke modified the story to make the structure less apparent. One modification placed the theme at the end of the story, so people would not encounter the goal until after they had read the plot and the resolution. People read or heard the story only once, so when they finally reached the information about the goal, they had to use it to interpret what they had previously read about the plot. A more extreme modification was to delete the goal statement entirely. People recalled less information when the goal statement occurred at the end of the story and still less information when the goal was deleted.

When a goal is included in a story, people use the goal to help themselves organize the actions described in the story. A character's attempts to achieve a goal result in the establishment of causal relations among many of the statements in a text. Work by Tom Trabasso and his students at the University of Chicago indicates that it is these causal relations that underlie what a reader judges to be important in a text. One event, A, is judged to be the cause of another event, B, if the absence of A implies the absence of B. Consider again the goal of walking into your house. You couldn't walk into your house unless you opened the door, which you couldn't do unless you unlocked the door, which you couldn't do unless you took out your keys. Thus all three actions are causally related (necessary) to walking into your house.

An important variable in determining the judged importance of statements in a story is the number of causal connections linked to the statement. Consider again the example of changing a flat. The six actions included in Figure 11.3 were take out the jack, position the jack, take off the hubcap, unscrew the lugs, remove the bad tire, and put away the jack. The first four actions are necessary for removing the bad tire. But in order to put away the jack, it is only necessary to have taken out the jack. Removing the bad tire therefore has many more causal connections than putting away the jack. We might therefore expect that removing the bad tire would be a more important event than putting away the jack, as is implied by Trabasso and Sperry's (1985) research. Trabasso and Sperry found that when subjects rated the importance of events in stories, the judged importance of an action was directly related to the number of causal connections associated with that action. The number of causal connections was also important in determining what people would recall from a story and what they would include in a summary of the story (Trabasso & van den Broek, 1985). These findings are consistent with the research discussed in Chapter 9 that showed how causal statements facilitate the integration and retrieval of information from LTM (Myers et al., 1984).

A Model of Comprehension

The first two sections of this chapter reviewed research on two very important components of comprehension—the prior knowledge of the reader and the organization of ideas in the text. This final section describes psychologists' attempts to develop detailed models of text comprehension. Because text comprehension requires the integration of ideas in the text, a model of text comprehension requires assumptions about how this integration occurs. We begin by examining research on the integration of ideas and then show how some of its findings can be accounted for by a model proposed by Walter Kintsch and his students at the University of Colorado.

Integration of Ideas

Haviland and Clark (1974) have effectively argued that a sentence is usually understood within the context of the sentences that precede it. For example, the statement *George thinks vanilla* is rather bizarre by itself but becomes understandable when preceded by the question *What kind of ice cream does Vivian like?* The understanding of a sentence should therefore depend on how easy it is to relate the ideas in the sentence to the ideas that came before it. This prediction can be illustrated by the following pairs of sentences:

1. Ed was given an alligator for his birthday. The alligator was his favorite present.
2. Ed was given lots of things for his birthday. The alligator was his favorite present.

In both cases the first sentence provides an appropriate context for the second sentence, but the first case makes it clear that Ed received an alligator for his birthday. The second case requires an inference that one of the things Ed received was an alligator.

Participants in Haviland and Clark's experiment saw pairs of sentences in a tachistoscope. After reading the first sentence, they pressed a button to see the second sentence. When they thought they understood the second sentence, they pushed another button, which stopped a clock that measured how long the second sentence had been displayed. As predicted by Haviland and Clark, it took significantly less time to comprehend the second sentence when the same idea (such as alligator) was mentioned in both sentences than when the relation between the two sentences had to be inferred.

The ease with which new ideas can be related to old ideas also depends on the order of the sentences in a paragraph (Kieras, 1978). Consider the sequence of sentences in Table 11.2. The letter preceding each sentence indicates whether the information in the sentence is given (g) or new (n). The sentence is classified as given if it contains at least one noun that appeared in the preceding sentences. The first example contains only one new sentence; all sentences but the first refer to information that preceded them. The second example contains four new sentences that do not refer to preceding information. Kieras predicted that the ideas in the first example should be easier to integrate and recall than the ideas in the second example, and the results supported his prediction.

You may have noticed that all but one of the given sentences in Example 1 repeat a noun from the immediately preceding sentence. The one exception—*The jelly was grape*—repeats a noun (*jelly*) from a sentence that occurred four steps earlier. This sentence may be more difficult to integrate with the preceding sentences because the given information may no longer be in STM, requiring a search of LTM to retrieve the first sentence. Evidence, in fact, suggests that comprehension is influenced by whether the preceding relevant information is still active in STM or whether it must be retrieved from LTM (Lesgold, Roth, & Curtis, 1979).

The following sentences should be easy to integrate because the first sentence contains relevant information that should still be available in STM when the reader encounters the second sentence.

1. A thick cloud of smoke hung over the forest. The forest was on fire [Lesgold, Roth, & Curtis, p. 294].

Now let's insert two sentences that change the topic and make it less likely that the information about the smoke over the forest is still in STM when the reader learns about the fire.

2. A thick cloud of black smoke hung over the forest. Glancing to one side, Carol could see a bee flying around the back seat. Both of the kids were jumping around but made no attempt to free the insect. The forest was on fire [p. 295].

Table 11.2   Examples of presentation orders, showing the given (g) or new (n) status of each sentence

Example 1	Example 2
n – The ants ate the jelly.	n – The kitchen was spotless.
g – The ants were hungry.	n – The table was wooden.
g – The ants were in the kitchen.	n – The ants were hungry.
g – The kitchen was spotless.	g – The ants were in the kitchen.
g – The jelly was grape.	n – The jelly was grape.
g – The jelly was on the table.	g – The jelly was on the table.
g – The table was wooden.	g – The ants ate the jelly.

The inserted information is irrelevant to the fire in the forest and should make it more difficult to comprehend the final sentence than in Case 1. Now consider the insertion of two sentences that are consistent with the initial topic.

3. A thick cloud of smoke hung over the forest. The smoke was thick and black, and began to fill the clear sky. Up ahead Carol could see a ranger directing traffic to slow down. The forest was on fire [p. 295].

The two inserted sentences continue the initial topic, making it easier for the reader to keep active in STM information about the cloud of black smoke. Lesgold, Roth, and Curtis predicted that less time should be required to comprehend the final sentence in Case 3 than in Case 2. Their results supported their predictions.

A number of variables influence comprehension, according to these studies. All the variables reflect how easy it is to integrate what a person is reading with what that person has already read. One variable is whether the reader can relate newly acquired information to ideas that were already expressed in the text. Kieras's (1978) research indicated that it was easier to recall ideas in the text if the sentences referred to previous information than if they contained only new information. A second variable is whether previously expressed ideas are still active in STM or whether they must be retrieved from LTM. Comprehension is easier when related ideas are still active in STM (Lesgold et al., 1979). A third variable is whether newly acquired information can be related directly to previous information or whether the reader must infer the relation. Inferences slow down comprehension (Haviland & Clark, 1974). A theory of comprehension should incorporate each of these three variables.

Kintsch's Model of Comprehension

The model of comprehension proposed by Kintsch is fairly complex. I will therefore give only a brief summary of its major assumptions, emphasizing those that are related to the previous three studies. Figure 11.4 illustrates a theoretical framework for discussing how the information-processing capabilities of the reader interact with the organization of the text. There are two inputs in the model—the text and the goals of the reader. The knowledge and goals of the reader are represented at the top of the figure by the *goal schema*. The goal schema indicates what is relevant; it establishes expectations, calls for certain facts, and may infer facts if they are not directly stated in the text. The text itself is represented in the model by *propositions*. The propositions divide the text into meaningful units; the *coherence rules* arrange them in a network called a *coherence graph* to show how they are related. The network is similar to the semantic networks discussed in Chapter 9. Propositions are grouped together whenever they belong to the same fact. The *macrostructure* of the text consists of a set of summarization rules called *macro-operators*, which indicate which facts are most relevant and are therefore determined by the reader's goals. For example, if we asked people to summarize the story about the two boys who stayed home from school (Anderson & Pichert, 1978), discussed earlier in this chapter, we would expect that the summaries would differ depending on whether people adopted the burglar or the homebuyer perspective.

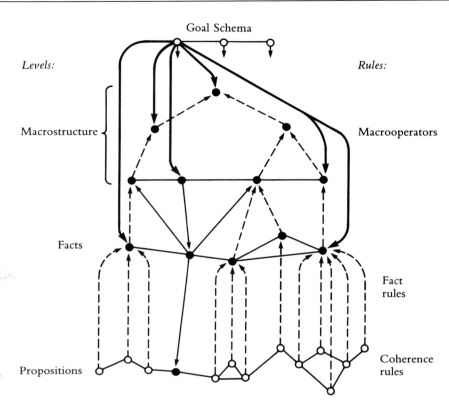

Figure 11.4   The global structure of Kintsch's model of comprehension

The general characteristics of the model can be illustrated with a simple example (Kintsch, 1979). Consider the following text:

> The Swazi tribe was at war with a neighboring tribe because of a dispute over cattle. Among the warriors were two unmarried men, Kakra and his younger brother Gum. Kakra was killed in a battle [p. 6].

The model specifies rules for dividing the text into propositions, but we will not be concerned with the details of these rules. We will consider word groups that correspond approximately to the underlying propositions. Figure 11.5 shows how the first sentence is divided into five groups and how the groups are related in a coherence graph. The proposition *was at war with* is the most important proposition, and the others are joined to it. An important parameter in the model is the number of propositions that can be kept active in STM. Since STM is limited in capacity, only a few propositions can be kept active; our example assumes that the capacity limit is three propositions, as indicated by the enclosed propositions in the figure. Propositions describing the plans and goals of the characters are particularly likely to be selected (Fletcher, 1986).

Coherence analysis: Cycle I

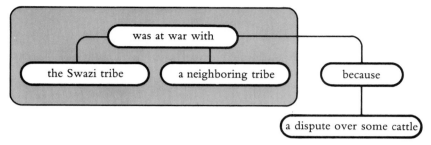

Figure 11.5 Analysis of the first sentence in the Swazi example

Figure 11.6 shows the propositions of the second sentence and the propositions from the first sentence that are still active in STM. The reader first tries to connect the new propositions with the old ones in STM, but the words in the second sentence don't match any of the words in STM. The reader next determines whether the new propositions can be related to any propositions in LTM. Kintsch proposes that the search of LTM, which he calls a *reinstatement search,* is one of the factors that make a text difficult to read. If information in the text can be related to ideas that are still active in STM, comprehension is easier than if the reader must search LTM in order to integrate new information with the old. This assumption is consistent with the findings of Lesgold et al. (1979).

Coherence analysis: Cycle II

Figure 11.6 Analysis of the second sentence in the Swazi example

The reinstatement search also fails for the example because there are no concepts that are common to the first two sentences. The model must therefore construct a new coherence graph rather than add on to the old graph. It may also make an inference at this point to interrelate the two graphs. The inference is that the warriors mentioned in the second sentence were members of the Swazi tribe. This seems like a reasonable inference, but it is not stated directly. Kintsch's model assumes that inferences, like reinstatement searches, slow down the reader and make comprehension more difficult. The evidence supports this assumption (for example, Haviland and Clark, 1974).

The model once again selects three propositions from the second sentence to keep active in STM. Figure 11.6 shows that the three selected specify the names of the two men. The third sentence—*Kakra was killed in battle*—is easy to relate to previous information because information about Kakra is still available in STM. The new information can therefore be added directly to the coherence graph without having to search LTM or make an inference.

This example should give you an approximate idea of how the model works. The major theme of the model is that incoming information can be understood more easily when it can be integrated with information that the reader has already encountered. The easiest case is when the new information can be related to information that is still active in STM. If it cannot be related, a reinstatement search attempts to relate the new information to propositions stored in LTM. If the reinstatement search fails, a new coherence graph must be started, resulting in a memory for ideas that are not very well integrated. The result should be poorer recall, as was found by Kieras (1978) when the new sentences could not be related to previous sentences. Integration of ideas can sometimes be achieved by an inference, but the need for inferences also contributes to the difficulty of the text.

Predicting Readability

One attractive aspect of Kintsch's model is that it is now complete enough to allow predictions about the ease of reading different kinds of text. Predicting readability is an important applied problem. The developers of educational materials want to be assured that their materials can be understood by the students who read them. A former professor of mine once wrote a chapter for *The Mind*, a book in one of the Time-Life series. His chapter required nine revisions before it satisfied the editors of Time-Life. Although he was a good writer and was familiar with the topic, he was inexperienced at writing for students in junior high school—the reading level selected for the series.

There have been many attempts to predict readability. According to Kintsch and Vipond (1979), the earliest formulas appeared in the 1920s. There are now about 50 readability formulas, most containing word and sentence variables—unfamiliar words and long sentences generally make a text harder to read. What the formulas lack, however, is a good way of measuring text organization. If someone placed all the words in a sentence in a scrambled order, the sentence would be very difficult to comprehend, but the predictions of most formulas would be unchanged because they don't consider the order of words in a sentence or the order of sentences in a paragraph. The formulas are limited because they are not based on a theory of text comprehension.

The theory currently being developed by Kintsch has already contributed to overcoming many of these limitations by providing an account of how the reader's information-processing capabilities interact with the organization of the text. Kintsch defined *readability* as the number of propositions recalled divided by the reading time. The measure takes into account both recall and reading time because it is easy to improve either measure at the expense of the other. Three parameters were estimated to make predictions. One parameter was the capacity of STM, which was usually about four propositions. Another parameter was the number of new propositions that were considered at one time. This number usually depended on the number of propositions in each sentence, since the model worked on one sentence at a time (as in the Swazi example) unless the sentence was too long. The maximum number ranged from 5 to 8 propositions, with a mean of 6.2. The final parameter was the probability that a proposition would be stored in LTM and recalled later—the "learning probability." The mean learning probability was rather high for the short texts and was equal to .64. The parameter estimates suggest that a reader processes all the propositions in a sentence unless the sentence contains more than six propositions; the probability of storing a given proposition in LTM is rather high for short paragraphs; and about four propositions can be kept active in STM.

Kintsch used his model, along with more traditional measures, to predict the readability of paragraphs. The two best predictors of readability were word frequency and the number of reinstatement searches. The first measure is contained in most readability formulas. As we might expect, the use of common words, those that occur frequently in the language, improves comprehension. The second measure—the number of reinstatement searches—is calculated from Kintsch's model. Application of the model determines how often a person must search LTM to relate new information to previous information. A reinstatement search is required only when the new information cannot be related to the propositions in STM. Another theoretical measure that improves the readability predictions is the number of inferences that are required. An inference is required whenever a concept is not directly repeated—for example, when *war* was mentioned in the first sentence and *warriors* in the second sentence. Kintsch found that the number of inferences influenced readability, though not as much as word frequency and the number of reinstatement searches. The required inferences were fairly easy, however; their influence might increase if they were more difficult.

The results show that a theory of comprehension can contribute to predicting readability. The theoretical measures—the number of reinstatement searches and the number of inferences—are determined by how well the ideas in the text relate to other ideas in the text. These measures were not included in the traditional measures of readability. Kintsch's model also provides a framework for considering the interaction between the reader and the text. The model implies that readability is not only determined by the text; it is also the result of the interaction between a particular reader and a particular text (Kintsch and Vipond, 1979). For example, a reinstatement search is required only when new information cannot be related to information in STM. A person who can retain many propositions in STM therefore has an advantage in having to make fewer reinstatement searches than a person with a more limited STM. There are several ways the facilitating effect of background knowledge could be incorporated into the model. Background knowledge might increase the number of propositions held in STM because of their greater familiarity. Background knowledge might also make it easier to make inferences in order to relate different concepts in the text.

Macrostructure

The story about Kakra and Gum illustrates the reader's attempt to understand the detailed meaning of a text by integrating phrases. For longer texts, understanding also occurs at a more global level as the reader attempts to grasp a summary of the main ideas. The macrostructure of the text consists of summarization rules that describe the "gist" of the text (see Figure 11.4).

Table 11.3 shows an example of a summary created by summarization rules. Notice that the summary includes causes for the failure to achieve a goal (election) and is therefore consistent with Trabasso and van den Broek's (1985) conclusion that causal connections are important in determining which information is retained in summaries generated by readers.

Vipond (1980) analyzed how both detailed (microstructure) and global (macrostructure) processing would influence text comprehension. He hypothesized that the same operations used to integrate the details of a text would be important in forming a summary of a text. Variables such as the number of reinstatement searches and the number of inferences might have similar effects at both levels in determining readability, as defined by considering both reading time and amount recalled.

Vipond tested his hypothesis by measuring the readability of 25 texts covering a variety of topics. As was found by Kintsch and Vipond (1979), the number of reinstatement searches was a major predictor of readability. Both the number of

Table 11.3   Example of a text and its summary

Text
    In New Brunswick, Premier Leonard Tilley had decided to call a provincial election and make Confederation the main issue. His opponents, although united in little else, joined in denouncing the Quebec plan. It was a scheme, they charged, for rescuing the Canadians from their difficulties at the expense of New Brunswick. Others warned that with both a federal and a provincial government to pay for, taxes would rise. New Brunswickers saw too few advantages and too many possible disadvantages in the plan to be willing to accept it as it stood. Tilley and his cabinet were overwhelmingly defeated in the election.

Summary
    In New Brunswick, Tilley called an election on Confederation. His opponents denounced the plan, saying it would cost New Brunswick money. New Brunswickers would not accept the plan as it stood; Tilley and his cabinet were defeated in the election.

reinstatement searches and the number of propositions that had to be reinstated correlated significantly with readability. The significant correlations occurred for reinstatements required to integrate the details and for reinstatements required to form the summary, supporting the hypothesis that similar operations occur at both levels of analysis. Operations at the micro- and macrolevels were equally important in determining readability. However, Vipond proposed that task demands could determine their relative importance; for example, forming a good summary might be more necessary for long-term retention than for the immediate recall required in his experiment.

Operations that create summaries are also important when we are not interested in details. In this case it would be beneficial to rapidly skim a text in order to pick out the most important information. Unfortunately, research suggests that this is easier said than done. People are not very good at selectively perceiving the most important information when they read a text rapidly (Masson, 1982). Reading the details may therefore be necessary in order to create a good summary.

As stated earlier, interaction between the fields of psychology and education was very apparent in the early part of this century but diminished during the following decades as psychologists began to study simple and somewhat artificial materials. The amount of current research activity on complex skills like comprehension suggests that the interaction between the two fields is increasing. In the next two chapters we will study another complex skill that has attracted the interest of both psychologists and educators—problem solving.

Summary

Psychologists study comprehension by investigating how people's prior knowledge and information-processing characteristics interact with the organization of ideas in a text. The importance of prior knowledge is evident when people have to comprehend very abstract ideas. A meaningful context improves recall if the context is given *before* people read abstract material. It is necessary to improve comprehension in order to improve recall. Recall of more concrete ideas may be improved by providing a context after people have read the text if the context causes a change in perspective. People's knowledge about everyday activities can be represented by scripts that describe the most common events associated with the activities. Scripts influence what a person emphasizes when reading a text. One disadvantage of prior knowledge is that it sometimes makes it hard to distinguish between recently read material and prior knowledge about the topic.

Comprehension is determined not only by what a person already knows but also by the organization of ideas in a text. The global structure of narrative stories includes setting, theme, plot, and resolution. The theme provides the general focus of the story and often consists of a goal that the main character tries to achieve. Comprehension is best when the theme precedes the plot; it deteriorates when the theme follows the plot and deteriorates even more when the theme is left out. Statements that have either a positive or a negative impact on the attainment of a goal are judged most important and are best remembered.

A model of text comprehension must account for how the reader attempts to relate the ideas in the text to ideas already read. Comprehension is easiest when the ideas can be related to ideas that are still available in STM. If no relations are found, the reader can search LTM to look for a relation. If no relations are found in LTM, the new material must be stored separately rather than integrated with the old material. Relations can sometimes be found by making inferences, but inferences slow down comprehension compared with direct repetition of the same concepts.

A model of comprehension proposed by Kintsch has been quite successful in predicting readability. The model can account for the organization of text by considering how many LTM searches and inferences are required. Its parameters include the number of propositions that are processed at one time, the probability of storing a proposition in LTM, and the number of propositions that can be kept active in STM. In addition to improving previous readability formulas, the model provides a theoretical framework for investigating how a person's information-processing characteristics interact with the organization of the text to influence comprehension.

Recommended Reading

Reder (1980) and Stein and Trabasso (1982) summarize research on the comprehension and retention of prose. Just and Carpenter (1980), Kieras (1983), and Haberlandt and Graesser (1985) have proposed detailed models to predict processing times for the different components of reading. Others have studied the effect of the reader's prior knowledge on learning information in a text (Chiesi, Spilich, & Voss, 1979; Spilich, Vesonder, Chiesi, & Voss, 1979). Alba and Hasher (1983), Brewer and Nakamura (1984), and Graesser and Nakamura (1982) discuss the impact of schema on comprehension and memory; Sharkey and Mitchell (1985) describe how scripts are used in reading. Buschke and Schaier (1979) and McKoon and Ratcliff (1980) studied the organization of text propositions in memory, and Walker and Meyer (1980a, 1980b) discuss the integration of text information. The model developed by Kintsch and his associates is discussed in papers by Kintsch and Van Dijk (1978), Miller and Kintsch (1980), Van Dijk and Kintsch (1983), and Keenan, Baillet, and Brown (1984). The psychology of reading is discussed in a recent book by Just and Carpenter (1987).

12

Problem Solving

Solving a problem means finding a way out of a difficulty, a way around an obstacle, attaining an aim that was not immediately understandable. Solving problems is the specific achievement of intelligence, and intelligence is the specific gift of mankind: Solving problems can be regarded as the most characteristically human activity.

GEORGE POLYA (1962)

Humans are not the only creatures who can solve problems, yet identifying problem solving as the most characteristically human activity, as Polya has done, emphasizes its importance in the development of civilization. The next two chapters discuss problem solving and emphasize recent progress in our attempt to understand how people solve problems. This chapter establishes the basic components of a theory of problem solving. The first section contains examples of different kinds of problems. A question that has interested psychologists is how general problem-solving skills are. At one extreme the answer is that the skills are very general, and a person who is good at solving one type of problem will also be very good at solving other types. At the other extreme is the claim that skills are very specific, and a person who is good at solving one type of problem may be poor at solving other types. The claim made in the first section falls between these two extremes. The proposed classification identifies three general kinds of problems on the basis of the skills required to solve them.

The second section describes the general characteristics of a theory of problem solving proposed by Newell and Simon (1972). The theory describes how problem solving is influenced by (1) people's information-processing capabilities as determined by STM and LTM, (2) the structure of the problem and its effect on the search for a solution, and (3) the effectiveness of different strategies and sources of information. The third section discusses general strategies such as the use of subgoals, analogy, and diagrams.

The problems discussed in this chapter are mainly puzzles. You may wonder why psychologists are interested in puzzles—wouldn't it be more appropriate to study the kinds of problems people encounter in school or work? One reason for studying problems like the anagram and series completion problems shown in Table 12.1 is that they often appear on intelligence tests. If we want to understand what intelligence tests really measure, we must take a closer look at the specific skills required to answer the questions. Another reason is that, when studying puzzles, psychologists can be less concerned about differences in people's education. Everyone should have more of an "equal chance" on puzzles than on problems taken from a textbook. However, psychologists have become more interested in classroom problems, as we will see in the next chapter. Fortunately, most of the issues discussed in this chapter will still be relevant when we discuss classroom problem solving.

Classifying Problems

Any attempt to improve problem-solving skills raises the question of what skills are needed for different kinds of problems. Students are taught how to solve statistics problems in a statistics class and chemistry problems in a chemistry class. Have they learned any general skills in a statistics class that can make them better problem solvers in a chemistry class, or do the problems in each class require a different set of skills? The question would be easier to answer if we could classify problems according to the skills needed to solve them.

Table 12.1 shows examples of problems that have been studied by psychologists. You will better understand this chapter if you try to solve these problems before reading further. When you have finished working on the problems, try to classify them according to the skills needed to solve them. We will examine one method of classification that proposes that the six problems can be divided into three categories.

The proposed classification is based on the general kinds of psychological skills and knowledge needed to solve different problems (Greeno, 1978). Greeno suggested that there are three types of problems: arrangement, inducing structure, and transformation. The classification does not imply that we will be able to classify every problem into one of the three categories. Rather, it provides three ideal types in order to determine whether a given problem requires primarily rearrangement, inducing structure, transformation, or some combination of the three skills. We will now consider examples of each type in order to see how the types differ.

Arrangement

Arrangement problems present some objects and require the problem solver to arrange them in a way that satisfies some criterion. The objects usually can be arranged in many different ways, but only one or a few of the arrangements forms a solution. An

Table 12.1   Examples of problems

A. Analogy
What word completes the analogy?
   Merchant : Sell :: Customer : _____
   Lawyer : Client :: Doctor : _____

B. String problem
Two strings hang from a ceiling but are too far apart to allow a person to hold one and walk to the other. On the floor are a book of matches, a screwdriver, and a few pieces of cotton. How could the strings be tied together?

C. Missionaries and cannibals
Five missionaries and five cannibals who have to cross a river find a boat, but the boat is so small that it can hold no more than three persons. If the missionaries on either bank of the river or in the boat are outnumbered at any time by cannibals, they will be eaten. Find the simplest schedule of crossings that will allow everyone to cross safely. At least one person must be in the boat at each crossing.

D. Water jar
You have an 8-gallon pail and a 5-gallon pail. How could you obtain 2 gallons of water?

E. Anagram
Rearrange the letters in each row to make an English word.
   RWAET
   KEROJ

F. Series completion
What number or letter continues each series?
   1 2 8 3 4 6 5 6 ____
   A B M C D M ____

excellent example is the rearrangement of the letters of an anagram to form a word—such as rearranging the letters KEROJ to spell JOKER and RWAET to spell WATER. Solving an arrangement problem often involves much trial and error, during which partial solutions are formed and evaluated. Greeno argued that the skills needed to solve arrangement problems include the following:

1. Fluency in generating possibilities. Flexibility is needed to generate many partial solutions and discard those that appear unpromising.
2. Retrieval of solution patterns. Ability to retrieve words from memory should be related to ability in solving anagrams.
3. Knowledge of principles that constrain search. Knowing the relative frequency with which various letters occur together should help guide the search. Since the pair J R is an unlikely combination, for instance, it should be avoided when forming partial solutions.

Gestalt psychologists were particularly interested in how people solve arrangement problems. Gestalt psychology, which began as the study of perception, emphasized the structure of patterns, and consequently it analyzed problem solving from this perspective. Many Gestalt tasks required the rearrangement of objects in order to find the correct relation among the parts.

A well-known example is the problem described by Köhler (1925) in his book *The Mentality of Apes*. Köhler hung some fruit from the top of a cage to investigate whether a chimpanzee or other ape could discover how to reach it. The cage contained several sticks and crates. The solution depended on finding a correct way to rearrange the objects—for example, standing on a crate and using a stick to knock down the fruit. According to the Gestalt analysis, solving the problem required the reorganization of the objects into a new structure.

Gestalt psychologists argued that discovering the correct organization usually occurred as a flash of insight. *Insight* is the sudden discovery of the correct solution following a period of incorrect attempts based primarily on trial and error. The key factor distinguishing insight from other forms of discovery is the suddenness of the solution. In contrast to solutions that are achieved through careful planning or a series of small steps, solutions based on insight seem to occur "in a flash."

Recent evidence supports the Gestalt argument that the correct arrangement of parts often occurs quite suddenly (Metcalfe, 1986b). Metcalfe gave her subjects anagrams to solve, such as *ssoia*, *pmuoi*, and *ttnua*. They were asked to assess how close they were to solving the problem, on a scale from 1 to 10, during the course of solving the anagrams. Every ten seconds a tap occurred and subjects recorded their ratings. The ratings remained very low until the discovery of the solution, implying that the correct answer suddenly appeared.

One factor that makes it difficult to find a correct arrangement is *functional fixedness*—the tendency to perceive an object only in terms of its most common use. The candle problem, studied by Duncker (1945), illustrates how functional fixedness can influence performance. The goal is to place three small candles at eye level on a door. Among other objects on a nearby table are a few tacks and three small boxes about the size of matchboxes. In one condition the boxes were filled with candles, tacks, and matches. In another condition the boxes were empty. The solution requires tacking the boxes to the door so they can serve as platforms for the candles (see Figure 12.1). More subjects solved the problem when the boxes were empty (Duncker, 1945; Adamson, 1952). The use of boxes as containers, rather than as platforms, was emphasized when they contained objects, and so it was more difficult to recognize their novel function.

The string problem in Table 12.1 requires finding a novel use for a tool. The screwdriver is tied to one string to create a pendulum that can be swung to the other string. One of the best examples of overcoming functional fixedness outside the laboratory is the attempt of prisoners to break out of jail. Since tools are not readily available in prison, prisoners have to use items that are available. Box 12.1 describes the ingenuity of two prisoners in finding novel uses for common objects.

Inducing Structure

Rearrangement problems require the rearrangement of objects to form a new relation among them. In problems of inducing structure, by contrast, the relation is fixed and the problem is to discover it. Some objects are given and the task is to discover how they are related. For example, series extrapolation problems consist of a series such as 1 2 8 3 4 6 5 6 _____ . The task is to find the next element of the series. Notice

Figure 12.1   The candle problem—initial state (a) and goal state (b)

that there are two series in the example. One is the ascending series 1 2, 3 4, 5 6; the other is the descending series 8, 6, ____ . So the correct answer is 4. Similarly, the answer to the letter series in Table 12.1 is E.

Another example of inducing structure is analogy problems like Merchant : Sell : : Customer : Buy. The instructions might indicate that the analogy should be labeled *true* or *false,* or the last word could be replaced by a blank, with instructions to fill in the word that best completes the analogy. Analogical reasoning is of particular interest because of its use in intelligence tests. The Miller Analogies Test, which is widely used for admission to graduate school, is composed exclusively of verbal analogies. Other ability tests, such as the GRE and the SAT, include analogies among the test items.

The psychological processes used in solving an analogy or series extrapolation problem involve identifying relations among the components and fitting the relations together in a pattern (Greeno, 1978). The importance of discovering relations among the terms of an analogy is illustrated in a model proposed by Sternberg (1977). There are four processes in Sternberg's model: encoding, inference, mapping, and application. Consider the problem *Washington is to 1 as Lincoln is to 10 or 5.* The task is to choose either 10 or 5 to complete the analogy. The *encoding* process identifies attri-

---

Box 12.1   Pair of crafty inmates melt way out of jail

SALINAS (AP)—Two crafty inmates used a length of shower pipe, a sheet and a wall socket to melt an unbreakable plastic window and escape from Monterey County's new jail, officials said Wednesday.

A sheriff's deputy said the pair escaped Tuesday night after using a makeshift cutting torch to reduce part of the cell window to mushy goo.

Lt. Ted Brown said the inmates wrapped a sheet around a piece of flattened shower pipe, wired the contraption and plugged it into a wall socket.

The gizmo heated up and the inmates pressed it against the window until its edge had melted away, Brown said.

Then they snapped a leg off the cell bed, placed it into the newly burned hole, pried out the entire window and skipped to freedom, Brown said.

From the *Los Angeles Times*, January 6, 1978. © Associated Press Newsfeatures. Reprinted by permission.

---

butes of the words that could be important in establishing relations. The first term, *Washington*, might be identified as a president, a portrait on a $1 bill, or a war hero. The *inference* process establishes valid relations between the first two terms. Washington was the first president of the United States, and his portrait appears on a $1 bill—two possible relations between Washington and 1. The *mapping* process establishes relations between the first and third terms. Both Washington and Lincoln were presidents, and portraits of both appear on bills, so both possibilities remain as the basis for the analogy. The *application* process attempts to establish a relation between Lincoln and 10 or 5 that is analogous to the one between Washington and 1. Since Lincoln was the 16th president of the United States, neither answer fits the presidential relation. However, Lincoln's portrait appears on a $5 bill, so the choice of 5 is consistent with the currency relation. This example reveals the importance of discovering relations. Suppose we had considered only the presidential relation. If we did not know that Lincoln was the 16th president, we would be more likely to guess that he was the tenth president than the fifth, and so we would have chosen the wrong answer.

Sternberg measured how quickly students were able to answer different kinds of problems in order to estimate how much time was needed to complete each of the four processes—encoding, inference, mapping, and application. One goal of his research is to study how these times vary across individuals and correlate the times with other measures of intellectual performance.

Sternberg and Gardner (1983) examined whether common components are involved in three different reasoning tasks that required inducing structure (series completion, analogy, and classification). Sternberg and Gardner combined the three central reasoning components—inference, mapping, and application—to form a single reasoning variable, which correlated significantly across the different tasks. In other words, students who were rapid in reasoning in one kind of induction task were also rapid in reasoning during other induction tasks. The results indicate that some common skills are involved in inducing structure across different tasks, as implied by Greeno's (1978) taxonomy.

Transformation Problems

Transformation problems consist of an initial state, a goal state, and a sequence of operations for changing the initial state into the goal state. Transformation problems differ from problems of inducing structure and arrangement by providing the goal state rather than requiring solvers to produce it. An anagram problem requires finding the word that solves the anagram, and Duncker's candle problem requires finding the correct arrangement of parts that supports the candle. In contrast, a transformation problem like the missionaries and cannibals problem provides the goal state.

The missionaries and cannibals problem requires transporting missionaries and cannibals across a river under the constraint that cannibals can never outnumber missionaries, in the boat or on either side of the river. In one version of this problem, the initial state consists of five missionaries, five cannibals, and a boat that can hold three persons, all on the left bank of the river. The goal state consists of the ten persons and the boat, all on the right bank of the river. The operations consist of moving from one to three persons in the boat back and forth across the river. The problem can be solved in 11 moves, but people usually require about 20 to 30 moves to reach a solution.

According to Greeno (1978), solving transformation problems primarily requires skills in planning based on a method called *means/end analysis*. Since a definite goal state is given in transformation problems, the problem solver can compare the current problem state with the goal state. Means/end analysis requires identifying differences that exist between the current state and the goal state and selecting operators that will reduce these differences.

The problems that we will consider in the rest of this chapter are mostly transformation problems. This will provide us the opportunity to study means/end analysis and alternative planning strategies. Much of what psychologists know about how people solve these problems is the result of the pioneering work of Simon and Newell at Carnegie-Mellon University. We will review the major aspects of their theory of human problem solving before looking at the applications of their ideas to particular problems.

Newell and Simon's Theory

Objectives and Method

The initial development of the theory was described in a paper titled "Elements of a Theory of Human Problem Solving" (Newell, Shaw, & Simon, 1958b), which, as we saw earlier, had an important influence on the development of information-processing theory. The paper described the first two years of a project that involved programming a digital computer to solve problems. One objective of the project, in fact, was to consider how programming a computer could contribute to a theory of human problem solving. The first step was to use all available evidence about human problem solving to program processes resembling those used by humans. The second step was to collect detailed data on how humans solve the same problems as those solved by the computer. The program could then be modified to provide a closer approximation of human behavior. Once success was achieved in simulating performance on a particular task, the investigators could examine a broader range of tasks, attempting to use the same set of elementary information processes and program organization in all the simulation programs. A long-term goal would be to draw implications from the theories for improving human performance.

Why does the computer play a central role in theory construction? Simon and Newell's (1971) answer is that much of our thinking is not directly observable. The covert nature of thought can make it seem magical or mysterious, leading to vague theories that obscure more than they clarify. The advantage of computer programs is that terms like *memory* and *strategy* can be defined in precisely stated instructions for a computer. Furthermore, the requirement that the programs must work—that is, must be able to solve the problem—provides a guarantee that no steps have been left unspecified. A successful program provides a measure of sufficiency—a test that the steps in the program are sufficient for solving the problem. A successful program does not guarantee that a person would solve the problem the same way; it is still necessary to make detailed observations on how people solve problems and modify the program to simulate their behavior.

To obtain details about how people solve problems, Newell and Simon (1972) usually collected verbal protocols from their subjects. They told the subjects to report verbally everything they thought about as they worked on the problem. The verbal statements often provided enough details to build a computer simulation program that would solve the problem in the same way that people solved it.

The method of collecting verbal protocols and constructing a simulation program has not been widely adopted by other investigators, although the approach is slowly gaining more appeal. One deterrent is simply that this method requires a lot of work for the investigator. The investigator therefore usually studies only a few subjects and assumes that they are fairly typical in the way they solve problems. Another limitation is that the method yields many details, and it is not always clear how to summarize the results in order to emphasize what is most important. Failure to collect verbal protocols, however, can result in the loss of valuable information because a subject's behavior may reveal little about what he is thinking.

Although the particular method used by Newell and Simon has not been widely adopted, their theory of problem solving has been very influential in determining how psychologists think about human information processing in general and problem solving in particular. The theory provides a general framework for specifying how information-processing characteristics, the structure of the problem, and different sources of knowledge interact to influence behavior.

Theoretical Assumptions

An important component of Newell and Simon's theory is the identification of the basic characteristics of human information processing that influence problem solving. These characteristics are the same ones that we discussed in earlier chapters: performance on a problem-solving task is influenced by the capacity, storage time, and retrieval time of short-term and long-term memory. The limited capacity of short-term memory (STM) places a constraint on the number of sequential operations that can be carried out mentally. Although most people can multiply 17 × 8 without using paper and pencil, multiplying 17 × 58 is much more difficult because the number of required operations (multiplying 17 × 8 and 17 × 5, storing the products, aligning, and adding) can exceed the limit of STM. Long-term memory (LTM) does not have these capacity limitations, but it takes time to enter new information into LTM. This can make it difficult to remember the steps that were used to solve a problem, causing us to repeat incorrect steps. Thus both the limited capacity of STM and the time required to store new information in LTM can greatly influence the efficiency of a human problem solver. The simulation model proposed by Atwood and Polson (1976) nicely demonstrates this point; we will return to this model later.

Simon and Newell's (1971) theory is concerned not only with the person but also with the task. The sequential nature of many problems raises the question of what options are available at each point in solving the problem. If there are many choices available, only a few of which lead to a solution, the problem can be very difficult. However, if one has a good plan for solving the problem and can therefore ignore unpromising paths, the number of unpromising paths will have little effect on performance. Simon and Newell illustrate this point by referring to the problem DONALD + GERALD = ROBERT.

$$
\begin{array}{r}
D\ O\ N\ A\ L\ D \\
+\ G\ E\ R\ A\ L\ D \\
\hline
R\ O\ B\ E\ R\ T
\end{array}
$$

The problem is to substitute a digit—0 to 9—for each of the ten letters in order to satisfy the constraint that the substitution obeys the rules of addition. The hint is $D = 5$. Therefore, $T = 0$, and a 1 has to be carried into the next column to the left. Although the number of possible choices is very large (there are 362,880 ways of assigning nine digits to nine letters), by following the rules of arithmetic and using accumulated information (such as that R must be odd), it is possible to explore relatively few promising choices. You can observe this for yourself by trying to solve the problem. What is important, therefore, is not the number of incorrect paths but how effectively one can discover a plan that avoids the incorrect paths. To use Newell and Simon's analogy, we need not be concerned how large the haystack is if we can identify a small part of it in which we are quite sure to find the needle.

Newell and Simon use the term *problem space* to refer to the choices that the problem solver evaluates while solving a problem. The problem itself determines the number of possible choices and paths that could be followed in searching for a solution, but the problem solver determines which of these he will actually explore. Among the sources of information that influence how a person constructs a problem space are the following:

1. The task instructions that give a description of the problem and may contain helpful information.
2. Previous experience with the same task or a nearly identical one.
3. Previous experience with analogous tasks.
4. Plans stored in LTM that generalize over a range of tasks.
5. Information accumulated while solving a problem.

Let us now take a closer look at how these sources of information influence problem solving. We will begin by showing how means/end analysis can be used to solve transformation problems.

Means/End Analysis

The use of means/end analysis is illustrated by a computer program called the General Problem Solver (Ernst & Newell, 1969). The program consists of general procedures that should apply across a variety of problems. A general procedure for solving transformation problems is to select operators that result in a problem state that is closer to the goal state. Operators are the allowed changes that can be made to solve the problem, such as moving missionaries and cannibals in the boat. Getting close to the goal is accomplished by trying to reduce the differences between the current problem state and the goal state. In order to follow this procedure, the General Problem Solver (GPS) must be given the differences that exist between problem states and the operators that are capable of eliminating these differences. A *table of connections* combines these two sets of information by showing which differences can be eliminated by each of the operators. The particular operators and differences will, of course, vary across problems, but the general strategy of consulting a table of connections in order to determine which operators are useful for reducing differences should remain the same across problems.

In most cases the principles used to construct GPS form a reasonable model of how people attempt to solve transformation problems. In fact, GPS was specifically used as a model of human performance on a symbol transformation task studied by Newell and Simon (1972). The problems were similar to the kind of derivations that students encounter in an introductory logic course. Students were given some initial statements, a set of 12 transformation rules, and a goal statement. The task was to use the rules to transform the initial statements in order to produce the goal statement. Newell and Simon identified six differences that distinguish logic statements. The table of connections specified which of these differences could be changed by each of the 12 transformation rules.

For example, a student might be asked to prove that if A implies B (A $\supset$ B), then the absence of B implies the absence of A ($-$B $\supset$ $-$A). Notice that there are two kinds of differences that distinguish the initial state (A ⊃ B) from the goal state (−B ⊃ −A). First, the two expressions differ in sign—there are negation signs before the A and the B in the goal state. Second, the positions of the A and the B have changed in the goal state. Students could use means/end analysis to solve this problem by applying transformation rules that changed either the sign or the position of the symbols. Newell and Simon (1972) asked their subjects to verbalize their strategies as they attempted to solve the symbol transformation problems. Students' solutions and verbal protocols revealed that many aspects of their thinking were similar to aspects of the means/end analysis used in the General Problem Solver.

Memory and Problem Solving

Computer programs such as the General Problem Solver provide a good source of ideas for how people might solve problems. However, we must be careful when we make use of a program that was not originally designed to simulate human thinking. As mentioned earlier, an important component of Newell and Simon's theory is the identification of basic characteristics of human memory that influence problem solving. Although the limited capacity of STM and the time required to store new information in LTM are not problems for a large computer, they can limit our progress toward becoming expert problem solvers.

The use of memory while solving problems is nicely illustrated in a model of an attempt to solve the water jar problem (Atwood & Polson, 1976). The water jar problem has a relatively small and well-defined search space, making it feasible to predict in detail how people will search for a solution. In one version of this problem, there are three pails, and the goal is to distribute the water equally between the two largest pails. Initially, the largest pail is full, and the other two pails are empty. For example, in the (8, 5, 3) problem, the pails can hold 8, 5, or 3 gallons of water. The goal is to divide the 8 gallons of water in the largest pail equally between the 8- and 5-gallon pails.

The Atwood and Polson model assumes that people will try to solve the problem by using a means/end heuristic. The means/end heuristic attempts to reduce the difference between the current content and the desired content of the two largest pails. If $C(A)$ and $C(B)$ are the current contents of the two largest pails, and $G(A)$ and $G(B)$ are the contents specified in the goal, the overall difference is given by $|C(A) - G(A)| + |C(B) - G(B)|$. In the initial state of the (8, 5, 3) problem, there are 8 gallons in A and 0 gallons in B. Since the goal state requires 4 gallons in each, the initial discrepancy is $|8 - 4| + |0 - 4|$, or 8 gallons. This discrepancy should be gradually reduced if the problem can be solved using a means/end analysis.

However, means/end analysis doesn't always work very well for the water jar problem; in fact, the solution of the (8, 5, 3) problem requires several violations of the means/end strategy. Another problem—one in which the pails hold 24, 21, or 3 gallons—has a similar search space but can be solved without violating the means/end strategy. If people use a means/end strategy, they should find the latter problem easier than the former. Atwood and Polson's results supported this prediction. People required over twice as many moves to solve the (8, 5, 3) problem even though it is possible to solve both problems in the same number of moves.

The optimal way of using the means/end strategy would be to evaluate all possible moves and select the one that minimizes the discrepancy between the resulting state and the goal state. However, the limited capacity of short-term memory places a constraint on the number of possible moves that can be evaluated and compared simultaneously. The model therefore assumes that people will simply look for a good move rather than always try to find the best move. If the discrepancy between the resulting state and the goal state is not too large, the probability of making the evaluated move depends on whether the problem solver recognizes the resulting problem state. The problem solver will recognize the problem state if she remembers being at that state. It is generally helpful to remember previously visited states in order not to return to them. Returning to old states generally implies that one is backing up and moving away from the goal state. Backing up is particularly detrimental in the problems studied by Atwood and Polson because it is possible to return all the way to the beginning states by making the wrong move.

To account for how people progress through the search space, Atwood and Polson estimated the probability of making a move to an old state as .20, the probability of making a move to a new state as .60, the probability of remembering previously visited states as .90, and the number of moves that can be evaluated in STM as three. These parameter estimates reveal that people do in fact prefer to move to new states rather than return to old states. They also reveal that people are able to recognize old states with fairly high accuracy. The estimate that only three moves can be compared in STM is consistent with previous estimates of STM capacity because, for each move, the problem solver has to remember not only the move but how much the resulting state differs from the goal state.

If the problem solver does not select a move during the first stage described above, the model specifies other criteria for move selection. The essential characteristics of the model are evident in this brief summary, however. First, there is the use of a means/end strategy to evaluate progress toward the goal. If the problem can be solved by gradually reducing the difference between the current state and the goal state, people solve it in fewer moves than if they are forced to make moves that violate the means/end strategy. Second, the limited capacity of STM places a constraint on the number of moves that can be evaluated. Even if you had a perfect strategy that enabled you always to select the best move at each point, you would not necessarily find the shortest solution if you could not evaluate all the moves at each decision point. For example, if there were four possible moves but you could evaluate only three because of the limitations of STM, the best move might be the one you did not evaluate.

Atwood and Polson's finding that people are much more likely to make a move if it leads to a new problem state is consistent with the idea that it is generally better to move to new states than to return to old states. However, an old state will appear to be a new state if the problem solver does not remember being there. It is therefore useful to remember what states you visited when solving a problem by storing this information in LTM. Atwood and Polson estimate that people were quite successful at storing such information as they solved the water jar problem.

General Strategies

Means/ends analysis is an example of a general strategy. A knowledge of general problem-solving strategies can be particularly useful because general strategies apply to many kinds of problems. For this reason books like Wickelgren's (1974) on how to solve problems emphasize general strategies such as forming subgoals or working backward.

Strategies like means/end analysis, forming subgoals, and working backward are called *heuristics* because they are often successful but do not guarantee success. In contrast, an algorithm is a procedure of steps that does guarantee a solution if one follows the steps correctly. The rules for multiplication constitute an algorithm because a correct answer is guaranteed if a person correctly follows the rules. We will first consider three general heuristics—forming subgoals, using analogy, and constructing diagrams—to evaluate both their potential usefulness and their limitations as general strategies.

Subgoals

A commonly suggested heuristic for solving problems is to divide the problem into parts—that is, to formulate subgoals. Subgoals are problem states intermediate between the initial state and the goal state; ideally they are on the solution path. Some problems have fairly obvious subgoals, and research has shown that people take advantage of them. Consider the puzzle called the Tower of Hanoi (see Figure 12.2). This puzzle consists of three pegs and a set of rings that vary in size. The initial state has all the rings stacked on peg A in order of decreasing size. The goal is to move the stack, one ring at a time, to peg C, under the constraint that a larger ring can never be placed on a smaller ring. A reasonable subgoal is to move the largest ring to peg C. But how does one begin in order to achieve this subgoal? The answer is not obvious, and people often make the wrong choice. But as they make other moves and come closer to achieving the subgoal, the correct moves become more obvious and errors decline (Egan & Greeno, 1974).

Using subgoals can make solving a problem easier because knowing that an intermediate problem state is on the solution path makes it possible to avoid searching many unpromising paths. Figure 12.3 shows a search space that contains 16 paths, each four steps in length. Only one path ends in the goal state. If we are given a subgoal state that we know can be reached in two steps, then we can reach the subgoal by searching only four paths, each two steps long. From the subgoal state there are another four paths, each two steps long. The search space has been reduced from 16 four-step paths to the 8 two-step paths represented by the shaded area in Figure 12.3.

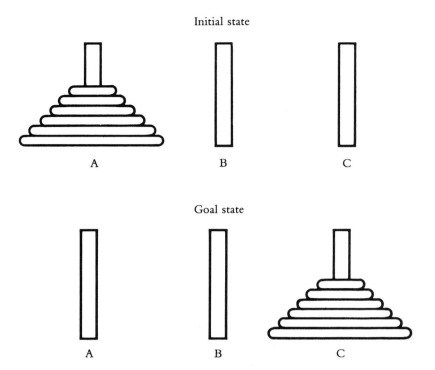

Initial state

Goal state

Figure 12.2   The Tower of Hanoi puzzle

Forming subgoals is often helpful, but it does not guarantee an easier solution. There are several limitations to keep in mind when using this method. First, it is not always obvious what are helpful intermediate problem states, as some problems do not have obvious subgoals. Second, reaching a subgoal may create confusion about what to do next. Hayes (1966) found that giving people a subgoal helped them solve the part of the problem that came before the subgoal. However, some problems actually took longer to solve with a subgoal because it took a long time to figure out what to do after reaching the subgoal.

An example of a problem in which a subgoal improved performance is the missionaries and cannibals problem (described in Table 12.1) requiring the transportation of five missionaries and five cannibals across a river using a boat that can hold three persons. Figure 12.4 shows the search space of legal moves for this problem (Simon & Reed, 1976). The ovals represent legal problem states—states in which cannibals do not outnumber missionaries (unless no missionaries are present). The first number is the number of missionaries on the left bank, the second number is the number of cannibals on the left bank, the third number is the number of missionaries on the right bank, and the fourth number is the number of cannibals on the right bank. The asterisk shows the location of the boat. State A is the initial state, and state Z is the goal state; *a* indicates a backward move—the problem solver

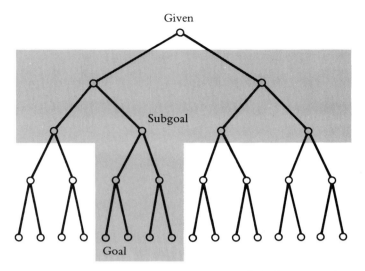

Figure 12.3   Search space. Knowledge of a subgoal limits search to the shaded area.

then must return to A. The numbers connecting the problem states show the number of missionaries (first number) and the number of cannibals (second number) being transported in the boat.

One group of students, the control group, were simply asked to solve the problem. Another group, the "subgoal" group, were told that, in order to solve the problem, they would have to reach a state in which there were three cannibals across the river by themselves and without the boat. This corresponds to state L in the search space. Students in the control group required an average of 30 moves to solve the problem, compared with an average of only 20 moves for students in the subgoal group.

Strategies and Subgoals

In order to try to understand why the subgoal was so effective, Simon and I developed a simulation model of the way students in the two groups explored the search space. The goal of the model was to predict, for each of the possible legal moves, the average number of times students in each group would make that particular move. We thought students would follow a means/end strategy in which they would move as many people across the river as possible and bring as few back as possible. A model based on the means/end strategy was fairly successful in predicting their choices, but some of their moves did not follow this strategy. For example, when at state A, students in the control group made an average of 0.5 moves to state B, 0.2 moves to state C, and 1.1 moves to state D. The means/end strategy would predict that subjects would move three persons across (to state B) rather than two persons (to state D), so why was moving one missionary and one cannibal such a popular choice? Violations of the

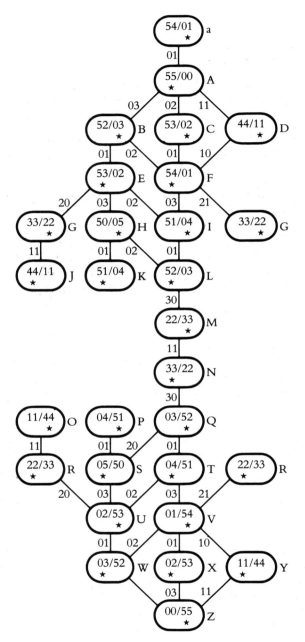

Figure 12.4   Search space for the five missionaries and cannibals problem

means/end strategy could be accounted for by proposing that people follow a *balance strategy*, which attempts to create equal numbers of missionaries and cannibals on each side of the river. The balance strategy makes it easy to avoid illegal moves because cannibals will never outnumber missionaries as long as the numbers of missionaries and cannibals are equal on both sides. The trouble with the balance strategy is that it tends to lead people away from the solution path and toward the blind alley represented by states G and J, both balanced states.

The model that we developed is called a *strategy shift model* because it proposes that students initially use a balance strategy but have to shift to a means/end strategy in order to avoid the blind alley and solve the problem. By shifting strategies sooner, they will make fewer bad moves and therefore require fewer moves to reach the solution. By assuming that students in the subgoal group would shift strategies after making only 4 moves (on the average) and students in the control group would shift strategies after making 15 moves (on the average), we were able to predict not only the total number of moves required by each group to solve the problem but exactly how each group would explore the search space. The fact that the subgoal—three missionaries and no cannibals—is an unbalanced state makes it intuitively likely that students in the subgoal group would not persist in following a balance strategy.

The research on the effectiveness of strategies reveals that the structure of the search space is one of the factors that influence the success of a particular strategy. It is not obvious, for example, that the balance strategy is a bad strategy. It is only after we examine the search space in Figure 12.4 that we realize the consequences of following the balance strategy.

Analogy

Analogy is another of the major heuristics for solving problems. Analogy requires that the problem solver use the solution of a similar problem to solve a current problem. Success in using analogy depends on both recognizing the similarity between two problems and recalling the solution of the analogous problem. Since the recall of a solution is required, analogy depends more on LTM than do means/end analysis and subgoals.

Let us look now at another version of the missionaries and cannibals problem, called the *jealous-husbands problem:*

> Three jealous husbands and their wives, having to cross a river at a ferry, find a boat. However, the boat is so small that it can hold no more than two persons. Find the simplest schedule of crossings that will permit all six persons to cross the river so that no woman is left in company with any other woman's husband unless her own husband is present. It is assumed that all passengers on the boat unboard before the next trip and that at least one person has to be in the boat for each crossing.

The jealous-husbands and the missionaries and cannibals problems are similar because the solution of one problem can be used to solve the other. Someone who knows the solution to the missionaries and cannibals problem can solve the jealous-husbands problem by (1) substituting husbands for missionaries, (2) substituting wives for cannibals, and (3) pairing the couples when men and women are on the same bank of the river. If people can make use of analogy to solve the problems, then it should be easier to solve either problem if a person first solved the analogous problem. However, experimental results indicated that people were in fact not better at solving one problem if they first solved the other problem (Reed, Ernst, & Banerji, 1974). Why not?

One reason may be that people did not know the relation between the two problems. In a second experiment the experimenter encouraged subjects to use their solution of the first problem to solve the second problem, informing them that husbands corresponded to missionaries and wives corresponded to cannibals. The information about how the problems were related helped subjects solve the missionaries and cannibals problem but did not help them solve the jealous-husbands problem.

These results show that successful use of analogy does not occur as readily as we might expect. Even when the instructions reveal the exact relation between two problems, the solution of one does not guarantee that it will be easier to solve the other. One explanation of this finding is that it is difficult to remember the correct solution when it consists of a long sequence of moves. This hypothesis suggests that the use of analogy should be more effective when the solution is easier to remember.

The problems studied by Gestalt psychologists typically were problems that could be solved in a few steps. Examples include the crate and stick (Köhler, 1925) and candle (Duncker, 1945) problems that we looked at earlier. Another problem studied by Duncker (1945) was the tumor, or radiation, problem. Table 12.2 describes this problem and a solution. The dispersion solution involves dividing the rays so they will have a high intensity only when they converge on the tumor. Although this is a clever solution, Duncker found that very few people solved the problem in this way.

Gick and Holyoak (1980) investigated whether more people would discover the dispersion solution if they were first exposed to an analogous solution. Their subjects read the attack-dispersion story before trying to solve the radiation problem. The attack-dispersion story described a solution to a military problem in which the army had to be divided in order to converge on a fortress. The instructions indicated that the first story might give subjects some hints for solving the radiation problem. The results showed that most people made use of the analogy. Over half of those who read the story included the dispersion solution among their proposed solutions, compared with only 8% of those who did not read the story before solving the radiation problem. But when Gick and Holyoak omitted the hint to use the story, the number of dispersion solutions greatly decreased. Their findings thus demonstrated that people could generate an analogous solution when prompted, but they did not spontaneously recognize the similarity between the two problems.

People's inability to spontaneously notice the relation between analogous problems poses a challenge for psychologists to make analogies more obvious. One reason

Table 12.2   A summary of the attack-dispersion story and of a corresponding solution to the radiation problem

Proposition number	
	Attack-dispersion story
1–2	A fortress was located in the center of the country.
2a	Many roads radiated out from the fortress.
3–4	A general wanted to capture the fortress with his army.
5–7	The general wanted to prevent mines on the roads from destroying his army and neighboring villages.
8	As a result the entire army could not attack the fortress along one road.
9–10	However, the entire army was needed to capture the fortress.
11	So an attack by one small group would not succeed.
12	The general therefore divided his army into several small groups.
13	He positioned the small groups at the heads of different roads.
14–15	The small groups simultaneously converged on the fortress.
16	In this way the army captured the fortress.
	Radiation problem and dispersion solution[a]
1′–2′	A tumor was located in the interior of a patient's body.
3′–4′	A doctor wanted to destroy the tumor with rays.
5′–7′	The doctor wanted to prevent the rays from destroying healthy tissue.
8′	As a result the high-intensity rays could not be applied to the tumor along one path.
9′–10′	However, high-intensity rays were needed to destroy the tumor.
11′	So applying one low-intensity ray would not succeed.
12′	*The doctor therefore divided the rays into several low-intensity rays.*
13′	*He positioned the low-intensity rays at multiple locations around the patient's body.*
14′–15′	*The low-intensity rays simultaneously converged on the tumor.*
16′	*In this way the rays destroyed the tumor.*

[a]Italicized propositions summarize the target dispersion solution.

that analogies are often not obvious is that the analogy preserves relations among the concepts in a problem but the concepts themselves differ (Gentner, 1983). This point is illustrated in Table 12.3 for the military and radiation problems. Although the concepts (army and fortress; rays and tumor) differ in the two problems, the solutions preserve the relations of breaking up and converging. The similarity of the two solutions is represented at the bottom of the table by the convergence schema, in which the concepts are described more generally. The solutions to both problems require breaking up a large force so weak forces can be simultaneously applied along multiple paths.

Gick and Holyoak (1983) discovered that people were likely to form this more general schema if they read and compared two analogous stories before trying to solve the radiation problem. For example, some students read the military story and a story about forming a circle around an oil fire in order to use many small hoses to spray foam on the fire. Students who described the relation between these two stories were much more likely to think of the convergence solution to the radiation problem than students who read only a single analogous story.

The advantage of creating a general schema, such as the convergence schema, is that it should be easier for subjects to recognize that the radiation problem is an

Table 12.3   Correspondences among the military problem, the radiation problem, and the convergence schema

Military problem
Initial state
  Goal: Use army to capture fortress.
  Resources: Sufficiently large army.
  Constraint: Unable to send entire army along one road.
  Solution plan: Send small groups along multiple roads simultaneously.
  Outcome: Fortress captured by army.

Radiation problem
Initial state
  Goal: Use rays to destroy tumor.
  Resources: Sufficiently powerful rays.
  Constraint: Unable to administer high-intensity rays from one direction.
  Solution plan: Administer low-intensity rays from multiple directions simultaneously.
  Outcome: Tumor destroyed by rays.

Convergence schema
Initial state
  Goal: Use force to overcome a central target.
  Resources: Sufficiently great force.
  Constraint: Unable to apply full force along one path.
  Solution plan: Apply weak forces along multiple paths simultaneously.
  Outcome: Central target overcome by force.

---

example of a general schema than to recognize how it relates to a particular problem. But psychologists are still investigating the extent to which people create general schemata as opposed to recalling a particular problem (Ross, 1984) as a basis for analogy. The outcome of this research should tell us how people can make better use of analogous solutions to solve problems.

Diagrams

Our final example of a general strategy for solving problems is the construction of diagrams. Diagrams can help us represent problems in a way that allows us to search efficiently for a solution. The importance of representation is illustrated by the fact that two problems with identical search spaces (problem isomorphs) may differ greatly in how easy they are to solve. One set of instructions may cause the solver to represent the problem in a way that leads to an easy solution, and another set of instructions may cause a representation that impedes finding the solution. Furthermore, a person who solves both of the problems may not recognize any similarity between them (Hayes & Simon, 1977).

Carroll, Thomas, and Malhotra (1980) studied the role of representation in design by creating two problem isomorphs. The *spatial version* involved designing a business office for seven employees. Each employee was to be assigned to a corridor a certain number of offices down from a central hallway containing a reception area at one end and accounting records at the other end. Subjects were told to try to assign compatible employees to the same corridor, assigning those with higher prestige nearer to the central hallway.

Problems of this kind are usually easier to solve by using a diagram like Figure 12.5. The top of the diagram shows the central hallway connecting the reception and accounting areas. The columns represent corridors. Examples of constraints that are satisfied by the arrangement in Figure 12.5 are that A uses the accounting records less than C, B and C are compatible, and C has more prestige than B.

The *temporal version* of the isomorph had equivalent constraints, but the constraints were placed on a manufacturing process that consisted of seven stages. The columns in Figure 12.5 can now be used to represent work shifts rather than corridors. The horizontal dimension represents time and the vertical dimension represents priority. Subjects were instructed to assign stages to the same work shift if the stages used the same resources. Some stages had to be assigned to earlier work shifts than others, and some stages had priority over others that belonged to the same work shift. Examples of constraints that are satisfied by the arrangement in Figure 12.5 are that stage A occurs before stage C, stages B and C use the same resources, and stage C has greater priority than stage B. Notice that distance from the accounting area in the spatial version corresponds to time in the temporal version, compatibility corresponds to use of the same resources, and prestige corresponds to priority.

Subjects who worked on the temporal version received 19 constraints that corresponded to the 19 constraints given to subjects who worked on the spatial version. Subjects were not instructed to use a diagram; they were able to select their own method for solving the problem. Performance was measured by how many constraints were satisfied in the design. The importance of representation is illustrated by the finding that subjects did significantly better on the spatial isomorph even though the two problems had equivalent constraints. Subjects given the spatial

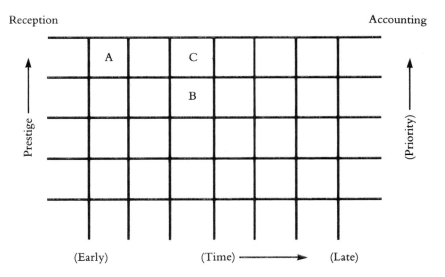

Figure 12.5   Graphic representation of a design problem. The labels in parentheses accompanied the temporal version.

isomorph not only satisfied more of the constraints but completed their design faster. All 17 subjects in the spatial task used a sketch of the business office to formulate their design, but only 2 of the 18 subjects in the temporal task used a graphic representation.

To determine whether graphic representation made the problem easier for the spatial group, the experimenters conducted a second experiment, in which both groups were instructed to use the matrix shown in Figure 12.5. This time there were no significant differences between the two groups, either in performance scores or in solution times. The differences in the first experiment therefore appear to have been caused by the facilitating effects of a graphic representation of the problem. The usefulness of the graphic representation was obvious in the spatial task, and students spontaneously adopted it. It was not obvious in the temporal task. Performance on the two tasks became equivalent only when both groups were required to use a graphic representation.

An interesting question raised by these findings is whether students could use analogy to improve their performance on the temporal task if they had first worked on the spatial task. Spontaneous use of a graphic procedure to solve the spatial task might then transfer to the temporal task. If students recognized the analogy between the two tasks, the experimenter would not have to tell them to use the graphic procedure on the temporal task.

In conclusion, the research reported in this section demonstrates the usefulness of employing general strategies like subgoal formation, analogy, and construction of diagrams. Most of the problems described in this chapter are puzzles in which the problem solver can search for a solution without having to know much about the subject matter. In contrast, many of the problems we encounter in the classroom require knowledge about a particular subject. Thus, both subject-matter knowledge and strategies have to be learned if one is to become a proficient problem solver (Glaser, 1984). The next chapter is concerned with classroom problem solving and emphasizes the differences between novices and experts.

Summary

Because there are many kinds of problems, constructing a theory of problem solving would be easier if we were able to classify problems according to the skills needed to solve them. One method of classification distinguishes among problems of arrangement, inducing structure, and transformation. Arrangement problems require the problem solver to arrange the elements of a problem in a way that satisfies some criterion. Anagrams are a good example because the letters have to be arranged to spell a word. In problems of inducing structure, some elements are given, and the task is to discover how the elements are related. Analogy or series completion problems are examples. Transformation problems consist of an initial state, a goal state, and operations for changing the initial state into the goal state. Many puzzles are of this type, including the missionaries and cannibals, Tower of Hanoi, and water jar problems.

Much of what psychologists know about how people solve problems is the result of the pioneering work of Newell and Simon. Their theory specifies how the basic characteristics of the human information processor, the search space, and different strategies affect problem solving. Performance on a task is influenced by the capacity, storage time, and retrieval time of short-term and long-term memory. It is also influenced by the search space, which determines the number of legal moves available at each point in solving the problem. Newell and Simon have depended on computer simulation models and verbal protocols for testing and developing the many details of their theory.

There are several ways that memory can influence success in solving a problem. Short-term memory is needed to evaluate the alternative choices at each point when searching for a solution. Memory is also needed to store information about previously visited problem states, previously evaluated hypotheses, and previously selected operators. The important role of memory in solving problems is revealed in a simulation model of how people solve the water jar problem.

Four general strategies for solving problems are means/end analysis, subgoals, analogy, and diagrams. These strategies are called heuristics because, although they are often useful, none guarantees a successful solution. The means/end strategy states that the problem solver should select operators that reduce the difference between the current problem state and the goal state. A table of connections shows which differences can be eliminated by each of the operators. Knowledge of subgoals is valuable because it reduces the size of the search space. A detailed simulation of how people solved the missionaries and cannibals problem revealed that a subgoal enabled them to avoid blind alleys by selecting a better strategy than the one that is frequently used. The use of an analogous solution is often useful, but people may not notice a potential analogy. Diagrams can be beneficial in design tasks.

Recommended Reading

The chapter on thinking by Greeno and Simon (in press) provides an extensive summary of work on reasoning and problem solving. The classic work on the effect of set on problem solving was conducted by Luchins (1942) in a study using the water jar problem. The Atwood-Polson model, originally developed for the water jar problem, was extended by Jeffries, Polson, Razran, and Atwood (1977) to describe performance on the missionaries and cannibals problem.

Information-processing models have also been developed to account for performance on Duncker's candle problem (Weisberg & Suls, 1973), on insight problems (Metcalfe, 1986a), and on geometric analogies (Mulholland, Pellegrino, & Glaser, 1980). Ericsson and Simon (1980) critically analyzed the role of verbal reports in constructing theories and argued that verbal reports can be very useful if they are treated like other kinds of data. Simon (1983) discusses the distinction between search and reasoning.

The past decade has witnessed a growing interest in developing information-processing models of how people answer questions on intelligence tests. This interest has been accompanied by the study of individual differences in problem solving. Articles by Hunt and Lansman (1975) and Pellegrino and Glaser (1979) provide an overview of work in this area. A book edited by Sternberg and Detterman (1979) contains a number of interesting chapters on the growing interaction between intelligence testing and cognitive psychology. Sternberg's (1985) book *Beyond IQ: A Theory of Human Intelligence* is particularly recommended.

13

Classroom Problem Solving

It is strange that we expect students to learn, yet seldom teach them anything about learning. We expect students to solve problems, yet seldom teach them about problem solving. And, similarly, we sometimes require students to remember a considerable body of material, yet seldom teach them the art of memory. It is time we made up for this lack, time that we developed the applied disciplines of learning and problem solving and memory. We need to develop the general principles of how to learn, how to remember, how to solve problems, then to develop applied courses, and then to establish the place of these methods in an academic curriculum.

DON NORMAN (1980)

How can we put cognitive psychology to use in improving instruction? Norman (1980) recommended four steps:

1. To understand enough about the psychology of learning or problem solving that applied techniques can be developed.
2. To develop applied methods and formal courses in these methods that can aid in the general problem-solving and learning abilities of our students.
3. To use this knowledge in two ways:
   a. To develop courses in methods of learning, memory, and problem solving to provide students with important cognitive tools.
   b. To develop better instructional systems for conventional teaching and make use of new technological developments and new techniques of cognitive science to make interactive, intelligent tutoring systems a reality.
4. To demonstrate the effectiveness of these techniques and to gain sufficient academic and public acceptance that not only will they be taught, they will be sought after.

273

Although courses on problem solving are not yet widespread, such courses already exist. One of the best known was first offered on the UCLA campus in 1969 to a class of 32 students (Rubinstein & Pfeiffer, 1979). The course was intended, first, to develop abilities to classify problems and, second, to identify and even restructure the skills needed to solve the problems. The organizers hoped that explicit instruction in a wide variety of practical applications of heuristic and algorithmic problem-solving methods would facilitate use of the methods and their generalization to new situations. They also felt that bringing together students with diverse majors would provide exposure to different problem-solving strategies. The course is based primarily on Rubinstein's (1975) book *Patterns of Problem Solving* and is taught by faculty members and teaching assistants from many disciplines. The popularity of the course is revealed by the fact that enrollment since 1976 has been about 1200 students a year, with 12 sections of the course taught each quarter.

Problem-solving courses are also popular at Carnegie-Mellon University, where they are currently taught in four of the colleges—science, engineering, humanities, and fine arts (Hayes, 1979). Some of the courses currently offered in different subject areas teach mainly specialized skills in the content area of the course. The history course, for example, makes explicit the search and evaluation procedures that should be used to find and evaluate historical information. The course taught in the psychology department assumes no prior knowledge and is not aimed at a particular field. It emphasizes general skills such as mnemonic techniques, decision making, representation and search, and creativity. The common theme of all the courses is their concern with *procedural knowledge*—knowledge of how to do something—rather than *declarative knowledge*, knowledge of facts and principles.

The attempt to teach good problem-solving techniques raises the question of how research on problem solving can improve instruction. Larkin (1980) has argued that attempts to teach problem solving in the classroom face three limitations. First, it is hard to teach people to solve problems, and even the best teachers often have limited success. Second, the methodologies most often used in educational research do not provide information about effective problem solving. Statistical comparisons of test scores, for instance, do not provide good insights into the processes of effective problem solving, the way these processes are acquired, and the kinds of deficits unskilled problem solvers experience. Third, although instructional programs in problem solving can achieve benefits, it is not clear how. If we could understand in detail how the instructional programs achieve their effects, then that knowledge could be applied to other programs and educational materials.

Larkin believes there has been impressive progress in understanding the detailed mechanisms of problem solving. However, since much of this progress has been achieved by studying puzzles and games, its direct application to the classroom is not immediately apparent. Nevertheless, the knowledge gained from this research is currently being used to study classroom problems, and a fruitful interaction between laboratory problem solving and classroom instruction is emerging.

This chapter discusses promising approaches to the study of how people solve classroom problems. The initial analysis of problems is discussed in the first section. The initial analysis usually requires categorization in order to identify the problem as belonging to a larger class of problems. Ability to categorize a problem correctly is one source of individual differences in performance. Another source is planning, discussed in the second section. People who solve classroom problems also differ widely in their specific knowledge about a particular subject. For example, a physics professor certainly knows much more about how to solve physics problems than an undergraduate who is taking an introductory physics course. Cognitive psychologists and educators have recently begun to study the differences between the ways a beginner and an expert approach a problem. Much of this work focuses on differences in formulating a plan for solution.

The third section examines how problem solving might be improved through instruction. There is some evidence that teaching heuristics can improve performance on mathematics problems. The search for problem-solving methods is becoming increasingly important as computers assume a more central role in education.

Initial Analysis and Categorization

One difference between a puzzle such as the missionary/cannibal problem and a classroom problem such as finding the concentration of a mixture is that we need considerable domain-specific knowledge to solve the latter problem. Domain-specific knowledge is knowledge about a particular subject matter. Most people could solve the standard version of the missionary/cannibal problem (three missionaries, three cannibals) without previous experience on this problem, but few people could solve a mixture problem without previous experience.

A central issue in classroom problem solving is how to balance instruction between teaching the general strategies discussed in the previous chapter and teaching the subject-matter knowledge required to solve classroom problems (Glaser, 1984; Polson & Jeffries, 1985). As Polson and Jeffries argue, good answers to this important practical question will depend on a better theoretical understanding of how people at different skill levels attempt to solve problems. One advantage that the more experienced problem solvers have is that they are better able to classify a problem as belonging to a particular category. We will begin by considering why categorization is important and will then look at how people differ in their ability to categorize problems.

Categorization of Algebra Word Problems

After we have learned how to solve different kinds of problems, it is useful to be able to categorize a new problem as belonging to a certain class of problems. We can then apply procedures for solving problems in that class. For example, a student in an algebra course might be given the following problem:

> One vegetable oil contains 6% saturated fats, and a second contains 26% saturated fats. In making a salad dressing, how many ounces of the second may be added to 10 ounces of the first if the percentage of saturated fats is not to exceed 16%?

The initial analysis of this problem should identify it as an example of a *mixture* problem. The student should then try to recall the procedure for solving mixture problems rather than the procedure for solving age, area, or interest problems. To determine whether students are able to classify algebra word problems systematically, Hinsley, Hayes, and Simon (1977) selected 76 problems from a high school algebra text. They then asked high school and college students to classify the problems by problem types, where the meaning of *problem types* was unspecified. When the students finished classifying the problems, they were asked to describe the properties of the categories they had identified. On the average, students identified 13.5 categories containing more than one problem, and there was considerable agreement among students about the identity of the categories. Examples included distance-rate-time, interest, ratio, triangle, area, mixture, and river-current problems.

Although the results showed that students are capable of categorizing algebra word problems, they did not show that the categories are used to formulate solutions. In fact, students may have had to formulate a solution before they could make a classification. This possibility would be very unlikely, however, if it could be shown that students can categorize a problem very early in the course of reading it. In a second experiment, problems were read to subjects one part at a time, and after each part subjects were asked to try to classify the problem. Half the subjects were able to classify the problems correctly after hearing less than one fifth of the problem. The results verified the assumption that students can categorize problems before they have enough information to formulate a solution.

The use of categories to guide the search for a solution was nicely demonstrated in a third experiment, which used a single, complex problem:

> Because of their quiet ways, the inhabitants of Smalltown were especially upset by the terrible New Year's Eve auto accident that claimed the life of one Smalltown resident. The facts were these. Both Smith and Jones were New Year's Eve babies, and each had planned a surprise visit to the other on their mutual birthday. Jones had started out for Smith's house traveling due east on Route 210 just 2 minutes after Smith had left for Jones's house. Smith was traveling directly south on Route 140. Jones was traveling 30 miles per hour faster than Smith even though their houses were only 5 miles apart as the crow flies. Their cars crashed at the right-angle intersection of the two highways. Officer Franklin, who observed the crash, determined that Jones was traveling half again as fast as Smith at the time of the crash. Smith had been driving for just 4 minutes at the time of the crash. The crash occurred nearer to the house of the dead man than to the house of the survivor. What was the name of the dead man? [Hinsley et al., 1977, p. 102].

The problem is an example of a distance-rate-time problem, but it contains some irrelevant information (their houses were 5 miles apart as the crow flies) that suggests that it might be a triangle problem. Verbal protocols collected from six subjects who solved the problem revealed that three of the six attended to the irrelevant triangle information. All three drew triangles and identified the 5-mile distance as the hypotenuse of the triangle. The other three subjects classified the problem as a distance-rate-time problem—in fact, initially formulating the problem as one driver going east and the other going west, a typical way of presenting problems belonging to this class. The knowledge associated with each of the two categories determined what the subject attended to in the problem, what information he expected, what information he regarded as relevant, and even what errors he made in reading the text.

From their findings the authors concluded:

1. Students can recognize problem categories and agree considerably on the categories.
2. They can usually recognize the categories early in reading the text. Sometimes reading as little as the initial noun phrase is sufficient.
3. Students have information about the problem categories that is useful for formulating solutions. This information includes knowledge about useful equations and diagrams and procedures for identifying relevant information.
4. They often use this information to solve algebra word problems when the instructions are simply to solve the problems and do not require classification.

Individual Differences in Categorization

The Smalltown problem illustrated individual differences in categorization: three of the students initially classified the problem as a distance-rate-time problem and three classified it as a triangle problem. The Smalltown problem was intentionally constructed to be complex and ambiguous in order to maximize the opportunity to study individual differences. Individual differences in categorization were not very apparent when standard problems were used.

Another approach to studying individual differences is to use standard problems but less sophisticated subjects. Silver (1981) asked seventh-grade students to form groups of problems that were "mathematically related" and to explain the basis for categorizing them. He used 16 problems that could be represented by a 4 × 4 matrix. The four problems in each horizontal row were mathematically related, and the same mathematical procedure could be used to solve each. The four problems in each vertical column described a similar story context but required different procedures to solve them. The first two problems in Table 13.1 are mathematically related, since the same procedure is used to solve each. The third problem has the same story context as the first but requires a different mathematical procedure.

Table 13.1   A word problem and related problems

Word problem	A farmer is counting the hens and rabbits in his barnyard. He counts a total of 50 heads and 140 feet. How many hens and how many rabbits does the farmer have?
Related structure	Bill has a collection of 20 coins that consists entirely of dimes and quarters. If the collection is worth $4.10, how many of each kind of coin are in the collection?
Related context	A farmer is counting the hens and rabbits in his barnyard. He counts six coops with four hens in each, two coops with three hens in each, five cages with six rabbits in each, and three cages with four rabbits in each. How many hens and how many rabbits does the farmer have?

Although Silver asked his students to classify mathematically related problems, students who had difficulty perceiving the mathematical structure of the problems might use story context as a basis of classification. Students were asked to solve 12 of the problems after they made their classification in order to determine whether there was any relation between the ability to classify and the ability to solve problems. Silver classified the students as good, average, or poor problem solvers on the basis of the number of problems they solved.

Table 13.2 illustrates the relation between the ability to classify problems and the ability to solve them. The *association* score was obtained by counting the related pairs that a student put into the same category. The *pure* category score was obtained by counting the categories that contained at least three related problems and no unrelated problems. The maximum association score was 24, and the maximum pure category score was 4. The results indicate that the better problem solvers formed categories on the basis of mathematical structure, and the poor problem solvers formed categories on the basis of story context.

Similar results were obtained when students were asked to recall information about story problems. Good problem solvers were able to recall information about mathematical structure. Poor problem solvers rarely recalled this information, even when the solutions were discussed prior to their recall. However, they could often remember details about the story context and were sometimes better than the good problem solvers at recalling these details. The results suggest that an important source of individual differences in mathematical problem solving is the ability to categorize problems initially according to the mathematical procedure needed to solve them.

Differences in ability to categorize problems according to their mathematical structure also distinguish novices from experts in more advanced courses. Chi, Glaser, and Rees (1982) asked eight novices and eight experts to sort 24 physics problems into categories based on similarity of solutions. The novices were under-graduates who had recently completed a physics course. The experts were advanced Ph.D. students from the physics department. Each group formed about the same number of categories, but the problems in the categories differed for the two groups. Novices tended to categorize problems on the basis of common objects, such as spring problems and inclined-plane problems. Experts tended to categorize problems on the basis of physics principles, such as problems that can be solved by applying the conservation of energy law or Newton's Second Law ($F = MA$). Thus, just as in

Table 13.2   Effect of ability on categorizing problems by structure and context

| Ability | Structure | | Context | |
	Association	Pure	Association	Pure
Good	17.0	3.1	0.6	0.1
Average	12.0	1.8	3.4	0.6
Poor	6.3	0.4	8.9	2.3

Silver's (1981) experiment with seventh-graders, the better problem solvers were more sensitive to the formal structure of the problem.

Planning and Solution Strategies

Most of the difficulty in solving a problem lies in the initial analysis if the solution requires standard procedures that are identified during this analysis. Little planning is necessary to solve a problem if its categorization reduces the number of relevant equations to one or two. The problem solver simply recalls the equations and substitutes the relevant values for the variables.

More complex problems, however, often require construction of a plan for producing the solution. Miller et al. (1960) defined a *plan* as a hierarchical process that controls the order in which a sequence of operations is to be performed. Planning implies that the problem solver is looking ahead and is not simply taking one step at a time. This, of course, is usually not possible the first time a person encounters a problem. Planning has not been emphasized in much of the research on puzzles because people usually do not have detailed knowledge about how to solve a particular puzzle. Successful models of puzzle solving have therefore been based on general strategies such as means/end analysis (Atwood & Polson, 1976; Simon & Reed, 1976). Once a person has solved a particular puzzle, however, subsequent solutions can use planning techniques such as forming subgoals or identifying sequences of moves (Reed & Johnsen, 1977).

Solving problems in courses like physics or engineering depends on a considerable degree of organized knowledge about a particular topic and how well this knowledge can be translated into efficient plans. Before examining how people make use of plans to solve problems, we will make the concept of planning more precise by looking at how it has been used in the field of artificial intelligence. As we saw in the previous chapter, the computer implementation of problem solving requires a detailed specification of the operations used to define a concept.

An Example from Artificial Intelligence

Many key ideas about planning have been formalized by Sacerdoti's work in artificial intelligence. His initial contribution was to modify a general-purpose problem-solving program called STRIPS to allow for planning. The modification was called AB-STRIPS (Abstraction Based Strips) because the planning took place in an abstraction of the search space that ignored many details (Sacerdoti, 1974). ABSTRIPS solved a problem in a hierarchy of abstraction spaces in which successively finer levels of details were introduced.

Figure 13.1 shows an example of a problem that was solved by ABSTRIPS. The problem is to use the robot to push box 1 next to box 2 and then put the robot in room A. Figure 13.1 shows the initial problem state. The robot is capable of performing operations such as pushing boxes, opening doors, and entering rooms. However,

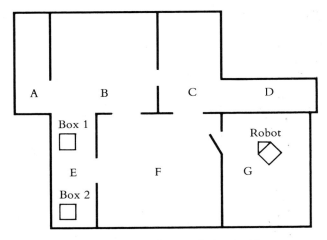

Figure 13.1   Initial state of robot problem

each operation has preconditions that must be satisfied before it can be used. For instance, in order to push box 1 to box 2, (1) box 1 must be a pushable object, (2) the two boxes and the robot must be in the same room, and (3) the robot must be next to box 1. Associated with each operation is a level of criticality. For this operation, precondition 1 is the most critical (the problem couldn't be solved if box 1 couldn't be pushed), precondition 2 is moderately critical, and precondition 3 is the least critical. ABSTRIPS plans solutions by first ignoring all but the most critical preconditions. It then uses its solution of the simpler problems to solve more complex problems as more details (preconditions) are introduced. Solution of the simpler problems provides subgoals for solving the more complex problems.

ABSTRIPS began solving the robot problem by first establishing two subgoals: (1) push box 1 to box 2 and (2) leave the robot in room A. In establishing these two subgoals, it checked only the most critical preconditions, such as that box 1 could be pushed and that there was a room A that could be entered. Since these preconditions were satisfied, it then attempted to reach the two subgoals by satisfying preconditions that had an intermediate level of criticality. A precondition for pushing box 1 is that the robot is in the same room as box 1; a new subgoal was therefore needed to move the robot to room E. A precondition for moving the robot to a room is that the robot is in an adjoining room. An attempt to move the robot to room B (an adjoining room) failed because the robot was not in a room next to room B. The attempt to move the robot to room F succeeded, thereby satisfying the precondition for moving the robot to room E. The intermediate preconditions for pushing box 1 to box 2 were now satisfied, and so this subgoal could be reached at an intermediate level of planning.

But two lesser preconditions had to be satisfied in order to reach the subgoal in the actual search space. A precondition for moving from one room to an adjacent room is that the door between the two rooms is open. It was therefore necessary to open the door between rooms F and G. It was also necessary to move the robot next to box 1 after it entered room E, since this is a lower-level precondition for moving objects.

Although many of these preconditions may seem rather trivial to us human problem solvers, they are important determinants of the effectiveness of a problem-solving program. Figure 13.2 illustrates the success of a hierarchical planning system. The original program, STRIPS, initially explored many unpromising paths in the search space before finding a path that resulted in the solution. It explored 119

a. STRIPS search tree for the sample problem

b. ABSTRIPS search tree in the space of criticality 6

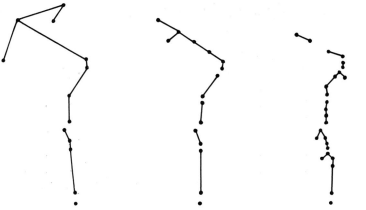

c. ABSTRIPS search tree in the space of criticality 5

d. ABSTRIPS search tree in the space of criticality 4

e. ABSTRIPS search tree in the problem space

Figure 13.2   Searches for a solution: STRIPS versus ABSTRIPS problem states in the search space, only 23 of which were on the successful path. The dots in Figure 13.2a represent problem states explored by STRIPS. You can see that many of the paths did not lead to a solution (represented by the dot at the bottom of the search tree).

ABSTRIPS first attempted to solve a simpler version of the problem by considering only the most important preconditions. It required only a few steps to solve the simpler problem (Figure 13.2b). By considering preconditions of lower criticality in subsequent searches (Figures 13.2c–13.2e), ABSTRIPS solved the problem without exploring unpromising paths. The procedure was successful because solution of the simpler problems provided subgoals that constrained the search as more details were added (Figures 13.2b–13.2e). ABSTRIPS required less than 6 minutes of computer time to solve this problem, compared with over 30 minutes for STRIPS.

This brief description of ABSTRIPS oversimplifies the nature of planning. One potential difficulty is that achieving one subgoal may make it impossible to achieve another. For example, if ABSTRIPS first tried to achieve the subgoal of leaving the robot in room A, it would have to abandon this subgoal in order to use the robot to move the box in room E.

Furthermore, ABSTRIPS cannot make use of the relationships among the various levels of plans; therefore it runs into trouble if its higher-level solutions are wrong. A more sophisticated program called NOAH (Network of Action Hierarchies) was designed to eliminate some of these deficiencies (Sacerdoti, 1977). NOAH performs its planning in a hierarchical fashion, as ABSTRIPS does, but tries not to overconstrain its search for a solution. NOAH is more flexible in the order in which subgoals are achieved, so it is less likely to have to abandon one subgoal because it must achieve another first. The ordering of subgoals is delayed until enough details have been obtained to specify the order. NOAH also saves the plans made at different levels in the hierarchy so that this information can be reused if it is necessary to modify a plan because some subgoals cannot be reached or are not part of the required solution.

Does Sacerdoti's work add to our knowledge of planning? As Sacerdoti points out in the concluding section of his book (1977), Miller, Galanter, and Pribram discussed the concept of planning in 1960. Their book discussed plan generation, execution monitoring, planning in spaces where details are ignored, integration of subplans into larger plans, and learning as the development of hierarchical structures.

Sacerdoti's contribution is that his computer program avoids the lack of specificity common to verbal formulations. There are so many ways even a small number of moves or problem states can interrelate that it is very easy for inconsistencies to go unnoticed or interrelationships to go unspecified. Although Miller, Galanter, and Pribram provided insights into the importance of planning, many of their concepts were insufficiently defined. Artificial intelligence provides a methodology for avoiding inconsistencies, for discovering new insights that were not apparent in a verbal description, and for testing variations in the initial formulation of a concept. In Sacerdoti's words, "The discipline imposed by computer implementation helps to debug our own insights" (1977, p. 107).

Hierarchical Planning as a Model of Human Problem Solving

Sacerdoti's theory provides a precise description of how planning can be efficiently organized, but are his ideas relevant to human behavior? Perhaps you can think of situations in which you wished you had planned more carefully before attempting a task. I can.

One example occurred on the morning that I left on my trip westward to spend a year at the University of California, Berkeley. Shortly before we left, the toilet broke and I had to repair a metal bar that connected the handle to a plunger. If we ignore the details, the task can be represented by two high-level subgoals: connect the bar to the handle and connect the plunger to the bar. One virtue of NOAH is that it can delay specifying the order of subgoals until it obtains information about lower-level details. I wasn't so smart.

After attaching the bar to the handle, I noticed that the bar was curved slightly upward, but it would have to curve downward in order to reach the plunger. I unscrewed the bar and once again attached it to the handle so it would curve downward. I then noticed that it still wouldn't reach the plunger unless I attached it before connecting the bar to the handle. Fortunately, the search space was small enough that having to start over twice did not delay my trip. Still, I wished I had planned before beginning.

Planning becomes more and more important as the search space grows larger. A good example of a task that depends on hierarchical planning is the writing of computer programs. Atwood, Polson, Jeffries, and Ramsey (1978) conducted an experiment to study this task. The theoretical assumptions that guided their research were greatly influenced by the ideas expressed in NOAH. They assumed:

1. A plan is a series of abstractions of the final solution, ranging from schematic high-level plans to detailed plans that produce the solution.
2. A plan is constructed by a process of stepwise refinement; that is, construction starts at the higher, more abstract levels, and the details are added later.
3. Planning involves utilization of previously learned knowledge structures.
4. Various components of the plan or even the entire plan can be retrieved from long-term memory and incorporated into a solution.
5. Planning involves the synthesis of many types of knowledge structures.

The subjects in this experiment were three highly experienced computer programmers. The task was to write a program that would accept as input the text of a book and would produce as output a list of specified index terms and page numbers on which each term appeared. The results showed that subjects differed in the extent to which they followed a hierarchical, top-down planning procedure. The protocols of the three subjects showed fairly clear differences in the overall quality, completeness, and organization of their knowledge. The knowledge of one subject was sufficiently developed to allow for the construction of plans in a top-down expansion. This subject's procedure was most similar to the procedure used by NOAH. The knowledge of a second subject was less well developed, and, as a result, backtracking was necessary in order to correct deficiencies in the design. The knowledge of the third subject was developed to such an extent that this subject was able to retrieve most of the design directly from memory and therefore required less planning than the other two subjects. These findings suggest that hierarchical planning is most likely to be carried out by someone who has enough knowledge to approach the task systematically but is unable to retrieve the solution directly from memory.

Individual Differences in Planning

The view that hierarchical planning is more characteristic of an expert than of a novice is supported by Larkin and Reif's (1979) research on how a novice and an expert solve physics (mechanics) problems. The expert was a physics professor who had recently taught a mechanics course. The "novice" was an excellent student who had recently completed his first university-level course in mechanics. Both subjects solved five problems, which were taken from a widely used textbook. Figure 13.3 shows one of the problems. The subjects were asked to work normally but to think aloud as much as possible. Both solved all five problems, but neither subject recognized any problem as having an immediately obvious solution.

Although both subjects solved all five problems, they did not proceed in the same way. The novice began immediately to identify relevant principles and apply them individually to generate equations. When relevant equations were identified, he combined them to eliminate undesirable quantities. The expert did not immediately construct a mathematical description of the problem. Instead, he used a more general planning procedure in which details were added by successive refinements. The expert did not try to write equations and eliminate undesirable quantities but used a more coherent approach to guide the subsequent construction of the relevant equations. The expert applied principles not individually but as part of a well-defined plan.

The result was that the equations generated by the expert were clustered together in time, corresponding to a rapid application of preplanned methods. In contrast, the novice generated equations more randomly in time. Figure 13.4 shows how much

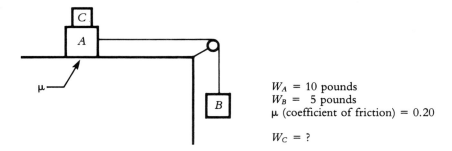

Figure 13.3   A physics problem requiring calculation of how much block C must weigh to keep block A from sliding off the table

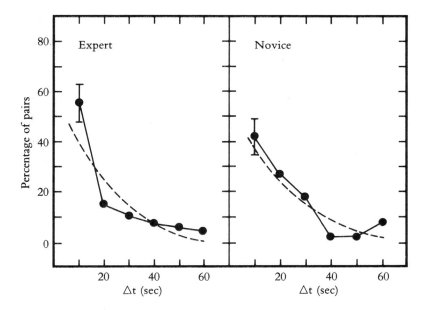

Figure 13.4   Percentage of equation pairs, as a function of intervening time (Δt), generated in problem solutions

time separated successive pairs of equations generated by the expert and the novice. The dashed lines are the curves that would occur if the equations had been generated randomly in time. The novice's graph closely corresponds to the prediction of random generation, whereas the expert's graph shows a large number of equation pairs with small intervening times, reflecting a significant amount of clustering.

The studies on individual differences in planning and problem solving have typically used a very limited number of subjects. These studies are continuing, and future theoretical models should be less tentative than current models. But some consistency is already emerging in interpretations of how the expert problem solver differs from the beginning problem solver. Heller and Greeno (1979) reviewed the evidence on individual differences in solving word problems in arithmetic, algebra, physics, and thermodynamics. They concluded that several characteristics of the solution procedures change as the problem solvers become more competent. Table 13.3 summarizes the differences for two ends of a continuum. Heller and Greeno's analysis provides a good first approximation of the differences between the novice and the expert and a useful summary of current knowledge.

Problem Solving and Instruction

The distinction between the operations used by the novice and the expert leads us to consider whether problem-solving strategies can be explicitly taught. If we can identify what the expert is doing, can we use this information to teach the novice to

Table 13.3   Hypothesized differences between a novice and an expert

	Novice	Expert
Problem representation	Rely on verbal problem statement; no use of semantic and auxiliary information	Construct diagram when useful; rely on strong spontaneous mediating representation
Knowledge structure	No problem category information used; principles stored separately	Strong problem category information available, with associated solution procedures
Initial analysis	No informal qualitative analysis; identify unknown and given values; go directly to equations	Qualitative elaboration of problem features to determine most promising procedure if solution is not immediately clear
Solution strategy	Nearly random search for equations containing desired quantities; substitute values until answer is isolated	Implement plan for solution; rarely need to rework by alternative procedure

become a better problem solver? The expert has acquired considerable knowledge over a long period, and it would be unreasonable to expect that the novice could acquire the same amount of knowledge over a short period. However, the expert may have learned some problem-solving strategies that, if explicitly taught, would make the novice a better problem solver.

Teaching Heuristics

A recent paper by Schoenfeld (1979) illustrates how we might teach heuristic strategies. Although Schoenfeld compared the performances of only seven students, his paper reflects both the potential benefits and the limitations of teaching heuristics.

The students were science mathematics majors who were recruited as volunteers from upper-division courses in mathematics. Four of the seven students were randomly assigned to a "heuristics" group and the remaining three to a "nonheuristics" group. All students took a pretest consisting of five challenging mathematics problems. They then participated in five instruction sessions spread over a two-week period, during which time they worked on and saw the solutions to 20 problems. All students spent the same amount of time working on the problems and saw the same solutions. After the instruction sessions, students took a posttest of five problems. All problems in the pretest, instruction sessions, and posttest were chosen from five classes of similar problems—similar in that they could be solved by a particular strategy.

At the first instruction session, the four heuristics students were given a list of the five strategies (see Table 13.4). They were then given the problems grouped according to strategy; each session was devoted to a particular strategy. Students in the nonheuristics group did not see the list of strategies and were given the 20

Table 13.4   The five problem-solving strategies

1. Draw a diagram if at all possible.
   Even if you finally solve the problem by algebraic or other means, a diagram can help give you a "feel" for the problem. It may suggest ideas or plausible answers. You may even solve a problem graphically.

2. If there is an integer paramèter, look for an inductive argument.
   Is there an "n" or other parameter in the problem which takes on integer values? If you need to find a formula for $f(n)$, you might try one of these:
   A. Calculate $f(1)$, $f(2)$, $f(3)$, $f(4)$, $f(5)$; list them in order, and see if there's a pattern. If there is, you might verify it by induction.
   B. See what happens as you pass from n objects to $n + 1$. If you can tell how to pass from $f(n)$ to $f(n + 1)$, you may build up $f(n)$ inductively.

3. Consider arguing by contradiction or contrapositive.
   Contrapositive: Instead of proving the statement "If X is true then Y is true," you can prove the equivalent statement "If Y is false then X must be false."
   Contradiction: Assume, for the sake of argument, that the statement you would like to prove is false. Using this assumption, go on to prove either that one of the given conditions in the problem is false, that something you know to be true is false, or that what you wish to prove is true. If you can do any of these, you have proved what you want.
   Both of these techniques are especially useful when you find it difficult to begin a direct argument because you have little to work with. If negating a statement gives you something solid to manipulate, this may be the technique to use.

4. Consider a similar problem with fewer variables.
   If the problem has a large number of variables and is too confusing to deal with comfortably, construct and solve a similar problem with fewer variables. You may then be able to
   A. Adapt the method of solution to the more complex problem.
   B. Take the result of the simpler problem and build up from there.

5. Try to establish subgoals.
   Can you obtain part of the answer, and perhaps go on from there? Can you decompose the problem so that a number of easier results can be combined to give the total result you want?

practice problems in random order. Although all students saw the same solutions, students in the heuristics group also saw an overlay to each solution that indicated where a particular strategy had been used.

The three students in the nonheuristics group successfully solved a total of five problems on the pretest and five problems on the posttest. The four students in the heuristics group correctly solved a total of four problems on the pretest and thirteen problems on the posttest. All four heuristics students improved their performance and had at least two more correct solutions on the posttest.

Schoenfeld is careful in interpreting his results and presents a balanced discussion of the implications of the study. The results are encouraging because they demonstrate that a training procedure can improve students' abilities to solve problems. Consequently, if we expect students to learn such strategies, we should label them explicitly and illustrate their use. But Schoenfeld also argues that we should not expect a dramatic improvement in performance on the basis of a limited number of practice sessions. There is no guarantee that students will use a particular technique or will know when to apply it even though they used it successfully during a practice session. In part, this is the fault of the vagueness of some of the strategies. The instruction to use subgoals, for example, did not transfer very well to other problems, because the strategy itself usually requires considerable specific knowledge to use effectively.

Schoenfeld's conclusion is therefore both cautious and optimistic:

> We are still a long way from success. If we can succeed in identifying truly useful problem-solving strategies (and here we have done well); if we can understand and exploit the mechanisms by which experts call these strategies into play; and if we can create efficient means by which this knowledge can be passed on to our students, the potential rewards are great indeed. The obstacles are many, the field vast. This experiment shows that, under appropriate circumstances, explicit instruction in general problem-solving strategies (heuristics) does have an impact on students' problem-solving performance. The rest will, with luck and work, come with time [1979, p. 186].

The Computer as Tutor

Contributions to a better understanding of problem solving have come from many disciplines. Rubinstein's problem-solving course at UCLA originated in the Department of Engineering, Hayes's course in the Department of Psychology. Carroll, Thomas, and Malhotra are psychologists who worked on design problems at the IBM Watson Research Center. The research on categorization of word problems was done by psychologists at Carnegie-Mellon University. Silver and Schoenfeld are both members of mathematics education departments, and Sacerdoti is a member of the artificial intelligence group at the Stanford Research Institute. Larkin and Reif have backgrounds in physics and did their study as members of the Group in Science and Mathematics Education at the University of California, Berkeley.

The multidisciplinary nature of research on complex skills has resulted in a multidisciplinary journal called *Cognitive Science,* first published in January 1977, with an emphasis on research in artificial intelligence, psychology, and language. The progress being made in these areas, combined with the rapid decline in costs of computers, should result in increasing use of the computer as an intelligent tutor that can help people solve problems. This goal is now attainable because the computer itself has become a good problem solver (see Box 13.1).

The initial development of computer-assisted instruction (CAI) in the 1960s was based on multiple-choice questions. A student's responses determined how that student would progress through the program, but there was no attempt to understand his or her misconceptions. Howe (1978) has characterized the most recent approaches to CAI as based on a "learning by doing" rather than a "learning by being told" philosophy. The newer view represents learning as an active construction of knowledge in which creativity and problem-solving skills play an important role. According to Howe, the major reason for the limitations of the traditional CAI program is that it neither knows nor understands the topic being taught. This means that it is unable to interpret alternative or interesting answers, to understand why a student made a mistake, or to supply the student with useful information. The goal of the most recent learner-based programs is to model the knowledge and skill acquired by an individual in order to best assist him or her in learning these skills.

Box 13.1 How smart can computers get?

On a Monday morning at Yale University, Margot Flowers sits down with her friend Abdul for another debate on Mideast politics:

MARGOT: Who started the 1967 war?

ABDUL: The Arabs did, by blockading the Strait of Tiran.

MARGOT: But Israel attacked first.

ABDUL: According to international law, blockades are acts of war.

MARGOT: Were we supposed to let you import American arms through the strait?

ABDUL: Israel was not importing arms through the strait. The reason for the blockade was to keep Israel from importing oil from Iran.

They don't have the finesse of U.N. diplomats, but then Margot Flowers is one of three scientists who created Abdul, a computer program that dips into its memory of data to reason out answers to questions. The dialogue is an exercise in a 25-year-old field called artificial intelligence (AI), and with the remarkable advances in computer technology at their command, hundreds of AI researchers are testing the potential of the new electronic brains. Their goal is as remarkable as their technology: to determine how close a computer can come to simulating the human mind and, perhaps, transcending it.

The results thus far are both tantalizing and reassuring. In scores of AI experiments, well-programed computers can play chess and backgammon, draw analogies among Shakespearean plays and understand tales involving friendship and adultery. Computers can use facts to make inferences and draw on experience to reach unprogramed conclusions. But only up to a point: what AI researchers are learning is that the human brain is even more astonishing than they thought—and that true intelligence involves elements of will, consciousness and creativity of which today's computers are incapable. "So far, artificial intelligence falls under the definition of problem solving," says AI scientist Terry Winograd of Stanford. "That's the first step."

The first "thinking" problem solver was probably a 1956 computer program called the Logic Theorist, which could choose from a set of facts and use logical operations to prove mathematical statements. Its first triumph was finding a proof of a theorem in mathematical logic that both Bertrand Russell and Alfred North Whitehead had missed.

Today's problem solvers are even more sophisticated. One of the most impressive is the backgammon champ programed by Hans J. Berliner of Carnegie-Mellon University of Pittsburgh. The program chooses among all possible legal moves by reducing each to a mathematical equation that measures threats and opportunities and then picks the move whose equation has the highest value. BACON, another program developed by Nobel laureate Herbert A. Simon and his colleagues at Carnegie-Mellon, looks for patterns in scientific data. On its own, BACON "discovered" a rule of planetary mechanics first established by Johannes Kepler in 1609. And when it was fed all the facts that were known about chemistry in the year 1800, BACON deduced the principle of atomic weight—a feat that took human scientists another 50 years.

From *Newsweek* (June 30, 1980). Reprinted by permission.

An example of this newer approach is Brown and Burton's (1978) diagnostic analysis of a student's misconceptions in basic mathematical skills. Using techniques developed in the field of artificial intelligence, they constructed a computer model for diagnosing why a student is making a mistake. Their model is based on the assumption that mistakes usually occur not because students do not follow procedures very well but because they often follow the wrong procedure. If students follow the wrong procedure, there should be a systematic pattern in their errors. A good diagnostic model should be able to identify the misconception ("bug") that causes the systematic pattern.

Brown and Burton's analysis revealed that there is a remarkable number of possible bugs even for relatively simple procedures like addition and subtraction. Furthermore, it's a challenging task for a teacher or a computer program to identify these bugs. Figure 13.5 shows three addition problems and three subtraction problems. Each set of three problems has a bug that produces the erroneous answers. See whether you can identify the two bugs before reading further.

Addition problems

17	18	43
+ 5	+ 6	+79
13	15	23

Subtraction problems

662	831	563
−357	−158	−241
215	583	322

Figure 13.5   Examples of an addition bug and a subtraction bug

If you tried diagnosing the errors, you will realize that error diagnosis can be difficult. The addition bug is that the student is treating each digit as a single digit. Thus 17 + 5 is treated as 1 + 7 + 5. The subtraction bug is that the student subtracts all borrows from the hundreds digits in the top number. Diagnosing bugs becomes even more difficult when (1) any one of several bugs can account for the errors, (2) there is more than one bug producing the errors, or (3) a student occasionally makes random errors when applying a buggy procedure.

Brown and Burton discuss three applications of their diagnostic model. The first is an instructional game for training student teachers. The prospective teachers were first shown a single problem with an incorrect answer. They then gave the computer new problems, and the computer gave buggy answers. When the students felt they had diagnosed the bug, the computer gave them problems and they had to produce buggy answers. The problems were selected so it would be difficult to give the correct buggy answers unless one had correctly diagnosed the bug. A second use of a diagnostic model was to analyze errors on subtraction problems made by elementary school pupils in order to identify bugs in their answers. A third application of the model was to judge the diagnostic quality of a test. If a test is used to diagnose specific misconceptions rather than simply to assign a numerical score, it is necessary to select problems that will reveal the misconceptions. A good diagnostic model can do this. The three applications illustrate the potential benefit of diagnostic models, computer tutors, and applications of theories in cognitive science to educational problems.

Combining Theory and Instruction

Another example of combining psychological theory and instructional programs is the work of John Anderson and his colleagues at Carnegie-Mellon University (Anderson, Boyle, & Reiser, 1985). Their work has focused on the design of intelligent tutoring systems for teaching high school geometry and the LISP programming language. The systems are based on the learning principles of ACT*, the most current version of the ACT theory described in Chapter 9.

ACT* consists of a set of assumptions about both declarative knowledge and procedural knowledge. The assumptions about declarative knowledge emphasize the representation and organization of factual information. We looked at this aspect of ACT in Chapter 9. The assumptions about procedural knowledge emphasize how we use this knowledge to carry out various tasks. The procedural assumptions of the theory are particularly relevant for tutoring cognitive skills.

The procedural component of the theory consists of a set of rules (usually called production rules) that specify which actions should be performed under a particular set of conditions. A production rule therefore consists of two parts—a condition part and an action part. The action is carried out whenever the condition is satisfied. An example of a production rule is "IF the goal is to generate the plural of a noun, THEN add an *s* to the noun." Notice that the condition specifies a goal and the action specifies a potential way to achieve the goal.

A problem with a production system consisting of many rules is that if more than one rule is applicable, it is necessary to select one. Two ways of resolving this conflict in ACT entail evaluating the specificity and strength of a rule (Anderson, 1982). The specificity principle states that if two productions can apply and one is more specific, then select the more specific one. A specific production rule for generating the plural of *man* is: "IF the goal is to generate the plural of *man*, THEN say *men*." The advantage of selecting a specific rule is that a general rule may not work in all cases, as illustrated by the rule that generated plurals by adding an *s* to the noun.

The second way to resolve conflicts is to select the production rule with the greatest strength. The strength reflects the frequency with which that production has been successfully applied. The production rules in ACT* are goal-directed, so success in achieving their goals would determine selections. A common goal in geometry problems is to prove that two triangles are congruent. The side-angle-side rule is one method for proving congruence, resulting in the production "IF the goal is to prove a pair of triangles congruent, THEN try to prove that their corresponding pairs of sides and included angles are congruent."

The computer tutor for geometry proofs constructed by Anderson and his colleagues contains 200 such rules, and the program executes the best rule that applies in a particular situation. Not all the rule applications are needed in the final proof, but when rules deviate from the final proof, they deviate in a way that is consistent with how students construct proofs. The tutor is therefore based on a model that consists of an effective and humanlike proof system containing a set of rules for making the most reasonable inference in a particular context.

Summary

Courses on improving problem-solving skills are currently being taught at a few universities, and many educational courses require problem solving. Many of the ideas we have discussed previously are being applied in the study of how people solve problems.

Both general strategies and domain-specific knowledge are needed to solve classroom problems, as demonstrated by individual differences in categorization and planning. College students' initial analysis of algebra word problems resulted in a categorization of each problem into one of about 14 categories. Students then used the information about the categories—including knowledge about useful equations, diagrams, and procedures for identifying relevant information—to formulate solutions. The development of categorization skills is illustrated by individual differences among seventh-graders who were given word problems and college students who were given physics problems. When asked to classify problems according to their mathematical structure, good problem solvers were able to form categories on the basis of the mathematical procedures used to solve the problems, whereas poor problem solvers formed categories on the basis of story context. Good problem solvers were also better at recalling the mathematical structure of problems.

As problems become more complex, the skilled use of planning becomes important in determining how efficiently they can be solved. Planning involves establishing subgoals that guide the search for a solution. Many of the key ideas used in planning have been formalized by work in artificial intelligence. Programs like NOAH use a hierarchical technique in which details are considered only after the initial solutions are formulated in an abstraction of the search space. A study of how computer programmers design software revealed three levels of performance—one characterized by considerable backtracking to correct incorrect procedures, one characterized by the efficient use of hierarchical planning, and one characterized by the retrieval of a detailed solution. Planning was also the main distinguishing characteristic between how a novice and an expert solved physics problems.

The distinction between the operations used by the novice and by the expert suggests that it might be beneficial to teach problem-solving strategies. As one example of this approach, upper-division science and mathematics majors were taught strategies about drawing a diagram, looking for an inductive argument, arguing by contradiction, formulating a simpler problem, and establishing subgoals. The group taught the strategies improved their performance on a posttest, whereas a control group did not. Another application of knowledge about problem solving is the design of intelligent computer tutors. Recent progress in the areas of artificial intelligence, education, and cognitive psychology has resulted in CAI programs that treat learning as an active construction of knowledge, involving skills in problem solving. Examples of this new approach include a program that diagnoses misconceptions about addition and subtraction and a program that uses the learning principles of ACT* to assist students in constructing geometry proofs.

Recommended Reading

Paige and Simon (1966) discuss cognitive processes in solving algebra word problems. The effect of meaningfulness on solving algebraic equations has been studied by Mayer and Greeno (1975) and Kieras and Greeno (1975). Mayer and Greeno (1972) have also investigated how different instructional procedures influence what people learn about a statistical formula called the *binominal theorem*. More recently, the construction of geometry proofs (Lewis & Anderson, 1985) and social science problems (Voss, Greene, Post, & Penner, 1983) have also been studied. The differences between experts and novices continue to be a popular topic of investigation in areas such as physics (Larkin, McDermott, Simon, & Simon, 1980) and computer programming (Adelson, 1984). A two-volume series, *Thinking and Learning Skills* (Chipman, Segal, & Glaser, 1985; Segal, Chipman, & Glaser, 1985), contains many interesting chapters. A review of research on instructional psychology occurs periodically in the *Annual Review of Psychology* (Pintrich, Cross, Kozma, & McKeachie, 1986).

14

Decision Making

I cannot, for want of sufficient premises, advise you what to determine, but if you please I will tell you how. . . . My way is to divide half a sheet of paper by a line into two columns; writing over one Pro, and over the other Con. Then, doing three or four days' consideration, I put down under the different heads short hints of the different motives, that at different times occur to me for or against the measure. When I have thus got them all together in one view, I endeavor to estimate the respective weights . . . [to] find at length where the balance lies. . . . And, though the weight of reasons cannot be taken with the precision of algebraic quantities, yet, when each is thus considered, separately and comparatively, and the whole matter lies before me, I think I can judge better, and am less liable to make a rash step; and in fact I have found great advantage for this kind of equation, in what may be called moral or prudential algebra.

BENJAMIN FRANKLIN (1772/1887)

Every day we make many decisions. Most of these are relatively unimportant—what to eat for breakfast, for example. Others—such as selecting a car, a home, or a job—are more important. Making decisions is often difficult because each alternative usually has many aspects, and very seldom does the best alternative excel on all of them. One way to simplify the decision process is to emphasize only a single aspect. Box 14.1 illustrates this approach. The Morrisons evaluated many features before buying a house, but they made their final selection on the basis of just one—the quality of the local school. Although this is a very important consideration for parents with school-age children, there was such a small difference in the quality of the schools that the Morrisons really overemphasized this feature.

The first section of this chapter describes models of how people select an alternative from a set of alternatives. Examples include selecting a dinner from a

Box 14.1 Dream home bypassed for school

KATHY O'TOOLE
Education Writer

Mike and Patty Morrison had hopes this time of getting their dream home—a new one, with carpeting in just the colors they wanted, with a fireplace in the family room and a breakfast area in the kitchen.

The Morrisons, newcomers from Southern California with two pre-school children, found their dream home in a new San Ramon subdivision.

But they didn't buy it.

The house lacked one feature. It wasn't near the elementary school whose pupils had the highest test scores in the San Ramon School District.

Instead, the Morrisons bought a more expensive home in Walnut Creek with a floor plan they didn't like, and the carpet a color they didn't like.

They made their decision based on standardized school test score information supplied by a San Ramon Valley real estate agent, Sherry Schiff.

The Morrisons' decision illustrates the relatively small differences parents sometimes consider in deciding what home to buy.

In state reading tests given last May, third-graders at the school near the home the Morrisons bought scored higher than those in 91 percent of the state's schools. The third-graders at the school near the home the Morrisons preferred scored better than those in 84 percent of the schools.

The Morrisons and their real estate agent have played a meaningless statistical game, contend several testing experts for Eastbay school districts and the state Department of Education.

The test scores of the two schools compared were so close, say the test experts, that they can't possibly tell parents in which school their child will do better.

Reproduced with permission from the *Oakland Tribune*, Oakland, California.

---

menu, a home, or a car. These models do not consider probabilities because they assume that a person knows the values of relevant dimensions, such as price, gas mileage, and optional equipment in the case of buying a car. The following two sections are concerned with examples of risky decision making—those in which the decision maker must consider probabilities. We will first examine how people make probability estimates, including ways they revise their estimates when they receive new information. We will then consider how people use the estimates to make decisions. The study of decision making has been influenced by both normative and descriptive models. Normative models specify what a person should do. They often provide a standard for comparing how closely actual decisions match normative decisions. Descriptive models seek to describe how people actually arrive at decisions. The relation between normative and descriptive models is a theme that occurs throughout the discussion of risky decision making. The final section of this chapter discusses medical decision making as an example of a complex skill. The discussion illustrates how psychological models can be used to describe medical diagnosis.

Making Choices

Compensatory Models

One reason decisions can be difficult is that alternatives usually have many attributes. If one of the attributes is not very attractive, the decision maker must decide whether to eliminate that alternative or continue to consider it because its other attributes may be very attractive. For example, a person may buy a car with low gas mileage because of the smooth ride and spaciousness of a large car. Decision-making models that allow attractive attributes to compensate for unattractive ones are called *compensatory models*. The advice by Benjamin Franklin quoted at the beginning of this chapter is consistent with a compensatory model because Franklin combined the pros and cons of each option.

An *additive model* is a kind of compensatory model. An additive model combines the attractive and unattractive attributes to arrive at a total score for each alternative. Consider the case of John Smith. John has lived in a college dormitory for three consecutive years. It is now his senior year, and he feels that it is time to enjoy the greater freedom that an apartment can offer. He has found two rather attractive apartments and must select one. John decides to follow Ben Franklin's advice and systematically list the advantages and disadvantages of each. First he lists the attributes that will influence his decision, and then he rates each on a scale that ranges from -3 (a very negative impression) to $+3$ (a very positive impression). Here are his ratings:

	Apartment A	Apartment B
Rent	$+1$	$+2$
Noise level	-2	$+3$
Distance to campus	$+3$	-1
Cleanliness	$+2$	$+2$
	$+4$	$+6$

The sums of the ratings for the various attributes of the two apartments reveal that John's best choice is to select apartment B, which is rated higher.

There are two ways of modifying the summation rule that could change the results. First, the four attributes were equally weighted in the example. If some attributes are more important to John than others, he will want to emphasize these attributes when making his decision. For instance, he might want to emphasize distance from campus if he lives in a cold climate and has to walk to classes. If this variable is twice as important as the others, he could multiply his ratings of distance by 2 to give this dimension greater emphasis. The sum of the ratings would then be $+7$ for apartment A and $+5$ for apartment B. Second, adding the ratings of the four attributes does not account for how the attributes might interact. Although apartment A is very noisy, it is so close to campus that the library would be a convenient place to study. The high noise level is therefore not as detrimental as it would be if the apartment were the only convenient place to study. The low rating for noise level should perhaps be modified to take into account the interaction between that dimension and distance to campus.

A model that is very similar to the additive model is called the *additive-difference model*. The latter compares two alternatives by totaling the differences between their values on each attribute. The values on each attribute are shown below. The third column shows the value obtained by subtracting the second column from the first.

	Apartment A	Apartment B	Difference
Rent	+1	+2	−1
Noise level	−2	+3	−5
Distance to campus	+3	−1	+4
Cleanliness	+2	+2	0
	+4	+6	−2

The sum of the differences is −2, which implies that apartment A is two units less attractive than apartment B. The additive model implies the same conclusion: the sum of the ratings for apartment A is 2 less than the sum of the ratings for apartment B. Although the additive and the additive-difference models result in the same conclusion, the search for information is different. The additive model evaluates all attributes of one alternative before considering the next alternative. The additive-difference model compares the two alternatives attribute by attribute. If there are more than two alternatives, a given alternative is compared with the best of the preceding alternatives.

Both the additive and the additive-difference models describe a good procedure for evaluating alternatives. Both evaluate alternatives on all their attributes and allow attractive values to compensate for unattractive values. The models can be used to make realistic decisions, as Box 14.2 illustrates. Box 14.2 describes an additive model in which points are assigned to six attributes depending on how much information each provides. The decision to proceed with further investigation is based on the sum of the points.

Although Benjamin Franklin's advice was good, we may question how often we follow it. The examples show that the additive model provides a systematic procedure for making decisions, but are we really this systematic in making decisions? How often do we take the time to make the kind of calculations required by the models? Perhaps some other model might better describe how we actually make choices. The alternative to a compensatory model is a *noncompensatory* model, in which unattractive attributes result in elimination of alternatives.

Noncompensatory Models

If we do not calculate, how *do* we make decisions? Tversky (1972) has proposed that we make choices by gradually eliminating less attractive alternatives. His theory is

**Box 14.2   Report says police can predict
which burglaries can be solved**

WASHINGTON (AP)—A new study indicates that police can reliably predict
which burglaries can be solved and recommends that they stop investigating cases
unlikely to lead to an arrest.

The report, released yesterday by the Police Executive Research Forum, said
"the characteristics of burglary cases, not follow-up investigations, determine the
overall success or failure rate of burglary investigations."

The FBI reported there were 3.1 million burglaries in 1978, but fewer than
one in five led to an arrest. It is the most common felony crime in the United
States.

The study recommends police departments consider six key elements of preliminary burglary reports to decide whether to investigate further.

The forum, a national organization of state and local police executives, used
police personnel in 26 cities, including Toledo, to test a rating system first developed
in 1972 by the Stanford Research Institute. . . .

The six elements and the numerical value assigned to them were:

- Police arrival at scene: Five points for police arrival less than one hour after
  the crime; one point for arrival between one and 12 hours after the crime;
  three-tenths of a point for arrival 12 to 24 hours afterwards; no points for
  arrival more than 24 hours later.
- Seven points for a civilian witness report.
- One point if a policeman discovered the crime.
- Seven points for usable fingerprints of a stranger at the scene.
- Nine points for the name or description of a suspect.
- One-tenth of a point for a description of a suspicious vehicle at the scene.
- No points for all other information.

If the preliminary report had a total value of 10 points or less, the study
predicted further investigation would not lead to an arrest. It predicted an arrest if
the total was more than 10 points.

Analyzing the results of 12,001 past burglary investigations, the forum found
that its method of weighing the factors was 85% accurate in predicting which cases
led to a suspect being arrested, charged and turned over for prosecution.

Under the screening procedure used by the forum, 86.7% of the burglary cases
would not be assigned for further investigation.

From the *Plain Dealer*, Cleveland, January 28, 1980. © Associated Press Newsfeatures.
Reprinted by permission.

called *elimination by aspects* because it assumes that the elimination is based on the sequential evaluation of the attributes, or aspects, of the alternatives. If the attribute of an alternative does not satisfy some minimum criterion, that alternative is eliminated from the set of choices.

Consider Mrs. Green, who is looking for a new car. If Mrs. Green has only $9000 to spend, she may first eliminate from her set of possible choices those cars that cost over $9000. She may also be interested in gas economy and eliminate cars that cannot travel at least 25 miles on a gallon on gas. By continuing to select attributes and rejecting those that do not satisfy some minimum criterion, she will continue to eliminate alternatives until there is only a single car remaining that satisfies all her criteria.

The final choice, based on this procedure, depends on the order in which the attributes are evaluated. If the price of the car is one of the last attributes Mrs. Green evaluates, she might eliminate all cars costing under $9000 early in her decision process—an undesirable situation if she has only $9000 to spend. The model therefore proposes that the attributes differ in importance, and the probability of selecting an attribute for evaluation depends on its importance. If price is a very important attribute, it has a high probability of being selected early in the sequence.

The elimination-by-aspects model has the advantage that it does not require any calculations. The decision maker simply selects an attribute according to some probability that depends on the importance of that attribute. She then determines whether an alternative satisfies a minimum criterion for that attribute and eliminates those alternatives that do not meet the criterion.

The *conjunctive model*—a variant of elimination by aspects—requires that all the attributes of an alternative satisfy minimum criteria before that alternative can be selected. It differs from elimination by aspects by proposing that people finish evaluating one alternative before considering another. The first alternative that satisfies all the minimum criteria is selected. The conjunctive model is an example of what Simon (1957) has called a *satisficing search*. Simon argued that limited capability to evaluate many alternatives often prevents people from selecting the best alternative. Instead, they are willing to settle for a good alternative—that is, one that satisfies all the minimum criteria. Other constraints, such as limits in time or availability, may also influence us to choose a good alternative rather than wait for the best alternative. For example, we may simply become tired of looking at apartments, or an apartment we liked may be rented by the time we return, so we will choose an available alternative rather than continue searching for a better one.

Selecting a Strategy

The four models we have looked at differ with respect to how people search for information. John Payne (1976) took advantage of this difference in designing a procedure for finding out which strategies people use. He presented information describing the attributes of apartments, such as rent, cleanliness, noise level, and distance from campus. The information describing each apartment was printed on the back of a card, which had to be turned over in order to reveal its value (see Figure 14.1). Subjects were allowed to turn over as many cards as they needed to make their decision. The order in which they turned over the cards should reveal how they searched for information. Payne gathered additional evidence about how they arrived at a decision by asking them to think aloud as they evaluated the information on the cards.

Payne proposed that the four decision-making models could be distinguished by the ways people search for information. Figure 14.2 shows a classification of the models according to whether the search is intradimensional or interdimensional and whether the number of dimensions searched is constant or variable across alternatives. This distinction can be clarified by comparing the additive model and the elimination-by-aspects model.

The additive model proposes that a person turns over cards representing one alternative and forms an overall score to represent the attractiveness of that alternative. The procedure is then repeated for the other alternatives. The search for information is *interdimensional* (across dimensions, or attributes) because all relevant dimensions are evaluated for one alternative before the next alternative is evaluated. This method would require turning over all the cards in one row before going on to the next row (see Figure 14.1). Although it is not necessary to turn over all cards in each row (since some dimensions may not be important), the decision maker should turn over the same number of cards in each row so all alternatives can be compared along the same dimensions. The search therefore involves looking at a "constant" number of dimensions across alternatives.

The elimination-by-aspects procedure uses an *intradimensional* (within dimensions) search. The decision maker selects a dimension and evaluates that dimension across all the alternatives remaining in the choice set. In other words, the cards in one column would be turned over before the decision maker went to another column. If some alternatives had already been eliminated, it would not be necessary to turn over the cards for those alternatives. This implies that the search evaluates a "variable" number of dimensions across alternatives. Some very expensive apartments could be eliminated after looking only at rent, whereas the final choice might require looking at many dimensions.

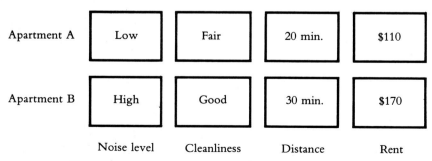

Figure 14.1   Information search task used by Payne (1976)

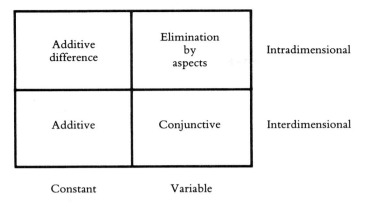

Additive difference	Elimination by aspects	Intradimensional
Additive	Conjunctive	Interdimensional
Constant	Variable	

Figure 14.2 Classification of decision models according to whether search is intra- or interdimensional across a constant or variable number of dimensions

The other two models—the additive-difference model and the conjunctive model—can also be classified along the two dimensions (see Figure 14.2). The additive-difference and elimination-by-aspects models propose that people search by dimensions, selecting a dimension and evaluating alternatives on that dimension before selecting another dimension. The search is intradimensional. The additive and conjunctive models propose that people search by alternatives, selecting an alternative and evaluating the dimensions of that alternative before selecting another alternative. The search is therefore interdimensional. The models can also be differentiated by whether the same or a different number of dimensions is evaluated for each alternative. The additive and additive-difference models evaluate the same number of dimensions for each alternative, whereas the conjunctive and elimination-by-aspects models evaluate a variable number of dimensions for each alternative—as soon as a dimension fails to satisfy the criterion, the alternative is no longer considered. Some alternatives might be rejected after evaluation of the first dimension, and other alternatives might remain in the choice set after many dimensions are evaluated.

Payne did not expect that everyone would follow the same strategy in searching for information. His expectations were influenced by work on problem solving that showed how individuals adapted their strategies to the demands of the task. An important characteristic of problem-solving strategies is that they attempt to keep the demands of the task within the limited capacity of the problem solver. Payne argued that the heuristics used by decision makers should also be adaptive to the information-processing demands of the task. One implication of this view is that the decision maker might change strategies as the demands of the task change.

Payne's results supported his expectations. Students were given a variety of tasks that differed in both the number of alternatives (2, 4, 8, or 12) and the number of dimensions (4, 8, or 12). Table 14.1 shows how the search strategies varied with the

Table 14.1   Classification of search patterns as a function of alternatives available

| Number of alternatives | Search pattern | | | |
| | Interdimensional | | Intradimensional | |
	Constant	Variable	Constant	Variable
2	12	3	18	3
4	6	11	2	17
8	3	15	0	18
12	2	12	0	22

number of alternatives in the choice set. The principal finding is that the students changed from searching a constant number of dimensions for two alternatives to a variable number of dimensions as the number of alternatives increased. The search strategies and verbal protocols revealed that, when asked to evaluate many alternatives, subjects reduced the complexity of the task by using the conjunctive or elimination-by-aspects procedure to eliminate some of the alternatives quickly. When only a few alternatives remained in the choice set, the subjects might then use one of the cognitively demanding procedures—such as the additive or additive-difference strategy—to make the final evaluation and choice.

The following excerpt from a protocol illustrates the use of the elimination-by-aspects model to reduce the number of alternatives:

> I'm going to look at landlord attitude. In H it's fair. In D it's poor. In B it's fair, and in A it's good. In L the attitude is poor. In K it's poor. In J it's good, and in I it's poor. . . . So, that's important to me. . . . So, I'm not going to live any place where it's poor [Payne, 1976, p. 379].

The subject never again examined alternatives D, I, K, and L. Contrast this protocol with an excerpt illustrating the use of the additive-difference model to compare two alternatives.

> O.K., we have an A and a B. First look at the rent for both of them. The rent for A is $170 and the rent for B is $140. $170 is a little steep, but it might have a low noise level. So we'll check A's noise level. A's noise level is low. We'll go to B's noise level. It's high. Gee, I can't really very well study with a lot of noise. So I'll ask myself the question, is it worth spending that extra $30 a month for, to be able to study in my apartment [p. 378].

The two protocols reveal how a low value on a dimension results in elimination of an alternative in the elimination-by-aspects model. However, when the additive-difference model is used, an alternative scoring low on one dimension might still be selected if it scores high on other dimensions; in the example above, the decision requires determining whether a lower rent will compensate for a high noise level.

Business Decisions

Payne's analysis revealed how the complexity of the task can determine how people select a decision strategy. Other factors that can influence strategy selection were discussed by Beach and Mitchell (1978) in an article on managerial decision making. Beach and Mitchell proposed that the strategies available to managers range from nonanalytic strategies consisting of simple rules to highly analytic strategies based on complex formulas. Although highly analytic strategies increase the probability of a correct decision, they also require more time, effort, and money to use. The manager must therefore decide whether the greater accuracy of analytic strategies compensates for their higher cost. Three factors that should influence the choice of a strategy, according to Beach and Mitchell, are the irreversibility of the decision, the significance of the decision, and the accountability of the decision maker.

McAllister, Mitchell, and Beach (1979) evaluated the effect of these three factors on strategy selection by presenting eight cases to 21 managers working in the Seattle area. The cases represented actual problems reported by managers—for example, whether they should approve a loan. The managers' task was to choose one of four decision strategies for each of the eight cases. The strategies were all variations of the additive rule used in Box 14.2 but varied in the complexity of the formula and the number of factors (loan amount, income, years in business) included in the formula.

The investigators hypothesized that the managers would select the more analytic (complex) strategies when (1) decisions are more significant, (2) the decision cannot be reversed, and (3) the decision maker is responsible for his or her actions. Each of these factors was varied across the eight cases, and each of the predictions was supported. The results are therefore consistent with Payne's finding that selection of decision strategies is influenced in a predictable way by different characteristics of the decision task.

Estimating Probabilities

We turn now to a somewhat more complex problem—making decisions under conditions of uncertainty. There was some amount of uncertainty in the previous examples. Although the distance of an apartment from campus is not likely to change, the noise level could change drastically if quiet neighbors were replaced by members of a rock band. In the examples discussed in the rest of the chapter, however, uncertainty is a major factor.

Box 14.3 gives an example of a situation in which there is much uncertainty. Using the best evidence available at that time, the National Aeronautics and Space Administration proposed that the odds were 152 to 1 against Skylab's injuring human beings. Odds are a ratio of two probabilities. In this particular case, the estimate of the probability that Skylab would not harm human life was 152 times as large as the estimate of the probability that it would.

The potential threat to human life caused by Skylab illustrates the importance of accurate estimates of probabilities in order to make wise decisions. Kahneman and Tversky have shown that probability estimates are based on heuristics that sometimes yield reasonable estimates but often do not. Two of these heuristics are availability and representativeness. Before reading further, answer the questions in Box 14.4 to determine how you might make use of these heuristics.

Box 14.3   152-to-1 Skylab will hurt no one

WASHINGTON (AP)—Skylab likely will tumble from orbit within weeks, but the odds are 152-to-1 against it harming human life anywhere in the world, space agency chief Robert A. Frosch said yesterday.

"For those who would like to know the likelihood that a particular person will be injured, it is about one chance in 600 billion," he said.

But Frosch, head of the National Aeronautics and Space Administration, conceded that the agency still has little idea exactly when or where the 79-ton space station will re-enter the earth's atmosphere.

He told a House Government Operations subcommittee that re-entry date "presently is predicted . . . between June 27 and July 21. There is a 50–50 probability that this will happen by July 9."

Scientists will have a better idea as time moves along, he said, but "at best we may be able to delay re-entry by a few hours through exercise of the spacecraft's stabilization system."

"The uncertainties are so large that nothing can be said at present as to where Skylab will re-enter, except that it will be within the limits of 50 degrees north and south latitude," he said. That includes all of the United States and Africa, much of Canada, and most of South America, Europe and Asia.

"Because 75 percent of the earth's surface in that band is water, it is quite likely re-entry will occur over water," he said.

From the *Oakland Tribune*, Oakland, California, June 5, 1979.

Availability

The *availability* heuristic proposes that we evaluate the probability of an event by judging the ease with which relevant instances come to mind (Tversky & Kahneman, 1973). For example, we may assess the divorce rate in a community by recalling divorces among our acquaintances. When availability is highly correlated with actual frequency, estimates should be accurate. But there are other factors besides actual frequency that can influence availability and cause systematic biases.

In the first experiment conducted by Tversky and Kahneman (1973), subjects were shown nine letters, which were to be used to construct words. They were given

---

Box 14.4 Questions about subjective probabilities

1. How many cities that begin with the letter F do you think you can recall? Give your estimate before you start recalling examples.
2. Are there more words in the English language that start with the letter K or that have a K as their third letter?
3. Which is the more likely cause of death—breast cancer or diabetes?
4. If a family has three boys (B) and three girls (G), which sequence of births is more likely—B B B G G G or B G G B G B?
5. Are you more likely to find 60 boys in a random sample of 100 children or 600 boys in a random sample of 1000 children?

---

seven seconds to estimate the number of words they believed they could produce in two minutes. The average number of words actually constructed varied from 1.3 (for the letters $X U Z O N L C J M$) to 22.4 (for $T A P C E R H O B O$). The correlation between the estimates and the number of words produced over 16 problems was .96.

In another experiment subjects were asked to estimate the number of instances they could recall from a category in two minutes. The average number of instances recalled varied from 4.1 (city names beginning with the letter F) to 23.7 (four-legged animals). The correlation between estimation and word production was .93 over 16 categories. The high correlation between estimation and production revealed that subjects were quite accurate in estimating the relative availability of instances in the different conditions.

Some instances, however, might be difficult to retrieve from memory even though they occur frequently. The availability hypothesis would predict that frequency should be underestimated in this case. Suppose you sample a word at random from an English text. Is it more likely that the word starts with a K or that K is its third letter? The availability hypothesis proposes that people try to answer this question by judging how easy it is to think of examples in each category. Since it is easier to think of words that begin with a certain letter, people should be biased toward responding that more words start with the letter K than have a K in the third position. The median estimated ratio for each of five letters was that there were twice as many words in which that letter was the first letter, rather than the third letter, in the word. The estimates were obtained despite the fact that all five letters are actually more frequent in the third position.

Slovic, Fischhoff, and Lichtenstein (1976) have used the availability hypothesis to account for how people estimated the relative probability of 41 causes of death—including diseases, accidents, homicide, suicide, and natural hazards—which were combined into 106 pairs. A large sample of college students judged which member of the pair was the more likely cause of death; Table 14.2 shows how often they were correct as a function of the relative frequency of the two events. Examination of the

Table 14.2   Judgments of relative frequency for selected pairs of lethal events

Less likely	More likely	True ratio	Percentage correct discrimination
Asthma	Firearm accident	1.20	80
Breast cancer	Diabetes	1.25	23
Lung cancer	Stomach cancer	1.25	25
Leukemia	Emphysema	1.49	47
Stroke	All cancer	1.57	83
All accidents	Stroke	1.85	20
Pregnancy	Appendicitis	2.00	17
Tuberculosis	Fire and flames	2.00	81
Emphysema	All accidents	5.19	88
Polio	Tornado	5.30	71
Drowning	Suicide	9.60	70
All accidents	All diseases	15.50	57
Diabetes	Heart disease	18.90	97
Tornado	Asthma	20.90	42
Syphilis	Homicide	46.00	86
Botulism	Lightning	52.00	37
Flood	Homicide	92.00	91
Syphilis	Diabetes	95.00	64
Botulism	Asthma	920.00	59
Excess cold	All cancer	982.00	95
Botulism	Emphysema	10,600.00	86

events most seriously misjudged provided indirect support for the hypothesis that availability, particularly as influenced by the media, biases probability estimates. The frequencies of accidents, cancer, botulism, and tornadoes—all of which receive heavy media coverage—were greatly overestimated. Asthma and diabetes, which receive less media coverage, were underestimated. Similarly, the spectacular event of fire—which often takes many victims and receives much media coverage—was perceived as considerably more frequent than the less spectacular event of drowning, even though they are about equally frequent causes of death.

Representativeness

The *representativeness* heuristic states that the probability of an event is estimated by evaluating how similar it is to the essential properties of its population. Let us clarify this definition by considering some specific examples.

Kahneman and Tversky (1972) studied representativeness through a questionnaire given to students in college-preparatory high schools. Some of the questions were designed to measure the concept of randomness. A major characteristic of apparent randomness is the absence of any systematic patterns. The representativeness heuristic implies that people should judge orderly events as having low probability if they believe the events were generated by a random process. This prediction was supported by the answers to one of the questions on the questionnaire:

On each round of a game, 20 marbles are distributed at random among five children: Alan, Ben, Carl, Dan and Ed. Consider the following distributions:

I		II	
Alan	4	Alan	4
Ben	4	Ben	4
Carl	5	Carl	4
Dan	4	Dan	4
Ed	3	Ed	4

In many rounds of the game will there be more results of type I or type II? [Kahneman & Tversky, 1972, p. 434]

The uniform distribution of marbles (II) is objectively more probable than the non-uniform distribution (I), but it appears too orderly to be generated by a random process. A significant majority of students selected distribution I as more probable than distribution II; the presence of some perturbation made the former seem more representative of a random process. Intuition regarding randomness is also illustrated by the fact that subjects estimated that the sequence of boy/girl births in the order B B B G G G was significantly less likely than the order G B B G B G, even though the two sequences are equally probable.

Furthermore, it was found that people ignore sample size when making probability estimates. A sample of events or objects is only part of the total population of those objects or events. Since the size of the sample does not reflect any particular property of its population, size should not influence representativeness. For example, finding 600 boys in a sample of 1000 babies was judged as likely as finding 60 boys in a sample of 100 babies, even though the latter event is much more likely. Although increasing sample size reduces the variance of a distribution, the students' estimates of probability distributions were uninfluenced by sample size.

This result was also obtained when students were asked to estimate posterior probabilities. Estimating posterior probabilities requires the revision of a probability on the basis of new evidence. A typical problem reads as follows:

Consider two very large decks of cards, denoted A and B. In deck A, ⅚ of the cards are marked X, and ⅙ are marked O. In deck B, ⅙ of the cards are marked X and ⅚ are marked O. One of the decks has been selected by chance and 12 cards have been drawn from it, of which 8 are marked X and 4 are marked O. What do you think the probability is that the 12 cards were drawn from deck A, that is, from the deck in which most of the cards are marked X? [Kahneman & Tversky, 1972, p. 447]

The question was repeated for samples containing 4 X's and 2 O's, 40 X's and 20 O's, and 5X's and 1 O. The median estimate that deck A was selected was .70 when the sample ratio of X : O was 4 : 2, 8 : 4, and 40 : 20. The estimate was .83 when the ratio of X : O was 5 : 1. The results reveal that the probability estimates were influenced by the ratio of X's to O's, which does not consider differences in sample size. The true posterior probabilities depend on the difference between the number of X's and O's. Notice that, for a constant ratio, the difference between X's and O's increases as the sample size increases. A sample of 40 X's and 20 O's provides the most evidence in favor of deck A, not the sample containing 5 X's and 1 O.

Expected Value

Estimating probabilities accurately is an important decision-making skill, but it is not sufficient for making good decisions. Imagine a situation in which the United States' oil interests in the Middle East are threatened. The response to this situation will depend in part on the probability that the threat is a real one. But the response also depends on the perceived consequences of various courses of action the government might take. For example, one response might be to increase American military forces in the Middle East. This course of action, like other alternative actions, has both advantages and disadvantages. It is therefore necessary to assess both the probability of events and the consequences of various actions when making decisions.

When we considered the different choice models in the first section of this chapter, we assigned values to the different dimensions of each alternative in the choice set. It is also necessary to assign values in risky decision making, but in addition we have to combine the values of different outcomes with the probabilities that they will occur. A normative procedure for combining probabilities and values is called *expected value*. Like other normative models, expected value provides a standard of reference against which psychologists can compare how people make decisions. Psychologists have usually made this comparison by designing rather simple gambling situations in which they can inform people about probabilities (of winning and losing) and values (amount won or lost). The expected value is the average amount of money people can expect to win or lose each time they decide to gamble. Let us see how it is calculated.

Calculating Expected Value

Expected value is calculated by multiplying the value of each possible outcome by its probability and adding the products. Its use can be illustrated by a simple game. I'm going to offer you the opportunity to play the game, and you must decide whether it would be to your advantage to play. I'm going to roll a fair die. If the number 6 appears, you win $5. If one of the other five numbers appears, you win nothing. It costs $1 every time you play. Should you participate?

Expected value allows you to estimate the average amount of money you can expect to win or lose on every roll of the die. You can calculate this amount if you know the probability of a win—$pr(W)$; the amount of a win—$v(W)$; the probability of a loss—$pr(L)$; and the amount of a loss—$v(L)$. Substituting these amounts into the equation below yields

$$\text{Expected value} = pr(W) \times v(W) + pr(L) \times v(L)$$
$$\text{Expected value} = \tfrac{1}{6} \times \$4 + \tfrac{5}{6} \times -\$1 = -\$\tfrac{1}{6}$$

The probability of a win is $\frac{1}{6}$, and the amount of a win is \$4 (\$5 minus the \$1 entry fee). The probability of a loss is $\frac{5}{6}$, and the value of a loss is \$1. The expected value of this game is $-\$\frac{1}{6}$, implying that you would lose an average of about 17 cents every time you played the game. A decision based on a normative model should be to play the game for a positive expected value and not to play the game for a negative expected value.

A problem with using expected value as a descriptive model is that it does not always predict behavior. Gambling casinos are usually crowded with people playing games that have negative expected values. People also buy insurance in spite of its negative expected value. Since insurance companies pay out less money in claims than they collect as premiums, a purchaser of insurance can expect to lose money. And yet the purchase of insurance can be justified on the basis that it provides protection against a large financial setback.

Subjective Expected Utility

Two changes were made in the concept of expected value in order to make it more descriptive of actual behavior. The first change replaced the value of an outcome by its utility. *Utility* is the subjective value of an outcome, or what the outcome is actually worth to an individual. If people enjoy gambling, the act of gambling has utility in addition to the money that is won or lost. If you enjoy winning money and don't mind losing money, then you could formulate a positive expected utility for the game I described earlier. If the utility of a win—$u(W)$—is \$6 rather than \$4, and the utility of a loss—$u(L)$—remains at \$1, the expected utility would be positive rather than negative.

$$\text{Expected utility} = pr(W) \times u(W) + pr(L) \times u(L)$$
$$\text{Expected utility} = \frac{1}{6} \times \$6 + \frac{5}{6} \times -\$1 = \$\frac{1}{6}$$

The expected-utility model could also explain why people buy insurance if the utility of money increases faster than the actual value of money as the amount increases. A person would then be more concerned about losing a substantial amount of money at one time than about paying out the much smaller premiums each year.

A second change in the expected-value model was to make it more descriptive by replacing probabilities by subjective probabilities. When decision makers don't know the actual probabilities, they must use subjective probabilities, or what they think the actual probabilities are. As we learned in the previous section, subjective probabilities often differ from actual probabilities. *Subjective expected utility* is calculated the same way as expected value, but probabilities are replaced by subjective probabilities (*spr*) and values are replaced by utilities. The subjective probability of each outcome is multiplied by its utility, and the products are added.

$$\text{Subjective expected utility} = spr(W) \times u(W) + spr(L) \times u(L)$$

By replacing probabilities with subjective probabilities and values with utilities, the subjective-expected-utility model bases its predictions on subjective information.

Therefore, it should be more accurate than the expected-value model in predicting people's decisions. Like the expected-value model, however, it assumes that people place an equal emphasis on the four components—$u(W)$, $spr(W)$, $u(L)$, and $spr(L)$. It also implies that people have to calculate, since it is necessary to multiply the utility of events by their subjective probabilities.

Information-Processing Models

We learned earlier that decision rules like elimination by aspects or the conjunctive rule simplify decision making by allowing the decision maker to eliminate alternatives without having to calculate. When evaluating the attractiveness of a gamble, people are likely to consider the probability of winning, the amount of a win, the probability of losing, and the amount of a loss. But they may find it difficult to mentally compute expected value or even to place equal emphasis on the four risk dimensions, as implied by the model.

Slovic and Lichtenstein (1968) tested the hypothesis that people will be more influenced by some dimensions than others. They had subjects evaluate the attractiveness of gambles, using a special type of gamble illustrated in Figure 14.3. A duplex gamble requires that the subject spin two spinners. The first spinner determines whether he will win money, and the second spinner determines whether he will lose money. There are four possible outcomes for the gamble shown in Figure 14.3: win $1 and lose $4 (a net loss of $3), win $1 and lose nothing, win nothing and lose nothing, or win nothing and lose $4. Slovic and Lichtenstein used duplex gambles in order to change the probability of winning and the probability of losing independently. This is not possible in a standard gamble (represented by only one spinner) because the probability of winning is equal to 1 minus the probability of losing. It is not possible to determine whether people are more influenced by the probability of winning or the probability of losing if the two probabilities cannot be varied independently.

Slovic and Lichtenstein used two methods to evaluate the attractiveness of gambles. One method used a simple rating scale that varied from -5 (strong preference for not playing) to $+5$ (strong preference for playing). The second method

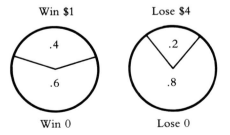

Figure 14.3   Example of a duplex gamble where $pr(W) = .4$, $v(W) = \$1$, $pr(L) = .2$, and $v(L) = \$4$

required that subjects indicate the largest amount of money they would be willing to pay the experimenter in order to play the gamble (for attractive gambles) or in order to not have to play the gamble (for unattractive gambles). In both cases Slovic and Lichtenstein correlated the judged attractiveness of gambles with the four risk dimensions. The correlations should be approximately equal if people were placing an equal emphasis on all four dimensions. The results indicated that there was a large difference in the correlations. A subject's highest correlation was, on the average, twice the size of the lowest correlation. The responses of many subjects were determined by one or two risk dimensions and were unresponsive to changes in the values of the less important dimensions.

The data also revealed that the particular dimension emphasized varied across subjects and that the most important dimension was influenced by whether the subject responded with a numerical rating or a monetary response. Table 14.3 shows that when subjects used a rating scale, the probability of a win was the most important dimension for 50% of the subjects. When subjects responded in terms of the amount of money they would be willing to pay the experimenter (bid), the amount of a loss was the most important dimension for 53% of the subjects. In other words, the response scale influences the way a gamble is evaluated. When responses were expressed in terms of money, subjects attended more to a monetary dimension— $v(L)$—than when the responses were numerical ratings.

Normative models cannot explain either the finding that people place an unequal emphasis on the risk dimensions or the finding that the dimension emphasized is influenced by the response scale. If people are not following normative models, do their ratings of relative attractiveness differ from the relative attractiveness of the gambles as determined by expected value? The average correlation between subjects' ratings and expected value was .79 for numerical ratings and .80 for monetary ratings. The correlations indicate that the expected-value model is a fairly accurate predictor of ratings even though subjects attend more to some dimensions than to others. Although models based on expected value are often useful in predicting responses, results like those obtained by Slovic and Lichtenstein help reveal how people simplify the task and how their decisions depart from expected value.

To summarize, expected-value models are reasonably good, though not perfect, predictors of decision-making behavior. The predictions can often be improved when utilities are substituted for values and subjective probabilities for probabilities. It should also be possible to improve their predictions by taking into account the fact that people may emphasize some dimensions of risk more than others.

Table 14.3 Percentage of subjects for whom a given risk dimension was most important

	Risk dimension			
	$pr(W)$	$v(W)$	$pr(L)$	$v(L)$
Rating group	50	9	15	26
Bidding group	18	19	10	53

Medical Decision Making

Medical diagnosis is an excellent example of a complex skill that we can relate to many of the issues raised in this chapter. A recent book, *Medical Problem Solving* (Elstein, Shulman, & Sprafka, 1978), summarizes the results of an extensive study of how doctors arrive at a diagnosis. The book is important not only because of the importance of medical decision making but also because the results are discussed within the context of models of human information processing and normative decision making.

Simulation of Medical Cases

Elstein, Shulman, and Sprafka report a series of experiments using various methodologies. Some experimenters used actors who played the role of patients; others simply used written descriptions of symptoms. Some allowed the physicians to request whatever information they wanted; others presented information in a fixed order. Some studied what the physicians did; others attempted to train medical students to become better decision makers.

I will summarize the results of one experiment that used "high-fidelity simulation": the simulation attempted to create a situation that closely resembled the actual world of the physician. Actors from the Department of Theater at Michigan State University were carefully trained to simulate patients. The cases were based on actual clinical records and presented problems that a general internist practicing in a community hospital could expect to see. Each physician could decide how much information to collect, including the results of (simulated) laboratory findings. The physicians knew the cases were simulated, but most of the 24 who participated thought the simulations were convincing.

The interactions between physicians and patients were recorded on videotape. The physicians were instructed to think aloud during the interaction and comment on what they had learned or were about to do and why. Additional information was obtained after the session, when an experimenter questioned each physician while both reviewed the videotape.

The simulation experiment presented three cases, all played by college students. The first case was a female student with three main complaints—extreme fatigue and excessive sleeping, poor appetite, and severe headache. Further history showed mild chills and fever with general aching of about five days' duration. Information that could be obtained from a physical examination included enlarged tonsils and mild jaundice.

Results of the Simulation

Table 14.4 shows the most frequent hypotheses for this case and the number of physicians who considered each during different stages of the examination. The initial hypotheses are general—infection, for example. One of the major findings across all the simulation experiments was that physicians start to form hypotheses early in the examination, before they have much information. The number of physicians who generated at least one hypothesis during the first five minutes was 20 (of 24) in simulation 1, 18 in simulation 2, and 23 in simulation 3. The process of gathering data can be thought of as a search through a large search space. If the physician simply gathered data unsystematically until a solution emerged, the search space would be so large that a diagnosis could never be reached in a reasonable amount of time. Forming hypotheses early in the sequence guides the acquisition of additional data, thus limiting the search by verifying or modifying current hypotheses. Table 14.4 reveals that the number of physicians who considered mononucleosis as a hypothesis increased as additional data were obtained.

The number of hypotheses that were considered at any one time was very consistent across problems; the means ranged between two and four. On all three simulations the average number of hypotheses considered at any one time remained relatively constant through various stages of the examination, implying that when a hypothesis was rejected, it was replaced by another or by a reformulation of the rejected hypothesis. It is likely that the hypotheses serve as organizers of data in STM, since the range of two to four is consistent with the number of chunks of complex material that can be retained at once in memory (Simon, 1974).

A central issue in the study was how physicians combine information to form hypotheses. Elstein's search for a model that describes what physicians do, rather than what they ought to do, began with the observation that in all the protocols the physicians were consistently able to rank hypotheses but were unable to give more precise estimates of probability.

Table 14.4   Hypotheses considered during various stages of the diagnosis

Hypothesis[a]	Total at any point	As first hypothesis	At quarter mark	At halfway mark	At conclusion
Infection[b]	21	14	15	19	5
Infectious mononucleosis	20	2	9	15	20
Infectious hepatitis	18	5	9	11	5
Hemolytic anemia	17				
Hereditary spherocytic anemia	10				8
Viral illness or viral respiratory infection	8		4	6	1
Meningitis	7		5	4	0
Anemia	6			3	
Influenza	4		3	1	0
Encephalitis	4		2	3	0
Leukemia	4			1	0
Lymphoma	4		0	0	1

[a]Twelve hypotheses in addition to those listed were each considered by one or two subjects at some point in the problem.
[b]Includes acute febrile illness, viral illness, bacterial infection, and viral respiratory infection.

The physicians did, however, spontaneously classify the cues as positive, negative, or noncontributory for each hypothesis. A simple additive model, in which cues that were interpreted as positive evidence were rated + 1, cues that were interpreted as negative evidence were rated − 1, and noncontributory cues were rated 0, was fairly successful in predicting which hypotheses would be selected. Note that this procedure is identical to the one suggested by Ben Franklin. Although it is possible to use probabilities in medical diagnosis, physicians apparently use a much simpler procedure to evaluate hypotheses. The simpler procedure avoids the cognitive demands of estimating the initial probabilities of diseases and revising the probabilities on the basis of evidence.

Heuristics for Medical Students

In the concluding chapter of their book Elstein and his coinvestigators offer a set of guidelines for medical students.

1. Generating a list of alternative hypotheses:
   a. *Multiple competing hypotheses.* Think of a number of diagnostic possibilities compatible with the major complaints and preliminary findings. Avoid making snap diagnoses.
   b. *Probability.* Consider the most common diagnoses first.
   c. *Utility.* Consider seriously those diagnoses for which effective therapies are available and in which failure to treat would be a serious omission.
2. Gathering data:
   d. *Planned testing.* Form a reasoned plan for testing your hypotheses, one that considers both probability and utility. Sequence laboratory tests to rule out first the most common diseases (probability) and next the diseases most needing treatment (utility).
   e. *Branching and screening.* The physical examination should use branching procedures. Develop adequate screening techniques to make overly detailed examinations unnecessary.
   f. *Cost/benefit calculation.* Consider the harm tests might do and their cost. Balance these against the information to be gained.
   g. *Precision.* Strive for the degree of reliability needed for the decision. More is unnecessary.
3. Combining data and selecting a course of action:
   h. *Disconfirmatory evidence.* Actively seek out and evaluate evidence that tends to rule out any hypothesis as well as the evidence that tends to confirm it.
   i. *Multiple diagnoses.* Don't forget the possibility that a patient with multiple complaints has more than one disease.
   j. *Revise probabilities.* Revise probabilities after collecting data. If the findings are relatively more likely in diagnosis A than in diagnosis B, revise your opinion in favor of A.

k. *Probability and utility.* When a course of action is selected, consider both the probability of the diagnoses for which the action is appropriate and the benefits and penalties that would follow. Combine these two considerations to estimate expected value and choose so as to maximize expected value.

These guidelines result from an attempt to combine the insights of normative decision models and cognitive psychology to formulate a practical tool for students. They are guidelines that should be useful for many tasks concerned with risky decision making. However, as the research of Elstein et al. (1978) shows, it is difficult even for experienced decision makers to combine probabilities. It would therefore be helpful if physicians had the aid of a computer-based system in making diagnoses. An example is described in Box 14.5. Future research should help us decide how human and computer can best work together to make important decisions.

Summary

Making decisions usually requires evaluating at least two alternatives, which differ on a number of attributes. Selecting an alternative requires the decision maker to combine this information to form an overall evaluation for each alternative. The study of how people search for information provides evidence about decision strategies.

Four of the more popular decision models can be differentiated by whether people compare the alternatives attribute by attribute (intradimensional) or alternative by alternative (interdimensional) and whether they evaluate the same number or a variable number of attributes for each alternative. In the elimination-by-aspects model alternatives are compared by attributes, and the number of attributes evaluated varies across alternatives. The conjunctive model is similar but considers only one alternative at a time; the first alternative that satisfies the minimum criteria for each attribute is selected. The additive and additive-difference models require that the same number of attributes be evaluated across alternatives. The additive model assigns a numerical score to each attribute and sums the scores to determine the relative attractiveness of each alternative. The additive-difference model compares alternatives attribute by attribute and determines the difference between the scores on each attribute; the sum of the differences determines which alternative is more attractive.

Research on how people select a decision strategy has shown that the choice of a strategy depends on task characteristics. People were likely to use a noncompensatory strategy such as elimination by aspects when there were many alternatives and a compensatory strategy such as the additive model when there were few alternatives. Managers were more likely to select a complex, analytic strategy if (1) the decision was significant, (2) the decision could not be reversed, and (3) they were personally responsible for the decision.

Box 14.5   Personal computers help diagnose illness

WILLIAM HARWOOD
United Press International

GAINESVILLE—A computer scientist and a physician have joined forces to develop a pioneering system to save time and money by letting doctors double check their diagnoses on inexpensive personal computers.

Unlike other more extensive diagnostic systems under development that require costly "main frame" computers, the system being designed at the University of Florida will run on IBM personal computers and compatible machines.

Doctors and hospitals could use the same computer to keep office records and patient information. "One of our aims was to try to develop a system that would be inexpensive that individual physicians would be able to afford," said Douglas Dankel, a University of Florida computer scientist who is working with Julian Russo, a St. Petersburg physician, to develop the system.

Most medical database computer systems are designed to mimic the process a doctor goes through to reach a diagnosis by analyzing all the available data. Using the Florida system, doctors would propose a diagnosis and then answer questions from the computer to confirm it.

Once the program is loaded, the computer asks for the patient's name and an identification number. It then asks the user to enter the patient's weight, height, temperature, race and sex and if the doctor has a preliminary diagnosis.

"Then the system would go through a series of questions, first off presenting all of the primary criteria that would need to be satisfied for the patient to have that particular disease," Dankel said.

The doctor can answer yes, no or unknown. He also can ask the computer why it wants the information and an answer is provided.

"If the physician says yes, all of those criteria are satisfied, the system says you have a confirmation of the disease and if a treatment's warranted, it will present a treatment to the physician."

If the doctor answers "no" to any of the primary criteria, for example because a lab test has not been conducted yet, the computer will ask more detailed questions.

The program then gives the probability of the patient having the disease and "it specifies any additional laboratory tests that it sees might be required," Dankel said. The final program also will suggest alternate diagnoses.

Risky decision making refers to decisions that are concerned with uncertainty—for example, evaluating the potential threat of a nuclear reactor, buying insurance, and diagnosing medical problems. In order to make good decisions, it is necessary to make accurate estimates of probabilities. Probability estimates are often based on heuristics, which sometimes yield reasonable estimates but often do not. Two heuristics are availability and representativeness. The availability heuristic proposes that we evaluate the probability of an event by judging the ease with which instances can be recalled. The representativeness heuristic states that the probability of an event is estimated by evaluating how similar it is to the essential properties of its population.

Expected value is a normative procedure for making decisions. Expected value is calculated by multiplying the value of events by their probability of occurring and summing the products. Subjective expected utility is a modified version of this procedure in which subjective values (utilities) replace values and subjective probabilities replace probabilities. The expected-value model can be further modified by allowing for the possibility that people may emphasize some components of the model more than others.

Physicians use several heuristics to simplify the task of diagnosing medical problems. They form hypotheses early in the diagnosis to guide their collection of data. They seem to use a simple additive model to combine the data, adding the number of positive cues and subtracting the number of negative cues. The authors of the book *Medical Problem Solving* use the results of their research to recommend a list of heuristics for training medical students. Future studies should focus on how well students can follow these heuristics and whether medical decision making can be improved if a computer is used to combine probabilities.

Recommended Reading

A review article by Pitz and Sachs (1984) summarizes recent research on decision making. A statistical model that has influenced many studies of decision making is multiple linear regression. Dawes (1979) evaluated the success of this approach, and Hammond (1971) recommended using the linear model and computer-implemented feedback to improve performance on decision-making tasks. The development of expected value as a psychological model was discussed by Payne (1973). Beach (1975) reviewed studies on the application of Bayesian models to military, business, and medical decisions. Other applications include the study of career (Pitz & Harren, 1980), jury (Penrod & Hastie, 1980), and medical (Fox, 1980) decision making. Recent work on heuristic biases in risky decision making is described by Kahneman and Tversky (1984) and Fischhoff and Bar-Hillel (1984).

References

ADAMS, M. J. (1979). Models of word recognition. *Cognitive Psychology, 11,* 133–176.

ADAMSON, R. E. (1952). Functional fixedness as related to problem solving: A repetition of three experiments. *Journal of Experimental Psychology, 44,* 288–291.

ADELSON, B. (1984). When novices surpass experts: The difficulty of a task may increase with expertise. *Journal of Experimental Psychology: Learning, Memory, and Cognition, 10,* 483–495.

ALBA, J. W., & HASHER, L. (1983). Is memory schematic? *Psychological Bulletin, 93,* 203–231.

ANDERSON, J. R. (1976). *Language, memory, and thought.* Hillsdale, NJ: Erlbaum.

ANDERSON, J. R. (1978). Arguments concerning representations for mental imagery. *Psychological Review, 85,* 249–277.

ANDERSON, J. R. (1982). Acquisition of cognitive skill. *Psychological Review, 89,* 369–406.

ANDERSON, J. R. (1983). *The architecture of cognition.* Cambridge, MA: Harvard University Press.

ANDERSON, J. R., BOYLE, C. F., & REISER, B. J. (1985). Intelligent tutoring systems. *Science, 228,* 456–462.

ANDERSON, J. R., & REDER, L. M. (1979). An elaborative processing explanation of depth of processing. In L. S. Cermak & F. I. M. Craik (Eds.), *Levels of processing in human memory.* Hillsdale, NJ: Erlbaum.

ANDERSON, R. C., & PICHERT, J. W. (1978). Recall of previously unrecallable information following a shift in perspective. *Journal of Verbal Learning and Verbal Behavior, 17,* 1–12.

ANDERSON, R. E. (1984). Did I do it or did I only imagine doing it? *Journal of Experimental Psychology: General, 113,* 594–613.

ARONSON, E. (1972). *The social animal.* New York: W. H. Freeman.

ATKINSON, R. C. (1972a). Ingredients for a theory of instruction. *American Psychologist, 27,* 921–931.

ATKINSON, R. C. (1972b). Optimizing the learning of a second-language vocabulary. *Journal of Experimental Psychology, 96,* 124–129.

ATKINSON, R. C., & RAUGH, M. R. (1975). An application of the mnemonic keyword method to the acquisition of a Russian vocabulary. *Journal of Experimental Psychology: Human Learning and Memory, 104,* 126–133.

ATKINSON, R. C., & SHIFFRIN, R. M. (1968). Human memory: A proposed system and its control processes. In K. W. Spence & J. T. Spence (Eds.), *The psychology of learning and motivation* (Vol. 2). Orlando, FL: Academic Press.

ATKINSON, R. C., & SHIFFRIN, R. M. (1971). The control of short-term memory. *Scientific American, 225,* 82–90.

ATWOOD, M. E., & POLSON, P. G. (1976). A process model for water jar problems. *Cognitive Psychology, 8,* 191–216.

ATWOOD, M. E., POLSON, P. G., JEFFRIES, R., & RAMSEY, H. R. (1978, December). Planning as a process of synthesis (Technical Report SAI–78–144–DEN). Englewood, CO: Science Applications.

BADDELEY, A. D. (1976). *The psychology of memory.* New York: Basic Books.

BADDELEY, A. D. (1978). The trouble with "levels":

A re-examination of Craik and Lockhart's framework for memory research. *Psychological Review, 85*, 139–152.

BADDELEY, A. D. (1982). Domains of recollection. *Psychological Review, 89*, 708–729.

BADDELEY, A., & HITCH, G. (1974). Working memory. In G. H. Bower (Ed.), *The psychology of learning and motivation* (Vol. 8). Orlando, FL: Academic Press.

BAHRICK, H. P. (1979). Maintenance of knowledge: Questions about memory we forgot to ask. *Journal of Experimental Psychology: General, 108*, 296–308.

BAHRICK, H. P., & BOUCHER, B. (1968). Retention of visual and verbal codes of the same stimuli. *Journal of Experimental Psychology, 78*, 417–422.

BARON, J. (1978). The word-superiority effect: Perceptual learning from reading. In W. K. Estes (Ed.), *Handbook of learning and cognitive processes*. Hillsdale, NJ: Erlbaum.

BARSALOU, L. W. (1985). Ideals, central tendency, and frequency of instantiation as determinants of graded structure in categories. *Journal of Experimental Psychology: Learning, Memory, & Cognition, 11*, 629–654.

BARTLETT, F. C. (1932). *Remembering: A study in experimental and social psychology*. New York: Macmillan.

BEACH, B. H. (1975). Expert judgment about uncertainty: Bayesian decision making in realistic settings. *Organizational Behavior and Human Performance, 14*, 10–59.

BEACH, L. R., & MITCHELL, T. R. (1978). A contingency model for the selection of decision strategies. *Academy of Management Review, 3*, 439–449.

BIEDERMAN, I. (1981). On the semantics of a glance at a scene. In M. Kubovy & J. R. Pomerantz (Eds.), *Perceptual organization*. Hillsdale, NJ: Erlbaum.

BIEDERMAN, I. (1985). Human image understanding: Recent research and a theory. *Computer Vision, Graphics, and Image Processing, 32*, 29–73.

BLANEY, P. H. (1986). Affect and memory: A review. *Psychological Bulletin, 99*, 229–246.

BLANK, M. S., & FOSS, D. J. (1978). Semantic facilitation and lexical access during sentence processing. *Memory & Cognition, 6*, 644–652.

BOCK, J. K. (1982). Toward a cognitive psychology of syntax: Information processing contributions to sentence formulation. *Psychological Review, 89*, 1–47.

BOURNE, L. E., JR. (1970). Knowing and using concepts. *Psychological Review, 77*, 546–556.

BOURNE, L. E., JR., EKSTRAND, B. R., LOVALLO, W. R., KELLOGG, R. T., HIEW, C. C., & YAROUSH, R. A. (1976). Frequency analysis of attribute identification. *Journal of Experimental Psychology: General, 105*, 294–312.

BOWER, G. H. (1970). Organizational factors in memory. *Cognitive Psychology, 1*, 18–46.

BOWER, G. H., BLACK, J. B., & TURNER, T. J. (1979). Scripts in memory for text. *Cognitive Psychology, 11*, 177–220.

BOWER, G. H., CLARK, M., WINZENZ, D., & LESGOLD, A. (1969). Hierarchical retrieval schemes in recall of categorized word lists. *Journal of Verbal Learning and Verbal Behavior, 8*, 323–343.

BOWER, G. H., & GLASS, A. L. (1976). Structural units and the reintegrative power of picture fragments. *Journal of Experimental Psychology, 2*, 456–466.

BOWER, G. H., & WINZENZ, D. (1970). Comparison of associative learning strategies. *Psychonomic Science, 20*, 119–120.

BRANSFORD, J. D., & FRANKS, J. J. (1971). The abstraction of linguistic ideas. *Cognitive Psychology, 2*, 331–350.

BRANSFORD, J. D., & JOHNSON, M. K. (1973). Considerations of some problems of comprehension. In W. G. Chase (Ed.), *Visual information processing*. Orlando, FL: Academic Press.

BREWER, W. F., & DUPREE, D. A. (1983). Use of plan schemata in the recall and recognition of goal-directed actions. *Journal of Experimental Psychology: Learning, Memory, & Cognition, 9*, 117–129.

BREWER, W. F., & NAKAMURA, G. V. (1984). The nature and function of schemas. In R. S. Wyer & T. K. Srull (Eds.), *Handbook of social cognition*. Hillsdale, NJ: Erlbaum.

BREWER, W. F., & PANI, J. R. (1983). The structure of human memory. In G. H. Bower (Ed.), *The psychology of learning and motivation* (Vol. 17). Orlando, FL: Academic Press.

BROADBENT, D. E. (1954). The role of auditory localization in attention and memory span. *Journal of Experimental Psychology, 47*, 191–196.

BROADBENT, D. E. (1957). A mechanical model for human attention and immediate memory. *Psychological Review, 64*, 205–215.

BROADBENT, D. E. (1958). *Perception and communication*. London: Pergamon Press.

BROADBENT, D. E. (1975). The magic number seven after fifteen years. In A. Kennedy & A. Wilkes (Eds.), *Studies in long term memory*. London: Wiley.

BROOKS, L. R. (1968). Spatial and verbal components of the act of recall. *Canadian Journal of Psychology, 22*, 349–368.

BROOKS, L. R. (1978). Nonanalytic concept formation and memory for instances. In E. Rosch & B. Lloyd (Eds.), *Cognition and categorization*. Hillsdale, NJ: Erlbaum.

BROWN, E., DEFFENBACHER, K., & STURGILL, W. (1977). Memory for faces and the circumstances of encounter. *Journal of Applied Psychology, 62*, 311–318.

BROWN, R., & MCNEILL, D. (1966). The "tip-of-the-tongue" phenomenon. *Journal of Verbal Learning and Verbal Behavior, 5*, 325–337.

BROWN, J. S., & BURTON, R. R. (1978). Diagnostic models for procedural bugs in basic mathematical skills. *Cognitive Science, 2*, 155–192.

BRUNER, J. S., GOODNOW, J. J., & AUSTIN, G. A. (1956). *A study of thinking*. New York: Wiley.

BUCKHOUT, R. (1974). Eyewitness testimony. *Scientific American, 231*, 23–31.

BUCKHOUT, R., EUGENIO, P., LICITRA, T., OLIVER, L., & KRAMER, T. H. (1981). Memory, hypnosis, and evidence: Research on eyewitnesses. *Social Action and the Law, 7*, 67–72.

BURKE, D. M., & LIGHT, L. L. (1981). Memory and aging: The role of retrieval processes. *Psychological Bulletin, 90*, 513–546.

BUSCHKE, H., & SCHAIER, A. H. (1979). Memory units, ideas, and propositions in semantic remembering. *Journal of Verbal Learning and Verbal Behavior, 18*, 549–563.

CANTOR, N., & MISCHEL, W. (1979). Prototypes in person perception. In L. Berkowitz (Ed.), *Advances in experimental social psychology* (Vol. 12). Orlando, FL: Academic Press.

CANTOR, N., SMITH, E. E., FRENCH, R., & MEZZICH, J. (1980). Psychiatric diagnosis as prototype categorization. *Journal of Abnormal Psychology, 89*, 181–193.

CARPENTER, P. A., & DANEMAN, M. (1981). Lexical retrieval and error recovery in reading: A model based on eye fixations. *Journal of Verbal Learning and Verbal Behavior, 20*, 137–160.

CARROLL, J. M., THOMAS, J. C., & MALHOTRA, A. (1980). Presentation and representation in design problem solving. *British Journal of Psychology, 71*, 143–153.

CAVANAGH, J. P. (1972). Relation between the immediate memory span and the memory search rate. *Psychological Review, 79*, 525–530.

CERMAK, L. S., & CRAIK, F. I. M. (Eds.) (1979). *Levels of processing in human memory.* Hillsdale, NJ: Erlbaum.

CHANG, T. M. (1986). Semantic memory: Facts and models. *Psychological Bulletin, 99*, 199–220.

CHAPANIS, A. (1965). *Man-machine engineering.* Monterey, CA: Brooks/Cole.

CHARNESS, N. (1976). Memory for chess positions: Resistance to interference. *Journal of Experimental Psychology: Human Learning and Memory, 2*, 641–653.

CHARROW, R. P., & CHARROW, V. R. (1979). Making legal language understandable: A psycholinguistic study of jury instructions. *Columbia Law Review, 79*, 1306–1374.

CHASE, W. G., & ERICSSON, K. A. (1979, November). *A mnemonic system for digit span: One year later.* Paper presented at the 20th annual meeting of the Psychonomic Society, Phoenix, AZ.

CHASE, W. G., & SIMON, H. A. (1973). Perception in chess. *Cognitive Psychology, 4*, 55–81.

CHERRY, C. (1953). Some experiments on the recognition of speech with one and with two ears. *Journal of the Acoustical Society of America, 25*, 975–979.

CHI, M. T. H., GLASER, R., & REES, E. (1982). Expertise in problem solving. In R. J. Sternberg (Ed.), *Advances in the psychology of human intelligence* (Vol. 1). Hillsdale, NJ: Erlbaum.

CHIESI, H. L., SPILICH, G. J., & VOSS, J. F. (1979). Acquisition of domain-related information in relation to high and low domain knowledge. *Journal of Verbal Learning and Verbal Behavior, 18*, 257–273.

CHIPMAN, S. F., SEGAL, J. W., & GLASER, R. (1985). *Thinking and learning skills* (Vol. 2). Hillsdale, NJ: Erlbaum.

CHOMSKY, N. (1957). *Syntactic structures.* The Hague: Mouton.

CHOMSKY, N. (1965). *Aspects of the theory of syntax.* Cambridge, MA: M.I.T. Press.

CLOWES, M. (1969). Transformational grammars and the organization of pictures. In A. Graselli (Ed.), *Automatic interpretation and the organization of pictures.* Orlando, FL: Academic Press.

COLLINS, A. M., & LOFTUS, E. F. (1975). A spreading activation theory of semantic processing. *Psychological Review, 82*, 407–428.

COLLINS, A. M., & QUILLIAN, M. R. (1969). Retrieval time from semantic memory. *Journal of Verbal Learning and Verbal Behavior, 8*, 240–248.

COLLINS, A. M., & QUILLIAN, M. R. (1970). Facilitating retrieval from semantic memory: The effect of repeating part of an inference. *Acta Psychologica, 33*, 304–314.

CONRAD, R. (1964). Acoustic confusions in immediate memory. *British Journal of Psychology, 55*, 75–84.

CONRAD, R. (1972). Speech and reading. In J. F. Kavanagh & I. G. Mattingly (Eds.), *Language by ear and by eye: The relationships between speech and reading.* Cambridge, MA: M.I.T. Press.

COOPER, L. A., & SHEPARD, R. N. (1973). Chronometric studies of the rotation of mental images. In W. G. Chase (Ed.), *Visual information processing.* Orlando, FL: Academic Press.

CRAIK, F. I. M. (1979a). Human memory. *Annual Review of Psychology, 30*, 63–102.

CRAIK, F. I. M. (1979b). Levels of processing: Overview and closing comments. In L. S. Cermak & F. I. M. Craik (Eds.), *Levels of processing in human memory.* Hillsdale, NJ: Erlbaum.

CRAIK, F. I. M., & LOCKHART, R. S. (1972). Levels of processing: A framework for memory research. *Journal of Verbal Learning and Verbal Behavior, 11*, 671–684.

CRAIK, F. I. M., & RABINOWITZ, J. C. (1983). Age differences in the acquisition and use of verbal information: A tutorial review. In H. Bouma & D. G. Bowwhuis (Eds.), *Attention and performance X.* Hillsdale, NJ: Erlbaum.

CRAIK, F. I. M., & TULVING, E. (1975). Depth of processing and the retention of words in episodic memory. *Journal of Experimental Psychology: General, 104*, 268–294.

CRAIK, F. I. M., & WATKINS, M. J. (1973). The role of rehearsal in short-term memory. *Journal of Verbal Learning and Verbal Behavior, 12*, 599–607.

CROVITZ, H. F. (1971). The capacity of memory loci in artificial memory. *Psychonomic Science, 24*, 187–188.

CROWDER, R. G. (1976). *Principles of learning and memory.* Hillsdale, NJ: Erlbaum.

CROWDER, R. G. (1982). The demise of short-term memory. *Acta Psychologica, 50,* 291–323.

DAWES, R. B. (1979). The robust beauty of improper linear models in decision making. *American Psychologist, 7,* 571–582.

DE GROOT, A. D. (1965). *Thought and choice in chess.* The Hague: Mouton.

DE GROOT, A. D. (1966). Perception and memory versus thought: Some old ideas and recent findings. In B. Kleinmuntz (Ed.), *Problem solving: Research, method, and theory.* New York: Wiley.

DENES, P. B., & PINSON, E. N. (1963). *The speech chain.* Bell Telephone Laboratories.

DEROSA, D. V., & TKACZ, D. (1976). Memory scanning of organized visual material. *Journal of Experimental Psychology: Human Learning and Memory, 2,* 688–694.

DETTERMAN, D. K., & RAMIG, P. (1978, November). *The relationship between vocabulary size and memory.* Paper presented at the 19th annual meeting of the Psychonomic Society, San Antonio, TX.

DEUTSCH, J. A., & DEUTSCH, D. (1963). Attention: Some theoretical considerations. *Psychological Review, 70,* 80–90.

DUNCKER, K. (1945). On problem solving. *Psychological Monographs, 58* (5, Whole No. 270).

D'YDEWALLE, G., & ROSSELLE, H. (1978). Text expectations in text learning. In M. M. Gruneberg, P. E. Morris, & R. N. Sykes (Eds.), *Practical aspects of memory.* Orlando, FL: Academic Press.

EGAN, D. E., & GREENO, J. G. (1974). Theory of rule induction: Knowledge acquired in concept learning, serial pattern learning, and problem solving. In L. Gregg (Ed.), *Knowledge and cognition.* Hillsdale, NJ: Erlbaum.

EGAN, D. E., & SCHWARTZ, B. J. (1979). Chunking in recall of symbolic drawings. *Memory & Cognition, 7,* 149–158.

EGAN, J. P. (1958). Recognition memory and the operating characteristic (Technical Note AFCR-TN 58-51). Bloomington: Indiana University Hearing and Communication Laboratory.

EGELAND, B. (1975). Effects of errorless training on teaching children to discriminate letters of the alphabet. *Journal of Applied Psychology, 60,* 533–536.

EICH, J. M. (1985). Levels of processing, encoding specificity, and CHARM. *Psychological Review, 92,* 1–38.

ELSTEIN, A. S., SHULMAN, L. S., & SPRAFKA, S. A. (1978). *Medical problem solving.* Cambridge, MA: Harvard University Press.

ERICKSON, J. R., & JONES, M. R. (1978). Thinking. *Annual Review of Psychology, 29,* 61–90.

ERICSSON, K. A. (1985). Memory skill. *Canadian Journal of Psychology, 39,* 188–231.

ERICSSON, K. A., & SIMON, H. A. (1980). Verbal reports as data. *Psychological Review, 87,* 215–251.

ERNST, G. W., & NEWELL, A. (1969). *GPS: A case study in generality and problem solving.* Orlando, FL: Academic Press.

ESTES, W. K. (1978a). The information processing approach to cognition: A confluence of metaphors and methods. In W. K. Estes (Ed.), *Handbook of learning and cognitive processes* (Vol. 5). Hillsdale, NJ: Erlbaum.

ESTES, W. K. (1978b). Perceptual processing in letter recognition and reading. In E. C. Carterette & M. P. Friedman (Eds.), *Handbook of perception* (Vol. 9). Orlando, FL: Academic Press.

ESTES, W. K., & TAYLOR, H. A. (1966). Visual detection in relation to display size and redundancy of critical elements. *Perception & Psychophysics, 1,* 9–16.

EYSENCK, M. W. (1978). Levels of processing: A critique. *British Journal of Psychology, 69,* 157–169.

EYSENCK, M. W. (1979). Depth, elaboration, and distinctiveness. In L. S. Cermak & F. I. M. Craik (Eds.), *Levels of processing in human memory.* Hillsdale, NJ: Erlbaum.

FINKE, R. A. (1980). Levels of equivalence in imagery and perception. *Psychological Review, 87,* 113–132.

FINKE, R. A. (1985). Theories relating mental imagery to perception. *Psychological Bulletin, 98,* 236–259.

FISCHHOFF, B., & BAR-HILLEL, M. (1984). Focusing techniques: A shortcut to improving probability judgments? *Organizational Behavior and Human Performance, 34,* 175–194.

FISCHLER, I., RUNDUS, D., & ATKINSON, R. C. (1970). Effects of overt rehearsal processes on free recall. *Psychonomic Science, 19,* 249–250.

FISHER, R. P., & CRAIK, F. I. M. (1977). Interaction between encoding and retrieval operations in cued recall. *Journal of Experimental Psychology: Human Learning and Memory, 3,* 701–711.

FLETCHER, C. R. (1986). Strategies for the allocation of short-term memory during comprehension. *Journal of Memory and Language, 25,* 43–58.

FOX, J. (1980). Making decisions under the influence of memory. *Psychological Review, 87,* 190–211.

FRANKLIN, B. (1887). *Complete works* (J. Bigelow, Ed.; Vol. 4). New York: Putnam.

FRAZIER, L., TAFT, L., ROEPER, T., CLIFTON, C., & EHRLICH, K. (1984). Parallel structure: A source of facilitation in sentence comprehension. *Memory & Cognition, 12,* 421–430.

GALAMBOS, J. A., & RIPS, L. J. (1982). Memory for routines. *Journal of Verbal Learning and Verbal Behavior, 21,* 260–281.

GARDNER, H. (1985). *The mind's new science: A history of the cognitive revolution.* New York: Basic Books.

GARNER, W. R. (1974). *The processing of information and structure.* Hillsdale, NJ: Erlbaum.

GARNER, W. R. (1979). Letter discrimination and identification. In A. D. Pick (Ed.), *Perception and its development: A tribute to Eleanor J. Gibson.* Hillsdale, NJ: Erlbaum.

GEISELMAN, R. E., FISHER, R. P., MACKINNON, D. P., & HOLLAND, H. L. (1985). Eyewitness memory enhancement in the police interview: Cognitive retrieval mnemonics versus hypnosis. *Journal of Applied Psychology, 70,* 401–412.

GENTNER, D. (1983). Structure-mapping: A theoretical framework for analogy. *Cognitive Science, 7,* 155–170.

GEYER, L. H., & DE WALD, C. G. (1973). Feature lists and confusion matrices. *Perception & Psychophysics, 14,* 479–482.

GIBSON, E. J. (1969). *Principles of perceptual learning and development.* New York:Appleton-Century-Crofts.

GIBSON, E. J., OSSER, H., SCHIFF, W., & SMITH, J. (1963). An analysis of critical features of letters, tested by a confusion matrix. In *A basic research program on reading* (Cooperative Research Project No. 639). Washington, DC: U.S. Office of Education.

GIBSON, E. J., SCHAPIRO, R., & YONAS, A. (1968). Confusion matrices for graphic patterns obtained with a latency measure. In *The analysis of reading skill: A program of basic and applied research* (Final Report, Project No. 5–1213). Ithaca, NY: Cornell University and U.S. Office of Education.

GICK, M. L., & HOLYOAK, K. (1980). Analogical problem solving. *Cognitive Psychology, 12,* 306–355.

GICK, M. L., & HOLYOAK, K. J. (1983). Schema induction and analogical transfer. *Cognitive Psychology, 15,* 1–38.

GLASER, R. (1984). Education and thinking: The role of knowledge. *American Psychologist, 39,* 93–104.

GLUCKSBERG, S., & MCCLOSKEY, M. (1981). Decisions about ignorance: Knowing that you don't know. *Journal of Experimental Psychology: Human Learning and Memory, 7,* 311–325.

GOLDBERG, L. R. (1986). The validity of ratings procedures to index the hierarchical level of categories. *Journal of Memory and Language, 25,* 323–347.

GOLDSTEIN, A. G. (1977). The fallibility of the eyewitness: Psychological evidence. In B. D. Sales (Ed.), *Psychology in the legal process.* New York: Spectrum.

GOPHER, D., & KAHNEMAN, D. (1971). Individual differences in attention and the prediction of flight criteria. *Perceptual and Motor Skills, 33,* 1335–1342.

GRAESSER, A. C., & NAKAMURA, G. V. (1982). The impact of a schema on comprehension and memory. In G. H. Bower (Ed.), *The psychology of learning and motivation* (Vol. 16). Orlando, FL: Academic Press.

GREENE, R. L. (1986). Sources of recency effects in free recall. *Psychological Bulletin, 99,* 221–228.

GREENO, J. G. (1978). Natures of problem solving abilities. In W. K. Estes (Ed.), *Handbook of learning and cognitive processes* (Vol. 5). Hillsdale, NJ: Erlbaum.

GREENO, J. G., & SIMON, H. A. (in press). Prob-

lem solving and reasoning. In R. C. Atkinson, R. J. Herrnstein, G. Lindzey, & R. D. Luce (Eds.), *Stevens' handbook of experimental psychology.* New York: Wiley.

GRIGGS, R. A., & COX, J. R. (1982). The elusive thematic-materials effect in Wason's selection task. *British Journal of Psychology, 73,* 407–420.

GROSSBERG, S., & STONE, G. (1986). Neural dynamics of word recognition and recall: Attentional priming, learning, and resonance. *Psychological Review, 93,* 46–74.

GRUNEBERG, M. M., MORRIS, P. E., & SYKES, R. N. (Eds.). (1978). *Practical aspects of memory.* Orlando, FL: Academic Press.

GUINDON, R., & KINTSCH, W. (1984). Priming macropropositions: Evidence for the primacy of macropropositions in the memory for text. *Journal of Verbal Learning and Verbal Behavior, 23,* 508–518.

GUNTER, B., CLIFFORD, B. R., & BERRY, C. (1980). Release from proactive interference with television news items: Evidence for encoding dimensions within televised news. *Journal of Experimental Psychology: Human Learning and Memory, 6,* 216–223.

GUTTENTAG, R. E. (1985). Memory and aging: Implications for theories of memory development during childhood. *Developmental Review, 5,* 56–82.

HABER, R. N. (1969). Introduction. In R. N. Haber (Ed.), *Information-processing approaches to visual perception.* New York: Holt, Rinehart and Winston.

HABERLANDT, K. F., & GRAESSER, A. C. (1985). Component processes in text comprehension and some of their interactions. *Journal of Experimental Psychology: General, 114,* 357–374.

HAMMOND, K. R. (1971). Computer graphics as an aid to learning. *Science, 172,* 903–908.

HARDYCK, C. D., & PETRINOVICH, L. F. (1970). Subvocal speech and comprehension levels as a function of the difficulty level of reading materials. *Journal of Verbal Learning and Verbal Behavior, 9,* 647–652.

HARRIS, R. J. (1977). Comprehension of pragmatic implications in advertising. *Journal of Applied Psychology, 62,* 603–608.

HARRIS, R. J. (1978). The effect of jury size and judge's instructions on memory for pragmatic implications from courtroom testimony. *Bulletin of the Psychonomic Society, 11,* 129–132.

HASHER, L., & ZACKS, R. T. (1979). Automatic and effortful processes in memory. *Journal of Experimental Psychology: General, 108,* 356–388.

HASHER, L., & ZACKS, R. T. (1984). Automatic processing of fundamental information: The case of frequency of occurrence. *American Psychologist, 39,* 1372–1388.

HAVILAND, S. E., & CLARK, H. H. (1974). What's new? Acquiring new information as a process of comprehension. *Journal of Verbal Learning and Verbal Behavior, 13,* 512–521.

HAYES, J. R. (1952). Memory span for several vocabularies as a function of vocabulary size. *Quarterly*

Progress Report, Acoustics Laboratory, Massachusetts Institute of Technology.

HAYES, J. R. (1966). Memory, goals, and problem solving. In B. Kleinmuntz (Ed.), *Problem solving: Research, method, and theory.* New York: Wiley.

HAYES, J. R. (1979, April). *Problem solving courses at Carnegie-Mellon University.* Paper presented at the annual meeting of the American Educational Research Association, San Francisco.

HAYES, J. R., & SIMON, H. A. (1977). Psychological differences among problem isomorphs. In N. J. Castellan, D. B. Pisoni, & G. R. Potts (Eds.), *Cognitive theory* (Vol. 2). Hillsdale, NJ: Erlbaum.

HAYES-ROTH, B., & HAYES-ROTH, F. (1977). Concept learning and the recognition and classification of examples. *Journal of Verbal Learning and Verbal Behavior, 16,* 321–338.

HAYGOOD, R. C., & BOURNE, L. E., JR. (1965). Attribute and rule learning aspects of conceptual behavior. *Psychological Review, 72,* 175–195.

HEALY, A. F. (1980). Proofreading errors on the word "The": New evidence on reading units. *Journal of Experimental Psychology: Human Perception and Performance, 6,* 45–57.

HEIDBREDER, E. (1961). *Seven psychologies.* New York: Appleton-Century-Crofts.

HELLER, J. I., & GREENO, J. G. (1979, January). *Information processing analyses of mathematical problem solving.* Paper presented at the Applied Problem Solving Conference, Evanston, IL.

HERRMANN, D. J., & NEISSER, U. (1978). An inventory of everyday memory experiences. In M. M. Gruneberg, P. E. Morris, & R. N. Sykes (Eds.), *Practical aspects of memory.* Orlando, FL: Academic Press.

HERTEL, P. T., ANOOSHIAN, L. J. & ASHBROOK, P. (1986). The accuracy of beliefs about retrieval cues. *Memory & Cognition, 14,* 265–269.

HINSLEY, D. A., HAYES, J. R., & SIMON, H. A. (1977). From words to equations: Meaning and representation in algebra word problems. In P. A. Carpenter & M. A. Just (Eds.), *Cognitive processes in comprehension.* Hillsdale, NJ: Erlbaum.

HIRST, W., SPELKE, E. S., REAVES, C. C., CAHARACK, G., & NEISSER, U. (1980). Dividing attention without alternation or automaticity. *Journal of Experimental Psychology: General, 109,* 98–117.

HITCH, G. J., & BADDELEY, A. D. (1976). Verbal reasoning and working memory. *Quarterly Journal of Experimental Psychology, 23,* 603–621.

HOCK, H. S., & TROMLEY, C. L. (1978). Mental rotation and perceptual uprightness. *Perception & Psychophysics, 24,* 529–533.

HOLBROOK, M. B. (1975). A comparison of methods for measuring the interletter similarity between capital letters. *Perception & Psychophysics, 17,* 532–536.

HOMA, D. (1984). On the nature of categories. In G. H. Bower (Ed.), *The psychology of learning and motivation* (Vol. 18). Orlando, FL: Academic Press.

HORTON, D. L., & MILLS, C. B. (1984). Human

learning and memory. *Annual Review of Psychology, 35,* 361–394.

HOWE, J. A. M. (1978). Artificial intelligence and computer-assisted learning: Ten years on. *Programmed Learning and Educational Technology, 15,* 114–125.

HUMPHREYS, M. S., & BAIN, J. D. (1983). Recognition memory: A cue and information analysis. *Memory & Cognition, 11,* 583–600.

HUNT, E., & LANSMAN, M. (1975). Cognitive theory applied to individual differences. In W. K. Estes (Ed.), *Handbook of learning and cognitive processes* (Vol. 1). Hillsdale, NJ: Erlbaum.

HUNT, R. R., & ELLIOTT, J. M. (1980). The role of nonsemantic information in memory: Orthographic distinctiveness effects on retention. *Journal of Experimental Psychology: General, 109,* 49–74.

HYDE, T. S., & JENKINS, J. J. (1969). The differential effects of incidental tasks on the organization of recall of a list of highly associated words. *Journal of Experimental Psychology, 82,* 472–481.

INTONS-PETERSON, M. J. (1983). Imagery paradigms: How vulnerable are they to experimenter's expectations? *Journal of Experimental Psychology: Human Perception and Performance, 9,* 394–412.

JACOBY, L. L., & BROOKS, L. R. (1984). Nonanalytic cognition: Memory, perception, and concept learning. In G. H. Bower (Ed.), *The psychology of learning and motivation* (Vol. 18). Orlando, FL: Academic Press.

JAMES, W. (1890). *The principles of psychology* (2 vols.). New York: Holt.

JARVELLA, R. J. (1979). Immediate memory and discourse processing. In G. H. Bower (Ed.), *The psychology of learning and motivation* (Vol. 13). Orlando, FL: Academic Press.

JEFFRIES, R., POLSON, P. G., RAZRAN, L., & ATWOOD, M. E. (1977). A process model for missionaries-cannibals and other river-crossing problems. *Cognitive Psychology, 9,* 412–440.

JENKINS, J. J. (1969). The acquisition of language. In D. A. Goslin (Ed.), *Handbook of socialization theory and research.* Skokie, IL: Rand McNally.

JOHNSON, M. K. (1983). A multiple-entry, modular memory system. In G. H. Bower (Ed.), *The psychology of learning and motivation* (Vol. 17). Orlando, FL: Academic Press.

JOHNSON, M. K., & HASHER, L. (in press). Human learning and memory. *Annual Review of Psychology, 38.*

JOHNSON, M. K., & RAYE, C. L. (1981). Reality monitoring. *Psychological Review, 88,* 67–85.

JOHNSON, M. K., RAYE, C. L., WANG, A. Y., & TAYLOR, T. T. (1979). Fact and fantasy: The roles of accuracy and variability in confusing imaginations with perceptual experiences. *Journal of Experimental Psychology: Human Learning and Memory, 5,* 229–240.

JOHNSON, S. (1967). Hierarchical clustering schemes. *Psychometrika, 32,* 241–254.

JOHNSON-LAIRD, P. N., LEGRENZI, P., & LEGRENZI, M. S. (1972). Reasoning and a sense of reality. *British Journal of Psychology, 63,* 395–400.

JOHNSTON, W. A., & DARK, V. J. (1986). Selective attention. *Annual Review of Psychology, 37,* 43–75.

JOHNSTON, W. A., & HEINZ, S. P. (1978). Flexibility and capacity demands of attention. *Journal of Experimental Psychology: General, 107,* 420–435.

JUST, M. A., & CARPENTER, P. A. (1980). A theory of reading: From eye fixations to comprehension. *Psychological Review, 87,* 329–354.

JUST, M. A., & CARPENTER, P. A. (1987). *The psychology of reading and language comprehension.* Newton, MA: Allyn & Bacon.

KAHNEMAN, D. (1973). *Attention and effort.* Englewood Cliffs, NJ: Prentice-Hall.

KAHNEMAN, D., BEN-ISHAI, R., & LOTAN, M. (1973). Relation of a test of attention to road accidents. *Journal of Applied Psychology, 58,* 113–115.

KAHNEMAN, D., & TVERSKY, A. (1972). Subjective probability: A judgment of representativeness. *Cognitive Psychology, 3,* 430–454.

KAHNEMAN, D., & TVERSKY, A. (1984). Choices, values, and frames. *American Psychologist, 39,* 341–350.

KEENAN, J. M., BAILLET, S. D., & BROWN, P. (1984). The effects of causal cohesion on comprehension and memory. *Journal of Verbal Learning and Verbal Behavior, 23,* 115–126.

KEENAN, J. M., MACWHINNEY, B., & MAYHEW, D. (1977). Pragmatics in memory: A study of natural conversation. *Journal of Verbal Learning and Verbal Behavior, 16,* 549–560.

KEMLER NELSON, D. G. K. (1984). The effect of intention on what concepts are acquired. *Journal of Verbal Learning and Verbal Behavior, 23,* 734–759.

KEPPEL, G., & UNDERWOOD, B. (1962). Proactive inhibition in short-term retention of single items. *Journal of Verbal Learning and Verbal Behavior, 1,* 153–161.

KIERAS, D. E. (1978). Good and bad structure in simple paragraphs: Effects on apparent theme, reading time, and recall. *Journal of Verbal Learning and Verbal Behavior, 17,* 13–28.

KIERAS, D. E. (1983). A simulation model for the comprehension of technical prose. In G. H. Bower (Ed.), *Psychology of learning and motivation* (Vol. 17). Orlando, FL: Academic Press.

KIERAS, D. E., & GREENO, J. G. (1975). Effect of meaningfulness on judgments of computability. *Memory & Cognition, 3,* 349–355.

KINTSCH, W. (1979). On modeling comprehension. *Educational Psychologist, 14,* 3–14.

KINTSCH, W., & BATES, E. (1977). Recognition memory for statements from a classroom lecture. *Journal of Experimental Psychology: Human Learning and Memory, 3,* 150–159.

KINTSCH, W., & VAN DIJK, T. A. (1978). Toward a model of text comprehension and production. *Psychological Review, 85,* 363–394.

KINTSCH, W., & VIPOND, D. (1979). Reading comprehension and readability in educational practice and psychological theory. In L. G. Nilsson (Ed.),

Perspectives on memory research. Hillsdale, NJ: Erlbaum.

KLAPP, S. T., MARSHBURN, E. A., & LESTER, P. T. (1983). Short-term memory does not involve the "working memory" of information processing: The demise of a common assumption. *Journal of Experimental Psychology: General, 112,* 204–264.

KLATZKY, R. L. (1980). *Human memory: Structures and processes* (2nd ed.). New York: W. H. Freeman.

KLATZKY, R. L. (1984). *Memory and awareness.* New York: W. H. Freeman.

KLEIMAN, G. M. (1975). Speech recoding in reading. *Journal of Verbal Learning and Verbal Behavior, 14,* 323–339.

KÖHLER, W. (1925). *The mentality of apes.* New York: Harcourt.

KOLERS, P. A. (1983). Perception and representation. *Annual Review of Psychology, 34,* 129–166.

KOSSLYN, S. M. (1975). Information representation in visual images. *Cognitive Psychology, 7,* 341–370.

KOSSLYN, S. M. (1981). The medium and the message in mental imagery: A theory. *Psychological Review, 88,* 46–66.

KOSSLYN. S. M. (1983). *Ghosts in the mind's machine: Creating and using images in the brain.* New York: Norton.

KOSSLYN, S. M., BALL, T. M., & REISER, B. J. (1978). Visual images preserve metric spatial information: Evidence from studies of image scanning. *Journal of Experimental Psychology: Human Perception and Performance, 4,* 47–60.

KOSSLYN, S. M., & POMERANTZ, J. R. (1977). Imagery, propositions, and the form of internal representations. *Cognitive Psychology, 9,* 52–76.

KROLL, N. E. A., & PARKS, T. E. (1978). Interference with short-term visual memory produced by concurrent central processing. *Journal of Experimental Psychology: Human Learning and Memory, 4,* 111–120.

KROLL, N. E. A., SCHEPELER, E. M., & ANGIN, K. T. (1986). Bizarre imagery: The misremembered mnemonic. *Journal of Experimental Psychology: Learning, Memory, and Cognition, 12,* 42–53.

LABERGE, D., & SAMUELS, S. J. (1974). Toward a theory of automatic information processing in reading. *Cognitive Psychology, 6,* 292–323.

LACHMAN, R., LACHMAN, J. L., & BUTTERFIELD, E. C. (1979). *Cognitive psychology and information processing: An introduction.* Hillsdale, NJ: Erlbaum.

LARKIN, J. H. (1980). Teaching problem solving in physics: The psychological laboratory and the practical classroom. In D. T. Tuma & F. Reif (Eds.), *Problem solving and education: Issues in teaching and research.* Hillsdale, NJ: Erlbaum.

LARKIN, J. H., MCDERMOTT, J., SIMON, D. P., & SIMON, H. A. (1980). Expert and novice performance in solving physics problems. *Science, 208,* 1335–1342.

LARKIN, J. H., & REIF, F. (1979). Understanding and teaching problem solving in physics. *European Journal of Science Education, 1,* 191–203.

LAUGHERY, K. R. (1969). Computer simulation of short-term memory: A component decay model. In G. H. Bower & J. T. Spence (Eds.), *The psychology of learning and motivation* (Vol. 3). Orlando, FL: Academic Press.

LESGOLD, A. M., ROTH, S. F., & CURTIS, M. E. (1979). Foregrounding effects in discourse comprehension. *Journal of Verbal Learning and Verbal Behavior, 18,* 291–308.

LEVINE, M. (1966). Hypothesis behavior by humans during discrimination learning. *Journal of Experimental Psychology, 71,* 331–338.

LEVY, B. A. (1978). Speech processing during reading. In A. M. Lesgold, J. W. Pellegrino, S. D. Fokkema, & R. Glaser (Eds.), *Cognitive psychology and instruction.* New York: Plenum.

LEWIS, M. W., & ANDERSON, J. R. (1985). Discrimination of operator schemata in problem solving: Learning from examples. *Cognitive Psychology, 17,* 26–65.

LIGHT, L. L., & CARTER-SOBELL, L. (1970). Effects of changed semantic context on recognition memory. *Journal of Verbal Learning and Verbal Behavior, 9,* 1–11.

LOCKHEAD, G. R., & CRIST, W. B. (1980). Making letters distinctive. *Journal of Educational Psychology, 72,* 483–493.

LOFTUS, E. F. (1975). Leading questions and the eyewitness report. *Cognitive Psychology, 7,* 560–572.

LOFTUS, G. R., SHIMAMURA, A. P., & JOHNSON, C. A. (1985). How much is an icon worth? *Journal of Experimental Psychology: Human Perception and Performance, 11,* 1–13.

LONG, G. M. (1980). Iconic memory: A review and critique of the study of short-term visual storage. *Psychological Bulletin, 88,* 785–820.

LORAYNE, H., & LUCAS, J. (1974). *The memory book.* New York: Ballantine Books.

LUCHINS, A. S. (1942). Mechanization in problem solving. *Psychological Monographs* (54, Whole No. 248).

LUTZ, K. A., & LUTZ, R. J. (1977). Effects of interactive imagery on learning: Applications to advertising. *Journal of Applied Psychology, 62,* 493–498.

LYONS, J. (1970). *Chomsky.* London: Collins.

MACKAY, D. G. (1966). To end ambiguous sentences. *Perception & Psychophysics, 1,* 426–435.

MACLEOD, C. M., HUNT, E. B., & MATHEWS, N. N. (1978). Individual differences in the verification of sentence-picture relationships. *Journal of Verbal Learning and Verbal Behavior, 17,* 493–507.

MALPASS, R. S., & DEVINE, P. G. (1981). Guided memory in eyewitness identification. *Journal of Applied Psychology, 66,* 343–350.

MANDLER, G. (1967). Organization and memory. In K. W. Spence & J. T. Spence (Eds.), *The psychology of learning and motivation* (Vol. 1). Orlando, FL: Academic Press.

MANDLER, G. (1980). Recognizing: The judgment of previous occurrence. *Psychological Review, 87,* 252–271.

MARCEL, A. J. (1983). Conscious and unconscious perception: An approach to the relations between phenomenal experience and perceptual processes. *Cognitive Psychology, 15,* 238–300.

MARSLEN-WILSON, M. D., & WELSH, A. (1978). Processing interactions and lexical access during word recognition in continuous speech. *Cognitive Psychology, 10,* 29–63.

MARTIN, R. C., & CARAMAZZA, A. (1980). Classification in well-defined and ill-defined categories: Evidence for common processing strategies. *Journal of Experimental Psychology: General, 109,* 320–353.

MASSARO, D. (1979). Letter information and orthographic context in word perception. *Journal of Experimental Psychology: Human Perception and Performance, 5,* 595–609.

MASSON, M. E. J. (1982). Cognitive processes in skimming stories. *Journal of Experimental Psychology: Learning, Memory, and Cognition, 8,* 400–417.

MAYER, R. E., & GREENO, J. G. (1972). Structural differences between learning outcomes produced by different instructional methods. *Journal of Experimental Psychology, 63,* 165–173.

MAYER, R. E., & GREENO, J. G. (1975). Effects of meaningfulness and organization on problem solving and computability judgments. *Memory & Cognition, 3,* 356–362.

MCALLISTER, D. W., MITCHELL, T. R., & BEACH, L. R. (1979). The contingency model for the selection of decision strategies: An empirical test of the effects of significance, accountability, and reversibility. *Organizational Behavior and Human Performance, 24,* 228–244.

MCCARTY, D. L. (1980). Investigation of a visual imagery mnemonic device for acquiring face-name associations. *Journal of Experimental Psychology: Human Learning and Memory, 6,* 145–155.

MCCLELLAND, J. L., & RUMELHART, D. E. (1981). An interactive-activation model of context effects in letter perception: Part 1. An account of basic findings. *Psychological Review, 88,* 375–407.

MCCLOSKEY, M., & GLUCKSBERG, S. (1979). Decision processes in verifying category membership statements: Implications for models of semantic memory. *Cognitive Psychology, 11,* 1–37.

MCDANIEL, M. A., & EINSTEIN, G. O. (1986). Bizarre imagery as an effective memory aid: The importance of distinctiveness. *Journal of Experimental Psychology: Learning, Memory, and Cognition, 12,* 54–65.

MCKOON, G., & RATCLIFF, R. (1980). Priming in item recognition: The organization of propositions in memory for text. *Journal of Verbal Learning and Verbal Behavior, 19,* 369–386.

MEDIN, D. L., ALTOM, M. W., EDELSON, S. M., & FREKO, D. (1982). Correlated symptoms and simulated medical classification. *Journal of Experimental Psychology: Learning, Memory, and Cognition, 8,* 37–50.

MEDIN, D. L., & SCHAFFER, M. M. (1978). Context theory of classification learning. *Psychological Review, 85,* 207–238.

MEDIN, D. L., & SMITH, E. E. (1984). Concepts and concept formation. *Annual Review of Psychology*, 35, 113–138.

MERVIS, C. B., & ROSCH, E. (1981). Categorization of natural objects. *Annual Review of Psychology*, 32, 89–115.

METCALFE, J. (1986a). Feeling of knowing in memory and problem solving. *Journal of Experimental Psychology: Human Perception and Performance, 6,* 58–66.

METCALFE, J. (1986b). Premonitions of insight predict impending error. *Journal of Experimental Psychology: Learning, Memory, and Cognition, 12,* 623–634.

MEYER, D. E., & SCHVANEVELDT, R. W. (1976). Meaning, memory structure, and mental processes. *Science, 192,* 27–33.

MIHAL, W. L., & BARETT, G. V. (1976). Individual differences in perceptual information processing and their relation to automobile accident involvement. *Journal of Applied Psychology, 61,* 229–233.

MILGRAM, S. (1970). The experience of living in cities. *Science, 167,* 1461–1468.

MILLER, G. A. (1956). The magical number seven, plus or minus two: Some limits on our capacity for processing information. *Psychological Review, 63,* 81–97.

MILLER, G. A., GALANTER, E., & PRIBRAM, K. (1960). *Plans and the structure of behavior.* New York: Holt, Rinehart and Winston.

MILLER, J. R., & KINTSCH, W. (1980). Readability and recall of short prose passages: A theoretical analysis. *Journal of Experimental Psychology: Human Learning and Memory, 6,* 335–354.

MITCHELL, D. B., & RICHMAN, C. L. (1980). Confirmed reservations: Mental travel. *Journal of Experimental Psychology: Human Perception and Performance, 6,* 58–66.

MORAY, N. (1959). Attention in dichotic listening: Affective cues and the influence of instructions. *Quarterly Journal of Experimental Psychology, 11,* 56–60.

MORRIS, C. D., BRANSFORD, J. D., & FRANKS, J. J. (1977). Levels of processing versus transfer appropriate processing. *Journal of Verbal Learning and Verbal Behavior, 16,* 519–533.

MORRIS, P. E., JONES, S., & HAMPSON, P. (1978). An imagery mnemonic for the learning of people's names. *British Journal of Psychology, 69,* 335–336.

MOSCOVITCH, M., & CRAIK, F. I. M. (1976). Depth of processing, retrieval cues, and uniqueness of encoding as factors in recall. *Journal of Verbal Learning and Verbal Behavior, 15,* 447–458.

MULHOLLAND, T. M., PELLEGRINO, J. W., & GLASER, R. (1980). Components of geometric analogy solution. *Cognitive Psychology, 12,* 252–284.

MURPHY, G. L., & MEDIN, D. L. (1985). The role of theories in conceptual coherence. *Psychological Review, 92,* 289–316.

MYERS, J. L., O'BRIEN, E. J., BALOTA, D. A., & TOYOFUKU, M. L. (1984). Memory search without interference: The role of integration. *Cognitive Psychology, 16,* 217–242.

NAVON, D., & GOPHER, D. (1979). On the economy of the human-processing system. *Psychological Review, 86,* 214–255.

NEISSER, U. (1967). *Cognitive psychology.* New York: Appleton-Century-Crofts.

NEISSER, U., & BECKLEN, R. (1975). Selective looking: Attending to visually specified events. *Cognitive Psychology, 7,* 480–494.

NELSON, T. O. (1977). Repetition and depth of processing. *Journal of Verbal Learning and Verbal Behavior, 16,* 151–171.

NELSON, T. O., & SMITH, E. E. (1972). Acquisition and forgetting of hierarchically organized information in long-term memory. *Journal of Experimental Psychology, 95,* 388–396.

NEUMANN, P. G. (1974). An attribute frequency model for the abstraction of prototypes. *Memory & Cognition, 2,* 241–248.

NEWELL, A., SHAW, J. C., & SIMON, H. A. (1958a). Chess-playing problems and the problem of complexity. *IBM Journal of Research and Development, 2,* 320–335.

NEWELL, A., SHAW, J. C., & SIMON, H. A. (1958b). Elements of a theory of human problem solving. *Psychological Review, 65,* 151–166.

NEWELL, A., & SIMON, H. A. (1972). *Human problem solving.* Englewood Cliffs, NJ: Prentice-Hall.

NICKERSON, R. S., & ADAMS, M. J. (1979). Long-term memory for a common object. *Cognitive Psychology, 11,* 287–307.

NIELSEN, G. D., & SMITH, E. E. (1973) Imaginal and verbal representations in short-term recognition of visual forms. *Journal of Experimental Psychology, 101,* 375–378.

NORMAN, D. A. (1968). Toward a theory of memory and attention. *Psychological Review, 75,* 522–536.

NORMAN, D. A. (1980). Cognitive engineering and education. In D. T. Tuma & F. Reif (Eds.), *Problem solving and education: Issues in teaching and research.* Hillsdale, NJ: Erlbaum.

PAAP, K. R., NEWSOME, S. L., MCDONALD, J. E., & SCHVANEVELDT, R. W. (1982). An activation-verification model for letter and word recognition: The word superiority effect. *Psychological Review, 89,* 573–594.

PAIGE, J. M., & SIMON, H. A. (1966). Cognitive processes in solving algebra word problems. In B. Kleinmuntz (Ed.), *Problem solving: Research, method, and theory.* New York: Wiley.

PAIVIO, A. (1969). Mental imagery in associative learning and memory. *Psychological Review, 76,* 241–263.

PAIVIO, A. (1971). *Imagery and verbal processes.* New York: Holt, Rinehart and Winston.

PAIVIO, A. (1975). Coding distinctions and repetition effects in memory. In G. H. Bower (Ed.), *Psychology of learning and motivation* (Vol. 9). Orlando, FL: Academic Press.

PAIVIO, A., SMYTHE, P. E., & YUILLE, J. C.

(1968). Imagery versus meaningfulness of nouns in paired-associate learning. *Canadian Journal of Psychology, 22*, 427–441.

PALMER, S. E. (1977). Hierarchical structure in perceptual representation. *Cognitive Psychology, 9*, 441–474.

PAYNE, J. W. (1973). Alternative approaches to decision making under risk. *Psychological Bulletin, 80*, 439–453.

PAYNE, J. W. (1976). Task complexity and contingent processing in decision making: An information search and protocol analysis. *Organizational Behavior and Human Performance, 16*, 366–387.

PELLEGRINO, J. W., & GLASER, R. (1979). Cognitive correlates and components in the analysis of individual differences. *Intelligence, 3*, 187–216.

PENROD, S., & HASTIE, R. (1980). A computer simulation of jury decision making. *Psychological Review, 87*, 133–159.

PETERSON, L. R., & PETERSON, M. J. (1959). Short-term retention of individual verbal items. *Journal of Experimental Psychology, 58*, 193–198.

PHILLIPS, W. A. (1974). On the distinction between sensory storage and short-term visual memory. *Perception & Psychophysics, 16*, 283–290.

PINTRICH, P. R., CROSS, D. R., KOZMA, R. B., & MCKEACHIE, W. J. (1986). Instructional psychology. *Annual Review of Psychology, 37*, 611–651.

PITTENGER, J. B., & SHAW, R. E. (1975). Aging faces as viscal-elastic events: Implications for a theory of nonrigid shape perception. *Journal of Experimental Psychology: Human Perception and Performance, 1*, 374–383.

PITZ, G. F., & HARREN, V. A. (1980). An analysis of career decision making from the point of view of information processing and decision theory. *Journal of Vocational Behavior, 16*, 320–346.

PITZ, G. F., & SACHS, N. J. (1984). Judgment and decision: Theory and application. *Annual Review of Psychology, 35*, 139–163.

POLSON, P. G, & JEFFRIES, R. (1985). Instruction in general problem-solving skills: An analysis of four approaches. In J. W. Segal, S. F. Chipman, & R. Glaser (Eds.), *Thinking and learning skills* (Vol. 1). Hillsdale, NJ: Erlbaum.

POLYA, G. (1962). *Mathematical discovery* (Vol. 1). New York: Wiley.

POSNER, M. I., BOIES, S. J., EICHELMAN, W. H., & TAYLOR, R. L. (1969). Retention of visual and name codes of single letters. *Journal of Experimental Psychology Monograph, 79*, 1–13.

POSNER, M. I., GOLDSMITH, R., & WELTON, K. E. (1967). Perceived distance and the classification of distorted patterns. *Journal of Experimental Psychology, 73*, 28–38.

POSNER, M. I., & KEELE, S. W. (1968). On the genesis of abstract ideas. *Journal of Experimental Psychology, 77*, 353–363.

POSNER, M. I., & SNYDER, C. R. R. (1975). Attention and cognitive control. In R. L. Solso (Ed.), *Information processing and cognition: The Loyola Symposium.* Hillsdale, NJ: Erlbaum.

POSTMAN, L., & PHILLIPS, L. W. (1965). Short term temporal changes in free recall. *Quarterly Journal of Experimental Psychology, 17*, 132–138.

POTTER, M. C., & FAULCONER, B. A. (1979). Understanding noun phrases. *Journal of Verbal Learning and Verbal Behavior, 18*, 509–521.

PRESSLEY, M., LEVIN, J. R., HALL, J. W., MILLER, G. E., & BERRY, J. K. (1980). The key word method and foreign word acquisition. *Journal of Experimental Psychology: Human Learning and Memory, 6*, 163–173.

PYLYSHYN, Z. W. (1973). What the mind's eye tells the mind's brain: A critique of mental imagery. *Psychological Bulletin, 80*, 1–24.

PYLYSHYN, Z. W. (1981). The imagery debate: Analogue media versus tacit knowledge. *Psychological Review, 88*, 16–45.

READ, J. D., & BRUCE, D. (1982). Longitudinal tracking of difficult memory retrievals. *Cognitive Psychology, 14*, 280–300.

REDER, L. M. (1980). The role of elaboration in the comprehension and retention of prose. *Review of Educational Research, 50*, 5–53.

REDER, L. M., & ANDERSON, J. R. (1980). Partial resolution of the paradox of interference: The role of integrating knowledge. *Cognitive Psychology, 12*, 447–472.

REDER, L. M., & ROSS, B. H. (1983). Integrated knowledge in different tasks: The role of retrieval strategy on fan effects. *Journal of Experimental Psychology: Learning, Memory, and Cognition, 9*, 55–72.

REED, S. K. (1972). Pattern recognition and categorization. *Cognitive Psychology, 3*, 382–407.

REED, S. K., ERNST, G. W., & BANERJI, R. (1974). The role of analogy in transfer between similar problem states. *Cognitive Psychology, 6*, 436–450.

REED, S. K., & FRIEDMAN, M. P. (1973). Perceptual vs. conceptual categorization. *Memory & Cognition, 1*, 157–163.

REED, S. K., HOCK, H., & LOCKHEAD, G. R. (1983). Tacit knowledge and the effect of pattern configuration on mental scanning. *Memory & Cognition, 11*, 137–143.

REED, S. K., & JOHNSEN, J. A. (1975). Detection of parts in patterns and images. *Memory & Cognition, 3*, 569–575.

REED, S. K., & JOHNSEN, J. A. (1977). Memory for problem solutions. In G. H. Bower (Ed.), *The psychology of learning and motivation* (Vol. 11). Orlando, FL: Academic Press.

REICHER, G. M. (1969). Perceptual recognition as a function of meaningfulness of stimulus material. *Journal of Experimental Psychology, 81*, 275–280.

REITMAN, J. S. (1974). Without surreptitious rehearsal, information in short-term memory decays. *Journal of Verbal Learning and Verbal Behavior, 13*, 365–377.

REITMAN, J. S., & BOWER, G. H. (1973). Storage and later recognition of exemplars of concepts. *Cognitive Psychology, 4*, 194–206.

ROEDIGER, H. L. (1980). Memory metaphors in cognitive psychology. *Memory & Cognition, 8,* 231–246.

ROSCH, E. (1973). Natural categories. *Cognitive Psychology, 4,* 328–350.

ROSCH, E. (1975). Cognitive representations of semantic categories. *Journal of Experimental Psychology: General, 3,* 192–233.

ROSCH, E., & MERVIS, C. B. (1975). Family resemblances: Studies in the internal structure of categories. *Cognitive Psychology, 7,* 573–605.

ROSCH, E., MERVIS, C. B., GRAY, W. D., JOHNSEN, D. M., & BOYES-BRAEM, P. (1976). Basic objects in natural categories. *Cognitive Psychology, 8,* 382–440.

ROSS, B. H. (1984). Remindings and their effects in learning a cognitive skill. *Cognitive Psychology, 16,* 371–416.

RUBINSTEIN, M. F. (1975). *Patterns of problem solving.* Englewood Cliffs, NJ: Prentice-Hall.

RUBINSTEIN, M. F., & PFEIFFER, K. R. (1979, April). *Theoretical and practical aspects of the UCLA problem solving course.* Paper presented at the annual meeting of the American Educational Research Association, San Francisco.

RUMELHART, D. E. (1970). A multicomponent theory of perception of briefly exposed stimulus displays. *Journal of Mathematical Psychology, 7,* 191–218.

RUMELHART, D. E. (1977). Toward an interactive model of reading. In S. Dornic (Ed.), *Attention and performance* (Vol. 6). Hillsdale, NJ: Erlbaum.

RUMELHART, D. E., & MCCLELLAND, J. L. (1982). An interactive-activation model of context effects in letter perception: Part 2. The contextual enhancement and some tests and extensions of the model. *Psychological Review, 89,* 60–94.

RUNDUS, D. (1971). Analysis of rehearsal processes in free recall. *Journal of Experimental Psychology, 89,* 63–77.

RUSHMER, R. F. (1970). *Cardiovascular dynamics.* Philadelphia: Saunders.

SACERDOTI, E. D. (1974). Planning in a hierarchy of abstraction spaces. *Artificial Intelligence, 5,* 115–135.

SACERDOTI, E. D. (1977). *A structure for plans and behavior.* Amsterdam: Elsevier.

SACHS, J. S. (1967). Recognition memory for syntactic and semantic aspects of connected discourse. *Perception & Psychophysics, 2,* 437–442.

SALASOO, A., & PISONI, D. B. (1985). Interaction of knowledge sources in spoken word identification. *Journal of Memory and Language, 24,* 210–231.

SANDERS, A. F., & SCHROOTS, J. J. F. (1969). Cognitive categories and memory span: III. Effects of similarity on recall. *Quarterly Journal of Experimental Psychology, 21,* 21–28.

SCHANK, R., & ABELSON, R. (1977). *Scripts, goals, and understanding.* Hillsdale, NJ: Erlbaum.

SCHNEIDER, W., & SHIFFRIN, R. M. (1977). Controlled and automatic human information processing: I. Detection, search, and attention. *Psychological Review, 84,* 1–66.

SCHOENFELD, A. H. (1979). Explicit heuristic training as a variable in problem-solving performances. *Journal for Research in Mathematics Education, 10,* 173–187.

SCHVANEVELDT, R. W., MEYER, D. E., & BECKER, C. A. (1976). Lexical ambiguity, semantic context, and visual word recognition. *Journal of Experimental Psychology: Human Perception and Performance, 2,* 243–256.

SCHWANENFLUGEL, P. J., & SHOBEN, E. J. (1985). The influence of sentence constraint on the scope of facilitation for upcoming words. *Journal of Memory and Language, 24,* 232–252.

SEGAL, J. W., CHIPMAN, S. F., & GLASER, R. (1985). *Thinking and learning skills* (Vol. 1). Hillsdale, NJ: Erlbaum.

SEIDENBERG, M. S., WATERS, G. S., SANDERS, M., & LANGER, P. (1984). Pre- and postlexical loci of contextual effects on word recognition. *Memory & Cognition, 12,* 315–328.

SHARKEY, N. E., & MITCHELL, D. C. (1985). Word recognition in a functional context: The use of scripts in reading. *Journal of Memory and Language, 24,* 253–270.

SHAUGHNESSY, J. J. (1981). Memory monitoring accuracy and modification of rehearsal strategies. *Journal of Verbal Learning and Verbal Behavior, 20,* 216–230.

SHEIKH, A. A. (Ed.). (1983). *Imagery: Current theory, research, and application.* New York: Wiley.

SHEPARD, R. N. (1967). Recognition memory for words, sentences, and pictures. *Journal of Verbal Learning and Verbal Behavior, 6,* 156–163.

SHEPARD, R. N., & METZLER, J. (1971). Mental rotation of three-dimensional objects. *Science, 171,* 701–703.

SHEPARD, R. N., & PODGORNY, P. (1978). Cognitive processes that resemble perceptual processes. In W. K. Estes (Ed.), *Handbook of learning and cognitive processes* (Vol. 5). Hillsdale, NJ: Erlbaum.

SHIFFRIN, R. M. (in press). Attention. In R. C. Atkinson, R. J. Hernstein, G. Lindzey, & R. D. Luce (Eds.), *Stevens' handbook of experimental psychology.* New York: Wiley.

SHIFFRIN, R. M., & SCHNEIDER, W. (1977). Controlled and automatic human information processing: II. Perceptual learning, automatic attending, and a general theory. *Psychological Review, 84,* 127–190.

SHULMAN, H. G. (1971). Similarity effects in short-term memory. *Psychological Bulletin, 75,* 399–415.

SIEGEL, J. A., & SIEGEL, W. (1972). Absolute judgment and paired-associate learning: Kissing cousins or identical twins? *Psychological Review, 79,* 300–316.

SILVER, E. A. (1981). Recall of mathematical problem information: Solving related problems. *Journal for Research in Mathematics Education, 12,* 54–64.

SIMON, H. A. (1957). *Models of man.* New York: Wiley.

SIMON, H. A. (1974). How big is a chunk? *Science, 183,* 482–488.

SIMON, H. A. (1983). Search and reasoning in problem solving. *Artificial Intelligence, 21,* 7–29.

SIMON, H. A., & GILMARTIN, K. (1973). A simulation of memory for chess positions. *Cognitive Psychology, 5,* 29–46.

SIMON, H. A., & NEWELL, A. (1971). Human problem solving: The state of the theory in 1970. *American Psychologist, 26,* 145–159.

SIMON, H. A., & REED, S. K. (1976). Modeling strategy shifts in a problem-solving task. *Cognitive Psychology, 8,* 86–97.

SLOVIC, P., FISCHHOFF, B., & LICHTENSTEIN, S. (1976). Cognitive processes and societal risk taking. In J. S. Carroll & J. W. Payne (Eds.), *Cognition and social behavior.* Hillsdale, NJ: Erlbaum.

SLOVIC, P., & LICHTENSTEIN, S. (1968). Relative importance of probabilities and payoffs in risk taking. *Journal of Experimental Psychology Monograph, 78*(3, Pt. 2).

SLOWIACZEK, M. L., & CLIFTON, C. (1980). Subvocalization and reading for meaning. *Journal of Verbal Learning and Verbal Behavior, 19,* 573–582.

SMITH, E. E. (1978). Theories of semantic memory. In W. K. Estes (Ed.), *Handbook of learning and cognitive processes* (Vol. 6). Hillsdale, NJ: Erlbaum.

SMITH, E. E., ADAMS, N., & SCHORR, D. (1978). Fact retrieval and the paradox of interference. *Cognitive Psychology, 10,* 438–464.

SMITH, E. E., & NIELSEN, G. D. (1970). Representation and retrieval processes in short-term memory: Recognition and recalls of faces. *Journal of Experimental Psychology, 85,* 397–405.

SMITH, E. E., SHOBEN, E. J., & RIPS, L. J. (1974). Structure and process in semantic memory: A featural model for semantic decision. *Psychological Review, 81,* 214–241.

SMITH, M. E. (1983). Hypnotic memory enhancement of witnesses: Does it work? *Psychological Bulletin, 94,* 387–407.

SPERLING, G. (1960). The information available in brief visual presentations. *Psychological Monographs, 74*(11, Whole No. 498).

SPERLING, G. (1963). A model for visual memory tasks. *Human Factors, 5,* 19–31.

SPERLING, G. (1976). Successive approximations to a model for short-term memory. *Acta Psychologica, 27,* 285–292.

SPILICH, G. J., VESONDER, G. T., CHIESI, H. L., & VOSS, J. F. (1979). Text processing of domain-related information for individuals with high and low domain knowledge. *Journal of Verbal Learning and Verbal Behavior, 18,* 275–290.

STANDING, L. (1973). Learning 10,000 pictures. *Quarterly Journal of Experimental Psychology, 25,* 207–222.

STANOVICH, K. E., & WEST, R. F. (1983). On priming by a sentence context. *Journal of Experimental Psychology: General, 112,* 1–36.

STEIN, B. S., & BRANSFORD, J. D. (1979). Constraints on effective elaboration: Effects of precision and subject generation. *Journal of Verbal Learning and Verbal Behavior, 18,* 769–777.

STEIN, N. L., & TRABASSO, T. (1982). What's in a story: An approach to comprehension and instruction. In R. Glaser (Ed.), *Advances in instructional psychology* (Vol. 2). Hillsdale, NJ: Erlbaum.

STERNBERG, R. J. (1977). Component processes in analogical reasoning. *Psychological Review, 84,* 353–378.

STERNBERG, R. J. (1985). *Beyond IQ: A theory of human intelligence.* Cambridge: Cambridge University Press.

STERNBERG, R. J., & DETTERMAN, D. K. (Eds.). (1979). *Human intelligence: Perspectives on its theory and measurement.* Norwood, NJ: Ablex.

STERNBERG, R. J., & GARDNER, M. K. (1983). Unities in inductive reasoning. *Journal of Experimental Psychology: General, 112,* 80–116.

STERNBERG, S. (1966). High-speed scanning in human memory. *Science, 153,* 652–654.

STERNBERG, S. (1967). Two operations in character recognition: Some evidence from reaction time measurements. *Perception & Psychophysics, 2,* 45–53.

STEVENS, A., & COUPE, P. (1978). Distortions in judged spatial relations. *Cognitive Psychology, 10,* 411–437.

STRAUSS, M. S. (1979). Abstraction of prototypical information by adults and 10-month-old infants. *Journal of Experimental Psychology: Human Learning and Memory, 5,* 618–632.

STROOP, J. R. (1935). Studies of interferences in serial verbal reactions. *Journal of Experimental Psychology, 18,* 643–662.

SUINN, R. M. (1983). Imagery and sports. In A. A. Sheikh (Ed.), *Imagery: Current theory, research, and application.* New York: Wiley.

SULIN, R. A., & DOOLING, D. J. (1974). Intrusion of a thematic idea in retention of prose. *Journal of Experimental Psychology, 103,* 255–262.

SUTHERLAND, N. S. (1968). Outlines of a theory of visual pattern recognition in animals and man. *Proceedings of the Royal Society, 171,* 297–317.

SWINNEY, D. A. (1979). Lexical access during sentence comprehension: Reconsideration of some context effects. *Journal of Verbal Learning and Verbal Behavior, 18,* 645–659.

SWINNEY, D. A., & HAKES, D. T. (1976). Effects of prior context upon lexical access during sentence comprehension. *Journal of Verbal Learning and Verbal Behavior, 15,* 681–689.

TAYLOR, S. E., & CROCKER, J. (1981). Schematic bases of social information processing. In E. T. Higgens, C. P. Herman, & M. P. Zanna (Eds.), *Social cognition: The Ontario Symposium* (Vol. 1). Hillsdale, NJ: Erlbaum.

THOMSON, D. M., & TULVING, E. (1970). Associative encoding and retrieval: Weak and strong cues. *Journal of Experimental Psychology, 86,* 255–262.

THORNDYKE, P. W. (1977). Cognitive structures in comprehension and memory of narrative discourse. *Cognitive Psychology, 9,* 77–110.

THORNDYKE, P. W., & STASZ, C. (1980). Individual differences in procedures for knowledge acquisition from maps. *Cognitive Psychology, 12,* 137–175.

TOWNSEND, J. T. (1971). Theoretical analysis of an alphabetic confusion matrix. *Perception & Psychophysics, 9,* 40–50.

TOWNSEND, J. T., & ASHBY, F. G. (1982). Experimental test of contemporary mathematical models of visual letter recognition. *Journal of Experimental Psychology: Human Perception and Performance, 6,* 834–864.

TOWNSEND, J. T., HU, G. G., & EVANS, R. J. (1984). Modeling feature perception in brief displays with evidence for positive interdependencies. *Perception & Psychophysics, 36,* 35–49.

TRABASSO, T., & SPERRY, L. L. (1985). The causal basis for deciding importance of story events. *Journal of Memory and Language, 24,* 595–611.

TRABASSO, T., & VAN DEN BROEK, P. (1985). Causal thinking and the representation of narrative events. *Journal of Memory and Language, 24,* 612–630.

TREISMAN, A. M. (1960). Contextual cues in encoding listening. *Quarterly Journal of Experimental Psychology, 12,* 242–248.

TREISMAN, A. M., & GELADE, G. (1980). A feature-integration theory of attention. *Cognitive Psychology, 12,* 97–136.

TREISMAN, A. M., & SCHMIDT, H. (1982). Illusory conjunctions in the perception of objects. *Cognitive Psychology, 14,* 107–141.

TULVING, E., & THOMSON, D. M. (1973). Encoding specificity and retrieval processes in episodic memory. *Psychological Review, 80,* 352–373.

TVERSKY, A. (1972). Elimination by aspects: A theory of choice. *Psychological Review, 79,* 281–299.

TVERSKY, A., & KAHNEMAN, D. (1973). Availability: A heuristic for judging frequency and probability. *Cognitive Psychology, 5,* 207–232.

TVERSKY, B. (1981). Distortions in memory for maps. *Cognitive Psychology, 13,* 407–433.

UHR, L. (1966). *Pattern recognition.* New York: Wiley.

VAN DIJK, T. A., & KINTSCH, W. (1983). *Strategies of discourse comprehension.* Orlando, FL: Academic Press.

VIPOND, D. (1980). Micro- and macroprocesses in text comprehension. *Journal of Verbal Learning and Verbal Behavior, 19,* 276–296.

VOSS, J. F., GREENE, T. R., POST, T. A., & PENNER, B. C. (1983). Problem-solving skill in the social sciences. In G. H. Bower (Ed.), *The psychology of learning and motivation* (Vol. 17). Orlando, FL: Academic Press.

WALKER, C. H., & MEYER, B. J. F. (1980a). Integrating different types of information in text. *Journal of Verbal Learning and Verbal Behavior, 19,* 263–275.

WALKER, C. H., & MEYER, B. J. F. (1980b). Integrating information from text: An evaluation of current theories. *Review of Educational Research, 50,* 421–437.

WASON, P. C., & JOHNSON-LAIRD, P. N. (1972). *Psychology of reasoning: Structure and content.* Cambridge, MA: Harvard University Press.

WASON, P. C., & SHAPIRO, D. (1971). Natural and contrived experience in a reasoning problem. *Quarterly Journal of Experimental Psychology, 23,* 63–71.

WATSON, J. B. (1924). *Behaviorism.* New York: Norton.

WAUGH, N. C., & NORMAN, D. A. (1965). Primary memory. *Psychological Review, 72,* 89–104.

WEBER, R. M. (1970). First graders' use of grammatical context in reading. In H. Levin & J. T. Williams (Eds.), *Basic studies in reading.* New York: Basic Books.

WEISBERG, R., & SULS, J. M. (1973). An information-processing model of Duncker's candle problem. *Cognitive Psychology, 4,* 255–276.

WICKELGREN, W. A. (1964). Size of rehearsal group and short-term memory. *Journal of Experimental Psychology, 68,* 413–419.

WICKELGREN, W. A. (1965). Acoustic similarity and intrusion errors in short-term memory. *Journal of Experimental Psychology, 70,* 102–108.

WICKELGREN, W. A. (1974). *How to solve problems.* New York: W. H. Freeman.

WICKENS, C. D., & KRAMER, A. (1985). Engineering psychology. *Annual Review of Psychology, 36,* 307–348.

WICKENS, D. D. (1972). Characteristics of word encoding. In A. W. Melton & E. Martin (Eds.), *Coding processes in human memory.* Washington, DC: Winston.

WICKENS, D. D., BORN, D. G., & ALLEN, C. K. (1963). Proactive inhibition and item similarity in short-term memory. *Journal of Verbal Learning and Verbal Behavior, 2,* 440–445.

YARMEY, A. D. (1979). *The psychology of eyewitness testimony.* New York: Free Press.

YATES, F. A. (1966). *The art of memory.* London: Routledge & Kegan Paul.

YERKES, R. M., & DODSON, J. D. (1908). The relation of strength of stimulus to rapidity of habit-formation. *Journal of Comparative Neurology of Psychology, 18,* 459–482.

ZACKS, R. T., HASHER, L., ALBA, J., SANFT, H., & ROSE, K. C. (1984). Is temporal order encoded automatically? *Memory & Cognition, 12,* 387–394.

ZECHMEISTER, E. B., & NYBERG, S. E. (1982). *Human memory: An introduction to research and theory.* Monterey, CA: Brooks/Cole.

Name Index

Subject Index

Credits

These pages constitute an extension of the copyright page. We have made every effort to trace the ownership of all copyrighted material and to secure permission from copyright holders. In the event of any question arising with regard to the use of any material, we will be pleased to make the necessary corrections in future printings.

CHAPTER 1. **8,** Figure 1.2 from *Plans and the Structure of Behavior*, by G. A. Miller, E. Galanter, and K. Pribram. Copyright 1960 by Holt, Rinehart, and Winston. Reprinted by permission of E. Galanter.

CHAPTER 2. **13,** Figure 2.1 from *Man Machine Engineering*, by A. Chapanis. Copyright © 1965 by Wadsworth, Inc. Reprinted by permission of the publisher, Brooks/Cole Publishing Company, Pacific Grove, California. **15,** Figure 2.2 from "On the Distinction between Sensory Storage and Short Term Visual Memory," by W. A. Phillips, *Perception and Psychophysics*, 1974, *16*, 283–290. Copyright 1974 by the Psychonomic Society, Inc. Reprinted by permission. **18,** Figure 2.3 from *Principles of Perceptual Learning and Development*, by E. Gibson, p. 88 © 1969 by Prentice-Hall, Inc., Englewood Cliffs, New Jersey. Reprinted by permission. **19,** Figure 2.4 from "Confusion Matrices for Graphic Patterns Obtained with a Latency Measure," by E. Gibson, R. Shapiro, and A. Yonas, in *The Analysis of Reading Skill: A Program of Basic and Applied Research*. Final report, project no. 5–1213, Cornell University and USOE, 1968. Reprinted by permission of Dr. Eleanor J. Gibson. **20,** Figure 2.5 from "Transformational Grammars and the Organization of Pictures," by M. Clowes, in A. Graselli (Ed.), *Automatic Interpretation and the Organization of Pictures*. Copyright 1969 by Academic Press, Inc. Reprinted by permission. **21,** Figure 2.6 from "Making Letters Distinctive," by G. R. Lockhead and W. B. Crist, *Journal of Educational Psychology*, 1980, *72*, 483–493. Copyright 1980 by the American Psychological Association. Reprinted by permission. **22,** Figures 2.7 and 2.8 from "Human Image Understanding: Recent Research and a Theory," by I. Biederman, *Computer Vision, Graphics and Image Processing*, 1985, *32*, 29–73. Copyright 1985 by Academic Press. Reprinted by permission. **24,** Figure 2.9 from "The Information Available in Brief Visual Presentations," by G. Sperling, *Psychological Monographs*, 1960, *74* (11, Whole No. 498). Copyright 1960 by the American Psychological Association. Reprinted by permission. **25,** Figure 2.10 from "Successive Approximations to a Model for Short-Term Memory," by G. Sperling, *Acta Psychologica*, 1967, *27*, 285–292. Copyright 1967 by North-Holland Publishing Company. Reprinted by permission. **28,** Figure 2.11 from *Cognitive Psychology*, by Robert L. Solso. Copyright © 1979 by Harcourt, Brace Jovanovich, Inc. Reprinted by permission of the publisher. **30,** Figures 2.12 through 2.15 from "Toward an Interactive Model of Reading," by D. E. Rumelhart. In S. Dornie (Ed.) *Attention and Performance* (Vol. 6). Copyright 1977 by Lawrence Erlbaum Associates, Inc., Publishers. Reprinted by permission.

CHAPTER 3. **37,** Figure 3.1 from "The Role of Auditory Localization in Attention and Memory Span," by D. E. Broadbent, *Journal of Experimental Psychology*, 1954, *47*, 191–196. Copyright 1954 by the American Psychological Association. Reprinted by permission. **38,** Figure 3.2 from "A Mechanical Model for Human Attention and Immediate Memory," by D. E. Broadbent, *Psychological Review*, 1957, *64*, 205–215. Copyright 1957 by the American Psychological Association. Reprinted by permission. **40,** Figure 3.3 from "Contextual Cues in Selective Listening," by A. M. Tretsman, *Quarterly Journal of Experimental Psychology*, 1970, *12*, 242–248. Copyright 1970 by the Experimental Psychology Society. Reprinted by permission. **41,** Figure 3.4 from "Toward a Theory of Memory and Attention," by D. A. Norman, *Psychological Review*, 1968, *75*, 522–536. Copyright 1968 by the American Psychological Association. Reprinted by permission. **43,** Figure 3.5 from Daniel Kahneman, *Attention and Force*, © 1973, p. 10. Reprinted by permission of Prentice-Hall, Inc., Englewood Cliffs, New Jersey. **48,** Figure 3.6 from "Toward a Theory of Automatic Information Processing in Reading," by D. LaBerge and S. J. Samuels, *Cognitive Psychology*, 1974, 6, 293–323. Copyright 1974 by Academic Press, Inc. Reprinted by permission.

CHAPTER 4. **56,** Figure 4.1 from "The Control of Short-Term Memory," by R. C. Atkinson and R. M. Shiffrin, *Scientific American*, 1971, *225*, 82–90. Copyright © by Scientific American, Inc. All rights reserved. Reprinted by permission. **57,** Figure 4.2 from "Short-Term Retention of Individual Verbal Items," by L. R. Peterson and M. J. Peterson, *Journal of Experimental Psychology*, 1959, *58*, 193–198. Copyright 1959 by the American Psychological Association. Reprinted by permission. **58,** Figure 4.3 from "Primary Memory," by N. C. Waugh and D. A. Norman, *Psychological Review*, 1965, *72*, 89–104. Copyright 1965 by the American Psychological Association. Reprinted by permission. **60,** Figure 4.4 from "Characteristics of Word Encoding," by D. D. Wickens. In A. W. Melton and E. Martin (Eds.), *Coding Processes in Human Memory*. Copyright 1972 by V. H. Winston & Sons. Reproduced with permission from Hemisphere Publishing Corporation, Washington, D. C. **63 and 64,** Figures 4.5 and 4.6

from "Perception and Memory versus Thought: Some Old Ideas and Recent Findings," by A. D. de Groot. In B. Kleinmuntz (Ed.), *Problem Solving: Research, Method and Theory*. Copyright 1966 by John Wiley & Sons, Inc. Reprinted by permission. **65** and **66,** Figures 4.7 and 4.8 from "Chunking in Recall of Symbolic Drawings," by D. E. Egan and B. J. Schwartz, *Memory & Cognition*, 1979, 7 149–158. Copyright 1979 by the Psychonomic Society, Inc. Reprinted by permission. **68,** Table 4.1 from *The Speech Chain*, by Peter B. Denes and Elliot N. Pinson. Copyright © 1963 by Bell Telephone Laboratories, Inc. Reproduced by permission of Doubleday & Company, Inc. **72,** Table 4.2 from "Speech Processing during Reading," by B. A. Levy, in A. M. Lesgold, J. W. Pellegrino, S. D. Fokkema, and R. Glaser (Eds.), *Cognitive Psychology and Instruction*. Copyright 1978 by Plenum Publishing Corporation. Reprinted by permission. **75** and **76,** Figures 4.9 and 4.10 from "Two Operations in Character Recognition: Some Evidence from Reaction Time Measurements," by S. Sternberg, *Perception & Psychophysics*, 1967, 2, 45–53. Copyright 1967 by the Psychonomic Society, Inc. Reprinted by permission. **77,** Figure 4.11 from "Relation between the Immediate Memory Span and the Memory Search Rate," by J. P. Cavanagh, *Psychological Review*, 1972, 79, 525–530. Copyright 1972 by the American Psychological Association. Reprinted by permission. **78,** Figure 4.12 from "Memory Scanning of Organized Visual Material," by D. V. DeRosa and D. Tkacz, *Journal of Experimental Psychology: Human Learning and Memory*, 1976, 2, 688–694. Copyright 1976 by the American Psychological Association. Reprinted by permission.

CHAPTER 5. **85,** Figure 5.2 from "Analysis of Rehearsal Processes in Free Recall," by D. Rundus, *Journal of Experimental Psychology*, 1971, 89, 63–77. Copyright 1971 by the American Psychological Association. Reprinted by permission. **86,** Table 5.1 from "The Control of Short-Term Memory," by R. C. Atkinson and R. M. Shiffrin, *Scientific American*, 1971, 225, 82–90. Copyright © 1971 by Scientific American, Inc. All rights reserved. Reprinted by permission. **87** and **89,** Figures 5.3 and 5.4 from "Ingredients for a Theory of Instruction," by R. C. Atkinson, *American Psychologist*, 1972, 27, 921–931. Copyright 1972 by the American Psychological Association. Reprinted by permission. **91,** Table 5.2 from "Automatic and Effortful Processes in Memory," by L. Hasher and R. T. Zacks, *Journal of Experimental Psychology: General*, 1979, 108, 356–388. Copyright 1979 by the American Psychological Association. Reprinted by permission.

CHAPTER 6. **104,** Table 6.1 from "Levels of Processing: A Framework for Memory Research," by F. I. M. Craik and R. S. Lockhart, *Journal of Verbal Learning and Verbal Behavior*, 1972, 11, 671–684. Copyright 1972 by Academic Press, Inc. Reprinted by permission. **109, 110,** and **112,** Table 6.2 and Figures 6.1 and 6.2 from "Depth of Processing and the Retention of Words in Episodic Memory," by F. I. M. Craik and E. Tulving, *Journal of Experimental Psychology: General*, 1975, 104, 268–294. Copyright 1975 by the American Psychological Association. Reprinted by permission. **117,** Table 6.3 from "Interaction between Encoding and Retrieval Operations in Cued Recall," by R. P. Fisher and F. I. M. Craik, *Journal of Experimental Psychology: Human Learning and Memory*, 1977, 3, 701–711. Copyright 1977 by the American Psychological Association. Reprinted by permission.

CHAPTER 7. **123,** Figure 7.1 reproduced with permission from the American Dental Association. **124** and **125,** Figures 7.2 and 7.3 from "Visual Images Preserve Metric Spatial Information: Evidence from Studies of Image Scanning," by S. M. Kosslyn, T. M. Ball, and B. J. Reiser, *Journal of Experimental Psychology: Human Perception and Performance*, 1978, 4, 47–60. Copyright 1978 by the American Psychological Association. Reprinted by permission. **127,** Figure 7.4 from "Representation and Retrieval Processes in Short-Term Memory: Recognition and Recall of Faces," by E. E. Smith and G. D. Nielsen, *Journal of Experimental Psychology*, 1970, 85, 397–405. Copyright 1970 by the American Psychological Association. Reprinted by permission. **128,** Figure 7.5 from "Imaginal and Verbal Representations in Short-Term Recognition of Visual Forms," by G. D. Nielsen and E. E. Smith, *Journal of Experimental Psychology*, 1973, 101, 375–378. Copyright 1973 by the American Psychological Association. Reprinted by permission. **129** and **130,** Figures 7.6 and 7.7 from "Mental Rotation of Three Dimensional Objects," by R. N. Shepard and J. Metzler, *Science*, 1971, 171, 701–703. Copyright 1971 by the American Association for the Advancement of Science. Reprinted by permission. **131** and **134,** Figures 7.8 and 7.9 from "Spatial and Verbal Components of the Act of Recall," by L. R. Brooks, *Canadian Journal of Psychology*, 1968, 22, 349–368. Copyright 1968 by the Canadian Psychological Association. Reprinted by permission. **137,** Figure 7.10 from "Effects of Interactive Imagery on Learning: Applications to Advertising," by K. A. Lutz and R. J. Lutz, *Journal of Applied Psychology*, 1977, 62, 493–498. Copyright 1977 by the American Psychological Association. Reprinted by permission. **139** and **140,** Figures 7.11 and 7.12 from "Imagery versus Meaningfulness of Nouns in Paired-Associate Learning," by A. Paivio, P. C. Smythe, and J. C. Yuille, *Canadian Journal of Psychology*, 1968, 22, 427–441. Copyright 1968 by the Canadian Psychological Association. Reprinted by permission. **143,** Table 7.1 from "An Application of the Mnemonic Keyword Method to the Acquisition of a Russian Vocabulary," by R. C. Atkinson and M. R. Raugh, *Journal of Experimental Psychology: Human Learning and Memory*, 1975, *104*, 126–133. Copyright 1975 by the American Psychological Association. Reprinted by permission.   **145,** quote from *The Art of Memory*, by Dame Frances Yates. Copyright 1966 by Routledge and Kegan Paul Ltd. and the University of Chicago Press. This and all other quotations from this source are reprinted by permission.   **146,** Figure 7.13 from "The Capacity of Memory Loci in Artificial Memory," by H. F. Crovitz, *Psychonomic Science*, 1971, *24*, 187–188. Copyright 1971 by the Psychonomic Society, Inc. Reprinted by permission.   **147,** Figure 7.14 from "Long-Term Memory for a Common Object," by R. S. Nickerson and M. J. Adams, *Cognitive Psychology*, 1979, *11*, 287–307. Copyright 1979 by Academic Press, Inc. Reprinted by permission.   **149,** Figure 7.15 from "Fact and Fantasy: The Roles of Accuracy and Variability in Confusing Imaginations with Perceptual Experiences," by M. K. Johnson, C. L. Raye, A. Y. Wang, and T. T. Taylor, *Journal of Experimental Psychology: Human Learning and Memory*, 1979, *5*, 229–240. Copyright 1979 by the American Psychological Association. Reprinted by permission.

CHAPTER 8.   **154** and **155,** Figures 8.1 and 8.2 from "Knowing and Using Concepts," by L. E. Bourne, Jr., *Psychological Review*, 1970, *77*, 546–556. Copyright 1970 by the American Psychological Association. Reprinted by permission.   **159, 160,** and **161,** Tables 8.1, 8.2, and 8.3 and Figure 8.3 from "Basic Objects in Natural Categories," by E. Rosch, C. B. Mervis, W. D. Gray, D. M. Johnsen, and P. Boyes-Braem, *Cognitive Psychology*, 1976, *8*, 382–440. Copyright 1976 by Academic Press, Inc. Reprinted by permission.   **162,** Table 8.4 from "Family Resemblances: Studies in the Internal Structure of Categories," by E. Rosch and C. B. Mervis, *Cognitive Psychology*, 1975, *7*, 573–605. Copyright 1975 by Academic Press, Inc. Reprinted by permission.   **166,** Figure 8.4 from "Perceptual vs. Conceptual Categorization," by S. K. Reed and M. P. Friedman, *Memory & Cognition*, 1973, *1*, 157–163. Copyright 1973 by the Psychonomic Society, Inc. Reprinted by permission.   **167** and **171,** Figure 8.5 and Table 8.5 from "Pattern Recognition and Categorization," by S. K. Reed, *Cognitive Psychology*, 1972, *3*, 382–407. Copyright 1972 by Academic Press, Inc. Reprinted by permission.   **168,** Figure 8.6 from "Perceived Distance and the Classification of Distorted Patterns," by M. I. Posner, R. Goldsmith, and K. E. Welton, *Journal of Experimental Psychology*, 1967, *73*, 28–38. Copyright 1967 by the American Psychological Association. Reprinted by permission.

CHAPTER 9.   **177,** Figures 9.1 and 9.2 from "Organizational Factors in Memory," by G. H. Bower, *Cognitive Psychology*, 1970, *1*, 18–46. Copyright 1970 by Academic Press, Inc. Reprinted by permission.   **181** and **183,** Figures 9.3 and 9.5 from "Retrieval Time from Semantic Memory," by A. M. Collins and M. R. Quillian, *Journal of Verbal Learning and Verbal Behavior*, 1969, *8*, 240–248. Copyright 1969 by Academic Press, Inc. Reprinted by permission.   **182,** Figure 9.4 from "Theories of Semantic Memory," by E. E. Smith, in W. K. Estes (Ed.), *Handbook of Learning and Cognitive Processes* (Vol. 6). Copyright 1978 by Lawrence Erlbaum Associates, Inc., Publishers. Reprinted by permission.   **188,** Figure 9.6 from "A Spreading Activation Theory of Semantic Processing," by A. M. Collins and E. F. Loftus, *Psychological Review*, 1975, *82*, 407–428. Copyright 1975 by the American Psychological Association. Reprinted by permission.   **191** and **193,** Table 9.1 and Figure 9.7 from *Language, Memory, and Thought*, by J. R. Anderson. Copyright 1976 by Lawrence Erlbaum Associates, Inc., Publishers. Reprinted by permission.   **195,** Figure 9.8 from "Partial Resolution of the Paradox of Interference: The Role of Integrating Knowledge," by L. Reder and J. R. Anderson, *Cognitive Psychology*, 1980, *12*, 447–472. Copyright 1980 by Academic Press, Inc. Reprinted by permission.   **197,** Table 9.2 from "Memory Search without Interference: The Role of Integration," by J. L. Myers, E. J. O'Brien, D. A. Balota, and M. L. Toyofuku, *Cognitive Psychology*, 1984, *16*, 217–242. Copyright 1984 by Academic Press, Inc. Reprinted by permission.

CHAPTER 10.   **209,** Figure 10.3 from "To End Ambiguous Sentences," by D. G. MacKay, *Perception & Psychophysics*, 1966, *1*, 426–435. Copyright 1966 by the Psychonomic Society, Inc. Reprinted by permission.   **212,** Figure 10.4 from "Lexical Retrieval and Error Recovery in Reading: A Model Based on Eye Fixations," by P. A. Carpenter and M. Daneman, *Journal of Verbal Learning and Verbal Behavior*, 1981, *20*, 137–160. Copyright 1981 by Academic Press, Inc. Reprinted by permission.   **216,** Figure 10.5 from "Understanding Noun Phrases," by M. C. Potter and B. A. Faulconer, *Journal of Verbal Learning and Verbal Behavior*, 1979, *18*, 509–521. Copyright 1979 by Academic Press, Inc. Reprinted by permission.

CHAPTER 11.   **228,** Figure 11.1 from "Considerations of Some Problems of Comprehension," by J. D. Bransford and M. K. Johnson, in W. G. Chase (Ed.), *Visual Information Processing*. Copyright 1973 by Academic Press, Inc. Reprinted by permission.   **229,** quote from "Considerations of Some Problems of Comprehension," by J. D. Bransford and M. K. Johnson, in W. G. Chase (Ed.), *Visual Information Processing*. Copyright 1973 by Academic Press, Inc. This and all other quotations from this source are reprinted by permission.   **232,** Figure 11.2 from "Intrusion of a Thematic Idea in Retention of Prose," by R. A. Sulin and D. J. Dooling, *Journal of Experimental Psychology,* 1974, *103,* 255–262. Copyright 1974 by the American Psychological Association. Reprinted by permission.   **234,** Table 11.1 from "Scripts in Memory for Text," by G. H. Bower, J. B. Black, and T. J. Turner, *Cognitive Psychology,* 1979, *11,* 177–220. Copyright 1979 by Academic Press, Inc. Reprinted by permission.   **237, 238,** quote from "Cognitive Structures in Comprehension and Memory of Narrative Discourse," by P. W. Thorndyke, *Cognitive Psychology,* 1977, *9,* 77–110. Copyright 1977 by Academic Press, Inc. Reprinted by permission.   **240,** Table 11.2 from "Good and Bad Structure in Simple Paragraphs: Effects on Apparent Theme, Reading Time, and Recall," by D. E. Kieras, *Journal of Verbal Learning and Verbal Behavior,* 1978, *17,* 13–28. Copyright 1978 by Academic Press, Inc. Reprinted by permission.   **242** and **243,** Figures 11.4, 11.5, and 11.6 from "On Modeling Comprehension," by W. Kintsch, *Educational Psychologist,* 1979, *14,* 3–14. Copyright 1979 by Division 15 of the American Psychological Association. Reprinted by permission.   **246,** Table 11.3 from "Micro- and Macroprocesses in Text Comprehension," by D. Vipond, *Journal of Verbal Learning and Verbal Behavior,* 1980, *19,* 276–296. Copyright 1980 by Academic Press, Inc. Reprinted by permission.

CHAPTER 12.   263, Figure 12.3 from *How to Solve Problems: Elements of a Theory of Problems and Problem Solving,* by W. W. Wickelgren. Copyright © 1974 by W. H. Freeman and Company. Reprinted by permission.   **264,** Figure 12.4 from "Modeling Strategy Shifts in a Problem-Solving Task," by H. A. Simon and S. K. Read, *Cognitive Psychology,* 1976, *8,* 86–97. Copyright 1976 by Academic Press, Inc. Reprinted by permission.   **267,** Table 12.2 from "Analogical Problem Solving," by M. L. Gick and K. Holyoak, *Cognitive Psychology,* 1980, *12,* 306–355. Copyright 1980 by Academic Press, Inc. Reprinted by permission.   **268,** Table 12.3 from "Schema Induction and Analogical Transfer," by M. L. Gick and K. Holyoak, *Cognitive Psychology,* 1983, *15,* 1–38. Copyright 1983 by Academic Press, Inc. Reprinted by permission.   **269,** Table 12.5 from "Presentation and Representation in Design Problem Solving," by J. M. Carroll, J. C. Thomas, and A. Malhotra, *British Journal of Psychology,* 1980, *71,* 143–153. Copyright 1980 by the British Psychological Society. Reprinted by permission.

CHAPTER 13.   273, quote from "Cognitive Engineering and Education," by D. A. Norman, in D. T. Tuma and F. Reif (Eds.), *Problem Solving and Education: Issues in Teaching and Research.* Copyright 1980 by Lawrence Erlbaum Associates, Inc., Publishers. This and all other quotations from this source are reprinted by permission.   **276,** quote from "Words to Equations: Meaning and Representation in Algebra Word Problems," by D. A. Kinsley, J. R. Hayes, and H. A. Simon, in P. A. Carpenter and M. A. Just (Eds.), *Cognitive Processes in Comprehension.* Copyright 1977 by Lawrence Erlbaum Associates, Inc., Publishers. Reprinted by permission.   **277** and **278,** Tables 13.1 and 13.2 from "Recall of Mathematical Problem Information: Solving Related Problems," by E. A. Silver, *Journal for Research in Mathematics Education,* 1981, *12,* 54–64. Copyright 1981 by the National Council of Teachers of Mathematics. Reprinted by permission.   **280** and **281,** Figures 13.1 and 13.2 from "Planning in a Hierarchy of Abstraction Spaces," by E. D. Sacerdoti, *Artificial Intelligence,* 1974, *5,* 115–135. Copyright 1974 by North-Holland Publishing Company, Amsterdam. Reprinted by permission.   **284** and **285,** Figures 13.3 and 13.4 from "Understanding and Teaching Problem Solving in Physics," by J. H. Larkin and F. Reif, *European Journal of Science Education,* 1979, *1,* 191–203. Copyright 1979 by the Institute for Science Education. Reprinted by permission.   **286,** Table 13.3 from "Information Processing Analysis of Mathematical Problem Solving," by J. I. Heller and J. G. Greeno. Paper presented at the Applied Problem Solving Conference, Evanston, Illinois, 1979. Reprinted by permission of Joan I. Heller.   **287,** Table 13.4 from "Explicit Heuristic Training as a Variable in Problem-Solving Performances," by A. H. Schoenfeld, *Journal for Research in Mathematics Education,* 1979, *10,* 173–187. Copyright 1979 by the National Council of Teachers of Mathematics. Reprinted by permission.

CHAPTER 14.   302, Table 14.1 from "Task Complexity and Contingent Processing in Decision Making: An Information Search and Protocol Analysis," by J. W. Payne, *Organizational Behavior and Human Performance,* 1976, *16,* 366–387. Copyright 1976 by Academic Press, Inc. Reprinted by permission.   **306,** Table 14.2 from "Cognitive Processes and Societal Risk Taking," by P. Slovic, B. Fischhoff, and S. Lichtenstein, in J. S. Carroll and J. W. Payne (Eds.), *Cognition and Social Behavior.* Copyright 1976 by Lawrence Erlbaum Associates, Inc., Publishers. Reprinted by permission.   **310** and **311,** Figure 14.3 and Table 14.3 from "Relative Importance of Probabilities and Payoffs in Risk Taking," by P. Slovic and S. Lichtenstein, *Journal of Experimental Psychology Monograph,* 1968, *78*(3, Pt. 2). Copyright 1968 by the American Psychological Association. Reprinted by permission.   **313,** Table 14.4 from *Medical Problem Solving,* by A. S. Elstein, L. S. Shulman, and S. A. Sprafka. Copyright 1978 by Harvard University Press. Reprinted by permission.